A Twentieth Century Life

previous books by the author:

1707: The Union of Scotland and England Chambers 1979
Walter Scott and Scotland Blackwood's 1981, pbk Saltire Society 1994
John Galt Scottish Academic Press 1985
In Bed with an Elephant Saltire Society 1985
The Thinking Nation University of Dundee 1989
Cultural Independence Scottish Ctr for Econ. and Soc. Research 1989
Towards Independence: Essays on Scotland Polygon1991, rpr 1996
Andrew Fletcher and the Treaty of Union John Donald 1992,
pbk Saltire Society 1994
Scotland in Europe: A Dialogue with a Sceptical Friend Canongate 1992
Defoe in Edinburgh and Other Papers Tuckwell Press 1995
A Mad God's Dream Edinburgh District Council 1997
Still in Bed with an Elephant Saltire Society 1998
The Boasted Advantages Saltire Society 1999

edited by the author:

(with AC Davis) *The Age of MacDiarmid* Mainstream 1980
Sir Walter Scott's The Letters of Malachi Malagrowther Blackwood's 1981
Andrew Fletcher's United and Separate Parliaments Saltire Society 1982
(with George Bruce) *A Scottish Postbag* Chambers 1979,
Saltire Society 2002
(with AC Davis) *Policy for the Arts: A Selection of AdCAS Papers* 1991
Scotland: A Concise Cultural History Mainstream 1993
(with Daniel Szechi) *Scotland's Ruine: Lockhart of Carnwath's
Memoirs of the Union* Association for Scottish Literary Studies 1995
(with Ian Gordon) *John Galt's The Member and The Radical*
Canongate 1996
Scotland: An Unwon Cause Canongate 1997
The Saltoun Papers: Reflections on Andrew Fletcher Saltire Society 2002

A Twentieth Century Life

Paul Henderson Scott

Argyll publishing

First published in 2002 by
Argyll Publishing
Glendaruel
Argyll PA22 3AE
Scotland
www.deliberatelythirsty.com

British Library Cataloguing-in-Publication Data.
A catalogue record for this book is available from
the British Library.

ISBN 1 902831 36 5

Cover Design: Alasdair Gray

Origination: Cordfall Ltd, Glasgow

Printing: Bell & Bain Ltd, Glasgow

For Laura

Paul Scott, Desert Rat, Brussels 1944

Contents

Introduction

I have called this book *A Twentieth Century Life* for two reasons. I lived through most of that tormented century and the circumstances of my life involved me in some of its most significant events. I hope that the book will give an impression of the age as well as of one individual. It falls into two parts, forty years abroad in the Army and Diplomatic Service, and another forty, about equally divided between before and after that period, in Scotland. I was more fortunate than many people in that century of outrage and disaster, fortunate in my place of birth and education, in surviving World War II, in the experiences of my diplomatic career, and in returning to Scotland in time to participate in a decisive phase of her recent history.

I am greatly indebted to many friends, acquaintances and colleagues. Two people in particular have made this book possible. Laura Fiorentini, who has shared my life for the last twenty years, has helped in innumerable ways. Dr Iain Brown of the National Library of Scotland, by suggesting that I should donate my large collection of personal papers to the Library, stimulated me into looking through them. It was this experience which made me realise that this was a book that I had to write. Perhaps the later Scottish chapters will, to some extent, provide for part of the twentieth century the same service that Henry Cockburn gave for part of the nineteenth in his *Memorials of his Time*.

Finally thanks are due to Anne Mason and Sheila Miller who helped with the difficult task of translating my scrawled manuscript into word-processed intelligibility.

Edinburgh, January 2002

(top) November 1922, Piershill
Studio, Edinburgh
(left) In Helensburgh, August 1934
(right) With cousin, Alison
Henderson, 1925

CHAPTER I

'The usual round of Edinburgh Boys'
1920 – 1939

I was born in Edinburgh on 7 November 1920. You might suppose that this was not the most auspicious time to emerge into the world. It meant being born in the aftermath of one World War, growing up in the years of depression and reaching military age just as the next War started. I have to admit that I was not conscious of any particular disadvantage at the time because I thoroughly enjoyed the first twenty years of my life in Edinburgh. With the place I had no quarrel. I have always loved both the idea and the reality of Edinburgh with a passion. The idea because of so much that has happened here in the past; the reality because of the dramatic beauty of the place and the solid decency and kindliness of the mass of its citizens.

There is nothing unusual about this feeling for Edinburgh. RL Stevenson found many things about it a sair trauchle – the prim disapproval of Victorian respectability for his Bohemian ways, and the snell east wind in what he called its draughty parallelograms of the New Town. Still his conclusion was that 'the place establishes an interest in people's hearts; go where they will, they find no city of the same distinction; go where they will, they take a pride in their old home.' I recognise the feeling. Sometimes in other countries, people ask where you come from. I was always uneasy that it sounded boastful when I replied Edinburgh, in as modest a tone as I could muster.

The Court of Session judge, Lord Cameron (Jock to his friends), felt in the same way about Edinburgh. He was President of the Edinburgh Sir Walter Scott Club in 1965. This is an office which has been held by a remarkable succession of people, writers, of course, but even Prime Ministers and the occasional Field Marshall or Archbishop. I arrived at this giddy height myself in 1995. The sole function of this office, which lasts a year, is to deliver an address at the annual dinner of the Club. Jock's address was mostly a celebration of his own, and Walter Scott's, love of Edinburgh. He began with a remark which certainly applies to both of us – 'When Edinburgh has laid her hand upon a man's shoulder, the memory of that touch does not readily fade or be easily forgot.'

Part of the imprint of Edinburgh that Jock Cameron was talking about is the sense in which we still live in the shadow of the eighteenth century. I plead guilty myself and others have noticed it. Bernard Crick in a review of my book *Towards Independence* wrote, 'Paul Scott . . . talks of Cockburn and Smith as if he has just drunk claret with them off the High Street.'

As a plea in mitigation, I would say that the eighteenth century Edinburgh, to which I look back with affection, was not only the home of the abstract intellectualism of David Hume and Adam Smith, but of the poetry of Allan Ramsay, Robert Fergusson and Robert Burns, rooted in Scottish tradition and in the real lives of living people. Why particularly in Edinburgh do we have this feel for the eighteenth century? I suppose it is partly because we are conscious that it was one of our great ages. Partly, also, the architecture must have an effect. Above all perhaps, it was the influence of the books we read and the style of education in which we were brought up and it was, I am sure, quite different from anything that now exists.

I cannot say that I remember very much about my life before I went to school when I was five. People like Casanova surprise me when in their memoirs they seem to have precise recall from their earliest days of every conversation and every event. I do not know how it is with other people, but I retain only a general picture of my childhood with very few episodes remaining in sharp detail. Although my birth certificate says that I was born in the Morningside district of Edinburgh, I think that we must have flitted very soon to Portobello.

This is a strange name, one might think, for a douce suburb of Edinburgh. Originally it was a village which grew up around a cottage built by a sailor, it is said, who had taken part in a sea battle off Puerto Bello in Panama in 1739. The streets of solid Georgian houses show that it was fashionable in the past, as you would expect for a place with fine sea views and a long sandy beach within easy reach of the Capital. Walter Scott's daughter and his son-in-law and biographer, John Gibson Lockhart, took a house ther e at one time, although Scott was surprised that they did not prefer the comfort of Abbotsford. In my childhood, Portobello, although sadly declined in the world, was still popular with summer visitors, especially from Glasgow in the week of the annual Fair Holiday.

We lived in a nineteenth century solid stone house in Hope Lane which ran into the High Street. On the opposite side of the lane was a much grander house, three stories to our two, with a larger garden. This was called Argyll House because it was said to have been the residence of the Edinburgh factor of one of the Dukes of Argyll. My maternal grandparents lived there. They came originally from Fife from farming people but my grandfather, Andrew Henderson, had moved firmly into the twentieth century. I am told that he was one of the first people in Scotland to own a motor car. A relic of the early days of cars was stored in an outhouse and I think was still there when I went off to the War. It had a strong family resemblance to its ancestors, horse drawn carriages, and had a rich aroma of polished leather and brass.

By the time that I was aware of my surroundings, Andrew Henderson ran a large garage at the foot of his garden and on the High Street of Portobello. It was the sort of garage which no longer exists because, in addition to selling and servicing cars, it had a large covered space for scores of them. It was before the days when people were prepared to leave these rare and valuable objects on the street. There was a workshop which repaired machinery for local industry and a real blacksmith's forge. At one entrance cars filled up with petrol; at the other horses came for new shoes. Horses were still a serious competitor to the petrol engine. There were more carts than lorries or vans on the streets. I remember being particularly frightened, when I was very young, by large cart wheels as they clattered over cobbled streets. The chief blacksmith, who had been with the Army in the Boer War, was a great, muscular, friendly man in a leather apron. I never tired of watching him as he hammered red hot iron, surrounded by sparks, or reassured a nervous giant of a cart horse as he held a hoof between his legs.

My father, Allan Scott, worked for some years in the management of this diverse enterprise. He had fought in World War I as a private in the Royal Scots Fusilliers and took part in the prolonged horror of the Battle of the Somme. This was something which he would never discuss, but his frigid reaction to any reference to war or armies was eloquence enough. He had been wounded by a rifle bullet in an arm and I imagine that was probably the reason why he survived with his life. He had a twin brother, Paul, who was in the Navy and had spent some hours in the sea, clinging to floating debris, after his ship had been torpedoed. After the war he went to live in Yorkshire to be close to a shipmate who had shared the same experience. He too never talked about any of this, although he was expansive on most subjects. He had artistic instincts, given to playing with words and paint. He kept a village shop which could be described as a hardware store, but somehow contrived to be an expression of his ebullient personality. A visit we paid to him in his Yorkshire village was one of the most memorable of my childhood holidays. Some years later, he married a sister of JB Priestley, the novelist.

There was some mystery about the parentage of these two twins, Allan and Paul. I was told that they had been born in Edinburgh and orphaned at an early age. That was all that I knew. It never occurred to me to enquire into it at the time and now it is too late.

The truth is that I had a very untroubled and uneventful childhood, surrounded by supportive and approving adults. I was free to follow my own inclinations, but whenever I needed their help they gave it to me without hesitation. My mother, Catherine, especially was always a powerful ally for whom nothing was too much trouble. Even my younger and only brother, Andrew, usually called Drew or Drewie, was more a companion than a competitor. Perhaps it was simply that I was not a threat or a nuisance to anyone because my disposition was studious and bookish and my tastes were simple and not expensive. I had the impression, even so, that effort and achievement was expected of me, but I accepted that as perfectly right and proper.

My father encouraged all my enthusiasms. I still have books that he gave me and that became lifelong companions. Our relationship was always cordial and unruffled, but at about the time I left school, I began to realise there were problems between him and my mother. They kept this to themselves and did not explain or attempt to enlist the support of my brother or me. It was an age when this sort of thing was less openly discussed than it would be now. Respectability demanded restraint and discretion. He took a job with a manufacturer of car components which involved a good deal of travelling and he was away from home for most of the time. Eventually he moved to the head office of the firm in England and more or less disappeared from our lives. He wrote to me from time to time, but I never saw him again. This was at the beginning of the war when life was disrupted and separation was normal. The trauma of it all was lost in the greater trauma of the war. He died while I was with the Army in Germany.

It was typical of the cocoon that surrounded me that my grandfather did not protest when I made it plain that I did not want to follow his footsteps into his business. He accepted that my interests and aptitudes lay elsewhere. Sustained by so much affection and understanding, my childhood was untroubled and uneventful. My clearest memories of it are associated with the beach of Portobello where summer days seem to have been endlessly long and constantly sunny. I remember only two small dramas. Once, when I must have been about six, I walked along the promenade with a girl employed to look after my brother as she pushed him in his pram. It was one of these capacious four-wheeled affairs that were usual at the time. She met a young man and became so involved in conversation that she let go of the pram. It sailed majestically towards the edge of the promenade and flew into space over the sand. I remember a moment of panic, but my brother in a nest of blankets and pillows was unharmed and undisturbed. The other incident must have been some years later. Two or three of us borrowed, without the formality of asking, a sailing dinghy belonging to the older brother of one of us. We succeeded in hoisting the sail and we went off at speed before a brisk wind. It was a different story as darkness fell and we tried to struggle back against wind and tide. We made it in the end, to find anxious parents, more relieved than furious, with their car headlights pointing out to sea. Once, much earlier than either of these episodes, I climbed out of bed on a summer evening and, having a penny or two at my disposal, walked to the local sweetshop in my pyjamas.

Of course in many ways, this was a simpler and softer world, even if that seems paradoxical of a short period between the two most destructive wars in the history of the world. For one thing, there were very few cars. As Robert Garioch says, you could play fitba in the street. There was no television to scare everybody with daily scenes of disaster and violent death. We hardly ever heard about crime, although of course it existed. The pressures were less: neither drugs to create an insatiable demand for money nor, television again, incessant advertising to stimulate consumerism. Nobody wants things that they have never heard about. Curiously too, all the new inventions which are supposed to make life easier or more comfortable, computers, mobile phones and all the rest of it, seem to have the opposite effect. Life was lived at an easier pace when we did not have the technology to speed it up.

I suppose that to a child of today our lives would sound impoverished, uncomfortable and miserable. No supermarkets with their vast range of exotic foods from the ends of the earth. Our shops had a very limited choice of mostly local produce, and fruits were strictly seasonal. We did not have either refrigerators or central heating. Cars were rare, but that of course was an advantage. We walked to school, or if it was too far, went by tram car.

We did not complain about any of these things because we did not know any better and there were compensations. A coal fire may only heat a small radius around it, but it is a living, companionable welcoming presence. We were spared the cacophonies of pop music which destroys the hearing and addles the brain of subsequent generations. In the absence of all electronic distraction, we had more time for books. A child today must find it difficult to escape long enough from the television or computer screen to discover the infinite delight, solace, information and stimulation of books. I feel the same way as Edward Gibbon when he says in his *Autobiography* that he would not exchange his 'early and invincible love of reading' for the 'treasure of India' and that his library was the foundation of his works and the best comfort of his life. Alan Taylor wrote recently in a newspaper article that reading was as natural to him as breathing and nearly as necessary. I agree with that.

Much of the literature which gives me most pleasure, and to which I constantly return, is Scottish. I discovered at quite an early age the Border ballads and the poetry of Fergusson and Burns, and the novels of Scott, Galt and Stevenson. Somewhat later, I added Dunbar, Henryson and Lindsay, the *Memoirs* of Cockburn, the *Journals* of Boswell, the poetry of Garioch and Sydney Smith. I have always responded with special delight to poetry or dialogue in Scots, a language which lives more in my head than on my tongue or in my ears.

I do not know how to explain this Scottish partiality, if it needs any explanation. No one tried to influence me or persuade me in this direction, although much later on I found that Hugh MacDiarmid was saying many things with which I agreed. It was a simple preference which by no means excluded other literature. I have always admired the sonority and assurance of Latin. Many writers from other countries give me much pleasure, especially Shakespeare, Swift, Fielding, Austen, Trollope, Michel de Montaigne, Molière and de Maupassant, Chekhov, Tolstoy, Shaw and Bertrand Russell.

Access to books was very easy. Edinburgh has several great libraries. If at first, I did not have access to the University Library and the National Library had not yet been established, the ordinary public library in Portobello had nearly everything I wanted. It was before the time when Penguin opened up the vast resources and convenience to the pocket (in both senses) of the paperback. There were several series of hardback repeats of classic titles which cost only a shilling or two, Nelson's Classics, World Classics and Everyman. The last two of these still survive, or have been revived, although now in a different format; and I still have, and still read, many of the earlier ones which I bought in the 20s and 30s. Also then, Edinburgh had many wonderful second-hand bookshops where you could pick up leather-bound eighteenth century books for a few pennies. Such shops hardly exist any longer. It is said that many sold out their entire stocks to the new universities on both sides of the Atlantic. My first substantial purchase of books was a handsome set of the Melrose Edition of the Waverley Novels, which I acquired at an auction sale for a few shillings when I was about ten.

Travelling on holiday for any distance was unusual before the War, except for the leisured rich. Paid holidays for workers of more than a week or two were unknown. Hardly anyone travelled by air. Until I joined the Army in 1941, I went abroad only once. That was when my Portobello grandfather took my cousin and me on a cruise from Newcastle to Bergen and the fjords in August 1935 on the handsome Norwegian ship, SY *Meteor*. I have had a special affection for Norway ever since. When we arrived back in Newcastle a porter stacked our luggage in a barrow. 'To the customs, Sir?' he asked. 'Nonsense,' said my grandfather in his most commanding tone. 'Put it in the train.' And he did. At least once, I was taken to visit my uncle with the village shop in Skipton in Yorkshire. We went to London and back by ship from Leith in September 1932. Otherwise, family holidays were all in Scotland. Even so, they were not very frequent and I can remember only two, one to a farm in Perthshire and the other in a boarding house in Helensburgh. When I went back to Helensburgh some fifty years later, I was pleased to discover that I still remembered where to find the flywheel of the first steamboat, the *Comet*, in a public park.

My grandfather used to take us all for a hurl in his car at the weekends. Usually we went to visit a relative who kept a shop, full of fascinating objects, in the High Street of Linlithgow or to Soutra Hill. There my cousin, brother and I would roam over the moors and paddle in the burns before we all had a copious lunch in the Carfraemill Inn. We had the roads mainly for ourselves. The main hazard of crossing the moor by car was to avoid the sheep which had not yet learned about the dangers of wandering about all over the road.

I was fortunate in my school, the Royal High School of Edinburgh, which I attended from the age of five to eighteen. At first the entire school was housed in Hamilton's splendid building, an early nineteenth century reinterpretation of classical Greece, below the Calton Hill. It is a building which echoes the intellectual self-confidence of Scotland in the age of the Enlightenment, the high value that was placed on education, and a sense of affinity with classical Greece and Rome. Also the situation, overlooking old Edinburgh and the Palace and looking up to St Giles and the Castle, makes you feel that you are in the heart of Scotland and enmeshed in its history. After I had been at school in this inspiring place from my first few years, the Preparatory and Junior classes, as they were then called, were moved in 1930 to a new building beside the school playing field of Jock's Lodge. We returned with relief two or three years later when we reached the dignity of the senior school.

Many years after I left the High School, the building was held to be unsuitable for modern needs and to be in the wrong place. The school moved to a undistinguished modern building in Barnton, an act, it seems to me, of cultural barbarism. The old building still stands there, sadly neglected and under-used, a monument to the aspirations of an earlier age. For a time in the 1970s it was prepared to be the seat of the Scottish Parliament, (or Assembly as it was then called) which was expected to follow the Referendum of 1979. When that achieved a majority, but an insufficiently large one to satisfy the notorious 40% rule, the building became the symbol of unsatisfied longings for political autonomy. The Campaign for a Scottish Assembly used it as their logo. Photographs of the great portico appeared on the covers of many books on the subject, including one of my own, *Towards Independence*.

After the Referendum of 11 September 1997 at last ensured the recovery of the Parliament, there was a general expectation that its seat would be in, or beside, the High School buildings. We held the assembly of delegates of the 1997 PEN Congress in the hall of the school and the final reception, with the permission of the Lord President of the Court of Session, in the old Parliament Hall by St Giles. In the programme we told the participants that they were therefore meeting in both the old and the new houses of the Scottish Parliament.

But we were wrong. Donald Dewar, the Labour Secretary of State for Scotland, had different ideas. He seemed determined at all costs to avoid the Calton Hill site, even when majority opinion was clearly in favour of it. It was central, prominent and accessible and there was plenty of Government office space in the immediate vicinity. The site by itself would have bestowed an air of significance and importance to the new Parliament. That perhaps was the trouble. The Labour Party were in a bad state of panic because the opinion polls were showing the SNP as the strongest party. They were anxious to prevent anything (such as the knighthood for Sean Connery proposed by the Tory Government) which might encourage nationalist feeling. A spokesman was quoted as saying that the High School had become a 'shiboleth of independence'. Even that was wrong. It was associated not with independence, but with devolution. Perhaps they had in mind a remark by Christopher Harvie in his *Scotland and Nationalism* that the High School had become a place of nationalist pilgrimage to rival Bannockburn, Arbroath or Elderslie.

As we were all conscious from the beginning, this was a school with a long and proud history, starting in Holyrood Abbey, probably in the twelfth century. At least from the time of the Reformation it became the 'tounis schule', which, like Edinburgh University, was under the control of the Town Council. Sir Walter Scott said that it was 'the pride and boast of our city'. Lord Brougham, at about the same time, said in a speech that it was the most important school in Scotland, and intimately connected with 'the literature and progress of the Kingdom'. As the leading school for centuries in the Capital, it produced so many distinguished men that a list of them reads like a biographical dictionary of Scottish achievement. Among writers, they include William Drummond, Robert Fergusson, Walter Scott, Francis Jeffrey and Henry Cockburn. Of course, the school lost it virtual monopoly long ago; but even in the twentieth century Robert Garioch, Norman MacCaig and James Allan Ford were educated there.

Since my time there, the school has lost much of its distinctive character. It no longer occupies the proud position in the centre of the city. In my day, the school confidently maintained its classical character with much emphasis on Latin and Greek. Now, there is no Greek and very little Latin. It was in my time for boys only; charged fees (although they were quite small) and had holidays at its own particular dates; it drew its pupils from the whole city and further afield, not from a local 'catchment area'. Now it has become to all appearances an ordinary comprehensive neighbourhood school. As I was writing this, I came across a cutting of a letter to the editor of *The Scotsman*, dated 21st April, 1973. This was inside my copy of JB Barclay's history of the school, *The Tounis Scule*. The writer, JC Keppie, argued that Schola Regia no longer existed and that it should be given a decent burial and a memorial.

Mr Keppie certainly had a point. The old High School has been sacrificed to modern educational theories or to Labour Party opposition to élitism and privilege. I am egalitarian by instinct and entirely opposed to inherited privilege, as displayed, for example, by the institution of monarchy. But the old High School was not a preserve of the rich or exclusive in spirit. Yes, there was a small fee and we bought our own books; but scholarships were readily available. It set high standards and by and large achieved them. To destroy such a school, or at least to fundamentally change its character, was, I think, a bad mistake. Planners, politicians and experts often do great damage with the best of intentions. Élitism, in the sense of aiming to achieve the best, should not be regarded as something shameful.

The writer Allan Massie recently made the same point and applied it to the High School of Glasgow, Aberdeen Grammar School and Dundee High School. All of them, he says, were victims of the mood of the sixties when élitism became a dirty word. These schools 'enjoyed deservedly high academic reputations. They were élitist. They might be democratic, but they were also formidably intellectual.'

I have come across an entry in my diary for 22nd December 1980 which records a conversation with Farquhar MacIntosh, then Rector of the school, who has been a valuable ally in many causes. He agreed that the translation to the nondescript new building, already showing more signs of decay than the old one ever did, was an undeniable loss. 'The harmony of the old building and the incomparable view from it were an inspiration in themselves and made it impossible not to feel part of a great tradition. How can anyone feel the same pride in the incipient slum in which they are now based?'

Farquhar went on to explain the reasons for the then Town Council's decision. They treated the school in the same way as any other under their control. This meant that it became 'comprehensive', which involved drawing its pupils from the immediate area; but that was an area of diminishing population. The school would have decayed as the population declined and it might even have been closed. Presumably the Labour administration which made these changes would have argued that they were acting on enlightened, democratic and egalitarian motives; but they have destroyed an irreplaceable asset in the intellectual life of Scotland.

Our schoolmasters, always in dark suits and academic robes, were nearly all serious and worthy men. The head of them all as Rector, William King Gillies, was remote and aloof with the air, I used to think, of a Roman Emperor. He had a marble bust of Julius Caesar in his study which perhaps suggested the comparison. There was no nonsense in those days of being allowed to choose the subjects you preferred. Each yearly intake was divided into two or three divisions, A, B, and, if necessary C, according to academic performance. This seems to me a sensible arrangement. If pupils of greatly different ability are in the same class, the brighter ones are doomed to boredom and the less able to a sense of inadequacy. In an A class, as I was, it was assumed that you would do Latin, Greek, French, English, mathematics, history, geography, art, music and crafts, and only a little science. On one prize day, King Gillies made a speech about this. (Now that I think about it, we half suspected that the 'King' was more a title than a mere family name). He said that the classics and mathematics were the only subjects worth teaching to boys who were worth teaching and that a mind so trained could pick up any other subjects without difficulty. How the teachers of the other subjects, or the boys in the B or C divisions, reacted to this, I have no idea. At that time I had a passing enthusiasm for chemistry and used to play around at home with retorts, flasks, Bunsen burners and such things. So I tried hard, without avail, to be allowed to do chemistry instead of Greek. My best friend, Donald Cameron, wanted to take medicine at the University. For the medical school, Highers in chemistry and physics was an entrance requirement. He too was not allowed to change subjects and left school a year early to prepare himself elsewhere.

At the time, I thought that the idea that everyone should concentrate on the classics and mathematics was a personal eccentricity of King Gillies. Years later George Davie's great book, *The Democratic Intellect* (which was published in 1961) gave me a new understanding. The theme of the book is the prolonged, and ultimately largely successful, campaign in the nineteenth century to make the Scottish universities conform to the English model. The tradition in Scotland was for a wide, general course, including philosophy and science as well as literature and languages. In England, the two universities specialised from the beginning; classics in Oxford and mathematics in Cambridge. As Davie says, the argument was pursued on both sides with 'sincerity and passion'. The Government was not prepared to finance the Scottish universities if they insisted on their own tradition. The Scots believed that the English approach was 'narrowing and illiberal' and unlikely to encourage a 'philosophical, open-minded and intellectually versatile attitude'. The English argued that diversity led to superficiality and a failure to attain sufficiently high standards either in the classics or in mathematics. These two subjects, and these alone, were regarded with particular reverence because, as King Gillies had argued, they were thought to be the best way to train the mind. King Gillies had evidently accepted the English theory.

You might say then that King Gillies was dictatorial and, that unfashionable word again, élitist. Such conduct is, of course, now unthinkable and his enthusiasm for early specialisation was misguided. Still, a case can be made for his point of view. If you are going to educate yourself to the maximum of your potential, I suspect that you have to discipline your mind to address subjects that do not come naturally or easily. Perhaps too much self-indulgence is debilitating. Things for which you have a natural aptitude require little effort and habits of effort have to be acquired. Also, I think that it is true that the classics and mathematics are good exercises for the mind. They both depend on the application of dispassionate logic. I remember that I could not see the point of grammar until I started to learn Latin, where you cannot understand a sentence without understanding the grammatical relationship between the parts of it. If you spend years learning Latin, you never lose the habit of trying to grasp the precise meaning of every sentence. In any case, Latin is a useful acquisition because it plays so large a part in our literature and in so many European languages, including English and Scots, as well as those derived from it. I went to South America in the Diplomatic Service without having time to learn any Spanish; but when I arrived I discovered that it was so close to Latin that I could understand the newspapers.

None of this means that I am in favour of early specialisation in these or any other subjects. We all need a rounded and general education. In particular, I think that a knowledge in some depth of the history of one's own country, and in more general outline of the rest of the world, is indispensable for an understanding of the circumstances in which we find ourselves. The neglect of Scottish history in most of our schools has been a serious deficiency.

The High School was divided into four 'Nations', as in the mediaeval universities. These were Angles, Picts, Britons and Scots, a reference to the early history of the territory which evolved into Scotland. We were arbitrarily allocated into one of these without any choice on the matter and without reference to anything else. It had no particular purpose, apart from providing teams for sport, and it determined where you sat in the Hall each morning. The Rector presided there and made the announcements of the day. There was a prayer and a hymn or two. Our allegiance was indicated by the colour of the rim of a badge with the device of the castle which the School shared with the City of Edinburgh in our coats of arms. I was an Angle which I used to think rather inappropriate.

One of our mathematics masters, Peter Thomsen, was a man of impressive intellectual force. I have never met anyone with such a passion and delight in the exercise of pure reason. When we first joined his class, he told us to forget all we thought we knew about arithmetical processes. Unless we understood what we were doing, we were wasting our time. He would teach us from first principles. George Davie is apposite again. He discusses the Scottish tradition of a philosophical approach to mathematics, or even arithmetic, treating them as 'a branch of liberal education'. That was certainly Peter Thomsen's attitude. His habit was to write out the proof of a proposition in geometry or a calculation in algebra on the blackboard. Quite often he would stand back and ask us to admire the sheer beauty of the logic. He was, I believe, a communist, but he made no attempt to indoctrinate us with his politics. He lived in a flat high above the promenade in Portobello and kept an old monster of a Buick in my grandfather's garage. They had many hard-hitting arguments together, to the evident pleasure of both of them. Like most of his colleagues, he was lavish with his time to help with ploys outside the classroom. In his case, it was not sport, but the school camera club, which had a dark-room in one of the basements, and the school library.

The destruction of that library is a sore point. It was housed in one of the two large rooms which balanced each other on both sides of the central great hall. There were handsome, glass-fronted, mahogany bookcases which entirely covered all the walls from floor to ceiling. There was an endless fascination in the collection of books, many dating from the eighteenth century, and on a great diversity of subjects. In the late 1970s, when the building was being prepared for the Scottish Assembly, as the Parliament was then to be called, the bookcases were removed and the room reduced to an empty space. I do not know what happened to the books, but the architect in charge made a deplorable confession when I went with a group from the Cockburn Association to inspect the alterations. He said that he had been away for a few days and when he come back he was horrified to see the shattered remains of the bookcases in skips outside the building.

The Deputy Rector and History Master was William CA Ross, known as the Bogue, presumably because of his initials and without any ill-will or derogatory intention. No-one could dislike him. He had two enthusiasms, the School and cricket. In pursuit of the first, he spent hours drawing up careful records about former pupils and their activities and wrote a history of the school which was published in 1934. My copy of it, before me as I write, has the signatures of the staff, headed by King Gillies, in the front and of my classmates at the back. Nearly all of them still evoke a clear picture in my mind as they were sixty years since. I remember Ross stopping me to give me some complicated details about university entrance or something of that sort. This puzzled me at first, but I began to realise from a hint he dropped that he thought he was talking to James Ford. By this time, it was too embarrassing to interrupt and explain the confusion, so I thanked him and then relayed the information to Jim, who was in the year above me. He is one of the very few people from the school with whom I am still in touch. He and his brother were in the Royal Scots in Hong Kong when it fell to the Japanese. His bother was tortured and killed by them because he tried to organise an escape from the prison camp. Jim survived and became a civil servant in the Scottish Office, head of their personnel department and then Registrar General of Scotland. Eventually he came to terms with his experiences at the hands of the Japanese by writing two novels about them, *The Brave White Flag* and *Season of Escape*. Another of his novels, *A Statue in a Public Place*, is a fine description of Edinburgh and of government service in it. 'The vows you are required to take were not far short of obedience, chastity and poverty; even outside the walls you had to avoid criticising your Ministers and your Department and had to be discreet in your fornication and in making money from other sources.' (I am not so sure about the poverty or the chastity these days.)

Many years later I often encountered Jim in the Scottish Arts Club when every Thursday he lunched with a diverse group of his old friends. He must have been an ideal civil servant, of unshakeable integrity and fairness, painstaking, warm, genial and kind, but intolerant of stupidity. Without complaint he gave much of his time helping wartime comrades, visiting them in hospital and so on. Now his eyesight is failing, a consequence perhaps of his years in the prison camp. Since he can no longer read he has disposed of all his books. I can imagine few things sadder than that.

Since I have mentioned Bogue's great passion for cricket, I should say a word about sport. We were kept fairly well exercised in a gymnasium and swimming pool which were the province of an agreeable eccentric, Tommy Lowe. He was a retired soldier who had fought in the Boer war, to which he often referred. Boys were sometimes reluctant to use the swimming pool, especially in the winter, because the heating was not very efficient. He would urge us to take the plunge with the warning that comrades of his in South Africa (where we thought it must be much warmer) had drowned in river crossings because they had never learned to swim. 'Don't let that happen to you.' When we were still not persuaded, he triumphantly produced a thermometer with a reading of 70^0; but we all knew that it was stuck permanently there.

The school played cricket in summer and rugby in winter. It was supposed at that time to be especially proud of its prowess on the rugby field, although my own circle were not persuaded that this was a matter of any consequence. I did not like the game myself very much because it was violent, muddy and uncomfortable. Cricket I quite enjoyed, but I was not much good at it. During the war, when I was stationed at Carnoustie, I actually played a game for the local county team because most of their players had disappeared into the forces. For most of my life I have been fond of boats of all kinds. While I was at school I joined a rowing club in Portobello where we rowed four-man Jolly boats, in the Firth of Forth, somewhat reminiscent of nineteenth century whalers. I organised a school team but we could not find any other school willing to compete.

I think sport is fine as long as one engages in it for exercise and the sheer physical pleasure of the activity. Skiing, to which the Army introduced me some years later, has given enormous satisfaction of this kind for the last sixty years or so. Watching other people play, on the other hand, has always seemed to me an absurdity. A still greater absurdity is the reporting of it at great length in the press, radio and television. This, I think is a sheer waste of paper and broadcasting time. I admit that I make an exception of rugby internationals in which Scotland is playing and of all skiing, but that is for the skiing itself, not for the competition. I dislike competitiveness of any kind. Sailing and skiing are delightful; but if you make a race of them, it destroys the essential pleasure.

It is often said, and it is true, that Scottish schools pay insufficient attention to Scottish history, language and literature and in fact to anything Scottish at all. Scottish schools have been slow to recognise that England is no longer the centre of the world. I cannot say, however, that this was true of the High School of Edinburgh as I knew it. It is true that we heard much about English literature and read Chaucer, Spenser, Shakespeare, Milton, Wordsworth and so forth. At the same time, Burns was not neglected and we used RL Mackie's *A Book of Scottish Verse* in the World's Classics series. I still have my copy, carefully preserved, dust jacket and all, in a transparent outer cover.

Of course we were often reminded of Walter Scott, perhaps the greatest of our predecessors on the school benches. I remember Ross remarking when someone had won a set of the Waverley Novels as a school prize, that they guaranteed stimulation and pleasure for a lifetime. Once a master, in despair over some inadequacy on the part of the class, told us that we had an obligation to measure up to the example set by Walter Scott, a formidable challenge, it seems to me. His *Quentin Durward* was a set book for our holiday reading, as was Stevenson's *Kidnapped* and *Catriona* and Munro's *The New Road*.

I came across Hugh MacDiarmid's collection of essays of 1934, *At The Sign of the Thistle*, in the school library, and in these I found much that reinforced my own evolving ideas. Perhaps it was a decisive influence. In fact, the atmosphere of the school was unquestionably Scottish, not as something self-conscious, studied or deliberate, but as a matter of course. How could it be otherwise in a school with such a history in such a setting and with such men as we had on the staff. They included Alexander Law, bursting with good nature and enthusiasm, and called Lofty because he was tall and not because he was aloof. He was an authority on eighteenth century Scotland particularly on the schools, about which he wrote a book, and above all on the poetry. He afterwards edited Allan Ramsay for the Scottish Text Society. When I came back to Edinburgh in 1980, he was still flourishing and I had several good conversations with him in his house and at meetings of the Friends of Edinburgh University Library.

Nor was the Highland part of our tradition ignored; there were some effective spokesmen for the Gaelic cause on the staff. One of the brothers of the great Gaelic poet, Sorley Maclean, was a classics master with an impressive record for precise scholarship. Then there was the very remarkable Hector MacIver from Lewis, a close friend of Sorley and one of these people who are more significant for their influence on others than for anything they do or write themselves. Sorley said that Hector 'was almost unique' in his ability to respond to both traditional and modern Gaelic poetry and because of 'his astonishing moral courage and his eloquence'. He could have been a star of stage or television because he had a spellbinding personality and a wonderful gift for storytelling. No one who heard him telling the story of the disappearance of the lighthouse keepers of Shannon Isle will ever forget it. After his death in 1966 at the age of 56 one of his former pupils, Karl Miller, afterwards editor of the *London Review of Books*, edited a collection of papers in his honour, to which one of my school friends, Robert Taubman, contributed an essay, with the title, 'Strangers', because that it is how, initially at least, he felt himself in Scotland. This book was entitled *Memoirs of a Modern Scotland*, rightly so because it was simultaneously an account of Hector MacIver and of the cultural and political transformation of Scotland in the 50s and 60s of which he was an important part.

Robert Taubman was unusual in the school because he was English and had been at a school in England. At that time such people were rare in Edinburgh. He comments in his essay on how different the atmosphere was from his English school:

> It was a place of conscious tradition, unlike the South-of-England school I came from, but not of amenity; tradition took the form of a good deal of antiquarianism and discomfort. Among the boys themselves there was perfect equality. In an unplanned, pre-comprehensive way, middle and working-class, toughs and scholars were all one, though not so in the official view; there was discrimination all right against those who did not do enough Latin and Greek to avoid having to do science. My English snobberies about tidiness or accent or what parents 'did' weren't, I think, particularly resented; they were just not understood.

I take that as a great compliment to the school. Taubman and I became friends because we had interests in common. He was fond of all literature, including Scottish. I had a high opinion of his talent and thought that he was likely to make a name for himself as a writer. This does not seem to have happened for some reason, although he reviewed novels at one time for the *New Statesman* or *The Spectator*. At university he won a scholarship for travel in Italy and he was supposed to produce some sort of work to show that he had spent the time in serious research. The story is that he was so beguiled by the sheer pleasure of Italy, which shows a right sense of value, that he did no work at all.

One of Robert's remarks in his essay 'Strangers' surprised me. He said that he found the boys in his form 'remarkable for their long trousers, experience with girls, independence and silence.' Among my own friends at least, I should have said quite the opposite about girls. In fact we lived a monastic existence. Unless you happened to have sisters, which I did not, you simply never encountered girls at all. At that time, too, there was much less emphasis on sex than there is now. There was no television continuously harping on about it and the cinema was still very prudish. We were, of course reasonably curious about sex and would raise questions about passages in Chaucer and Spenser, although probably more for the fun of embarrassing the master than to acquire information. Donald Cameron, however, did have a sister, Suzanne, who was the first girl to send me into that turmoil of delight, mixed with longings and apprehensions, which is youthful love. I think that I met her for the first time when Donald brought her along when we went to a theatre together. Our relationship, which was passionate but chaste, developed in intensity when we were both students at the University together. She was not only beautiful and charming, but intellectually alert and enthusiastic for Ibsen, Shaw and the *New Statesman*. What more could one wish?

The unselfconscious Scottishness of the school was true of Scotland as a whole. The Scotland which I grew up was in many ways more Scottish in reality than the Scotland of today, although we are now more aware of it. In the 1920s and 30s not only a pronounced Scottish accent, but a large measure of Scots vocabulary, were commonplace, even in Edinburgh. Before the days of wireless and talking pictures in the cinema, few of us had much experience of English or American voices. Our shops were mostly small family businesses, owned and staffed by Scots. Industry was largely Scottish owned and controlled. Our social habits and celebrations were little influenced by what happened elsewhere. Factories worked, and shops and offices were open on Christmas day; but the visiting and emotion of Hogmanay made it a very special day indeed. When I came back to live in Scotland in 1980, I was astonished to discover that Guy Fawkes day on 5th November was being celebrated there. When I was at school, we should have thought that absurd because it was obvious that this English celebration had nothing to do with us. The different attitude in 1980 brought home to me very vividly just how far radio and television, and the pressure of advertising, had advanced the processes of Anglicisation and Americanisation. It is a strange paradox that the Scotland of the 1980s and 1990s is less Scottish in practice, but more consciously and deliberately determined to preserve and advance the national character. It is like our attitude to a threatened species of plant or animal; the closer they come to extinction, the more determined we are to help them to survive.

Neither Hector MacIver nor any other master in the school ever made the slightest attempt to influence our political views or made the case for Scottish independence. I suppose that the Scottish constitutional question was much in the air, although still only among a small minority, because my last years at school coincided with the events which led to the fusion of the other parties to form the Scottish National Party in 1934. I had reached my own conclusion that Scotland should be independent and was delighted to find that there were other individuals and organisations who agreed with me. It seemed to me that Scotland had made a considerable contribution to civilisation, but could do still more if we were free to make our own decisions in accordance with our own attitudes and values. The Union had been imposed on Scotland, against the wishes of the great majority of the people, and in the interest of our powerful neighbour to the south. Tom Scott, in the introduction to the *Penguin Book of Scottish Verse*, which he edited, has a sentence which expresses my own feeling:

> To MacDiarmid the English ascendancy was a historical iniquity with no right but might behind it, and to be overthrown by all good men and true.

At school I contested a mock election on behalf of the SNP and at university I helped to establish a student organisation. My views on this matter have been constant and consistent, but I was not alone in this respect. When I first got in touch with the Edinburgh Branch of the SNP the chairman was Frank Yeaman. When I came back to Edinburgh in 1980 he was still in the same position and as I write in April 1999 he still is. Against the might and wealth of the British state and of the established political parties and of their propaganda machines, the SNP has had to struggle on for decades. Many people have given time, effort and money to it throughout their lives without seeing much in the way of progress. No one with mercenary or career objectives would have given it a second thought. This is why it has remained an association of patriots and idealists. I hope that it does not lose this purity of motive when now at last we seem to be close to achievement.

One of my favourite activities at school was the Literary and Debating Society of which I became President. This was run entirely by the boys without any interference by the staff. Sometimes we invited outside speakers, although they tended to be alumni of the school. One I remember was Henry Harvey Wood. He edited an edition of Robert Henryson in 1933 which contributed greatly to the rediscovery of a mediaeval makar whom Edwin Muir thought was the greatest of all Scottish poets. Harvey Wood was then a lecturer at the Department of (so-called) English Literature at Edinburgh University. During the war he worked for the British Council and was one of the people responsible for the establishment of the Edinburgh Festival.

With a European war becoming increasingly inevitable, we decided in the Debating Society in the autumn of 1937 to invite other Edinburgh schools, Heriots, Stewart's and Watson's to take part in a joint debate. We wanted to discuss the question that we expected to have to face quite soon in harsh reality, as it was expressed in the resolution: 'That this House would not fight for any cause and under any circumstances.' Inevitably the press began to take an interest, and that alarmed the heads of the schools. To their credit, they agreed that we should hold the debate, but the press were not to be admitted. The press reacted by calling it a 'secret schoolboy debate'.

I resented the idea of secrecy and so I agreed to write a report for the *Scottish Daily Express*. That is the reason why I still have a note of the details in a reporter's notebook, which I probably bought specially for the purpose, and which I have carefully preserved. The *Express* even paid me 10/6d, which is the first money that I ever earned. The 'remittance advice' survives inside the notebook and shows that the debate was held on 19th November 1937. From these notes, it seems that most of the speakers in the debate were in favour of pacifism and they made a strong case. One was unrealistic enough to suggest that if Britain set a good example by disarming completely, all other countries would do the same. Somewhat surprisingly, because he was as gentle a creature as you would hope to find, Robert Taubman seconded for the negative. He said that the pacifism was an inadequate response to the situation in the world. There were, he said, causes for which it was right to fight. From my notes he does not seem to have mentioned the need to resist Nazism, but he said that Ireland was right to fight for freedom. The final count was 50 votes for the motion, but 62 against which rather spoiled the story for the press. Still, it does suggest that opinion was fairly evenly divided among the age group that would be the first conscripts only two or three years later.

In the following two years we all became increasingly aware of the horrifying events that were evolving in Germany and of their probable consequences. My own instinct bent towards pacifism, a cause for which Suzanne's mother was an active and persuasive propagandist. I needed no persuasion to convince me that war was usually futile and always massively destructive of life and of everything that was civilised. Among my SNP friends at the time, and they included two men, outstanding in different ways but both fine poets, Douglas Young and George Campbell Hay, there was much discussion of the whole question. Would it be right to go to war with Germany? Did a British Government have any right, under the Treaty of Union to conscript Scots for service outside Scotland?

Douglas Young would almost certainly have been exempt from conscription because of his health, but as a matter of principle he opposed the right of the government to apply it in Scotland. He took the matter to the Court of Session, where, I am told, the Judges congratulated him on the subtlety and erudition of his argument, but regretted that they had to accept the right of Parliament, under the prevailing (but not Scottish) doctrine of parliamentary sovereignty. He was a tall, bearded, kenspeckle and genial giant of a man with a ready wit. His poetry in Scots included translations from many languages, especially Greek, including a version of Aristophanes's *The Frogs* and *The Birds*. At that time he was a lecturer in Greek at Aberdeen University, but afterwards took chairs in universities in Canada and then America where he died in 1973.

George Campbell Hay was a very different character. He too was a scholar, but sensitive and rather shy and a wholly delightful companion. Although not a native speaker of Gaelic, he learnt the language and wrote poetry in it, as well as in Scots, English, French, Italian and Norwegian. During the war he resisted conscription, but eventually joined the army and served in North Africa and the Middle East. His experiences there caused a serious breakdown in his physical and mental health. One of his Gaelic poems, translated into Scots by Douglas Young, is about a man from the Hebrides drowned during the war. It ends:

> Sair the price maun be dounpitten
> by the island-fowks for the greatness of Britain.

That was true of his own life. When I came back to Edinburgh in 1980 I heard that he was living there and, of course, I tried to find him. Everyone I asked told me that he was in such a delicate mental state that any voice from the past would upset him even more. I accepted this advice, but regretted it when I heard that he had died, apparently isolated and alone. At that time I was taking a Gaelic class and one of my fellow pupils told us a lamentable story. He had opened a suitcase that was being offered for sale at one of Lyon and Turnbull's lane sales, where they disposed of articles of small value. It was full of

Campbell Hay's manuscripts. They might easily have been thrown away if they had fallen into other hands.

Much as I instinctively detested militarism and violence, I reached the obvious conclusion while I was still at school that Hitler's Germany had to be resisted. We all realised that we would almost certainly find ourselves in the forces before long and that we were of the generation that would provide the second lieutenants and the fighter pilots. In other words, our expectation of life was probably fairly short and planning for anything else was futile. Strangely, enough, I do not remember that we were particularly depressed by the thought. That was how life was and we accepted it, as our fathers had done, just over twenty years before. I took the logical step and joined the school Officers' Training Corps, of which I had disapproved for years.

The OTC turned out not to be so bad as I had imagined. If it was soldiering, it was soldiering of a very gentle and theoretical kind. When one of us accidentally hurt himself with his bayonet, they were withdrawn to avoid such a thing happening again. We wore the uniform of the Royal Scots with the kilt and we had a pipe band. Days spent on exercises or at a camp with other schools by the seaside at Elie in Fife were a pleasant change from the classroom. Instruction on infantry tactics came easily to a generation brought up on Caesar's *Gallic Wars*.

When the time came for us to leave school in July 1939 the war had not yet started. We ended our school days with the annual ceremony at which speeches were made and prizes given. These, in our time at least, were very generous. The dux in English, for instance, was traditionally awarded with a large and handsome pocket watch in solid gold. Since it was decided that James Kinsley and I had merited this with complete equality, we were given one each. Book prizes too were plentiful and well chosen. Kinsley was afterwards Professor of English in Nottingham University and edited the standard edition of Robert Burns and one of William Dunbar. In the Preface of the latter, he records that he was awarded a copy of Mackay Mackenzie's edition of Dunbar and that this 'began one of the most intense literary affections' of his life. I can say the same. That is true as well of a fine set of Jane Austen's novels, *The Oxford Book of English Verse* and Agnes Mackenzie's *Scottish Literature to 1714*. They have been part of my library and my life ever since.

The senior form leaving the school went through a simple but impressive ceremony. At the end of the Hall there was a Greek doorway in white marble which was used only once a year when the departing boys shook hands with the Rector and passed through it to be received on the great portico outside by the Chairman of the Royal High School Club. Perhaps it was especially moving in our year because the doorway was also a memorial to the boys of the school who were killed in World War I.

CHAPTER 2
Edinburgh University
October 1939 – July 1941

A month after the declaration of war, I became a student at Edinburgh University in October 1939. At first, this was the so-called 'phoney war' where the two sides glared at one another across the Maginot Line, but appeared to do very little else. We knew that this would not last and that we were living on borrowed time. James Kinsley, as a candidate for the ministry of the Church, was exempt from the call-up to the forces. The rest of us knew that we should find ourselves in uniform before very long. I was able to complete two academic years of the four of the Honours English course.

In the spirit of the old Scottish tradition of diversity, I did from time to time drop into lectures on other subjects. I remember in particular those on political economy by Alexander Gray, one of the few economists who was also an accomplished poet, and in Scots at that. In all subjects it was the practice for the Professor himself to give a course of lectures to the first year students. For English Literature, it was Dover Wilson, a Shakespearean scholar and editor. His lectures tended to the sentimental. He told us once that he had noticed that the most worn volume of Shakespeare in University libraries was invariably *Romeo and Juliet*. Although he gave the impression that he thought that his mission was to bring English civilisation to the savage barbarians of the North, we must have converted him a little because he stayed in Scotland when he retired. British History was also in the hands of an Englishman, VH Galbraith. He was much more robust and outspoken. 'It is all very well to be romantic about the past,' he once said, 'but even the romantics take good care to choose their friends from among people who wash.' Galbraith also understood Scotland. I have kept a cutting from *The Scotsman* of 2nd March 1944 which reported a speech he made when he retired; serious newspapers used to do that sort of thing. Already in 1944 he was discussing English and Scottish nationality in the sort of terms that have become commonplace today.

> England has lost its nationality altogether, and the people who talk about the Englishman are talking about a past which is dead and gone. There is no such thing as an Englishman in the sense that there is a Scot. Scotland is a nation and it has a great tradition and stands for something. That something is just what there is not in England. What I find in Scotland is a tremendous steadiness about people, and a reliability and saneness. That is what I call a rock-like quality. They are not lop-sided and not specialised.

I hope that he was right about Scotland, but I am always surprised when people talk as he did about England. It seems to me that the English are so confident of their identity that they do not feel the need to assert or discuss it.

Galbraith's remark about specialisation suggests that he was aware of the long nineteenth century debate over the Scottish tradition in university education which was afterwards the subject of George Davie's book, *The Democratic Intellect*. In fact Galbraith went on to say:

> You have the most marvellous universities – potentially – and they are not English universities. You must resist those rascals they will send you after the war, who will tell you what you have to do with education. No proposal with regard to education which comes up here from England is worth a damn to you. . . I am perfectly sure that the future of Scotland lies in a sort of tremendous development of its own affairs, and having the powers to do that.

I think that he was absolutely right. As it happens, when I was in my first Department of the Foreign Office in 1950 a daughter of Vincent Galbraith, Mary, joined the Department. She was one of the first women to be appointed to the Senior Branch. At first, she was strangely reserved, if not hostile. She told us afterwards, when she discovered that we were quite harmless and human, that this was because her mother had told her to expect resentment from the men. She had been encouraged by her mother to try for the Diplomatic Service as one more male bastion that had to be stormed. She was on guard against a male conspiracy to do her down. In no time at all, she discovered that we were only too delighted to have a bright and lively girl in our midst. We were all intrigued when the office messengers delivered flowers from an admirer in another department. I do not know what happed to her afterwards. Presumably she married and had to resign as was the rule in those benighted times.

The Scottish History class was very different from the British, in style, size and manner. The Professor, Robert K err Hannay, preferred the tutorial approach to formal prepared lectures. This, in any case, was encouraged by the small number of students, about twenty in the ordinary class, compared to about ten times that number in the first ordinary British. Since many of the students were preparing to be school teachers, it is not surprising that most of the history taught in Scottish schools has been British, which usually means English.

Hannay had been Curator of the Historical Department of Register House and the study of the original sources remained his chief interest and the core of his teaching. We should never trust 'the books', by which he meant all secondary publications. At the time when I was in his class, he was working on a calendar of the correspondence of James IV, which the Scottish History Society eventually published, many years later, in 1953. I think that it must have been from Hannay that I first acquired a particular interest in that brilliant and ultimately tragic period. We were an intimate, happy crew in Hannay's class and did not realise at the time that he was already suffering from the illness that killed him towards the end of the first academic year.

The somewhat staid atmosphere of the Old Quad in those days was enlivened by a member of the class with the improbable name, Honor Mary Pape. She was given to wearing outrageous clothes and making even more outrageous remarks in an all too audible whisper in the silence of the reading room.

In the second of my two years at the University, most of our lectures on literature were by two men of completely opposite style, Arthur Melville Clark and Geor ge Kitchin. Melville Clark was always impeccably dressed and his lecture style was equally meticulous. Everything he said was carefully researched, and carefully composed and delivered. Nothing was unexpected or startling. No sudden insights. Kitchin was always disorganised and so full of ideas that he hardly ever finished a sentence without rushing off at a tangent in pursuit of a new thought.

It was not fashionable at the time in academic circles to confess to enthusiasm for Scottish literature, although, with Hugh MacDiarmid bellowing in the wings, things were beginning to change. After all it was at Edinburgh University that I was introduced to the poetry of Robert Henryson. Probably this was due to Henry Harvey Wood who edited an edition of Henryson in 1933. We used as a text a very handsome edition of his *Testament of Cresseid*, edited by Bruce Dickins, a treasure of a book in design as well as content. This was published by the Porpoise Press who were pioneers in the publication of the writers of the Scottish Renaissance. I still have both books and I see that I bought them in 1939 because it used to be my habit to write the date of purchase on the fly leaves.

Both Melville Clark and Kitchin were, I think, secret, or at least discrete, enthusiasts for Scottish literature. Clark in 1969 published *Sir Walter Scott: The Formative Years*, a painstakingly scholarly account of Scott's formal and informal education. In spite of the scholarship, his love for the subject is obvious. In it, he remarks, by the way, that Walter Scott and his Edinburgh contemporaries had less devotion to the University than to the High School. They had none of the affection and sense of belonging for the university which they had for the school. From my own experience I think that is probably still true. After all you stay longer at school and at a more impressionable time of life. If Clark was enthusiastic, like so many of us, about Walter Scott, Kitchin's enthusiasms ranged more widely. He edited a collection of essays on Scottish literature past and present, at a time when such a thing was still unusual.

Strangely enough, as I was writing about my first student days in Edinburgh University, I came across an old file from that time. I have no idea how it has survived all my movements and vicissitudes. There are Certificates of Merit from various classes, including one signed by Melville Clark, from which I see that I was fourth in the English class in 1940-41. Among them there is also a list of the signatures of the Scots Nationalist Association in 1939-40, which I helped to form very soon after the formation of the Scottish National Party itself. There were only thirteen members and they include my school friends, Tom Kydd, Robert Taubman, Donald Cameron (who was afterwards a member of the Communist Party for many years) but not his sister,

Suzanne. In spite of our closeness in many things and lifelong friendship, she has never shared my political ideas nor my feelings for Scotland.

During the whole of my time at the University, Suzanne and I had a very intense relationship. We met almost every day and spent most of our free time together, walking on the Pentland Hills, theatres and cinemas and endlessly talking. Our feelings were heightened by the fact that I would soon have to go to the Army with all that involved. I still have the letters which she sent me after I left Edinburgh. There are hundreds of them; we seem to have written to one another every two or three days.

In April 1940 her brother Donald and I went off to Argyll in the sturdy Hillman car which my grandfather gave me while I was still at school. Our purpose was to help the SNP in a by-election in which William Power was the candidate. We stayed at the youth hostel on the shore of Loch Eck and went to public meetings, which were then still an important part of election campaigns. I remember in particular a crowded one in a large theatre in Dunoon where our questions and heckling reduced the Conservative candidate to incoherent rage. Power got 7,000 votes against the Tory's 12,000 which was the best SNP performance so far.

In the same file there was also a letter of 1950 from Bruce Cooper who was Secretary of the Dialectic Society. He wrote in reply to my apology for not being able to come to a reunion dinner because I was in Germany, and he remarked that two of my contemporaries would be there, Robert Taubman and Alastair Dunnett. The Dialectic was, and perhaps still is, one of these debating societies where a small group of like-minded students sit round a table and debate some proposition in a fairly formal manner. David Daiches, who was a member some years before me, had theories – as he did about most literary matters – about the formality of Scottish students, of our generation at least. He said that it was not uncommon for a speaker at the Dialectic to begin, 'I rise to homologate the sentiments of the previous speaker.'

The best known such society in Edinburgh was the Speculative. I have always regretted that somehow I failed to have any contact with it when I was a student. Perhaps the quality of the debate there was no better, but I confess that I have a weakness for historical associations. There must be a special satisfaction in being a member of the same society, as well as the same University, as Walter Scott and RL Stevenson, the two writers who had probably given me more pleasure than any others. I have since felt about the Speculative as LE Jones says of All Souls in his autobiography, *An Edwardian Faith*: 'the place which I felt myself uniquely fitted, not indeed to deserve or adorn, but to savour and enjoy.' I feel like that about the Scottish Parliament.

Robert Taubman was indeed a contemporary, but who was the Alastair Dunnett? I did, many years later, have a very good friend of that name, the editor of *The Scotsman* from 1956 to 1972. It must have been a different Alastair Dunnett at the dinner because the Alastair I have just mentioned went to no university and could not have been a member of the Dialectic. They might, of course, have had the sense to invite him as a guest because he would be a delight at any dinner table. Cooper's letter mentions that the next debate, in the presence of Field Marshall Earl Wavell, no less, was to be on the question: 'That Burns would have benefitted from a university education.'

That is an admirable subject for debate, it seems to me, because there is much to be said on both sides. I have always delighted in universities and have been involved with them, in one way or another, for most of my life. George Bruce once told me a relevant anecdote about Maurice Lindsay. 'Why,' Maurice asked him, 'do my books of poems get such bad reviews?' George, who has all the directness of his Fraserburgh upbringing, replied that it was because many of the poems were not much good. 'My trouble,' said Maurice, 'is that because I did not go to a university, I do no know which are good and which are bad.' From then onwards, Maurice never published anything, and he has published many books, without submitting the text first to George for his approval.

This shows a touching faith in the advantages of a university education, although, whatever their qualities, I do not suppose they can confer infallibility in critical judgement. Nor do I suppose that Alastair Dunnett would have been a better editor or stronger force for good if he had been to a university. Walter Scott in his *Journal*, which is one of the most delightful and fascinating of all such books, says: 'many a clever boy is flogged into a dunce and many an original composition corrected into mediocrity.'

De Lancey Ferguson has a remark, which is even more relevant, in the Introduction to his selection of the letters of Robert Burns: 'Had he received a formal education, it would have been in the anglifying mould that was standard in late eighteen-century Scotland. So trained, the poet might have become another Thomson, but he would have been taught to despise the folk tradition which has made him immortal.'

Ferguson wrote this in 1951, a year after Cooper's letter. The idea must have been in the air at the time. I am not sure that Ferguson was right. Burns, after all, was well read in the fashionable books of his time and he resisted the pressure of the leading pundits in Edinburgh, who thought he should write in English, and I imagine that his boyhood teacher, John Murdoch, did his best in the same direction. Many lesser men certainly yielded to such pressures, but Burns was of sterner stuff.

The Dialectic Society was not the only forum for debate. There was a much larger audience and a more confrontational style in the University Union. Once too, I was part of a team to represent Edinburgh at a debate in the Glasgow Union where John MacCormick was a guest speaker. He was for years a leader of the movement for self-government and he was Power's election agent in Argyll. His son Neil, is a close friend and colleague in the SNP, an academic lawyer of international distinction and now a member of the European Parliament.

Rectorial elections are one of the great institutions of the older Scottish universities. They give the students an opportunity to elect someone of their choice to represent them on the Court, the governing body of the university. They are also the opportunity to make a political gesture or merely have fun and hilarity in a sort of mockery of the political process. It is the latter instinct, I think, which prompts the regrettable nomination, and sometimes the election, of pop stars or television presenters. There was a Rectorial election in my time. It was a virtual certainty, and so indeed it turned out, that Sir Donald Pollock would be elected, if only because he was well known in the University as a wealthy benefactor. His opponents during the campaign published what they claimed was a postcard from Bernard Shaw, declining nomination on the grounds that 'any candidate of the slightest intelligence would be ignominiously defeated by Sir Donald Pollock.' I was naive enough at the time to be impressed that Shaw had such an understanding of our petty concerns; but I suppose that it was no more than a squib by the anti-Pollock camp.

A number of us were determined to put up a candidate who was a worthy representative of the cultural life of Scotland. A majority, I think on the proposal of Robert Taubman, favoured Edwin Muir. He would not have been my first choice. It was, after all, only a few years after the publication of his book, *Scott and Scotland*, with which I disagreed and to which I eventually wrote a reply. At all events, Robert and I went to St Andrews to invite Edwin to stand. The conversation was dominated by his wife, Willa, notoriously the stronger personality. Both seemed to be pleased by the proposal and Edwin formally accepted.

We did not win, but we had an enjoyable campaign. Our master stroke was to be the display on polling day of a large banner, 'Edwin Muir for Rector,' suspended in mid-air over the middle of the Old Quad. To achieve this, Donald Cameron and I somehow managed during the night to get ourselves onto the roof of the building surrounding the quadrangle and manipulate an ingenious contrivance of wires to pull the banner across. We left it fluttering proudly there, well pleased with the night's work. Unfortunately, it was all for nothing. A strong squall in the early morning blew the banner into a hopeless and illegible jumble across the wires. It is to the credit of the university that they subsequently removed the sorry mess without any attempt to look for the culprits. A high degree of tolerance is part of the Rectorial tradition.

I was a member of the editorial board of the university magazine, *The Student*. With an exuberant Irishman, whose name if I remember rightly was Docherty, I spent some happy weeks planning a new review that was to reinvigorate the intellectual life of Scotland. We did publish the first, and last, number, which produced no reaction at all. I have forgotten its name, like that of my partner in the endeavour.

It was about this time too that I first came across the Saltire Society, 'founded in 1936', as it says in the Syllabus, 'to encourage everything that might improve the quality of life in Scotland and restore the country to its proper place as a creative force in European civilisation.' This accords so much with my own feelings and aspirations that the Society has been part of my life ever since.

At the end of the academic year in 1941, for the call-up authorities allowed us to finish the year, the time came for me to leave the university for the army. Perhaps because of this abrupt and involuntary transition, or perhaps just because the environment suits me, I have never entirely severed my connections with academic life. I have taken university courses in most places where I have been in my subsequent career and I have taken part in scores of academic conferences. In 1989 I was elected Rector of Dundee University. I took a postgraduate degree of M.Litt after I retired. Even in the army, I remember making expeditions to the universities of St Andrews, Aberystwyth and Oxford. It is one of the advantages of living in Edinburgh, as, I suppose, of any university town, that there are frequently public lectures and always the society of well-stocked and active minds. I return to that atmosphere very frequently. In some ways I have never left it.

CHAPTER 3

The Army in training
July 1941 – October 1944

Someone writing about World War I said that, although the Army could involve you in misery and horror, it could also be quite kind and generous to you now and again. My first posting was such a case. I did not have to go far, only to Dreghorn Barracks. This is within the confines of Edinburgh and on the edge of the Pentland Hills, where I often used to go for country walks. There I was to join the Royal Artillery on 17th July 1941 and to be trained to drive heavy gun tractors, which were not unlike ordinary large lorries. My fellow recruits were mostly Scots from all sorts of backgrounds, urban and rural. I think that most of us were a bit apprehensive at first, but we soon relaxed. The atmosphere was more like a scout camp than military indoctrination.

After a month or so, those of us who lived nearby were given 'sleeping-out' passes. This meant that we could stay at home, turn up in the morning and leave in the evening, like an ordinary job. We were even given rations to take home in compensation for missing the evening meal. Army training in the films was never like this. When we graduated to spending most of the driving in the town in these gun tractors, it was accepted practice that we should drop off at a point convenient for the bus home.

Of course it was too good to last. My past record in the school and university Officer Training Corps caught up with me. It meant that I was destined for the more demanding life as an officer cadet instead of the indulgence of Dreghorn. I was summoned before the CO who congratulated me and said that I was to join the pre-OCTU (Officer Cadet Training Unit) of the Artists' Rifles at Morecambe. The sudden wrench of leaving Edinburgh and Suzanne and everything that was familiar hardly seemed to me a matter for congratulations. But I could not complain after such a gentle introduction to the military life.

This new unit was curious and unexpected as well. The Artists' Rifles had apparently been a Territorial regiment which had produced combatant forces in World War I, but was now reduced, or elevated, to this training role. Most of the officers had been masters at English public schools and most of the cadets, like me, had had a year or two at a university. The general atmosphere was hearty, but also slightly intellectual and slightly pretentious. I was conscious of an Englishness that I had not encountered before. It made you think of English school stories. It was more strenuous than Dreghorn because we did battle courses, route marches and infantry tactical exercises but the conversation was better. Debate and discussion was positively encouraged. We used to do guard duty walking round the camp in pairs during the night, demonstrating our cleverness to one another. One of my partners in this exercise was Theo Peters, afterwards a colleague in the Foreign Office. Another, Paul Hanbury, invited me for a weekend in his family's splendid Tudor mansion, Upham House near Marlborough. Most of it was being used as a convalescent home for officers. In our spare time in Morecambe, some of us made friends in the local repertory theatre. Thora Hird, who was the star, and her husband held open house for us. They had a baby girl who as Jeanette Scott became a film actress in Holywood.

Some of our colleagues seemed to have indulged more basic amusements. The CO felt that he had to call a meeting to tell us that there had been complaints from local people about fornication on the beach at Morecambe. He broached the subject with circumlocution and evident embarrassment. At last he got to the point. 'Damn it all, chaps, it's true. I took a walk along the promenade the other night and the truth is this, I have never seen so many naked bottoms bouncing in the moonlight.'

Intellectual and worthy it might have been, but the accommodation was Spartan enough. We lived in the so-called chalets of a Butlin's Holiday Camp surrounding a house, called Heysham Towers. This was all right in summer, but rather a cold winter followed. Our huts had plywood walls, no heating and ill-fitting doors and windows. In the morning our towels were often frozen rigid and our boots were so stuck with ice to the floor that we had to lever them free with our bayonets. We treated the whole thing more as a joke than a hardship and anyway it was better than sleeping in the open on an exercise.

Those of us who survived the trial by Heysham Towers were then sent on to OCTUs proper. Since I had been recruited into the Artillery, that is where I remained, not the Sandhurst of the Infantry but the Shrivenham of the gunners. Having no heroic urge, I was not sorry about this. I had great respect for these men who endured so much, but the poor, bloody infantry always have the worst of it. They walk on their feet, carry their kit on their backs and come into close contact with the enemy. The gunner may not be as remote as the bomber in his aircraft, but at least he is at some distance and he travels on wheels.

Shrivenham lies between Swindon and Marlborough in Wiltshire in the deep south of England. It was a group of modern barrack buildings, rather more lavish than most, evidently built at a time when urgency and economy were not all that mattered. It lies in pleasant country on the Salisbury Plain with all its military associations. I should like to have seen more of the surroundings and the agreeable country towns, but we had little free time and no private transport. Even the army had to be careful with its petrol supplies. Many of our exercises we did by bicycle and amused ourselves by using cavalry words of command as though they were horses.

The general atmosphere was not unlike a university, but one run by fanatical puritans – an early start each day; strict code of dress; rigid timetable; no women or other distractions; much physical training as well as lectures on such things as the intricacies of the Bofors guns or military law. There was an ethos of efficiency and strenuous endeavour. I suppose the spur was the thought that you could be sent back to the ranks, 'r.t.ued' in the jargon – returned to unit – if you failed to make the grade. As far as I can remember that happened to only one of my group and we were very sorry for him. He was older than the rest of us and perhaps found the battle courses and such like more demanding. To support an appeal against this rejection, he produced press cuttings, testimonials and photographs about his past achievements. But in the eyes of the authorities that only made him seem more inadequate and unsuitable.

One of my school or university friends – I can't remember who it was – ran into me during these days. I heard afterwards that he had reported to mutual friends in Edinburgh that I was quite unchanged and behaved as though I did not know that there was a war. 'There he is, still spending every available minute with a book – Burns, Tolstoy or Fisher, if one could believe it.' This was accurate. During all my time in the army, I had with me the World Classics Burns, *War and Peace* and, a larger volume, Fisher's *History of Europe*.

One of our instructors was a young actor from one of the theatrical dynasties, Terry, if I remember rightly. He played the part of the effete young man in the film of Shaw's *Pygmalion* who invited Eliza Doolittle to walk through the park. To which she made the memorable reply, 'Not bloody likely. I'm for a taxi.' In real life, he looked just as effete, but he was given to doing tricks with live grenades. I am told that he eventually blew off one of his hands.

We were being trained to become officers in regiments of Light Anti-Aircraft Artillery equipped with Bofors guns. They were capable of a very high rate of fire of small shells, and would have been a very effective defence against the Stuka dive-bomb attacks which did great physical and psychological damage to the British and French forces in the German *Blitzkreig* in the summer of 1940. The British Army, and perhaps all armies everywhere have a reputation of preparing to fight, not the next campaign, when conditions might be very different, but the one before. This was a classic case. To manufacture the guns and train the officers and men to give every infantry and armoured division a regiment of Bofors was a mammoth undertaking. It was achieved with skill, expense and effort. But by the time it was achieved it was unnecessary. Long before the D-Day invasion of Europe, the Allies had supremacy in the air and the dive bombers were no longer a threat.

This is the sort of thing that gives the Army a reputation for stupidity, the subject of endless satire. Lions led by donkeys, someone said of the infantry in World War I. Career Army officers, in the past at least, had a reputation for snobbery, mental rigidity and limited imagination. They were thought to have more courage and dash than common sense, as in the charge of the Light Brigade in the Crimea. At the same time, the Army also has a reputation for careful planning and efficiency, as in the phrase 'with military precision'. The two reputations are not necessarily inconsistent. You can be efficient in matters that can be regulated by rules, but fail to see that your efforts are misguided.

The wartime Army is, of course, quite different from peace time. Only a few highly intelligent people are likely to choose the Army as a career, but during the war people of all kinds and qualities were conscripted. I suspect that the result was an injection of imagination and intelligence. Certainly, as in any large organisation, there was much for the people on the ground to complain about. 'Order, disorder and confusion'; 'Haven't you heard? It's all been changed'; 'The usual bloody cock-up.' Such phrases as these were commonplace. Still, in my own experience there was more efficiency than confusion. I was more often impressed by the intelligence and ability of our instructors at Shrivenham, for example, than irritated by the opposite. The force that invaded Europe on 6th June 1944 was well equipped, highly trained and meticulously planned. It had, after all, had four years to prepare.

But I anticipate. My course at Shrivenham was moved for its last month or two to much more humble surroundings in a military camp at Towyn in North Wales. Perhaps someone had realised that officers for regiments of Bofors guns did not deserve a very high priority. I enjoyed the change. For one thing, I felt more at home among the mountains and coast of Wales than in the 'tame and domestic' countryside of Wiltshire. Sometimes it was too wild; it nearly always seemed to pour with rain when we had to sleep out in the open air on exercises. One free day I escaped on a pilgrimage to Abersystwyth, a complicated journey by public transport, to see the university and because I had heard of a good bookshop there.

I was commissioned as a 2nd Lieutenant on 8th October 1942 and posted along with two or three fellow graduates to join the 108 Light Anti-Aircraft Regiment in Cruden Bay about fifteen miles north of Aberdeen. Once again, the Army was being kind to me. The Regiment was part of the 52nd (Lowland) Division, one of the two Scottish divisions, (the other was 51st Highland). It was Lowland in the sense that consisted of Regiments associated with the Lowlands of Scotland. In function it was, or became, a mountain division, the first, strangely enough, in the history of the British Army. The divisional sign, which we wore on our sleeves, was the Saltire of Scotland in a shield, surrounded by the word, Mountain. If one had to go to war, it was some consolation to do it under your own national colours. Also, it was good to be back in Scotland. The Division was spread all over the North East which we had many opportunities to explore during most of the next two years.

The mountain business had many consequences. We were dressed in a comfortable compromise between military uniform and the garb of the enthusiastic hill walker. We had thick jerseys and anoraks instead of battle dress blouses, ski caps with a large peak and camouflage suits, both white and brown and green. We had an Indian Army supply column with horses and had to adapt our pace of mobile operations to their speed. We experimented with husky dogs. Above all, some of us were lucky enough (although not everyone saw it like that) to spend a winter in tents at a ski-school near Aviemore. For my part, this started a life-long addiction.

I have to admit that many of the troops did not share my enthusiasm. At first, with the devotion and determination which was usual at that time, we worked every day. Living in tents in the mountains, remote from girls, cinemas and pubs, the troops began to be a little restive. They were not convinced when I told them how lucky they were to be skiing at Government expense. Admittedly, it involved climbing 1,000 feet every day to reach the snow or the top, with a rucksack, a change of clothes, a rifle and fifty rounds of ammunition. There were very few days in the season when we had sunshine, bright skies and snow down to the valley. Eventually, we relented and arranged a free day and a half each week and persuaded the railway company to stop the trains at the nearest signal box. The joys of Inverness and Perth were then within reach. I even managed a day in Edinburgh and caused a little sensation when I arrived, with Robert Taubman I think, to lunch in the De Guise restaurant in my mountain uniform, previously unseen in the metropolis.

Of course, we never fought in mountains or in the Arctic after all this preparation. When the Division first went into action against the enemy, it was below sea-level in Zuid Beveland and Walcheren in western Holland. But this was not another example of military ineptitude. It was partly a precaution in case it became desirable to send a force to Norway again, but it was also an elaborate bluff. We made no secret that we had our eyes on Norway. Maps of Norway were visible through the windows of our Divisional HQ. We had a Norwegian field battery, a Norwegian field hospital, and Norwegian instructors in the ski school. Several of us started to learn the language. Norwegians were constantly crossing the North Sea in small boats and landing in the Moray Firth. Some of our Norwegian colleagues even disappeared from time to time to return to Norway on clandestine missions. No quisling was safe from them. We were congratulated afterwards on the success of the bluff. The Germans kept a substantial force inactive in Norway, in case our intentions were as they seemed.

Among the new 2nd Lts who joined the Regiment with me from Towyn was one, Bill Garden by name, who had been the golf correspondent of *The Scotsman* newspaper. He had covered all the important golf tournaments for years and had interviewed not only the golf champions but many other people whose names appeared in the headlines. He used to drop a few of these names into his conversations in a way which impressed people who were not used to it. He could play golf fairly well himself. These talents so beguiled the commandant at Towyn that the two of them quite often played golf together, while the rest of us were off on some exercise or other.

Quite soon after our arrival in Cruden Bay, Garden was given a few days leave. To our surprise, because officers were not supposed to behave like that, he failed to return. After a week or two, the military police in Aberdeen telephoned to say that they had one of our officers under arrest. He was brought back and had to have another officer permanently with him until his fate was decided. This was not too onerous a responsibility because they spent most of their time playing golf. Then he had to appear before the Divisional Commander who told him not to be a bloody fool, not to let the side down, and not to do it again.

But he did, and this time he was not found for months. Instead we started to get letters of complaint from the police and from hotels and other places, usually in the better golfing resorts. He evidently still used his own name. His technique was to stay in the best hotels, borrow money from other guests, and then disappear without paying his bill. Many of us remember that he had borrowed money from us as well, but with such charm and plausibility that you hardly noticed. Once when the Regiment was moving into Carnoustie in November 1943, for we seemed to specialise in golfing places, a sergeant reported that he had caught a glimpse of Garden. Again he vanished. Eventually he was caught by the police in the South of England and sent for trial. We never saw him again.

I mention this little episode, at some length because it was so exceptional. The general atmosphere was one of strenuous endeavour. In my papers I have come across a letter of Sept 1945 in which the adjutant, Tony Foreman, who was once my Troop Commander, sent me photographs of myself which had been found in the Regimental files (they must have been weeding them) along with a pamphlet which was a short history of the Regiment from 1 January 1942 to 8 May

1945. I knew that it had been converted to LAA from a battalion of the Green Howards and we still wore green lanyards to commemorate it. But I had forgotten that this had happened only in January 1942 and that the Regiment joined the 52nd Division in March, just seven months before I arrived there myself.

The Regiment were therefore newcomers to the mysteries of light anti-aircraft artillery, which was quite a complex science. This is presumably why the graduates from Shrivenham or Towyn were received with such enthusiasm. It probably explains, too, why I acted as an umpire in a divisional exercise called 'Goliath' which was held over a wide area of the Highlands in December. I know this because miraculously I still have the full notebook with carbon copies of my reports. The exercise was meant to try us under difficult circumstances and terrain and weather and it evidently did. The Regimental history says only that 'valuable experience was gained in the art of removing gun wheels deep in the apparently bottomless bogs of the Scottish Highlands.'

The same source tells me that the Regiment covered about 3,000 miles in the first five months of 1943. Twice we moved from the Highlands to the south coast of England to add to the air defence, then to a practice camp to fire the guns at Clacton, and then to 'Spartan' a large exercise over the south of England. Just before one of these moves an Instructor in Gunnery was posted to us as a troop commander. These men ruled the roost in practice camps. They wore red bands round their hats like generals, and denounced the failings of practising regiments with an air of scorn and superiority. They tended to be rather unpopular in consequence.

Not long after this particular one joined us, we set off in one of our long convoy journeys to the south of England. The CO as was his habit, parked his staff car at the side of the road to review, like Napoleon, his men as they went past. The new troop commander was observed to be sitting comfortably in a jeep, an unacceptable indulgence for a troop officer. A dispatch rider was sent off to present the CO's compliments and to say that he expected to see his troop officers on motor cycles.

Now it is true that we lived on motor cycles, the modern equivalent of the horse, and had learned the hard way how to cope with them. To ride up and down a convoy of guns, which tended at speed to bounce from side to side, was at first a very alarming experience. The poor Instructor in Gunnery did his best, but by the time we reached the south coast of England he was a nervous wreck and had to be sent to hospital. That was the last we saw of him because the CO sent round a report, for him to initial, saying that he was not acceptable as an officer in a combatant unit. The commandant of the hospital complained to the War Office about this harassment of a patient in his care. Perhaps the patient thought it was no so much harassment as a merciful escape.

Strangely enough though, I do not think that most of us were looking for an escape. We had no illusions about war and knew that it was often miserable, tedious and dangerous with a high risk of injury or death. For some reason, we accepted that this was something which had to be done and we were ready to work, train and plan to do it as efficiently as possible. But why? It was nothing to do with patriotic fervour. Recently Andrew Wilson at an SNP Conference in Inverness raised a slight stir by referring to the Union Jack in terms similar to Bernard Shaw in *John Bull's Other Island*, 'that detestable symbol of a decadent imperialism'. The pompous and insufferable, John Reid, the Labour Minister, said that this was an insult to those who fought under it during the war. I can assure him that in the wartime Army we never saw a Union flag, or any flag for that matter, even if we had a Saltire in our divisional sign. In fact, the symbol of the allied army was a large white star painted on the top of all our vehicles so that it would be recognised from the air. We assumed at the time, and it was probably right, that this was adapted from the American flag.

Certainly we (by which I mean my friends and colleagues) did not think that we were fighting, or about to fight, for the idea of Britishness. It seems to be a common assumption that experience as a member of the British Forces is likely to make people more British than Scottish. In fact, the effect was very often the opposite. Partly this was because involvement in a British organisation quite often brought home the way in which Scotland was taken for granted as a docile dependency. One of the popular songs on the BBC of the time was, 'There'll always be an England.' Also, as Hugh MacDiarmid remarked in one of his letters about World War I, it was being fought in defence of the rights of the small nations and Scotland was a small nation too. There were contingents from many countries in the so-called British forces, and not only from the Commonwealth, but from countries, such as Poland or Norway, over-run by the German advance. They had their own units and the name of their country on their uniforms. Even before the Americans joined us after the Japanese attack on Pearl Harbour, we were part of an international allied force, of which Scotland formed a not insignificant part.

There was remarkably little talk in the barracks or camps about the justice of the cause. No doubt, we were all convinced that Hitler's Germany was a threat to civilisation that had to be resisted. All of that was taken for granted and hardly discussed. In our nomadic existence we had few opportunities to read newspapers or listen to the BBC and so we were much less subjected to propaganda than the civilians at home. There was very little sign of crusading fervour.

Oddly enough, I think that most of us had simply transferred to the army, the habits acquired at school. Most of us had gone more or less straight from one to the other. At that time, certainly in Scotland, but to some extent, I think, in England too, discipline, good order and attention to the task in hand were taken for granted in our schools. In the classroom, as on the sports field, the natural thing was to do as well as you could. From all that one hears or observes, these attitudes have disappeared in the postwar world. The change of attitude in the schools is not the fault of the politicians and educational bureaucrats alone. Society as a whole has become less deferential, less inclined to use their heads and make an effort, more distracted by the hype of the advertisers and by brainless entertainment on television. Perhaps this is irreversible and there is no easy answer but the intellectual pleasures are more satisfying and more enduring than any others. For that reason, Scotland may, one of these days, recover its passion for education and for ideas.

In addition to the continuous training and practice, our military education was continued by specialist courses all over the country. I went, for instance, to the Army School of Signals at Catterick. There I was instructed in the maintenance and use of radio transmitters and receivers. We acquired an unnecessary fluency in the morse code by having to go to practice classes every morning before breakfast until we had mastered the required speed. An intelligent colleague taught me chess for which he had a fanatical enthusiam. So had I, for a while, but I eventually decided that it took too much of the time which could be better employed in reading. I went also to a motor-cycle school in Llandudno where we rode across rivers and up unbelievably steep slopes in the mountains. Once a group of us on these noisy machines destroyed the peace of some climbers who thought they had reached a pinnacle of tranquility on the top of a Welsh mountain.

One of the decisive turning points in life, sexual initiation, I also attained in Wales. This was while I was at a battle-school just across the border, not far from Hereford. We were living in huts, with much healthy exercise and, of course, we were, quite literally, fighting-fit. It was our habit on our free Saturday afternoons to go into the nearest town for the cinema and that sort of thing. Somehow I met a luscious and bright land-girl. These were girls, recruited to replace men on the farms, who were dressed in a fetching uniform of breeches and jersey. This particular one, Kathleen, had been the secretary of a well-known trade-union leader. When I took her to dinner in the local hotel, she started talking about an episode in a sleeping-bag in a film of a Hemingway novel, *For Whom the Bell Tolls*, I think. It struck me that she was suggesting that we might try something similar. So we did, in the open air, in an orchard. Her body was very white in the moonlight. It was my first time and I think hers as well. I was about 23 and she was about the same age, late by modern standards, but not so uncommon at that time.

As the invasion approached, our training became more concerned with the means of crossing the North Sea or the Channel. We spent an agreeable two or three weeks in a school for amphibious operations in Inveraray. The splendour of Loch Fyne and the surrounding hills was our introduction to landing craft.

Reality came closer in July 1943 when we took part in an exercise in the south of England called Harlequin. This time we sailed with our guns to within a close distance of the French coast, only to turn round and come back again. The idea was to provoke the Germans into revealing their defence strength in artillery and air-power. Fortunately for us, as the potential target, they refused to play and there was no reaction at all. Either they were all asleep or they knew what we were about.

Before and after this affair we slept in the open among the trees of the New Forest. Once during the night I woke to find one of the wild horses gazing at me curiously with its face a few inches from mine. The landing craft were commanded by young naval officers who were evidently anxious to display both their authority on their ship and traditional naval hospitality. When we had established ourselves on board, I was welcomed and offered a drink. It was half a tumbler full of pink gin. How, I wondered, do the navy see straight enough to handle their navigation.

Shortly after this, the powers that be decided that 52nd Division were not to invade by sea at all, but by air. We were to practise the difficult art of loading the guns and the jeeps that pulled them into Dakota aircraft. This was not easy. The guns could only be fitted in by removing their barrels and other bits and pieces, and even the wheels once they had reached the top of the ramp. A moment of carelessness or impatience could damage the fuselage and incapacitate the aircraft.

While all this was going on, a number of officers from the Division, including me, were mysteriously summoned to Troon on the Ayrshire coast. We were told that we were needed for a mission of the highest secrecy and importance. There was nothing heroic or dangerous about it. It was highly entertaining play acting. What we had to do was to devise a series of imaginary landings on an enemy occupied coast. Then we would act them out entirely by radio transmission, from radio cars scattered around Ayrshire and up into Argyll. It was to be as authentic as possible, with reverses, confusion and disasters as well as successfully established beachheads and sweeps inland. We devised and carried out two or three scenarios of this kind, all of us giving free play to the imagination, and happy as schoolboys with cowboys and Indians. We once even had time for lunch in Rogano's in Glasgow on the way to one of our sites north of the Clyde.

The object, of course, was to confuse the enemy. We were told that they would be so confused by these broadcasts that they would not react quickly to the real invasion. I was always a bit sceptical about this. Surely even the most elementary technology could distinguish between transmissions from the Clyde coast and the English Channel. Still, the morning when we returned to our units at the end of this pleasant interlude was the morning of 6th June 1944, D-Day of the Normandy landings, and we received congratulations for a very successful deception from the highest possible source.

Back into what passed for normal life, we moved to the south coast for the real thing. We were to be part of the back-up to an airborne landing. The parachutists would capture an airfield, then the air-portable forces, including us, would follow. Several such operations were planned in detail. Each time, we were held in waiting in a camp, cut off from all communication with the outside world. One operation after another was abandoned because the battle on the ground had surged forward. We might have been among the first troops to liberate Paris, but again we were not needed. The final attempt was Arnheim in September 1944. We went as far as loading our guns in the Dakotas and we sat waiting. This time the opposite happened. Instead of the ground battle moving too fast, it was too slow. The Germans had unexpected strength on the ground and our airfield was not captured.

Now those who planned such things decided that we were not, after all, to be airborne. Perhaps the losses at Arnheim were too heavy to permit any further such attempts. At all events, we were to join the battle in a more conventional manner by sea. So in the following month, on 16 October 1944, still in our mountain clothes and with our mountain equipment, we sailed by cross-channel steamers from Dover to Ostend, which was by then safely in allied hands. I shared a cabin with Jimmy Blackie, from Edinburgh, an ideal colleague, entirely reliable and irrepressibly optimistic and friendly. After the war, he became Church of Scotland chaplin to Edinburgh University and I am sure that he was admirable at the job .

CHAPTER 4

The Army in action
October 1944 – May 1945

When we arrived in Ostend in October 1944, on a pleasant Autumn afternoon, we marched through the town to a staging camp. We must have been an incongruous sight with our rucksacks, anoraks and ski-caps. Except for my cruise to Norway years before, it was the first time that I had set foot on the European mainland. It was an exhilarating moment, not so much because we were embarking on a military campaign with unpredictable consequences, but because of the sheer thrill of the strange and unknown.

We were on territory which had been under German occupation and was now restored to the world. At that time, it seems to me, countries were more distinct from one another than they are now. They even had a different smell, mainly I think, because people smoked different cigarettes and cooked different food. Now such perfumes are displaced by the stench of car exhausts which is the same everywhere, and every supermarket sells a great diversity of products, but the same diversity almost all over the world. Then everything abroad was still new and unexpected.

After a day or two we were united again with our guns and jeeps and the Division moved to an area near Ghent to prepare for our first deployment in action. My troop was lucky enough to be billeted in an elegant Château with formal gardens and a surrounding forest. There was even a marble bath, fit for a Roman emperor, in a bathroom on the first floor. No water came out of the taps and it had to be filled by buckets carried upstairs.

Ghent is a fascinating town. One night it was enlivened by some Canadians firing their machine guns in the streets out of sheer *joie de vivre*. I do not know why my social encounters tended to be highly respectable, but I was invited by an attractive young woman to meet her family – a pattern which tended to repeat itself across Europe. They were lively and civilised and well aware of the ancient links between Flanders and Scotland.

At that time, Belgium south of the Scheldt was in Allied hands, but the Germans were still on the other side of the estuary in the peninsula of Sud Beveland and the island of Walcheren. They had to be removed before the port of Antwerp could be used. This was to be the first objective of 52nd (Lowland) Mountain Division, a contradiction both in name and in function. Sud Beveland, mostly at sea-level and largely flooded, was as different as possible from a mountain.

I was duly summoned one night to an orders group in a fashionable hotel in Antwerp. I arrived with all the military clutter of map cases and the like. The foyer was full of well-dressed people drinking their aperitifs. Quite often war collided with ordinary life. The concierge took one look at me. 'You want the observation post, sir? Kindly take the lift to the top floor.' There indeed was the command post of the operation with a fine view of the surrounding area. 356 Battery was to drive before first light through Antwerp and into Sud Beveland. My troop was to deploy its guns to defend a bridge, reported to be still intact, on the main road which ran through the centre of the peninsula towards the island of Walcheren.

As we approached that point in the early morning, an RAF Mosquito swept along the line of the convoy and fired canon shells at the leading vehicles. The first attack against us had come from our own side. Men, who had been my companions for months, were dead or horribly wounded within a fraction of a second. I was speechless with pity and rage at first, but then I realised that the Germans were at that moment retreating across a causeway to Walcheren. We were on a road with flooding on both sides and from the air at speed it must have looked very similar. A day or two later a Mosquito crash landed close to our position and we rescued the pilot who was obviously surprised to find that he was still alive and in friendly hands. Even to us, he looked so young, and so frightened, that we did not have the heart to tell him what we thought about Mosquito pilots.

On the morning after this initiation, as I was visiting our gun positions by motor cycle, I encountered an apparition. This was Gerda Gastra Gerber, a very beautiful, young, blonde girl, who was collecting milk from a farmhouse. True to form, she invited me to her house that evening – to meet her mother. For several evenings all three of us talked about the German occupation, the war, the future, schools and universities, Edinburgh, Walter Scott and RL Stevenson.

Admittedly, she did begin to linger on the doorstep as she said good night as I left on each occasion at a respectable hour. A few days later, there was cause for a memorable celebration. The Germans in Walcheren had surrendered on 3rd November. In this part of Holland, the misery of the occupation was over. The Battery reassembled in a fishing village called Yrseke on the north shore of Sud Beveland, famous for its oysters. The battery major, Gerry Butler, ate fifty of them and had cause to regret it. Yrseke had emerged unscathed from the war because it had been by-passed by the fighting. So there was to be a great party involving all of us and the whole village. We sent trucks to Antwerp to buy beer. People dug up stores of wine, spirits and liqueurs which they had buried in their gardens. Free and unlimited drinking in all the cafes was to be the order of the night. I was billeted in a comfortable and friendly house and they invited Gerda. Bliss it was to be alive.

At least it all started off very well. We cheered and sang. We drank toast after toast. We danced in the streets. Then Gerda suggested that we should head towards a certain cafe where her local band was to play. We collected a group of people and went down the street shouting, 'We go to the band of Kruinigen.'

But that was the last I remember, until I woke alone in bed in my billet. The mixture of strong drinks had been too much for me. They had carried me home and put me to bed. The party had gone on without me. Pity that I missed it. Still, there would be more days when we could at last be alone together.

But, with the Army's genius for the unexpected and the infuriating, an order reached us (I can't imagine how) that we were to leave that day for some place on the mainland. How were we to do it? The whole battery was scattered in private houses all over the village, and no doubt, all of them with bad hangovers. All we could do was to pass the word round and hope for the best. Miraculously all appeared in time, even if some had to be carried out, still unconscious, by their Dutch hosts. Tearful farewells in all directions, not least between Gerda and me. Oh! The cruelty of war!

We were now to be involved in an operation which the newspapers at the time called the battle of the Sittard Triangle. Sittard is a small town to the north of Maastricht at a base of a triangle defined by the convergence of the River Maas and one of its tributaries. The intention was to drive the Germans back from their bridgeheads to the west of the Rhine as preparation of the allied advance across it. Movement in the whole area was difficult because of flooding, but the planners thought that a frost in early December gave us an opportunity. If we were relying on that and on surprise, we were disappointed in both. Just after the launch of the attack, there was a sudden thaw which reduced the tracks to mud again and the BBC announced to the world that the British Army had began an offensive north of Sittard.

My role in this affair was to monitor progress of the forces through a village on the main axis. I was sent in an armoured car with a sergeant, a wireless operator and a driver to station ourselves at a crossroads and call vehicles forward at a rate which avoided congestion. A photograph of me (from behind) appeared in *The Times*. I looked like Napoleon reviewing the troops, but I was only controlling the flow of traffic.

The crossroads were an obvious target for the enemy mortar and artillery fire and some of it came quite close. When this happened and dust, debris and shattered glass was scattered around, a woman emerged from a cafe on the corner and began to clean it up. I did my best to persuade her to look for a safer place, but she persisted with her brushing. Habits of good housekeeping seemed to be stronger than the instinct for survival. I am happy to say that she was still alive and cleaning up next day when the battle had moved on.

A little before that our headquarters had graciously said by radio that we could relax and get some sleep. The four of us took over a deserted house near the crossroads and put down our sleeping bags in a room in the front. We woke up abruptly, not long afterwards, to the sound of male, guttural voices outside the window. The front door of the house opened and we heard heavy footsteps in the corridor. Without a word, we were all out of the sleeping bags in a flash, standing with our sten guns pointed at the door and expecting it to be kicked open followed by a grenade. It can only have been a few seconds, but it seemed like an age. The footsteps went down through the corridor and then silence. More by body language than by words we agreed that it was better to investigate than to wait for the grenade. The sergeant and I went down the corridor, very gingerly and not feeling at all heroic. Anti-climax. Two men of the house, at least as frightened

'Like Napolean reviewing the troops' – P aul Scott in the battle of the Sittard Triangle, December 1944

as we were, had ventured back. There were making a fire in the kitchen to keep themselves warm and cook something to eat.

The battle of the Sittard Triangle was successful in its limited objective, but the clearing up of the German bridgeheads had to be postponed because of signs that they were massing a large force for a counter attack. The Division was sent to defend a large sector to the east of Maastricht. We drove through that famous frontier place late at night with the streets dark and deserted and without a sign of life. Fortunately for us, because we were very thin on the ground, the expected attack came well to the south of us. This was the Ardenne Offensive, which began on 16th December 1944, with ten armoured and fourteen infantry divisions. It was aimed at Antwerp with the intention of cutting the allied forces in two and denying us the use of the port, a last desperate attempt by the Germans to hold the Western front. When it failed, they must have realised that their defeat was now inevitable.

I suppose that it was shortly after this that my colleague from Edinburgh, Jimmy Blackie, and I were given two days leave in Brussels.

It was not quite the scene of great merrymaking of the kind which Byron and Thackeray describe on the night before Waterloo. Even so, it had been liberated not long before by a rapid surge of the allied advance. It is said that the operation order for the Guards Armoured Division had been the most laconic in military history – 'Intention: Guards Armoured Division will liberate Brussels. Method: Guards Armoured Division will get there first.' There had been no fighting in or around it and the town was undamaged by war. For me, it has never lost that feel of normality, civilisation and security which it had in these first two days.

Perhaps it was even a little dull. While we had savoured the then unusual pleasures of a bath, sleep in a comfortable bed and breakfast we set off to explore the town. We soon discovered that all the theatres and cinemas were closed because of a shortage of electricity or something of that kind. When we asked the hotel concierge what might be open, he wrote an address on a piece of paper. 'I think that you might find this interesting gentlemen.' We were so innocent that we had not imagined that it would be a high class brothel. We made embarrassed but polite conversation with some elegantly dressed but, to us, matronly and not very tempting ladies of a mature age. Since we were prudent, and frankly somewhat inexperienced, Edinburgh boys, we made our excuses and left.

At about this time, it was decided that since 52nd Division was clearly not going to be used in the mountains, it was time to reduce its establishment to the normal format of an infantry division. This meant less artillery and so some of us were posted to other divisions. On 1st January 1945 I joined 15th LAA Regiment in 7th Armoured Division, the Desert Rats, which, as all the world knew at that time, had fought in North Africa and through Italy.

This was something of a culture shock. I reported, as instructed, to the Divisional HQ. There I was received, politely but languidly by officers with practically no trace of ordinary uniform, but with jerseys down to their knees, scarves down to their ankles, corduroy trousers and suede desert boots. 'Decent of you to join us, old boy. Care for a drink?' I still have a book of cartoons, *The Two Types* by Jan, published by the British Army Newspaper Unit in Italy, I suppose in 1943. This shows their style to perfection. In one cartoon, the two are gazing in astonishment at an officer in battledress, 'You know – the things we used to wear in England.' That was the situation precisely. In the 52nd

Division, with no desert experience behind us, we followed the rules like the rest of the Army known to us. Now I was the strange creature among these exotic types.

The atmosphere was similar when I joined the other two officers of the troop I had been assigned to. They seemed to intend to spend the afternoon relaxing over a bottle of wine without rushing around to see if everything was under control. Even when the troop sergeant looked in a day or two later to remark that we were moving next morning, there was still no great activity. The troop ran itself. They all had done it so often that there was no need for fuss. Experience had taught them that the best way to survive was to take it easy and not exert yourself too much. There were complaints from above about this time that the division was not sufficiently aggressive. The old hands were untroubled; they knew that they had nothing to prove. I found after a few days that they were not as arrogant as they appeared and were quite ready to accept me as long as I was patient with their endless tales of the desert.

A vast number of officers were summoned at about this time to a cinema to hear a pep talk from Montgomery. One chance bomb might have incapacitated the entire division. 'We are going to cross the Rhine and I – with God's help – will knock the enemy for six.' 'Nice of him', someone remarked, 'to include God in the troops under command.' One unfortunate at the end of a row fell asleep and collapsed noisely on to the floor.

Now that the allied armies were advancing into Germany itself, it was obvious that emphasis would soon turn from combat to the administration of the occupied territories, with all the problems caused by massive destruction and by the displacement of populations. There was already an embryonic structure of military government in being, but it would have to be strengthened. I volunteered in response to a circular, was interviewed by a Selection Board and accepted, almost simultaneously with the major British advance across the Rhine on 23 March 1945. Events moved fast in the next few weeks.

My copies of some official letters from this time have survived. They are typed on the flimsy paper of the time and are yellow with age. It is impressive to see such a vast organisation as the wartime army, moving into enemy country where there was so much confusion calmly conducting its affairs by meticulous and carefully cross-referenced correspondence. It is because of these letters that I know the dates of various moves, postings, promotions and the like.

A number of these letters are signed by Major David Morrison, of the Argyll and Sutherland Highlanders, Commander 202 Military Government Detachment in Holzminden. He was a laconic Scot, from Helensburgh, unperturbable among all the chaos, the type that ran the Empire, I suppose. He evidently approved of me because he wrote several letters in August 1945 to plead against a demand from 7th Armoured Division that I should join them in Berlin as a Staff Officer, Military Government. He gives some information in a letter of 4 August about the events of the months immediately after the crossing of the Rhine:

> Lt. P.H. Scott was attached at our request to this unit by A/Q 7 Armd Div in March 45 for Mil Gov duties. He was allotted the duties of an Admin officer and which duties he carried out with distinction from the crossing of the Rhine to the surrender of Hamburg and then to Tonning in May 45 after the capitulation. At Tonning Lt. Scott was mostly concerned with the evacuation of D.Ps. At Holzminden where we moved on 2 June 45 Lt. Scott has carried out, again with distinction, the function of Det. Admin., Civil Admin., Education, Trade & Industry, D.P.s, and Food & Agriculture.

Montgomery says in his book, *Normandy to the Baltic*, that further resistance by the Germans after we had crossed the Rhine was 'obviously futile'. Although, as he says, the German forces were approaching disintegration, there were isolated episodes of stubborn opposition. In one small town, heavy firing continued from a building that was already destroyed and in flames, and this from a group of very young schoolboys. Once, after spending a peaceful night in a village to the south of Bremen, we discovered next morning that we had been isolated by a counter attack behind us, but not for long.

There was very little sign of hostility or resentment on the part of the civil population. Just after we crossed the Rhine a woman threw a bucket of water over the occupants of a jeep, but I heard of nothing more serious than that. Most people had evidently lost any stomach for resistance and that was not surprising. Our arrival in a place meant that for the inhabitants the war was over and there was no more risk of shelling or bombing. Much of that had been devastating. More than one village, which happened to be an important road junction, had been reduced to a heap of rubble through which a passage had to be made by bulldozers. When you were only a few miles from a heavy air raid, the sky was livid with flames and the ground trembled under your feet. Also, the Soviet forces were now advancing rapidly in the east and our occupation was regarded as infinitely preferable.

As we approached the River Elbe near Hamburg, I was asked to go in an armoured car to establish contact with the division on our right. This meant driving through country which in theory was free from troops of either side. Still, it was a fairly hare-brained venture. The driver and I were alone in unknown territory. When I stopped, standing up in the turret to consult the map, a German soldier suddenly emerged from a wood at the side of the road. Instinctively, I drew my revolver, but fortunately he had the good sense to run away. Shortly afterwards, I was stopped by a man who said he was the burgermeister. He wanted to welcome me and surrendered a stock of rifles and ammunition. This had been intended for a last-ditch resistance, but he and the people of the place did not propose to do anything so stupid.

In fact, complete German surrender was already imminent. Shortly after I got back to our headquarters, I heard that the German commander in Hamburg had sent a party to offer the surrender of the city. In fact, it was his second attempt, because the first negotiating party had unfortunately been mistaken by our forward troops as an attack. When they arrived on 2nd May 1945, they said that their superior command also wished to surrender their entire forces in the west. For this we passed them on to Montgomery at his tactical headquarters on Lüneberg Heide.

Meanwhile, we agreed arrangements for our entry into Hamburg. The streets were to be deserted, except for the police force. A small party (in which I was included) would drive straight to the Rathaus to accept the surrender. We should have an armoured escort which would leave a tank at all major road junctions. This all happened precisely to plan on 3rd May. The Germans not only formally surrendered the city, but immediately produced champagne and sponge biscuits, as though it was some sort of celebration. I was very lucky to be there, the culmination of our efforts and one of the most dramatic episodes in the war. On the next evening, Montgomery at his headquarters accepted the wider surrender. I do not know if he provided champagne. An order was issued for a cease fire at 0800 hours next morning.

Hamburg was a sorry spectacle. Whole streets were lined with the burnt-out and roofless remains of once solid buildings. Strangely enough, among all this destruction, some of the most prominent buildings, such as the Rathaus itself, had survived more or less intact. They included two of the largest and best hotels, the Atlantic and the Vierjahrezeiten. We were comfortably installed in the latter and I thought once again that we might be able to rest on our laurels for a few days. As in Yrseke, our superiors had other ideas. We were to take over the Landkreis (administrative district) of Eiderstedt, a peninsula protruding into the North Sea, just south of the Danish border. Here the German occupation forces in Denmark were to be disarmed and assembled before they could be demobilised and sent home. The main town was Tonning which is mentioned in Major Morrison's letter. As we approached the place in a jeep, we rounded a bend and saw ahead a road block, manned by German soldiers. Had they heard of the cease fire? Presumably they had, because they immediately raised the barriers as we approached, stood to attention and saluted.

When we looked round our new domain, it was at once obvious that we had many problems. Apart from the disposal of the German troops from Denmark, there were several camps, in various degrees of squalor, of prisoners of war and displaced persons of several nationalities, including Russian, Yugoslav and French. There was also a small German airforce base with staff and buildings which could be useful. We decided that the first step was to summon the commander of this base to a meeting with our brigadier. He duly arrived with a couple of supporting officers. None of us knew quite how to behave. We had been at war with them only a few days before. Our official policy was 'non-fraternisation'; we were forbidden to have any friendly or social relations with Germans; we were supposed to be formal, stiff and aloof.

In accordance with this policy, our brigadier proceeded to lay down the law through an interpreter and gave a long list of what was needed. When he finished, the German exploded and said in perfect idiomatic English: 'Well, if I may say so, Brigadier, it is all very well for you to sit there and issue all these orders, but am I the poor bastard that's supposed to carry them out?' For a moment, stunned silence. What do you do with such a rebellious ex-enemy at the start of our relationship? But then we all laughed. He explained that he had both British and German nationality and had been educated in England. If he had been there when the war started, he might have been in the British, instead of the German, airforce – as good an illustration as you could wish of the absurdity of war. With the ice broken, we drew up a sensible plan of action.

The Handbook for Military Government in Germany, of which I still have a copy, is a substantial volume of over 1,000 paragraphs and many appendices. It begins by listing the 'primary objectives of Military Government.' The first was 'the imposition of the will of the Allies upon occupied Germany', and begins to list such points as the repatriation of United Nations displaced persons, the apprehension of war criminals, the elimination of Nazisim, and German Militarism, the restoration of law and order and so on. 'Preservation and establishment of suitable Civil Administration', is the last of the points; but, of course, it rapidly became our main preoccupation. The *Handbook*, which was written well before anyone had to face the problem on the ground, was harsh in its terms. It says that no steps towards the economic rehabilitation of Germany are to be undertaken, no relief supplies are to be imported or distributed for the German population; Germany will always be treated as a defeated, and not as a liberated, country.

Of course, in the atmosphere of the time that is easy to understand. Hitler's Germany had not only unleashed a destructive war over the whole of Europe, which it had conducted, especially in the Soviet Union, with hideous brutality, but had tyrannised its own people and had undertaken the systematic slaughter of the entire Jewish population of several millions. This was brutality on a scale unparalleled in history, except perhaps almost simultaneously in the Soviet Union of Stalin. It goes well beyond the imagination of any tragedian that two ruthless dictators, who placed no value on human life, should have been inflicted on the world at the same time.

In the following days, it soon became apparent that we badly needed interpreters in many languages. Another request to our German colleague. A corporal in the German equivalent of the Pioneer Corps appeared and told us that he had come to be our interpreter. 'But we need interpreters for Russian, Serbo-Croat, French and probably several other languages and all into and out of both English and German.' He told us that he could do all of this and Welsh, but not Gaelic, as well. He had been a Professor in the University of Vienna until he had been sacked for political unreliability after the *Anschluss* with Germany. His passion was the acquisition of languages and the study of their relationships. He told us that learning languages was easy after the first fifteen or so, but admitted that he was still working on Finnish. Hans, as we called him, was not only a superb interpreter but a source of information on all sorts of subjects. He could be fluent, witty and entertaining in all of his multiple languages. We enjoyed his company so much that we virtually made him an honorary member of the officers' mess, even as a corporal and a German one at that.

The first task was to attend to the needs of the groups of prisoners and displaced persons. The Soviet prisoners had obviously been treated more harshly than the others, crowded in the most insalubrious conditions and pitifully badly fed. I managed to find a comfortable building for them and decent supplies of food. They presented me with an eloquent letter of gratitude in Russian, which I am sorry to say, I have not yet found among my papers. Perhaps I could have used it to ease my later relations with the Soviets in Berlin; but perhaps, not, because I heard later that their Government treated returning prisoners as criminals. They were sent to imprisonment in Siberia for years, if not shot.

Fortunately, as long as I was in Tonning we did not arrange to send home any of the Soviet prisoners. I do not know what happened to them, but I hope that they were treated sympathetically. They certainly deserved it. Other nationalities had fewer problems and all they wanted was to be sent home. Of them all, the best organised and self-confident were the Yugoslavs. When I told them that I expected to be able to provide transport for them within a few days, they thanked me, but said that they had already arranged it. I did not ask how.

As David Morrison records in his letter, our Military Government Detachment moved to Holzminden, which is to the south of Hannover, on 2nd June 1945. This was a comparatively tranquil interlude. Holzminden was a pleasant, undamaged town in fine country and there were no pressing problems of disarmament or repatriation. We were a small group of about five officers and we all had to turn our hand to everything. We seemed to have been visited by journalists in search of local stories because I have a cutting from the *Edinburgh Evening Dispatch*. It reports that David Morrison wears the kilt to the evident admiration of the women.

The tone of the *Military Government Handbook*, and of the policy of 'no fraternisation', was to attach blame to the entire German people. Neither Hitler nor Stalin could have achieved their purposes without the enthusiastic support of thousands of loyal acolytes and the compliant participation, or at least acceptance, of the mass of the people. Some resisted and suffered for their resistance. An unknown number of others may have detested in silence the horrors that were being perpetrated in their name. It is easy to blame, and more difficult to imagine the intimidation and the pressures which forced people to comply or to stay silent. As Norman Davies says in his book *Europe: A History*, 'a totalitarian regime drives everyone in its power to varying degrees of complicity. Unfree people should not be judged by the criteria of free societies.' Judgement apart, it is impossible to be surrounded by defeated, humiliated and hungry people, often living among the ruins of their bombed cities, without feeling compassion and the need to help.

Opinion in the outside world had been slow to believe the unspeakable outrages that were perpetrated in the German extermination camps. It was only when the advancing allied armies liberated them and photographs of the heaps of emaciated corpses appeared in the press that the full horror was understood. I had no such dreadful encounters myself, for which I am grateful, but somewhere between the Rhine at the Elbe we did come across an abandoned prison camp, surrounded by barbed wire and watch towers. In a wood close to it, there were tidy rows of mounds of earth which were almost certainly mass graves.

I was left in the comparative tranquillity of Holzminden for only two months before 7th Armoured Division reclaimed me to join them in Berlin. Among my papers there is a copy of a strange letter from David Morrison, dated 4th August 1945:

> This certifies that Capt. J.C.Frank R.A. and two O.R.s arrived at this HQ on Wedensday 1st August with orders to collect Lt. P.H. Scott. It was on my own authority but agreed by A/Q 7 Armd. Div. that I detained Capt. Frank until AM Sunday 5th Aug., it being impossible for Lt. Scott to hand over his duties in less time.

Why I needed an escort, I have no idea but I set off for the unknown complications of Berlin under four-power occupation.

CHAPTER 5

Berlin, Spandau
August 1945 – August 1946

In advance of the German surrender, the Allied Powers had agreed
that the country should be divided into four Zones of occupation,
and Berlin itself into Sectors, American, British, French and Soviet.
Berlin was in the heart of the Soviet zone and could be reached by
road only by crossing about one hundred miles of Soviet-occupied
territory. In the final months of the war all the capitals of Eastern
Europe were liberated, as the language of the time expressed it, by
the Soviet Army.

In April 1945, the Soviets had not yet entered the part of Germany
which was to be their Zone, but the Americans were already a hundred
miles inside it. Even so, the western armies halted to allow the Soviets
to liberate Berlin. On various pretexts, they delayed the entry of the
first Western troops for ten weeks. The British element was provided
by 7th Armoured Division.

On a sunny day in early August 1945 a driver and I drove to Berlin
in an army vehicle through an apparently empty countryside. For most
of the way we saw no other vehicle on the wide, straight autobahn and
no other sign of life. When we stopped to eat our haversack rations,
as the army calls them, a Russian soldier appeared out of the woods.
He came towards us waving a bundle of German marks. They were
then more or less worthless, but he had so many that we thought he
might want to buy our truck. As far as we could make out from his
rudimentary German, it was only our watches he wanted. He was
perfectly happy when we gave him a few packets of cigarettes, which
were then a much more valuable currency than his marks. He shared
our tea and sandwiches and we parted on terms of undying allied
friendship and solidarity. It was my first encounter with a Soviet soldier.

In fact, I think that it was probably the first time that I had met a

Russian of any kind. My only acquaintance with them was through the pages of Tolstoy, but that is probably as informative an introduction as one could find. I was to have endless discussions with them in the next few years in Berlin.

Just before I began to write this chapter, BBC Scotland broadcast two radio programmes, which they called the Scottish-Russian love affair, about the extraordinary involvement of Scots in Russia since the eighteenth century. By coincidence, Duncan Thomson's subject in a recent Scottish National Portrait Gallery lecture was John Rogerson, a Scottish doctor at the court of Catherine the Great. Many Scots with experience in Russian, such as Diarmid Gunn, the son of Neil Gunn, who was a naval attaché in Moscow, believe that there is a special affinity between Scots and Russians. They think that there are many similarities in our characters and attitudes. The same is said about many other peoples, the French, Flemings, Norwegians and Irish, for example. Perhaps the truth is simply that the Scots are very adaptable, enjoy other societies and are ready to fit in anywhere.

At the end of the war, there was a particular reason why Western opinion generally was well-disposed towards the Soviet Union. Since 1941 the Russians (if I can use that word for convenience to mean Soviet citizens) had faced the full fury of German military force and ruthlessness. The German advance had reached the outskirts of Moscow and Leningrad and had inflicted enormous slaughter and destruction. From November 1942 the Russians, at great cost, had begun to throw the Germans back and by August 1944 the last of them had been expelled from the prewar Soviet territory. All of this mammoth and heroic struggle had cost the Soviet Union nearly nine million lives. Meanwhile, British forces were advancing in North Africa and Italy, but the Allies were not ready to launch the second front in Europe until the Normandy landings in June 1944. By then, the military strength of Germany had been substantially reduced and our task and our casualties were correspondingly diminished. Naturally Western opinion looked on the Soviet Union with admiration and gratitude.

In retrospect, it is easy to see that the Soviet Union won most of its objectives in the wartime negotiations with the West about the conduct of the war and the future of Europe. They aimed at the political domination of Eastern Europe and they succeeded, partly by force of arms, and partly by single-minded determination in the negotiations.

The way in which this came about is the subject of a brilliant book by Chester Wilmot, *The Struggle for Europe*. He quotes a prophetic remark by Liddell Hart in 1941:

> Where there is no longer the counter-balance of an opposing force to control the appetites of the victors, there is no check on the conflict of views and interests between the parties to the alliance. The divergence is then apt to become so acute as to turn the comradeship of common danger into the hostility of mutual dissatisfaction – so that the ally of one war becomes the enemy of the next.

Fortunately, the mutual dissatisfaction in this case did not lead to actual war, but it came close. With nuclear weapons that might easily have meant the virtual end of civilised human life. It did not take long for the Western powers to realise that they had disposed of one aggressive tyranny only to be faced with the threat of another and with the division of Europe into two opposing camps. Berlin was one of the arenas where this transformation of comradeship into hostility first became apparent. There, and for most of my subsequent professional career, I was involved in various aspects of this troubled relationship.

For my four years in Berlin, from August 1945 to the end of 1950, I do not have to rely entirely on memory. I have a small archive of papers, rather more than for any subsequent postings around the world. I think this is because they did not accompany me on these travels. They had been safely deposited in my mother's house in Edinburgh.

I see from them that before I reached Berlin I had been promoted to Acting/Captain on 12th April 1945. I was now officially a staff officer with staff pay (which I don't think amounted to much).

My first job in Berlin from August 1945 was as Deputy Commander of the Military Government Detachment responsible for the district of Spandau. Until that time the word had meant to me the notorious and deadly machine gun made there and named after it. Later it became famous as the site of the prison, under four-power control, but happily not involving our Detachment, where Hess and others, condemned to imprisonment at the Nuremberg Trials, were elaborately and expensively housed. Spandau lies on the west of Berlin with a long border with the Soviet Zone. It had been less damaged than the centre of the city which had been massively reduced by bombing to ruins and burnt-out empty walls. The officers of the Detachment lived together in a comfortable and undamaged surburban villa.

The Russians had been very active in a number of diverse ways in the weeks before our arrival. The introduction to a printed official report on the Blockade of 1948 described the situation succinctly as follows:

> The Russians occupied Berlin for ten weeks before the Western Allies entered. During that time they despoiled much of what remained of the city, stripping its modern factories and its most modern power station, Berlin West, in the British Sector. Private property and the women of the city did not escape Russian attention. Thus was set up a deep antagonism.

These last two sentences are a rather coy reference to the orgy of rape and looting in which soldiers of the Soviet army had indulged during, and for some time after, their seizure of Berlin. They presumably thought of it as a due retaliation for the outrages that the Germans had committed in their own country.

Among my papers is a brief record which I was asked to write of Military Government in Berlin/Spandau from our entry in July to 31st December 1945. It begins also by a reference to the Soviet actions before we arrived and acknowledges that they had their positive side:

> When British Military Government arrived in Spandau in July 45, the foundations of Allied Military Government had already been firmly laid by the Russians in the three months since their entry. A new body of local officials had been appointed, food supply had been organised and the essential services of the district were working. A considerable degree of de-Nazification had been carried out. Political Parties, a Trade Union, newspapers, cinemas and theatres were in full operation. The initial tasks of British Military Government in Berlin were therefore different from those in the districts of western Germany occupied during the advance. The problem was not to create order out of chaos, but to take over a working organisation

already set up by an Ally with different political and economic conceptions to our own. As events were soon to show this was a problem with its own peculiar difficulties.

From the beginning, it was obvious that the Russians had exploited the first three months in Berlin to consolidate their position in a way which gave them a powerful advantage over the other Allies. The Magistrat, the Police Präsidium, the HQs of all four political parties, and the publishing offices of all the newspapers were in the Russian Sector. Moreover city officials all over Berlin had been appointed by the Russians with due regard to their political opinions. In Spandau, as elsewhere, the majority of local officials were old members of the Communist or Social Democratic Parties, but of little or no administrative experience. Spandau, however, was fortunate in its Bürgermeister, Dr Münch, a man of integrity, good intention and clear understanding.

The Russians, in other words, had attended to their own political and economic advantage, but they had also taken the first steps to clear up the immediate chaos and destruction of the bombing and street fighting. Some corpses still lay under the ruins and there was a noisome dust on windy days, but the streets had been cleared from the rubble and the people, hungry and ill clothed, were going about their daily lives. As so often, the human spirit was proving its capacity to survive in the most adverse circumstances. It was impossible not to feel compassion and even admiration. Also, they were welcoming to us because we were a lesser evil. We were seen more as a liberating force, than a conquering enemy.

From the beginning in Berlin, we made no serious attempt to follow the impossible and repugnant policy of no fraternisation. Ordinary human feelings prevailed. We had friends among the Germans with whom we worked and among the women, whom we soon discovered were much less sexually inhibited than girls at home still were in those distant days.

The commander of this Military Government Detachment was Lt Col FPB Sangster , a professional cavalry officer of the old school, who had been, and in a sense still was, the commanding officer of a unit of the Iniskilling Dragoon Guards. It was said that he had been sacked from his combative command by Montgomery because of his refusal to modify his ideas about cavalry tactics to suit tanks instead of horses. In spite of that, he was nobody's fool. His shrewd insights into human motivation and probable reaction was a great asset in coping with all the problems that faced us. He believed in hard play as well as hard work and was always ready for a party. I have a copy of a confidential report which he wrote about me in which he says that I would make a good Staff Officer and he recommends me for the Staff College. By his standards, that was a real compliment.

We had a legal officer to preside over our Military Government Court, who had been an English barrister before the War and two public safety officers who had been in the police force. They really were strong, silent men, saying very little, unsurprised and undismayed by outrage and crisis.

Then there was Geoffrey Seggie, a Captain in the Durham Light Infantry in 131 Brigade of the 7th Armoured Division, a wild daredevil who became one of my closest friends. He had been sent to our Detachment for the most unlikely of tasks, the organisation of the food supply to the population. This had to be organised from virtually nothing, because at the handover the Russians had told us that they were withdrawing all the staff and all the transport that had been engaged in it.

I say that Geoffrey was an unlikely appointment, not because he was inefficient, but because his known talents were more war-like. He had been a commander of a bren-gun carrier platoon, usually in the forefront of the infantry advance. He had been wounded once, just slightly in the arm, and had won the MC. Even before he joined us, I had heard tales about his reckless courage.

In fact, his wildness landed me in one or two scrapes. He had acquired by requisition an eight-cylinder Horch, a mammoth of a car, a sort of compromise between a Rolls Royce and a tank. On Sundays after things had settled down a little, we had the habit of going to concerts of the Berlin Philharmonic. One afternoon, as we were driving there at high speed, because there was virtually no other traffic about, an army 3-ton lorry suddenly emerged from a side street. We hit it on the side, and knocked it clean over. Its cargo of potatoes (probably part of Geoffrey's organisation) spilled out over the street. The blow of the collision had been more on Geoffrey's side than on mine. He was unconscious and his face, which had hit the steering wheel, was covered in blood. A less solid vehicle would have crumpled altogether.

An army car happened to pass and with some difficulty we

extracted Geoffrey and took him to the military hospital in Spandau. When he had been cleaned up and put to bed, the nurse looked at me. 'Are you all right? You don't look it.' I assured her that I was quite unhurt. When we got back to our suburban villa, they looked at me in surprise because a report had already recorded that we had both been killed. I joined the others who were sitting around having a drink before dinner. 'You don't look too well,' said Hook, 'you had better go to bed.' A little later, 'Look, go to bed; that's an order.' I had to confess that I had lost control of my legs and could not stand. I was still in bed some days later, when Geoffrey emerged from hospital.

Another episode arose from a rather elegant party in the American Sector to which Geoffrey and I had been invited. A war correspondent of the *Daily Telegraph* was there and was clearly trying to impress the girls by tales of desperate military adventure which he claimed to have seen at close quarters. This was too much for Geoffrey.

'I know your sort,' he said, 'You sit in comfort and safety miles from any fighting and use your imagination. The only time I ever saw any war correspondents during the whole war was in a bar in Brussels when I went there for two days leave.' The man from the *Daily Telegraph* was furious. A week or two later two stories appeared side by side on the front page of his newspaper. One said that supplies of Spandau machine guns had reached Jewish extremists in Palestine and were being used against British troops. The other said that Military Government in Spandau had authorised the release of machine guns from the factory. In fact, we had agreed to the transfer of some partly processed parts to be used for quite a different and harmless purpose in another factory. Of course, the newspaper story caused enough fuss to require an investigation and much waste of time by a Court of Inquiry.

Geoffrey and I arrived at this party as a consequence of a visit from a school friend of mine, Tom Kydd. He walked into my office one day in RAF uniform. Members of bomber crews were flying to Berlin in their bombers in theory, he said, to study the results of their bombing on the ground, but in practice to help to keep them occupied until they were demobilised. He had seized the chance to come because his mother wanted him to try to trace a woman that she had tried to help before the war. At that time, Tom's mother had been running a sort of Scarlet Pimpernel service to rescue Germans who were likely to suffer Nazi persecution. This particular woman was partly Jewish and, for that reason, had been abandoned by her husband who was of high rank in some Government service or other. Tom had the woman's prewar address.

I said that I should be glad to help, but of course it would be miraculous if she was still alive and living at the same address, or even if the house was still standing. But anything was possible.

Tom himself was a miraculous survivor. At the beginning of the war he had been a conscientious objector to military service, really because his sympathies were with the Soviet Union, at that time an ally of Germany. He drove an ambulance during the blitz on London. When Germany invaded Russia, he volunteered for military service and became in due course a navigator in a bomber. On one raid his plane was shot down over Holland and the whole crew reported as missing, presumed dead. Tom had landed by parachute and in the early morning he encountered a man on a bicycle who, by luck, was Dutch and well-disposed. For the next two years the local people had fed and concealed him until one day British troops arrived. 'Good morning,' he said, 'I am an RAF officer.' 'You don't bloody well look like it,' was the reply. But they sent him back to Britain very quickly and he telephoned his mother who had never given up hope.

So Tom and I went in search of this house which turned out to be in the American Sector, spacious and undamaged with a large garden. The lady in question was still there with her two sons, bright if rather arrogant young men, who had found well-paid jobs with the Americans. They were all doing quite nicely, thank you. It was at a party in their house that we met the man from the *Daily Telegraph*. The prima ballerina of the Berlin ballet was there and so was an incredibly beautiful girl, Erika Pick, who had arrived from Dresden. Both came sailing with us next morning, which was a Sunday, in the yacht which we kept at the harbour of the Water Police in Spandau.

It gradually became apparent that Erika, who had an air of angelic purity about her and who was not in the least demanding or assertive, had come to Berlin with two purposes. The first was to have her father posted to Berlin because he was Jewish and he had escaped from Germany and was now a sergeant in the Pioneer Corps in the British Army. The second was to find a flat in Berlin and to bring her mother from Dresden so that all the family could be united.

She thought that it would be a long and difficult process to arrange all this. Apart from anything else, the Russians had strict controls over anyone moving from their Zone to Berlin. As it happened, I was in a position where I could arrange the whole thing by just a few letters. The British Army were sympathetic about posting the father and he would be entitled to Army family accommodation in Berlin. The Russians too were sympathetic when I pointed out that the father had good anti-fascist credentials. So Erika achieved her two wishes in a matter of weeks and her family regarded me a sort of benevolent demi-god who could work miracles. Even that was not enough to overcome Erika's stern virginity. We were good and close friends, but that was all. What else was to be expected of a gorgeous girl who could survive unscathed during the Soviet occupation of Dresden and a journey through their Zone to Berlin. I was to meet her again later in London and the United States.

After the first few weeks of crisis and the unexpected, life in Spandau began to settle down into something approaching routine. Rape and violent robbery by Soviet soldiers gradually ceased, probably because their authorities had tightened discipline and also because the local police became more confident, encouraged by our public safety officers and supported by British Army patrols. One night a Russian officer was noticed going into the house next door. A little later there were screams, but, as was quite obvious from one of our upstairs windows, they were of enthusiastic participation. *'Noch einmal, Herr Hauptmann, noch einmal!'* Do it again, Captain, do it again.!

By this time, we encountered Russians quite rarely, although the agreement was that members of all the occupying powers could travel freely through all four sectors. Once the car of three young officers broke down outside our house. We invited them in, although communication was difficult. They spoke very little German and our Russian interpreter was not there. It must have been winter, because they had great coats and fur hats. As we sat together, one of us remarked on these splendid hats. The senior Russians gave a sharp command to the youngest officer who collected the hats and took them outside to hang them up. I am afraid that they thought we had remarked on their uncultivated behaviour.

We evolved a style of life that was demanding but by no means uncomfortable. In some ways it was even luxurious. From the NAAFI, which attended to such things, we bought a large supply of champagne from a German army stock at an absurdly low price. To some visiting MPs who asked for beer, we had to say that we were sorry we had no beer; would champagne do? It must have confirmed their suspicions that, as conquerors, we were living the life of Riley.

We did have one officer who became an alcoholic. He had played rugby football for Wales and was excellent company when he was sober, but that was increasingly rare. One morning he told us that he was very worried because he had tried late at night to visit a nurse of his acquaintance at the British Military hospital which was close to us. The guard had been turned out and there had been a great disturbance. He expected a court martial and disgrace. We advised him to go at once and apologise with his best Welsh charm to the Matron. This worked. She told him that she well understood that these things happened after a party. 'Boys will be boys. But don't worry. I shall withdraw the report.'

That was not the end of his troubles. He had little patience with our Russian interpreter who was a Canadian civilian of Armenian origin, called Afanassieff. He was quiet, inoffensive and rather pedantic. His favourite evening occupation was to sit in the mess typing interminable letters (or was it a novel?) on a portable typewriter. Our Welshman had no patience with this sort of behaviour. He came back one evening in his usual state and told Afanassieff to stop at once. This was a mess, not an office. When Afanassieff refused, he threw the typewriter out of the window and things became very violent. Guy Courage, of the brewing family, who was the senior officer present, tried to restore order. In the course of this, he struck the Welshman, who fell, hit his head against a table and passed out. Obviously this kind of thing could not go on. We arranged for our Welsh friend, whom we liked in spite of it all, to be sent off for psychiatric treatment. He did not return.

The Sadler Wells Ballet, soon to become the Royal Ballet, came to play in a Berlin theatre. Geoffrey and I were entranced and we invited the company to a party. Margot Fonteyn, Robert Helpman, Beryl Grey, Moira Shearer and a whole host of these wonderful dancers. I enjoyed particularly the company of Beryl Grey. She could not only dance divinely, but had the ability to explain what it felt like and meant to her, in a straightforward way with no trace of pretension. The ballet was her whole life, but she was not obsessive about it. She wrote to me a few times and we met afterwards once or twice in London.

The army, anxious, no doubt to keep us out of mischief, but concerned also to preserve hierarchy, soon established clubs for officers and other ranks. Among my papers is the text of a speech that Winston Churchill made at the opening of one of the latter, the Winston Club. It is Churchillian rhetoric at its most florid, addressed to the Desert Rats, the 7th Armoured Division. They were, he said, established in Berlin, 'from which, as from a volcano, fire and smoke and poisonous fumes have erupted all over Europe twice in a generation.' He ended, 'Dear Desert Rats! May your glory ever shine! May your laurels never fade! May the memory of this glorious pilgrimage of war which you have made from Alamein, via the Baltic to Berlin, never die! It is a march unsurpassed through all the story of war so far as my reading of history leads me to believe.'

For the officers there were three clubs. One called the Embassy was in fact in the building which had been the Embassy of the puppet state of Croatia. In the entrance it had a map of the country in inlaid wood. Another had been the leading tennis club of Berlin with many courts, some of which were flooded for skating in winter. The third was a sailing club on the Havel lake in Gatow, an elegant place with bedrooms. By the time this was established, some wives had arrived to join their men. One of these had expressed concern that the bedrooms might encourage officers to sleep with their girlfriends, a practice which in those censorious days was still regarded with disapproval. But the general's wife was more realistic. 'Don't worry,' she said, 'They will do that anyway and it is better that they should do it with some style and comfort.' How right she was. I remember some delightful weekends there with Dorothy, a nurse fom the Military hospital, who was warm, affectionate and full of the joy of life.

But life was not all cakes and ale. We worked hard at the job of repairing a shattered society, freeing it from Nazi control and influence and preparing it from the restoration of democracy. Military Government was always seen as a temporary expedient. We were working, in a sense, to deprive ourselves of a job. This was not difficult, because few of us looked on the army as a permanent occupation. We were wartime soldiers who wanted to go home as soon as possible.

I have copies of two of the monthly reports from Military Government Spandau which we sent to our Berlin headquarters, those for January and May 1946. I probably wrote most of them myself, but I am astonished, when I read them again, by their range, detail and comprehensiveness. There is plenty of evidence of the pitifully meagre supplies of food and fuel for the population. There were arrangements to cut wood in the forest and ration its distribution as fuel. Children and their mothers were sent to the British Zone for the winter because conditions were easier there. There was no fodder for horses which were still used in those days to pull carts. They were being fed only on potato peelings and were dying at the rate of seven to ten a week. Those still alive were 'rapidly becoming too weak to walk, let alone attempt to work.'

Still, conditions were gradually improving. Two theatres and five cinemas were open, a symphony orchestra was being formed and there were plans to rebuild a municipal theatre. The local newspaper, the *Spandauer Volksblatt*, began publication again in March 1946.

The report on the first six months of Military Government, which I wrote in December 1945, had ended by saying that although material conditions were improving, there were signs of an approaching political crisis. This was a reference to the Soviet campaign to force the fusion of the German Communist Party with the Social Democrats (SPD) to make a new party, the *Sozialistiche Einheits Partie* (Socialist Unity Party (SEP). This was a transparent attempt to help the communists into power and neutralize the much more popular SPD. So far, in all five Zones of Germany and Sectors of Berlin, power was in the hands of the occupying powers, but we were all committed to democratic elections and transfer of responsibility to the Germans themselves before very long. It was already clear that the Soviets meant to do everything they could to exercise control through the new party which they were creating. In their own Zone and Sector they had a free hand. They were trying to achieve the same result in the western Sectors through their communist friends.

This political issue was to become my main responsibility because in August 1946 I was transferred to the Headquarters of Military Government, Berlin, and made a temporary Major and Staff Officer II (Political).

CHAPTER 6

Berlin: the Allied Kommandatura
and the Blockade
August 1946 – December 1950

So in August 1946 I moved from the outer suburb of Spandau to
Douglas Strasse in the Grunewald, a street of substantial houses,
almost entirely occupied by the staff of Military Government. Each of
us had a bed-sittingroom, and, if you were lucky (as I was) a bathroom
and balcony. They were cleaned and kept in order by a matronly
German. The largest house at the end of the street with the largest
garden was the mess where we took our meals. I had the service too of
a Volkswagen with a German ex-Navy driver who finally disgraced
himself by a plot, which failed, to steal the car.

My responsibilities were defined at the time as political affairs in
the Allied Kommandatura, liaison with Political Division and with
political parties and organisations. I suppose that my qualification
for all of this was the interest which I had displayed in political
developments in the reports which I had written from Spandau. The
Political Division was part of the British element of the Control Council
for Germany as a whole. It was staffed mainly by members of the
Diplomatic Service headed by Christopher Steel. We had frequent
meetings to discuss the political situation in Berlin.

What, you might ask, was the Allied Kommandatura? Before the
end of the war the allied governments reached agreement on the
'control machinery' that was to exercise authority in Germany after
its surrender. Germany was to be divided into four Zones each under
the control of the commander in chief of the occupying power. The
four of them together, American, British, French and Soviet, were to
constitute the Central Council 'to ensure appropriate uniformity of
action' and 'to direct the administration of Greater Berlin through
appropriate organs.' These were defined as 'an Inter-Allied Governing

Authority (Kommandatura) consisting of four commandants, one from each Power . . . to direct jointly the administration of the Greater Berlin area. Each of the Commandants will serve in rotation in the position of Chief Commandant or head of the Inter Allied Governing Authority.'

It might sound from this that what was intended was an integrated authority where the Allied Powers would work together. In practice it was quite different. From the beginning, it was organised as a complicated form of permanent international conference. Each Power controlled its own Sector and they met in the Kommandatura to discuss matters of city-wide concern which were executed through the Magistrat, the Soviet-nominated city administration. All decisions by the Kommandatura were required to be unanimous, which meant that they could be vetoed by any one of the four powers. This may sound like an incredibly cumbersome way to run a city, as indeed it was, but it was more than that. Berlin for the next few years was the chief focus of the breakdown of the relationship between the Soviet Union and the Western powers and of the struggle for supremacy between them. Municipal politics never had such an international significance as in postwar Berlin, where the appointment of an official or a change in food rations was an aspect of the relations between the world powers.

In the previous chapter I mentioned the way in which the Russians had energetically exploited the advantage of entering Berlin first and securing by negotiation two months delay between May and July 1945 before the entry of the British and Americans, followed by the French in August. I think that the West was naive at first and anxious to maintain a spirit of wartime cooperation. It was only gradually that we realised how thorough and effective the Russian preparations had been.

The studios of Radio Berlin were one important asset irremovably placed in the Sector which was to become British. Russian control over this was, however, assured by a gentlemen's agreement in the first few days after the British entry and it remained as an important part of the Russian propaganda machine within a stone's throw of British Military Government Headquarters. On their arrival, therefore, the Western Allies found a ruined city with the wounds of war still raw, but still living and already re-organised to suit Russian policy.

All this in two months! This should have been an adequate warning that the Russians were not only ruthless, but determined and single-minded in working for the expansion of Soviet power. The episode of Radio Berlin is an example of Western naivety and anxiety to preserve allied co-operation. It is said that shortly after his arrival in Berlin, the British commandant was warmly entertained by his Soviet counterpart. In the course of the exchange of toasts the Russian remarked that his people had been working hard in repairing that station in the interests of democracy and were prepared to carry on. 'Jolly good, by all means' or words to that effect from our man. 'That's agreed then?' 'Certainly.'

A rather more formal agreement, but somewhat similar in its consequences, followed at the first meeting of the Kommandatura on 11th July 1945, and, of course, the adoption of the Russian name for the institution was itself significant. The three generals (because their French colleague had not yet arrived) issued a joint document, headed 'ORDER', that 'until special notice, all existing regulations and ordinances issued by the Commander of the Soviet Army Garrison and Military Commandant of the City of Berlin' were to remain in force. As an interim measure to avoid chaos this was perfectly reasonable, but it was combined with the rule of unanimity over future decisions. This meant that the Russians could veto any move that they did not like. It was much easier for them to preserve the status quo, which they had established, than for any change to be introduced.

By virtue of my new job, I became part of the Allied Kommandatura in August 1946. It was housed in a building in the Thiel Allee in the American Sector, which was formerly the headquarters of the Nazi Labour Front, but which might have been designed for its new purpose. It had a handsome, panelled room for the meetings of the Commandants or their Deputies and had plenty of other suitable rooms for the committees. There was even a restaurant where we all had lunch together on the days when we had meetings.

The committees dealt with various subject areas, including one on local government, on which I was one of the two British delegates. Our responsibility was to prepare for the restoration of representative self-government to the people of Berlin by agreeing an interim constitution and electoral law and preparing any regulations that might be needed for the recognition and conduct of political parties. The Committee reported to the Deputy Commandants who, if necessary, referred decisions to the Commandants. The chairmanship on all levels rotated monthly between the Powers and even extended to the kitchens. So we had the pleasure of a change of cuisine each month, with the chefs of each country in healthy competition.

I do not suppose that any more elaborate and complex method of running a city has ever been devised, and beneath all this was the German structure of the Magistrat and the district administrations. Admittedly Berlin was a city of substantial size, 548 square miles, and of a population of 4.3 million, as large as many small states. The four power control of Germany as a whole hardly functioned at all, with the Soviet Zone soon following a separate course from the rest. In Berlin it did function, if laboriously and slowly, for about three years. I see from my notes that in that time the Allied Kommandatura issued 1,164 agreed orders. The rehabilitation of the city and steps towards representative government gradually progressed.

By the time I joined the Local Government Committee it had received a draft constitution from the Magistrat and had debated it for months, article by article. At first the Russians were obstructive, but they had a sudden change of policy and began to seem even more eager than the rest of us for an early election and a transfer of power to the elected assemblies. They seem to have been misled by their own propaganda and to believe that the election would give power to the new party which they were creating and through which, as in their Zone, they could exercise control. The new Constitution was approved by the Kommandatura and sent to the Magistrat on 13 August 1946. The covering letter said that it was 'a temporary document intended to restore political freedom and place it in the hands of the people of Berlin. It places a concentration of authority in the hands of the elected representatives of the people.'

These high-sounding phrases were frequently quoted by the city authorities in the following months when it began to appear that the freedom and authority allowed to the city was even less than it had been before the grant of the new Constitution and the first elections under it.

The problem lay in the disappointment of Soviet expectations in that election and in the final article of the Constitution, Article 36, which they were able to use as an opportunity for increased interference. It said that 'the independent administration of Berlin is subordinate to the Allied Kommandatura' and that: 'Alterations in the Constitution, resignation of the Magistrat or any of its members, as well as the appointment and discharge of leading officials of the city administration can only take effect with the sanction of the Allied Kommandatura Berlin.'

My work in the Local Government Committee began with the discussion on the Electoral Law that was to govern the conduct of the first election. The atmosphere on the Comittee was, at that stage at least, entirely friendly and cooperative. The Soviet members were jovial with the agreeable habit of quoting proverbs to support their arguments. Their interpreter for English was a bright and formidable young woman. Her name, as I can see from a magazine article that has survived, was Senior Lieutenant Clara Roshki. She was much admired by her colleagues because, among other qualities, she had won several decorations as a sniper, a fact which I found somewhat intimidating.

Apart from the sessions of the committee and the lunches, we had very few social contacts with our Soviet colleagues. They gave one or two parties with large quantities of vodka, which we soon learned was a hazard to security as well as to health and sobriety. They sent cards for the New Year. Our Deputy Commandant, Brigadier 'Loonie' Hinde, a man with all the virtues and none of the vices of the best kind of Army officer, once decided to improve relations by a party to end all parties. Army lorries were sent to Denmark to collect vast supplies of food and drink. A local film company was employed to transform the Douglas Strasse mess into a convincing jungle, complete with stuffed monkeys and recorded bird song in the trees. Everyone was duly impressed, except an unsympathetic Army audit office which calculated the cost of sending the lorries to Denmark and sent a large bill to Loonie. But we all contributed.

My particular friend on the committee was the French member, Victor Ziegelmeyer. He was normally charming and placid, but he also had the unusual ability, when driven to an explosion of rage by Soviet intransigence, to persuade even them to give way by the sheer force of his personality. We had a passion for skiing in common, although he was in quite a different league from me. He had been a member of the French national ski team when, with Emile Allais as captain, they were dominant in international competition. There seemed to be few peaks in the Alps which he had not climbed on skis. We went once together for a ski holiday in Zürs in Austria with the other friends from Berlin, Tom Stables and Celia Sharpe. It was the cheapest holiday we ever had because the Army insisted that we should

The Local Government Committee of the Allied Kommandatura, Berlin 1946.
The French member, Victor Ziegelmeyer, is at the front on the left

take with us a huge box of rations. We presented this to the hotel
keeper when we arrived and he was so impressed that he gave us free
board and lodging. Zielgemeyer did have the unfortunate habit of
pressing us to get up in the middle of the night to climb some peak
before the sun reached it. I suppose it was good for us. On one of
these climbs he found a bra lying in the snow, dropped presumably
by a woman who had stripped to the waist as she was climbing in the
sun. That night Ziegelmeyer went round everyone's table in the dining
room and asked politely 'Excuse me, Madame, is this by any chance
yours?' He was also one of the first people to take up water ski-ing.
Once he gave a demonstration to an admiring audience at the sailing
club in Gatow. This was a little marred because he sank ignominiously
within a foot or two of the jetty onto which he had planned to step
gracefully. I have to admit that he had a tendency to show off. In Zürs
he intimidated even the local experts by the sheer brilliance of his
technique on skis. With him, showing off was curiously part of his
charm.

The Soviets were conducting a campaign to bring about the fusion of the Communists (KPD) and Social Democrats (SPD) to form a combined workers' party (SED) under Communist, and therefore under their own, control. In their own Zone, where opposition to Soviet policies was not tolerated, the fusion was carried through and the SPD suppressed. In the three Western Sectors the SPD was able to organise a plebiscite of its members on 31 March 1946 which decided against the fusion by a very large majority. As a compromise, the Allied Kommandatura agreed to recognise both the SPD and SED in Berlin. The way was now open for the first elections under the temporary constitution which were to be held on 20th October 1946. In the Local Government Committee of the Kommandatura we agreed an electoral law for the purpose without too much difficulty. The Russians still seemed to be confident of an SED victory and the party certainly appeared to dominate the campaign. With Russian support, it had far more resources than the other parties and was able, quite literally, to distribute free food and beer at its meetings.

It had been agreed that the conduct of the election would be open to inspection by all four allies in all four Sectors. Accordingly on the polling day, which was a Sunday, a colleague, Major Ken Spenser, and I toured the polling stations in the Soviet Sector. All was going smoothly until at one of the stations we were approached by a young Russian officer, who had an escort of armed soldiers. 'Would you please accompany me to my headquarters?' We clearly had little choice and drove there with a Soviet Army vehicle in front and behind. On arrival we protested about this interference with an activity agreed by all four Allies and insisted that they connect us by telephone to one of our Soviet colleagues in the Kommandatura. We were released with profuse apologies and decided that the episode was too trivial to be worth a fuss. I see that the preliminary report on the election for the Committee, which I signed myself as the British member, says: 'No incident however slight, no cases of intimidation or pressure have been reported up to the present.' The Allied observers and all four political parties agreed that the conduct of the election was entirely free and satisfactory.

The result was a clear setback for Soviet policy. The SPD had 48.8%; the CDU (Christian Democrats) 22.3%; the SED 19.5% and the LDP (Liberals) 9.4%. When the result was announced, the SPD leaders were, of course, delighted, but also, as they told me, apprehensive about the responsibility which now fell on them. We all knew that the Russians would fight back. They reacted both in the Kommandatura and in the general political arena outside. In the Kommandatura they reversed their policy and sought to keep as stringent a grip as they could on the Magistrat, using Article 36 of the Constitution to its maximum extent.

The Magistrat, consisting of the heads of the departments of the administration for the whole city of Berlin, was a form of cabinet government. Under the temporary constitution, all parties represented in the elected city assembly had the right to representation in the Magistrat so that it formed a coalition. The new Magistrat following the election had 10 SPD members, 4 CDU, 4SED and 2 LDP. It had been assumed by the western allies, the political parties and the public generally that they would automatically take office. The Kommandatura itself had given that impression by saying that the intention of the Constitution was 'to restore political freedom.' The Russians, faced with the loss of the Magistrat which they had originally appointed, issued an unilateral order that the old Magistrat must not hand over to the new without the approval of the Kommandatura.

This was a breach of the agreement for the four power control of the city, but the Russians had now put the other allies in a difficult position. If they repudiated the Russian action, all pretence of a unified Berlin under four power supervision would collapse. The consequence was again a compromise which gave the Russians a tactical advantage. The Kommandatura issued an order agreeing to the resignation of the old Magistrat and approving the new with the exception of some members to whom the Russians had objections. This established a precedent that elected members could not take office without previous Kommandatura approval. The Russians had obtained a veto over appointments to the Magistrat and they now proceeded to use similar tactics to obtain the same power over its acts.

We had endless debates in the Kommandatura, of medieval subtlety and prolixity, whether in particular cases prior approval or post approval applied, the Soviet veto working in different ways in each case. They used these procedures to veto Ernst Reuter's election as Oberburgemeister, but his Deputy, Louise Schroeder, and the Assembly Chairman of the City, Otto Suhr, all members of the SPD, were also resolute and courageous upholders of democratic rights. They, and the population of West Berlin generally, refused to yield to Soviet pressure or inducements.

Inside the Soviet Sector and Zone conditions were utterly different; there was no freedom of expression and resistance was not tolerated. In December 1947 a body known as the Volkscongress was set up in the Soviet Zone under SED influence. It claimed to represent the whole of the German people but in fact it included only the SED and its affiliated organisations along with the LDP of the Soviet Zone which was under Soviet control. The refusal of the CDU in the Soviet Zone to join the Volkscongress provoked a Soviet campaign against it which finally deprived it of independence. The consequence was a clean break between the LDP and CDU in the West and the parties of the same name in the Soviet Sector and Zone.

This was only one of the ways in which Berlin, Germany and Europe were being divided into two halves, the West and the East, with increasing discrepancy in political, economic and social conditions between the two. The Allied Control Council for Germany as a whole scarcely ever succeeded in reaching agreement on anything. In Berlin the allied Kommandatura still continued to function and the City was still governed as a unit, but with increasing difficulty. I was so closely involved with all of this that I could not bring myself to leave it. I was due for release from the Army in November 1946, but I was offered, and accepted, deferment of this for six months. Towards the end of this period I transferred to the Control Commission as a civilian, but still doing the same job. On 5th May 1947 I was appointed a COI and Deputy Head of the Governmental Structure Branch.

This was a drastic change in the course of my life. I had always assumed that I would leave the Army as soon as possible and go back to Scotland and to Edinburgh University. I still kept in touch with Scotland and regarded my mother's house in Edinburgh as my home from which my absence was only temporary. The decision to stay on for a time in Berlin led to a much longer diversion. Through my association with the diplomats from the Foreign Office in Political Division of the Control Commission, I was urged to apply for the Reconstruction Examination for the Senior Branch of the Diplomatic Service. Apart from the fascination of the work I was doing at Berlin, I was attracted in any case by diplomacy. One of my friends at school, Charles Johnston, afterwards a Sheriff in Glasgow, had done his best to persuade me that it was the most interesting of careers. On his recommendation, I read Harold Nicolson's book, *Diplomacy*, which I see that I bought in October 1942 on my visit to Aberystwyth. It had given me the idea that Charles was probably right. A life spent in the study of other countries and in the conduct of relations with them seemed to me to offer a variety of challenges and experiences and my appetite for it was whetted by the continuous international conference of the Kommandatura.

The Kommandatura continued to function with endless debates and uneasy compromises and the pretence that Berlin was being administered as a unified city was maintained. Developments outside the city subjected its status to increasing pressure. The city was surrounded by the Soviet Zone, which was moving increasingly in a different direction from the three Western Zones. A conference of the four Powers in London in December 1947 was virtually a final attempt to preserve an agreed allied policy towards the whole of Germany. It failed and at the same time the Russians were sponsoring the Volkscongress, evidently intended as an embryonic German Government with its capital in Berlin. From the Russian point of view, the presence of the western allies in Berlin was at its best a nuisance, if not a serious obstacle to their plans.

On 19 December 1947 I sent the following letter to Brigadier Hinde, the Deputy Commandant and effective head of British Military Government in Berlin:

> There is very little I can add to the paper which you read to Mr
> Foggan, Lt Col Fletcher and myself last night. The whole
> question of course depends on whether the Russians have in fact
> finally abandoned all intention of endeavouring to reach an
> agreement with the West. If they still have that intention, then I
> should think that the Control Council and the Allied
> Kommandatura will continue to function very much as at
> present. If they have abandoned the intention, then I should
> think that their object would be to remove the other Allies from
> Berlin as quickly as possible.
>
> In the latter case the method employed might well be a
> gradual process of economic pressure designed to force us to
> leave on our own decision. It would for instance be only too easy
> for a 'breakdown' to occur in the railway system between Berlin
> and the British zone. At the same time they would probably avoid
> any drastic action which it would be difficult for them to justify to
> world opinion.

> If it has not already been done, it would seem desirable that
> we should prepare a plan to meet those possibilities. In
> particular, this plan should prepare means for the supply of the
> Western Sectors entirely by road. It would also seem desirable
> that a plan should be prepared in the case of a withdrawal from
> Berlin becoming inevitable. This plan should include
> arrangements for the evacuation of the German politicians and
> others to whom we have a moral obligation.

At the time this letter was regarded as excessively pessimistic. Our personal relations with the Russians on the Allied Kommandatura, at all levels, were friendly enough and it was difficult to imagine that they were plotting to expel us altogether from Berlin. The open split between East and West first became apparent in the Allied Control Council which was supposed to control Germany as a whole. It had long been apparent that the German economy had no hope of recovery without a currency reform to replace the existing one which had become almost worthless. Proposals for this purpose had been under discussion for months in the Council, but on 20th March 1948 the Soviets walked out. The Western Powers therefore decided to go ahead with the reform in their Zones, which they did on 18th June 1948.

Even before the Western currency reform, although they afterwards tended to use it as an excuse, the Russians began progressively to impose restrictions on travel between the Western Zones and Berlin. They began, as I had expected, on the railways. In a minor way at first on 24th January 1948 then more strongly from 1st April when barge traffic was also restricted. More regulations, and so-called technical difficulties and breakdowns followed until by 24th June all rail, barge and road traffic was effectively stopped altogether. When I wrote my letter in the previous December I had not expected the Russians to take the risk of stopping road as well as rail traffic. The Russians remained in the Allied Kommandatura, presumably because they were able to use it to make problems for the SPD-dominated Magistrat. They finally withdrew from it on 1st July.

So began the blockade of Berlin, which was, of course, a major international crisis involving the risk of a war with the Soviet Union. What was the West to do? If they accepted defeat and withdrew, which was perhaps what the Russians expected, they would abandon the Berliners, who had resisted Soviet pressure for three years, and allow the Soviet Union a great increase in power and prestige and an enhancement of their world-wide influence. With undisputed control of Berlin they could aim at German unification on their terms. There was no possibility of the West simply trying to force communication by land. The allied armies were largely disbanded, but the Soviets had their forces in strength on the ground. In any case, a war of this kind, so soon after the last, was simply unthinkable. It would have caused still more slaughter and destruction without benefit to anybody. There remained the only alternative, fantastic as it at first seemed, of supplying the Western Sectors entirely by air. That would mean flying into the two airports – one in the British and one in the American Sector – food and everything else necessary for a population of over 2 million people, including fuel for the approaching winter.

This remarkable feat was in fact accomplished with planes using the two airfields to their maximum capacity, day and night. One took off at one end to be immediately replaced by one landing at the other. There were flying-boats as well on the Havel. By February 1949 the Russian sought talks and the blockade was lifted on 12th May 1949, after nearly a whole year.

Life during the blockade was fairly austere and Spartan, almost as if we were the garrison of a besieged castle. We were never reduced to actual hunger, but we had very little fresh food and had to eat such things as powdered eggs and powdered potatoes. Once when two or three of us were on some mission to the Zone we went to a somewhat pretentious officers' club for lunch. 'What did we want'? 'Potatoes.' 'How were they to be cooked?' 'Any way, as long as they are real.' A colleague of mine, James Lowndes, somehow acquired a few fresh eggs and generously decided to invite some friends to dinner to share them. Unfortunately he made them into a Mexican dish that was so hot that we could not swallow it. James was of one those people for whom things tend to go wrong. At about this time he was engaged to the sort of girl who used to be called a flapper. She was Canadian and had a rather more senior job in the Control Commission than his own. Her chief claim to fame was a huge collection of shoes, rows and rows of them. James's ardour began to cool when he discovered that her idea of a fair marriage arrangement was that she would keep her own salary for her own pleasure, but that James's would meet all the household bills. It was just as well. Her flamboyance and the solidity of James would not have mixed.

Conditions were, of course, much more difficult in winter. Before the blockade nearly 90% of the electrical supply to Berlin had come from power stations in the Soviet Sector and Zone. On 23rd June 1948 the Soviet authorities cut off the supply. This put an enormous strain on old power stations in the Western Sector, especially as they were coal fired and the coal now had to come by air. With the exception of hospitals, radio transmitters and some other public services, power cuts had to be introduced. The civilian population had four hours of supply per day and the occupation authorities eight, and these hours were not always at the most convenient times. The winter was a test of endurance; but the people as a whole made it very clear that they preferred hardship to surrender.

Journalists, politicians and other people likely to influence opinion were brought to Berlin from time to time so they could see for themselves the prodigious effort of the airlift. Once I was entertaining a group of journalists at a reception in the officers club on their first day. It had to stop very early because of the power cut. Three or four of them were in no mood to go back to their hotel so I took them to my place to have a few more drinks. They brightened up when the unmistakable sound of a lively party emerged from the next set of rooms so we had to join in. Here the host was a rumbustious character, one of the stalwarts who had been brought to Berlin to help to organise the handling of incoming flights at the airport. As star guests he had acquired the chorus girls from a nightclub. Before long they were quite literally dancing naked on the table. The journalists stayed longer at the party than I did. Next morning, I found a note from one of them under my door, 'thanks for the local colour'. I began to imagine the headlines, 'naked girls at Military Government debauchery'. Some hours later, I had to face the journalists again to give them a talk about Berlin politics. They behaved impeccably there and afterwards. As far as I heard, none of them even printed a word about the party.

Bertrand Russell was another of our visitors whom I was delighted to look after for two or three days. I had for years been an enthusiastic reader of his several volumes of essays and his *History of Western Philosophy* but not, I regret to say, his *Principia Mathematica*. His wit and his scepticism delighted me. In fact, he and Bernard Shaw at one time probably had a considerable influence on my general attitude to life. Russell was 76 when he came to Berlin in 1948 and he had just had a narrow escape from death in Norway. He had been flying to

Trondheim in a flying-boat which landed and started to sink in the fjord. He escaped by swimming, but nineteen other passengers had been drowned. He made light of this episode when he was asked about it, as though it had been a perfectly normal occurrence. At all the receptions and so forth that we arranged for him, he was the perfect guest, charming and entertaining. Admittedly he clearly took pleasure in teasing people when his eyes would light up with a particular sparkle. With an American he discussed education there and said that one of his grandchildren had been to school in the States after starting her education in England: 'She found that all the work was already perfectly familiar to her, except one quite new subject.' 'What was that?' 'It was about the alleged advantages of the capitalist system.' To someone who dismissed detective stories: 'Oh really, I read nothing else.' He gave a lecture in German at the university, although he confessed that his German was a little rusty because he had not used it for about fifty years.

Harold Nicolson, whose book, *Diplomacy*, I have mentioned, was a visitor of whom I also had high expectations. As it happened, I had read two of his books not long before, *Friday Mornings*, a selection of his contributions to *The Spectator* and his *Congress of Vienna*. I had long admired the studied elegance of his broadcast talks. I remember, too, a remark of his in some other book where he had said of David Hume, how pleasurable it was to refresh the mind by contact with a clear Scottish intelligence. I arranged a lunch for him with the leading Berlin politicians and expected a flow of brilliant conversation. It did not work. The politicians were eager to talk about the current situation in Berlin, which we all thought at that time must be the major preoccupation of the whole world. Nicolson only wanted to discuss his own experiences in the Embassy in Berlin just after World War I. Each side was bored by the other.

TS Eliot came on a visit organised by the British Council. He was entertained to dinner in the Press Club and gave a public lecture afterwards. The dinner ran a little late, as the assembled audience were able to observe whenever a connecting door was opened. He began his lecture by apologising for the delay, 'due to reasons which were only too painfully obvious.'

Of course, there were visits by Ministers and other politicians. Ernest Bevin came at least once. He was an ungainly bear of a man, but genial, the most improbable of all Foreign Secretaries. Those who worked closely with him obviously liked him, which is more than can be said for some of his suave successors. Harold Macmillan came shortly after his time as Minister Resident in North Africa. He had a distinct air of effortless superiority and of indifference to the concerns of lesser beings. This seemed to be a deliberate pose, but his conversation soon revealed an intelligent and sensitive response to the realities of the situation.

When the Russians walked out of the Allied Kommandatura on 1st July 1948, the question naturally arose whether we should continue with the remaining three members or accept that the organisation had collapsed. My view was that we should continue, partly to have a means of preserving coordination between the three Western Sectors, and partly to leave open the framework for the resumption of quadripartite cooperation. I drafted a statement which I proposed should be issued by the three commandants. It began by saying that 'the Allied Kommandatura, which was established by agreement between the four Allied Governments, can only be dissolved by these four Governments.' It would therefore continue to function. We should like to see the return of the Soviet delegation, but their absence from the Kommandatura could not be permitted to stop its work.

For some reason, we failed to reach an agreement on such a statement. Among my papers is a report of a conversation I had with Otto Suhr, the President of the City Assembly, on 23rd July. He said he was worried that 'the administration of the Western Sectors was falling to pieces because of a lack of coordination.' He thought that 'the situaton would be gradually improved if the City could continue to deal with the Allied Kommandatura, whether the Russians are represented there or not.' In spite of this support, it was not until 21st December 1948 that the three Commandants issued a statement substantially on the lines of my original draft. Until then the Kommandatura had in effect been in suspense since the Soviets walked out.

Berlin was now in a curious state of multiple contradiction between theory and practice. The Allied Kommandatura was in theory in control of the whole of Berlin, but in practice now only of the three Western Sectors. The Magistrat and City Assembly, with their buildings in the Soviet Sector, still functioned for the whole of Berlin. Increasingly, the Soviet Sector in practice, and the whole of Berlin in theory, were being treated by the Soviets as part of their Zone. Since the election in 1946 the Soviet-controlled press and radio had done its best to discredit the Magistrat and these attacks now increased in virulence. In a report which I wrote at the end of July I said that it was likely that the Russians would impose an alternative Magistrat under their own control at an opportune moment. The SPD, CDU and LDP were determined, in spite of the personal risk to their leaders, to keep the Magistrat and Assembly in full operation in the Soviet Sector as long as possible. If Berlin was to be divided, they wanted it to be evident that it was the Soviets who had imposed the division.

As an additional complication, the Temporary Constitution of 1946 had a lifespan of only two years. Under its provisions, the City Assembly was required to prepare a new draft Constitution for submission to the Allies before 1st May 1948. This had been done but the discussion of the draft was interrupted by the Soviet withdrawal on 1st July. Even so, elections were due to be held by November 1948 under the terms of the Temporary Constitution. On 2nd September the City Assembly forwarded a copy of the Election Regulations to each of the four Commandants for their approval. The British, French and American approved. The Soviet Commandant, General Kotikov, replied on 20th October. He agreed that elections were necessary because the promises made to the electors in 1946 'have been grossly violated'. New elections could be held, provided among other points, 'organisations and formations of a military and fascist characters are dissolved'.

Since the Soviet licensed press habitually described the political parties other than the SED as 'warmongers and fascists', it followed that the Soviet condition was a demand for their suppression. The City Assembly therefore decided that the election could only be carried out in the Western Sectors. The deputies elected in 1946 in the Soviet Sector would retain their seats until a free election could be held there as well.

The election in the Western Sectors was slightly delayed because Soviet-inspired mob violence disrupted the meeting of the City Assembly called to approve the date, but it was carried out on 5th December 1948, again with elaborate measures to inspect its conduct. The SPD had an even greater lead than in 1946, 64.5%, with the CDU at 19.4% and the LDP at 16.1%. Participation was 86.3% of the electorate, a sharp rejection of the SED who had campaigned for abstention.

The SED had responded in advance by calling a meeting in the opera house in the Soviet Sector on 30th November to elect, with no constitutional authority, a new Magistrat. On 21st December the Soviet authorities officially recognised them as 'the only legal administrative body of Berlin'. The political division of Berlin was therefore now complete, although it was not until August 1961 that it was given physical recognition by the erection of the Berlin Wall.

The movement towards the transformation of the Western Zones into the German Federal Republic, which was eventually established on 23rd May 1949, required a new definition of a much less restrictive relationship between the occupying Powers and the German administration. This was the purpose of a document, known as the Occupation Statute, agreed by the three Military Governors, who also decided that something similar should be drawn up for Berlin. The drafting of this fell to me because I was the Chairman of the Local Government Committee at the time. I produced a document to which I gave the good Scottish title of A Statement of Principles.

Part of a verbatim record of the discussion when it was introduced to the Committee still exists in my papers. Both the Americans and the French delegates began by saying that it was an excellent document, but that did not stop a complex debate which goes on for 16 pages. We all finally agreed more or less on my text, but the debate had been an interesting intellectual exercise. Essentially the point of issue was that the French were more anxious than the Americans and ourselves to preserve control. The document, rather like the Act establishing the Scottish Parliament, in fact allowed Berlin to act except on a list of reserved subjects.

Meanwhile my application for the examination for appointment to the Senior Branch of the Foreign Service, to use the official title, was catching up with me. To be eligible to apply, you had either to have a university degree with 'at least 2nd class honours' or a certificate that you would have been expected to reach this level if war service had not interrupted the course. Arthur Melville Clark gave me the certificate. It was then a process in three stages. The first was a qualifying examination in basic literacy and numeracy with an intelligence test. I was summoned to appear for this in Victoria Halls, Bloomsbury Square, London on 9th and 10th November 1948. This was said to be an examination designed for people who had spent the last few years in the Forces and which did not need any particular preparation. I had little time for that in any case, but I did read an introduction to mathematics. Unfortunately I cannot remember the author or title and I seem to have lost the book. It made me realise that Peter Thomsen's logical approach to the subject had given me a basic foundation. There was also a language test, for which I chose German, with dictation and conversation.

This first step, which was not very demanding, I duly passed and was then invited for the next two, the celebrated country house weekend and the final interview. The Manor House, Stoke D'Abernon, Cobham, Surrey, was the site for some years of these weekend interrogations. I have come across a letter of 25th September 1947 from a friend of mine which gives such an accurate account of what went on there that I quote it in full:

My dear Paul,

It was extraordinarily good to see you again in Edinburgh, and to listen once more to your usual extravagant statements! I still feel slightly imbued with Scottish Nationalist propaganda, but my more fervent thoughts on the subject are beginning to wear off! Since returning home, life has been so hectic that I have had no chance to get down seriously to reading the opinions and thoughts (if any!) of Messrs Douglas Young and Maurice Lindsay! However, I hope to do so 'ere long, and will then become again an ardent supporter of the cause, I feel sure!

Now, as you will remember, I promised you some information on the FO Country-Houseparty, so here it is.

You are recommended to travel down to Cobham by the 10.52 am train from (I think) Waterloo, but my informant advises at least the 10.32, which allows you a little time at the house to adjust yourself before becoming caught up in the most exhausting whirl of the 48-hour 'course'.

The house itself is very pleasant, standing in charming grounds, and is run on the lines of an officers' mess. It is very well run apparently – witness my friend was offered coffee immediately on arrival. Candidates sleep in huts in the grounds, which contain single rooms and the usual offices. These huts, I gather, are similar to the officers' Messes and Quarters one used to meet on RAF Stations. In the house, there is a dining-room and a common-room etc, as well as lecture rooms.

In your room on arrival you find two numbers which you have

to pin on to yourself – one in the front, one on the back. This is, of course, so that you can be identified from all sides, and taken up on every word you let slip in an unguarded moment.

The party itself starts at noon with an opening address by the Commandant, the theme of which is that 'We do NOT watch you eat and drink here' – which is apparently the idea that most people have. Then you are divided into groups of approximately seven each, in which you work for the remainder of the 48 hours. Each group has a Directing Staff consisting of:

Group Chairman.

Group Psychologist.

Group Observer.

and one or two odd bodies, who also do a bit of observing when you are not looking!

The next item on the programme is a 2 hour psychological test – which contains all the usual dodges about which you will know already including the picture test, wherein you look at a picture for half-a-minute and write your impressions for a minute. You also have to describe yourself as seen by:–

a. A penetrating critic.

b. Your best friend.

Next you retire to a common-room for a period of discussion. This is quite informal. One of the staff throws out a subject for discussion, and the candidates just chew over it amongst themselves, whilst the observers sit in the background, pencils and note-books poised, writing 'No. 42 (Scott) – this man is a congenital idiot'!

In the evening of the first day, you are given a talk on the Civil Service by some expert.

I ought to mention that the food is very good and that there is an excellent bar, but, unfortunately you do not have the time to appreciate either. My friend told me that they all went to bed at about 10 pm on both nights, and that they were all completely exhausted. His brain was turning around at such a rate that he could not get to sleep until about 1 am – and he is a very quiet, phlegmatic type, I can assure you. It is, apparently, an exhausting business, which I find hard to convey in this very dull recital of such facts as I can cull from the very illegible notes I took in a Manchester restaurant! However, to continue with the story.

The next day, you are presented with a folder, called the 'Island Story'. This is all the dope on an imaginary island of the West Indies type. First of all you are to imagine that you are the PA (or whatever it is called) to a new Governor of this island. On leaving London by air, you are presented with this file, which you have to read and you are given half-an-hour (I think) to ascertain the six most important problems with which the Governor will have to deal on arrival at the island.

In discussion, the group solution is decided upon and you then go into committee and elect a chairman and secretary. Each problem of the six is then debated in committee with a different chairman and secretary for each problem – so that each one has a chance of acting in both capacities. When acting as chairman, you have to present the problem in all its aspects, give your personal solution, conduct the discussion of the committee and then sum up. This apparently takes most of the second day, although there are other problems set concerning the 'Island Story'.

I should tell you that while all these extremely ?interesting? activities are going on, each candidate is called away for interviews of approximately an hour's duration with each of the three principals of the Group Directing Staff. The Psychologist plumbs the depths of your life – both intimate and not-so-intimate, the other two talk to you in more general terms. One more thing, which you have to do, is to give a talk on a subject concerned with Art, Culture or Thought. (Here I foresee Scottish Nationalism rearing its ugly head, although I don't know whether this would be quite the thing for a FO party!).

Whilst with the Group Staff, you have to fill in several forms, stating your interests, your ideas of leisure etc etc.

After 48 hours, you leave Cobham a sadly disillusioned and exhausted man, I gather, and you wonder why you ever thought you had a chance of getting through!

Well, broadly speaking, Paul, that is the 'gen'. I am sorry if it is not very clear, but I had only a short time with my friend to get through a lot, and my mushroom omelette kept getting in the way. However, I hope it is of some use to you as a general guide. There is, of course, no guarantee that the plan will be the same when you go to Cobham, but my informant thinks that it will be more or less of the same order.

I hope all goes well in Berlin and that you have managed your trip to Paris.

I must stop now and do some work, but I hope to hear from you in the not too distant future.

All good wishes,

Tony

Who this helpful friend was I am sorry to say I have forgotten, but he had briefed me so well that I knew in advance exactly what to expect. The final interview took place at the Commission in 6 Burlington Gardens in London. Here we were summoned in, one by one, to sit at the end of a long table for cross-examination for thirty minutes or so by about a dozen assorted academics, pundits and retired senior civil servants. They were all very polite, but they had clearly been well briefed by the Stoke D'Aberon people to probe into points where we might be vulnerable. I emerged from all of this successfully, but, after all, my work in Berlin might have been designed as training for it.

This is how I came to spend the next thirty years or so as a diplomat. In a sense I regret it because I think that I might have achieved more in, and for, Scotland, if I had returned there when I could have left the army in November 1946. This would have been a more normal sort of life among my own friends, developing friendships and mutual interests steadily over many years. I should probably have started writing for publication very much sooner, instead of drafting dispatches for internal circulation in the Foreign Office and Whitehall. On the other hand, the Diplomatic Service provided me with a career, full of interest, in an atmosphere of mutual support, for which I am very grateful. My colleagues were generally admirable people who enlivened life with intelligent conversation, which is one of the greatest of pleasures. The Service not only enabled me to see much of the world, but by its nature, introduced me to leading people in many countries and gave me an insight into diverse societies. It was a continuous education. Still it meant that I have spent the best part of forty years of my life in a sort of comfortable and interesting exile. It had its advantages, but it deprived me of the experience of Scotland for all of that time.

I have written about my time in postwar Berlin in greater detail than I apply to other places where my career has taken me. There are several reasons for this. I have a much larger archive of papers about Berlin than I have for all the other places together. Also at the time when I was there, Berlin was the major point of contact between the Soviet Union and the West and the place where the split between them revealed itself most dramatically, and this split dominated international relations for the next forty years. The process in Berlin was obvious and rapid. That is unusual in diplomatic life. As Lord Strang said once, diplomacy is normally a matter of ploughing the sand. You deal either with routine matters of little interest or importance or with a small part of an intractable problem which drags on for years.

Berlin affected the course of my life in more ways than the diversion into diplomacy. It was there that I met Celia Sharpe whom I married two or three years later in London. She was working in the Education Branch of Military Government. The tabloid press would have called her an English rose and she certainly was English. Her father, a barrister, had been a judge in Burma and lived in Sussex. Perhaps unusually for a woman from such a background, she acquired an enthusiasm, which I know was genuine, for most things Scottish, especially the music and dance, and to an extent, the history, and the literature. She was kind and generous to a fault; perhaps the adoption of Scottishness was an aspect of that. In the long run the marriage did not survive and we have not lived together for more than twenty years; but we still remain friends and she comes to Edinburgh for a day or so every year. She has probably been kinder to me than I deserve.

At my last meeting of the Kommandatura committee Ziegelmeyer, who was in the chair, made an elaborate farewell speech. He said, with wild exaggeration, that my name would always be associated with the restoration of democratic government in Berlin. In fact few people, apart from the members of the committee itself, knew anything about our activities.

CHAPTER 7
Interludes – Edinburgh, Paris, Prague
1947 – 1950

From the end of the War, I was able to go back to Edinburgh quite frequently on leave. One of the most memorable of these visits was to the first Edinburgh Festival in 1947. The Festival was a triumph which no one who was there will ever forget, a defiance of the greyness and austerity of the war, a reaffirmation, as a leader in the *Manchester Guardian* said, of the unconquerable spirit of European civilisation. The Lord Provost, Sir John Falconer, said in a note in the programme of the first Festival that the aim was to provide the world with a place where every year the best in music, drama and the visual arts could be seen and heard in ideal surroundings. So it was from the beginning.

The Louis Jouvet Company came from Paris. The Vienna Philharmonic was reunited with Bruno Walter and there has been an infinity of such things over the years. The spirit of the Auld Alliance was revived. At one of the early Festivals Louis Jouvet (or was it Jean Louis Barrault?), gave a speech at a closing ceremony in the Usher Hall with which he concluded, 'Merci á tois, Ecosse fidèle', and many people in the audience were in tears. There was a profusion of flowers in every venue, and a club, which somehow escaped from wartime restrictions, in the Assembly Rooms in George Street where the audience and the stars mingled. The sun shone every day. We had at last emerged from the shadows.

As Robert Garioch said in 'Embro to the Ploy'.

> There's monie hartsom braw high-jinks
> mixed up in this alloy
> in simmer, when aa sorts foregether
> in Embro to the ploy.

The international content of the Festival has not been confined to Europe, but has embraced virtually the whole world, but what about Scotland itself? Hugh MacDiarmid said of this first festival that there was nothing Scottish about it except that one-man band playing on the High Street. This was not quite true because from the beginning the Saltire Society, determined to give Scotland a voice, staged programmes of Scottish music and poetry from the Makars to the present. Ian Gilmour and his wife, Meta Forrest, arranged and took part in these Saltire programmes for many years. They made the speaking of Scottish poetry of all periods a sophisticated art form that was an inspiration and delight. I have cherished them as friends for more than forty years.

It was not until the second year that David Lyndsay's *Ane Satyre of the Thrie Estaitis* burst upon an astonished world. This production by Tyrone Guthrie of a text adapted by Robert Kemp was probably the first since the sixteenth century. Sir David Lyndsay of the Mount, diplomat and Lord Lyon King of Arms to King James V, as well as a prolific poet, was no establishment conformist. His play is full of energy, humour and satirical wit and it is merciless in its satire of the inadequacies of King and lords spiritual and temporal, merchants, burghers and rulers. Scottish egalitarianism and passion for social justice has no more powerful expression. Scotland in the sixteenth century must have been a self-confident and sophisticated society to have allowed its public performance, even apparently one before the King and Court in the Palace of Linlithgow. In all the great performances which the Edinburgh Festival has given in the more than fifty years of its existence, none has made a greater impact than the revival (since repeated many times, but not often enough) of this once forgotten play. In Scotland it has contributed to our cultural and political self-confidence and to a new appreciation of the expressive power of the Scots language. Tyrone Guthrie's use of a stage surrounded by the audience in the Assembly Hall of the Church of Scotland has had an international influence on the technique of dramatic production.

Then there is the extraordinary phenomenon of the Fringe. The central core of the Edinburgh International Festival, to give it the official title, is planned and selective. Around it has grown up spontaneously an accumulation of events, exhibitions and performance of all kinds, free from all control or selection. This began in a small way at first when the Saltire Society and a few others saw a new opportunity. Since then it has expanded in all directions. Now the Fringe by itself has become the largest festival of the arts in the world with hundreds of companies and thousands of performances. Its quality is as diverse as its nature. It can be astonishing and brilliant or atrocious or simply incompetent and boring. These events happen all over Edinburgh, and sometimes outside, in all sorts of unlikely places. In the Disruption of 1842 the Church of Scotland split in two and the Free Church, which rebelled against the patronage imposed by the British Parliament, set about building its own kirks and church halls all over Scotland. It is one of the unexpected consequences that Edinburgh now has an abundance of such places that can be pressed into use as uncomfortable and sometimes cold but acceptable theatres.

You might suppose that with so much going on it would be difficult to find audiences. It is true that competition is intense and some Fringe shows attract almost no audience at all. On the other hand, the atmosphere of Festival persuades usually staid citizens that it is normal to go to several shows a day and that is what most of the thousands of visitors do. Consequently, other annual festivals have joined in. From the early days there has been a Military Tattoo on the lofty stage of the Castle Esplanade, a superb setting, but often so battered by wind and rain that it proves that the spectators, as well as the performers, are made of stern stuff. The combination of pipe bands, marching soldiers, Scottish dancing, all spiced with exotica from foreign parts, attracts bus loads from England and many visitors from America and other places who have seen it at home on television. Many of them think that the Tattoo is the Festival. But there are also Film and Jazz Festivals, and more recently a Book Festival. All of these are important events in themselves, each of which could take up your entire time.

The effect of all this frenzy of activity on Edinburgh and on Scotland generally is incalculable. It used to be said that the season for the arts in Edinburgh lasted only for these three weeks. There was a song which said:

> If you think this place is culture's crown
> you should come here in the winter.

Now there are other festivals, of science, folk music, children's theatre and Hogmanay at other times of the year. The stimulation of all of this on ideas and artistic creativity must be great. Add to it, the free, public lectures provided by the three universities, the public libraries and many organisations and the whole place becomes a cauldron of inspiration. Edinburgh used to bask on the laurels of the past, the Scottish Enlightenment, the *Edinburgh Review* and *Blackwood's*, Sir Walter Scott, RL Stevenson. Now I am inclined to think that the present is even more interesting than the past.

I said in the last chapter that my time in Berlin had an influence on the subsequent course of my life. So, thrust into the middle of it, has had the Edinburgh Festival. No matter where I have been in the world, I have contrived to be in Edinburgh for the Festival, if sometimes only for a few days. I may have missed one or two, but no more. I have concentrated on the Scottish events, which can be found nowhere else in the world, those of the Saltire Society and of the Clarsach Society, the Royal Scottish Country Dance Society and many others who have followed their example. For most of this time I have been part of the audience only, but after I came back to Scotland I became involved in other ways.

My holiday excursions from Berlin were not only to Edinburgh. One of the first was a weekend visit to Paris in December 1946. This was my first visit to Paris, but I felt at home from the start because I had long been familiar with it from books and films. Somebody once said that everyone has two capitals, his own and Paris. I feel like that and I am conscious of a need to go there are least once a year. I have not always succeeded.

On this first visit I was asked by one of my colleagues in Military Government, Francis Cammaerts, to do a small service for him. Cammaerts afterwards gave evidence in defence of Penguin Books when they were prosecuted for the publication of *Lady Chatterley's Lover*. He was the son of a Belgian poet, Emil Cammaerts. At the beginning of the War he had been a conscientious objector, but then changed his mind and became one of the secret agents parachuted into France to assist the resistance. He had said very little about this before, but he now told me why he wanted me to take some papers to Paris. They were for a woman whose name I do not remember with confidence, but I think it was Christine. She needed some papers for a divorce action and Cammaerts had been able to persuade some authority in East Germany or Poland to produce them. She had been one of the group of agents working with him in occupied France and, Cammaerts said as though it were an everyday occurrence, 'She saved my life from the Gestapo.'

Cammaerts had been arrested by the Gestapo after the Allied break-out from Normandy. When Christine discovered this she went herself to the Gestapo and demanded to see the commander. 'I know that you have arrested Colonel Cammaerts and I want you to release him immediately. My headquarters in London know all about this and they know your full name and description. You must realise that Germany is losing the war. If you do not do as I say, you will be arrested after the War and tried as a war criminal and we have enough evidence about your activities to make the verdict certain. If you release my Colonel now, we may take a more lenient view.' Incredible as it may seem, they both walked free.

So I duly met Christine and handed over the papers. Through her, I met a number of other former secret agents who had been working for months with the constant risk of arrest, torture, death or the concentration camp hanging over them. Now the grateful Government had said, in effect, thank you very much; well done; here is a medal; but we don't need you anymore. None had any idea what they were going to do next. Ordinary peacetime life was too much of an anti-climax.

Some time afterwards, as I learned from the newspapers, Christine had a very sad end. It sounds too melodramatic to be credible, but after all the risks of resistance in occupied France, she was murdered outside her own flat in peacetime London. After her work in France she had taken a job as an assistant purser on a passenger liner. She had an affair with another member of the crew but had tired of him. He shot her in a jealous rage.

Christine was not my only contact on this memorable first visit to Paris. Our Russian interpreter in Spandau, Afanasieff, had given me an introduction to his two brothers who were living in Paris. They could not have been more different from one another. One was a saintly character in a religious order devoted to work for the poor and needy. The other was flamboyant and extrovert. He made no secret of the fact that he was flourishing on the black market, operating some mysterious currency deals with Switzerland. We had dinner in the Hotel George V and then went to a Russian nightclub. He insisted on paying for everything on the grounds that I had to work for the pittance the Government paid me. When I told him that I was thinking of taking the Foreign Office examination he said, 'You are bound to succeed. You are Scottish. That is a tremendous advantage.' That proves, I suppose, that he knew how to win friends and influence people.

I took every opportunity I could to ski each winter, sometimes for a weekend in the Harz Mountains, but often further away for two weeks or so. I have mentioned Zürs already and I went to Chamonix at least once. In January 1947 the Czechoslovak Legion (like the British Legion, an organisation of former members of the armed services), sent an invitation for a group of officers and other ranks to come as their guests to ski in the High Tatra, as a gesture to repay the hospitality which they had experienced in Britain during the war. I seized the chance and went on a long and complicated train journey which was the usual way of travel at that time. We spent the first couple of days in Prague, my first experience of that beautiful and mysterious place. Because this part of the world had been cut off from us for so long (and did not Chamberlain once describe it as a distant land of which we know little?) I felt that I was experiencing something quite new. To my surprise, I thought that there was on the contrary something familiar about the dining room when I went down to dinner. There was a group of Church of Scotland ministers who had come to renew their links with the Hussite Church.

Our enthusiastic and welcoming Czech hosts took us first to ski in some hills not far from Prague. We spent quite a long part of the afternoon drinking a steaming and potent punch. It was only as it was getting dark that they set off at high speed, over ground familiar to them, to lead the way down the hill. It was the sort of experience that sharpens up your reactions. Then we went to the real mountains, Strebzke Pleso in the Tatra.

There I encountered an attractive girl, Alexandra Albrechtova, who was staying in the hotel with some members of her family. Another British Officer and I competed for her attentions, but she concentrated on me when she discovered that we could communicate in French. Sasa asked me to come to her room at midnight when most other people would be safely in bed. This I did and I confess for once I started skiing rather late next day. She invited me too to visit her in her house in Bratislava at the end of the week. We made love on sacks of hay in the stables. Some years later, (it must have been in the early

1950s), she sought me out in London and I was able to help her to establish herself there. She had arrived with only the summer clothes she was wearing at the time. The Gottwald regime was becoming increasingly repressive and her brother, who had taken part in student demonstrations, had been arrested. Her father had immediately sent her to London on the first available plane before new travel restrictions would have made escape impossible.

In his confidential report, Hook Sangster said that I was 'keen on sport, particularly skiing and sailing'. This was true, as far as it goes, but it depends what you mean by sport. In the sense of hunting or shooting animals, it is utterly repugnant to me. Also, as I have said before, watching other people playing games, or taking a passionate interest in the affairs of a professional football team, are to my mind are both the height of absurdity and a deplorable waste of time. But if by sport you mean participating in some activity which is agreeable in itself as healthy exercise which takes you to the mountains or the sea, that is a different matter. Skiing is an example. In Berlin I discovered the pleasure of horse riding in the woods of the Grunewald, which I did first thing in the morning several times a week. We had a variety of sailing boats in a yacht club on the Havel, a lake on the edge of the town. In the winter we skated usually on a frozen tennis court, but sometimes on a pond.

Tom Stables of the Military Government Secretariat was a man of invincible high spirits who treated life as a constant comedy of which he wanted all of us to share the absurdity. He was also a natural athlete and, in particular, a spectacular skater. It was typical of his clowning that he would go on to a crowded ice-rink and stagger round as though he was about to crash in a heap, but then he would suddenly begin to pirouette or leap in the air with effortless ease. Once when a number of us were skating on a pond, some small boys told us that one of our friends had fallen through the ice at the other end. He was quite close to the edge and we were trying to reach him with planks and other objects that were lying around. As we were doing this, he suddenly said in a tone that made us realise that he really was near the end, 'I am sorry chaps. I'm afraid I can't hold out much longer .' Tom without hesitation dashed into the icy water up to his shoulders, breaking the ice as he went and pulled the victim out by the hand. I have seldom seen such a courageous and instantaneous reaction.

CHAPTER 8

Bonn and the Foreign Office
November 1949 – June 1953

The three Western Zones of postwar occupied Germany became the German Federal Republic on 23rd May 1949 with its capital in Bonn. The American, British and French still retained some powers under the Occupation Statute but the new Republic was intended soon to become a normal state, as independent as any other. I was transferred to Bonn on 6th November 1949 to join the office which was in effect the British Embassy to the new Federal Republic of Germany.

The whole atmosphere when I arrived was very different from Berlin. You had the feeling of solid progress towards normality and a brighter future. Germans and allies alike felt that they were involved at the gestation of a new Germany which would take its place in the world, free from the madness with which it had been infected for years. Soviet pressure was the remote cause of the division of Germany, not the constant threat which it had been in Berlin.

Most of my colleagues and I lived in a grand nineteenth century mansion, called (for reasons which I never discovered) the Villa Spiritus, close to the River Rhine and to one of the bridges which crossed it. We had not yet reached the normality where diplomats lived like other people with their own wives and children in separate flats and houses. Our offices were not normal either because they were in huts in a former army and air force camp. This was known officially as Chancery, Office of the UK High Commissioner, Wahn, although it was known locally as Wahnerheide.

There was a small group of diplomats, headed by Kit Steel and including some of my other friends from Berlin such as John Killick. They accepted me as one of themselves, although I had not yet been appointed officially. Life in the Villa Spiritus was never dull. At almost every meal, even breakfast, one or other of us had usually invited a journalist, politician or official for a working session. We were constantly immersed in the affairs of the new republic. Three or four of us joined with equal enthusiasm in the celebration of Carnival and would appear for a serious discussion at breakfast, bleary-eyed and in fancy dress.

I see from the few papers which I still have from this period that I was allocated three subjects: Berlin and the Soviet Zone, left-wing politics and liaison with the Federal Ministry for all-German-Affairs. The usual Foreign Office system applied. The desk officer is responsible in the first instance for his own group of subjects or countries. He (and of course I use that term generally to include the feminine as well as the masculine) is expected to become the recognised expert in these matters. All incoming documents, letters, dispatches or telegrams on his subjects go first to him. He can either deal with each paper, either alone or after consultation with other departments, or he can decide to refer it to his immediate superior. If he does that, he must write a minute which gives his views and recommends a course of action. If that involves a written reply, he must supply a draft. These minutes and drafts can go up through the chain of command, perhaps to the top, and at each stage, the official involved can take the responsibility to make the decision. I suppose that other Government departments and other organisations work in a similar way. Of course, in time of crisis the system may be suspended with rapid action taken at the top, but then it is essential for the man at the bottom to be kept informed.

This system has many advantages. The new recruit is thrown in at the deep end and has to learn fast. He has to distinguish the trivial and routine from the important and dangerous. He has to avoid the opposite extremes of troubling his superior by referring to him matters which he should decide for himself or, on the other hand, failing to refer important and potentially dangerous questions which are beyond his competence. If his drafting is slack, inelegant, or long-winded, or ambiguous (unless ambiguity is deliberate and necessary) he will soon suffer the indignity of finding it slashed or rewritten.

So the system is an education, apart from anything else, in literary composition. Much of it is a curious sort of composition, because the readership is very restricted and it usually appears under the name of someone else. This can apply even to routine letters because the official who signs is not necessarily the author. With dispatches this is almost invariably the case. These are fairly long and elaborate reports addressed to the Foreign Secretary and signed by the Ambassador or other head of post. What happens to them depends largely on the appropriate desk officer in the Foreign Office. He may read them simply for his own information and initial them off for no further action, mark them for copies to be sent to other departments, send them up through the chain of command or recommend them for Foreign Office Print, with various different degrees of distribution. In this last case, they are printed and copies are sent widely around in Whitehall, to Ministers and to the Palace and the posts abroad. It does not mean that all these people actually read them, of course. Most of them are subjected to floods of paper from all directions and do not have time to read much of it. Still, it is a potentially wide and influential readership and eventually the dispatches and other papers are available to the historians. I see that while I was in Bonn, or Wahn, I drafted several such dispatches, one on the problem of refugees and a series on the political parties.

I do not know to what extent this system still exists. It may be that with modern instant communication, e-mail and the rest, that the comparatively leisurely methods of the past no longer prevail. It may be that dispatches and Foreign Office Print are now regarded as picturesque antiquities. I have described the system, which I first encountered at Wahn, in some detail because it was the background to my life for the next thirty years or so.

It was in April 1950 that I first reported to the Foreign Office. This is the building designed in the 1870s for both the Foreign and the Indian Offices and which reflects the comfortable self-assurance of the Victorian imperial age. There is a ceremonial staircase surrounded by the symbols of past glory and one or two grand and spacious offices for ministers. Some years later my son, Alastair, was admitted with some other children to watch the trooping of the colour ceremony on the Horse Guards' Parade from the windows of the Secretary of State's room. He looked around with approval and remarked that I had 'quite a nice office'. In fact, of course, my actual room was much less magnificent, but seductively comfortable for all that. The Foreign Office generally had the air of a gentlemen's club, like the Travellers or the Athenaeum. The furniture was a bit shabby, but solid and of good quality in its day. Perhaps the Government has sold it off by now for its antique value. Heating was still by coal fire.

When India became independent the Foreign Office had expanded from Downing Street to King Charles Street to incorporate the space of the old India Office. Particularly in that part of the building there were some fine pictures, mostly portraits of eighteenth century conquerors and administrators in European costumes, wigs and embroidered waistcoats, highly inappropriate for the climate of India. No wonder that many of them died young.

In the 1950s we still worked on Saturday forenoons. The convention was that we could then wear tweed jackets instead of dark suits, presumably a relic of the days when everyone would be impatient to rush off to their country houses. The Foreign Office had been that sort of place and some of the old habits still clung to it.

A Foreign Office Department usually consisted of about ten people dispersed between three rooms. The head of the department had one for himself. His deputy probably shared one with another more senior member. The rest were in what was known as the Third Room where six or more people had their desks, each with two telephones, one internal and one external. With several people talking on the telephone or dictating to a secretary simultaneously, it could be very noisy. The advantages were that we all got to know one another very well and had some idea of what was going on at the other desks. The secretaries came from a typing pool and the papers were registered and filed in a separate office attached to each Department and called its Division. Each incoming document arrived in its own paper file cover on which you wrote the minutes and instruction about its distribution and the action to be taken, or simply initialled it off. We had large presses (significantly it is the Scots word which is used) in which our papers were locked up at night. Papers were circulated to other rooms in locked dispatch boxes, which were covered in red leather.

The Third Room might sound like a turmoil in which concentration was impossible. In fact, we got used to working in the noise as it was generally a stimulating and happy confusion. Each desk dealt with one or two countries or one or two subjects. If your own desk was going through a dull patch, there was usually something interesting at another. When there was a crisis, everything expanded at once, not only dealing with the event, but also with the sudden increase in interest by the press, the public and the parliamentarians. Usually the desk officer was dealing with routine and dull affairs in which no one could be persuaded to take an interest. With a coup, a natural disaster, a political scandal, there could be a sudden explosion in telegrams, telephone calls, parliamentary questions, enquiries to ministers and so forth. The whole Third Room was interested. Everyone lent a hand and the working day was as long as it took. There were never any fixed hours, anyway.

At any time, the company in the Third Room was a pleasure in itself. That may come as a surprise because diplomats have a bad reputation, as arrogant, pompous stuffed-shirts. It was true that some did succumb to pomposity. The trappings of diplomatic life abroad could give some people an inflated idea of their importance. I have encountered a few bad examples myself, usually among Ambassadors. After all, they live, in some posts at least, in virtual palaces with many servants and give lavish dinners to the great and the good of the country. They are often treated with elaborate deference. You have to have your feet firmly on the ground to keep a grip on reality, but it was not like that in the Third Room. The new entrants to the service had been selected by a painstaking process designed to find people who were intelligent, articulate, capable of rapid, precise and rational thought and good at relations with other people of all kinds. It would be surprising if they were not good company. Some were even witty; all were irreverent. It was not an atmosphere in which pomposity could survive.

Then it was said that most members of the service were the products of the English, so-called public, schools and of the universities of Oxford or Cambridge. I think statistically that such people are, or were, in the majority. I do not remember any sign of them ganging up against the rest of us. There were Scots all over the place. Of course, promotion boards and the like might be largely composed of Oxbridge people, who naturally tended, perhaps unconsciously, to favour their own kind.

One of the stalwarts of my first department, Horace Phillips, had been educated at Hillhead High School in Glasgow and at no university at all. He was one of those who had been merged into the Senior Branch of the Diplomatic Service through internal promotion. He revelled in hard work and was usually the first to arrive in the morning and the last to leave at night, and always ready to volunteer for duty on public holidays. In spite of that, he was invincibly amiable and cheerful. He told us once that he had come up from the south coast in a railway compartment with a group of Iranian naval cadets. Confident that no one would understand, they had spent the time denigrating their British instructors and in bawdy observations about every woman in sight. Horace, whose Persian was fluent, listened to this in silence until the train was pulling into the station. Then a polite request in their language that he might take his suitcase from the rack threw the cadets into a panic and they ran for dear life along the platform. Horace ended his career as Ambassador in Turkey.

Our first action each morning was to read the telegrams from posts abroad which had accumulated during the night. For some of them you might have to take immediate action. Foreign Office telegrams were not short and cryptic but written in coherent, if preferably succinct, prose. Through them posts reported important developments in their countries or negotiations in which they were engaged. They could be unclassified and *en clair*, but they were usually confidential or secret and sent in cypher which was, normally, translated into ordinary language before it reached your desk. Depending on the importance of the subject, they were distributed to a few or to many departments in the Foreign Office and throughout Whitehall. Like Foreign Office print they were one of the means by which everyone in the Office could keep in touch with current events everywhere in the world. I speak, of course, of my own time. Modern technology has no doubt transformed the system.

The Department I joined, South-East Asia, was concerned with a part of the world about which I knew practically nothing. Its Head was a heroic man with a name and initials almost the same as my own, Robert Heatlie Scott. He came originally from Inverness. Like my friend Jim Ford, he had fallen into Japanese hands when Hong Kong surrendered to them. Since at that time he had been working for the Ministry of Information, the Japanese regarded him with particular suspicion and treated him with even more than their usual brutality. He wrote a chilling but unemotional account of it. After the war, since he was an expert on the Far East, he was involved in relations with Japan. These he handled without any sign of bitterness or resentment. The similarity of our initials, RH and PH, sometimes caused confusion. When I had been in the Department only a few months I was delighted to get an invitation to lunch from Kingsley Martin, the very distinguished editor of the *New Statesman*, at that time the most intelligent of periodicals which I had read with pleasure and admiration for years. Of course, it was apparent when I arrived to meet him and his collaborators that he had been expecting RH. Still, he adjusted to the shock with aplomb and we had a lively conversation about Burma, which was my speciality at the time.

Shortly after I joined the office, I was summoned to take part in a training course for new entrants to the Senior Branch, the programme of which has miraculously survived among my papers. It lasted five weeks and took up most of every day. There were visits and and lectures all over the office and in the Board of Trade and the World Service of the BBC. The opening talk was by the Permanent Under Secretary, William Strang. Probably because most of us had spent the war in the Army, Navy or Air Force, where quite different customs prevail, he cautioned us against excessive deference. We were all colleagues together and all should be addressed by their first names.

Strang, the most senior official in the Office, was another of the Scots who infiltrated it so thoroughly. In his autobiography, *Home and Abroad*, he explains that he was born into 'a Scottish household in a rural English environment'. This was because his father was a Scottish farmer who had moved to England. He says that this meant that he was 'faced with a need for adaptation and adjustment, conscious or unconscious, going beyond what is normally called for in the formation of personality.' His family were bilingual, speaking both English with a West-of-Scotland accent, and Scots, or, as he very properly calls it, Lallans. It is, he says, 'a widely spoken but not fully surviving literary language with its own variations in vocabulary, its own tune and intonations, its own turns of expression and its own characteristic ways of thought.' It is clear from this that Strang and I had much in common. At the time I did not know it because *Home and Abroad* was not published until 1956 and I was a much too junior an official to meet him socially. As it happens, I did meet his daughter and took her out to dinner a couple of times. She was not very communicative and nothing came of it.

At the beginning of *Home and Abroad*, Strang describes the laborious and frugal lives of the dairy farmers in the west of Scotland from which he sprang and he says, 'These severe conditions of life produced men and women vigorous in mind and body, hard-working, thrifty, secure in their opinions to the point of aggressiveness, self-respecting, cheerful, alert, pungent of speech and sparing of praise, honourable, upright and devout.' I mention this because the first of his phrases reminds me of a remark about myself which I once happened to see in a letter from Personel Department to an Ambassador in a post I was about to join, 'robust in body and mind'. I thought at the time that this was not too comfortable reputation to have because it suggested that I was the sort of character who could be sent to places that were dangerous or unpleasant.

I was in South East Asia Department from April 1950 until June 1953. We were concerned with a very disturbed part of the world. India, Pakistan and Burma had recently achieved independence from British rule and there were still many questions arising from the handover of power. Indonesia was escaping with difficulty from Dutch control. The French were at war with the Viet-Minh in Indo-China. In June 1950 the Korean war began when North Korea invaded the South. The Chinese invaded Tibet with ruthless brutality in October 1950. In most of these matters we were more or less impotent observers. I remember feeling this particularly when we received an eloquent and pathetic request from Tibet for help against the Chinese invader. We could only observe, deplore and regret. At the time the Chinese produced a rather crude propagandist magazine in English. One had a photograph of a Chinese soldier fondling the breasts of a Tibetan girl. The caption below it said that it showed the Chinese Army giving medical assistance to the grateful population.

My own desk was concerned with Burma. I became so immersed in their affairs that I almost felt that I was living in the place. I also became very fond of the people from my meetings with the staff of the Burmese Embassy and with officials and journalists who visited London. Most of them had a convivial, carefree attitude to life which was very refreshing. At a party given by the First Secretary we were invited to change into Burmese costume and discovered that all the buttons were rubies, which were apparently plentiful in his part of the country. It is sad that so happy and relaxed a people should have fallen years later into the hands of a thuggish government.

In the 1950s we still felt in the Foreign Office that the Americans welcomed our opinions and paid attention to them. To some extent, it was a consequence of the war in which there had been combined US/British headquarters. It was said that the usual situation in them was an American nominally in charge with a British deputy who did all the work. At the time this was natural enough because the British had longer active experience of war and Britain was still a major power which had run the show alone. After the war all of that began gradually to change. The Americans became increasingly conscious of their growing strength and of British decline. They were willing to accept Britain as a docile ally, but less and less as a mentor whose views had to be taken into account. At one point during the Korean War we were apprehensive that the Americans might resort to nuclear weapons. We solemnly, and quite rightly, advised against it. Whether that made any difference to the American decision, I have no idea.

In the year when I joined the Foreign Office I was spending Christmas with Celia Sharpe's family in Sussex. This was the Christmas when Ian Hamilton and his friends removed the Stone of Destiny from Westminster Abbey. I was delighted by this as the perfectly proper recovery of property looted from Scotland, as an admirable tweaking of the nose of establishment pomposity, and as an assertion of a will to reassert our political identity. The reactions of the people I met at Sussex Christmas parties was utterly different. They seemed quite genuinely to regard it with horror an act of sedition and sacrilege. That too was the tone of comment at the BBC.

In 1996 Michael Forsyth, as Scottish Secretary in the last days of a declining Conservative administration, persuaded his cabinet colleagues to agree to return the Stone to Scotland officially. He evidently hoped that this would restore the electoral fortunes of his party by demonstrating that they were not, after all, anti-Scottish. The contrast with 1950 could not have been more complete. In England, apart for one or two letters in *The Times*, no one seemed to notice or care. In Scotland, it was regarded as the appropriate righting of an ancient wrong, but nothing to get very excited about. Events had moved too far for what would once have been a bold gesture to have a noticeable effect on support for a discredited government. Attitudes to both the monarchy and the constitutional position of Scotland had changed radically in these forty six years.

During my time in South East Asia Department, I had a very pleasant interlude in Paris. The Office assumed that those of us who had joined under the postwar reconstruction scheme, as the Wilton Park procedure was known, would have had little opportunity to acquire fluent French. That was still the one foreign language of which a knowledge was assumed. Papers arriving in French, unlike other languages, were not regarded as requiring translation. So there was an arrangement to allow us to apply to spend a month or so with a family in Paris, selected for the purpose by the Embassy. I had two such visits. The first was in the house, near the Parc Monceau, of the family of an aged sculptor from Brittany who had been a pupil of Rodin. He had abandoned sculpture because he said that he was too old and feeble for the physical effort. His wife, who was much younger, ran the place benevolently and efficiently as a sort of finishing school for young aspirants anxious to acquire fluency. They were of diverse nationalities, but the rule was that all had to speak nothing but French. She told us there was once a young man from Wales had refused to speak at all for several days. He had an honours degree in French, acquired during the War when foreign travel was impossible, but when he arrived in Paris he had been struck dumb by the horror of discovering that his French was apparently unintelligible to the natives. It is true, of course, that the French are usually not very understanding in such cases. There was an English woman barrister from London who, for that period, was remarkably frank in the confession of her sexual appetites, which seemed to distract her very badly from her French studies. I had not realised so clearly before that women had this problem as much as men.

My second residence in Paris was with two sisters, of mature age, who lived in a flat with two boisterous poodles in the Rue Villersexel, close to the *Assemblée Nationale*. One of the sisters had been a leader of the resistance during the occupation. After a warning that the Gestapo were waiting for her in her flat, she had been hidden for months in a monastery on the outskirts of Paris. This belonged to an order who do not normally allow women to enter their monastery, where her brother was a monk. The order aspired to high intellectual standards and the brother was a keen student of contemporary French theatre. He invited me to the monastery for lunch and I was allowed, with other visitors, to witness the mass, from the gallery in the back of the Church. It was choreographed like a ballet with the monks in white habits at moments prostrating themselves flat on the floor. The lunch, and the wines and liqueurs, were excellent.

The sisters were very keen that I should experience all aspects of French life. I attended some very enjoyable courses in the Sorbonne and sessions in the law courts. I had tea with the *Secretaire Perpetuel* of the *Academie Française*. He was a historian with an enthusiasm for the Auld Alliance. When he first visited Scotland, he told me that he went, as a Frenchman always should, without putting his feet on the soil of

England by finding a boat which sailed from Calais to Leith. I was also, thanks to the sisters, invited to take part in the annual ball of the *Ecole des Beaux Arts*. This was an event of unbridled licence, expected and permitted by the police, metro officials, night club owners and the public at large. You spend the first two or three hours careering around Paris, charging into all sorts of establishments and paying for nothing. Eventually you arrive at a hall near the Etoile where elaborate tableaux are torn apart and so are most of the costumes. The difficulty is getting home in the early morning in a highly unpresentable state.

These three years were the first time that I had lived for more than a day or two in London. I had been there on holiday when I was at school and I had passed through several times during the war. It is, of course, a city that is immensely rich in almost everything, history, theatres, art galleries. museums, book shops and anything else that can be imagined. Samuel Johnson was quite right to say that if your are tired of London, you are tired of life. I accept all that and during all the time I spent there I kept on discovering new treasures; but for me it is a city more to be admired than loved. It is better to visit London that to live in it; but I have never felt any desire to go back for a visit since I last worked there. I have never felt entirely at home in London, as I have, for instance in Edinburgh, Paris, Vienna or even Montreal. Why that is, I am not quite sure. I suspect that it has something to do with the sheer size of the place and the way in which most people, most of the time, look harassed and unhappy. These two points are connected because I think that it is the problem of moving about in the traffic and the crowds which upset people.

The first place I found to live was a very small flat, about the size of a ship's cabin, near Baker Street underground station. It is associated in my mind with a very beautiful Dutch girl, of such striking appearance that heads turned wherever I went with her. Ken Spencer, one of my Berlin colleagues, had introduced us. At first I was surprised that he seemed to be ready to surrender her to me without a struggle, but I soon understood why. She was kind and anxious to please, but of such an impenetrable stupidity that conversation with her was tedious beyond endurance. Oscar Wilde said that there was no sin except stupidity. She proved that he had a point.

This episode suggests something also about sex. It can be a very intense pleasure, so intense that I have often found myself wondering why does anyone ever do anything else. How is it that people find the time or the inclination to write the books and build bridges? It is true also in other moods, perhaps when a relationship is reaching the end of its course, that you begin to agree with Lord Chesterfield when he said that the position was ridiculous, the expense damnable and the pleasure momentary.

At about this time, I met James Lowndes, another friend from Berlin. James was a man for whom things tended to go wrong. He had a difficult start to life. His family had, but lost, a large country house, Newton Valence Manor in Hampshire. His father had made, and again lost, a fortune in Brazil, where I believe that a bank still has the family name. So do some streets in London. His mother, whom I have met and who in her advanced age was still very charming, was apparently impetuous and forgetful. In an absent-minded moment she sent James to a Catholic boarding school, Ampleforth, where they disturbed him by praying publicly for his conversion. Quite often when he came home from school for holidays, he found that his mother had changed lover and residence without telling him. The consequence was that James was a man clearly in search of stability and status. He had the complication of a clash between his political ideas, which were idealistic liberal, and his social aspirations, which were focussed on that lost country house, of which he carried around a photograph.

When he came back from Berlin, James made several applications for government jobs, including one in Malaya, then in the grip of the jungle war against the communists. He even applied for a commission with a fashionable territorial regiment in London, which shows how desperate he was. These applications usually went smoothly, until they suddenly hit an invisible and inpenetrable barrier. James was at a loss to understand this, until he met a school friend who was in one of the personnel departments concerned. 'Look, I am not supposed to tell you this, but the fact is that the security services have a black mark against you.' 'Why, what on earth is the reason for that?' 'Well it seems, old boy, that you were reported as supporting the Communist party during the war.' It was in vain that James pointed out that it was the Commonwealth, not the Communist, party. The abbreviations used in the records apparently did not distinguish them. So James eventually accepted a humble job in the Stationery Office. He said that he never saw words in this work only numbers in accounts, which he had to check after they had already been checked by someone else. He said that he was surrounded by people who had no interest in anything which interested him.

So I could hardly refuse when James asked me to share a suburban villa which he had rented in Wembley. We soon both realised that it was a mistake. It is a miserable part of outer London and the journey to and from the centre was tedious. What did I say about the unhappiness of Londoners? Fortunately, James encountered an old acquaintance, a widow living on a large pension from an oil company. He moved in with her in a flat in Upper Berkeley Street. Eventually he was able to buy back the family country house and divide into flats, and then he disappeared. I once met a man in Switzerland who had rented one of the flats, but I never saw James again.

I went to share a flat in Fairfax Road, near the Swiss Cottage underground station, with Peter Wagner, a stockbroker. This may seem an unlikely association for me since I have never had any interest in, or connection with, the Stock Exchange. I had met Peter when I was skiing in Klosters in Switzerland, a place which I first visited in January 1951 and to which I have returned nearly every year since. My introduction to it was due to Celia Sharpe who had taught in a finishing school there before she came to Berlin. Peter was a stockbroker of unusually wide interests. It was in his family house in the country that I first came across Hugh MacDiarmid's autobiography, and galimaufry, *Lucky Poet*. A third occupant of the flat was another friend of Peter, Tony Jalowicz, a barrister who taught law at Trinity College, Cambridge. He was highly intelligent, but once nearly blew the place up when he tried to put out a fire in a pan of hot fat in which he was about to cook chips.

The beautiful Erika Pick came to London from Berlin at about this time. She took a job as a fashion model. She said that it was the most boring and mindless occupation on earth, but it paid for her art classes. A family from America, who had known her father when he worked in New York, wrote to invite her to accompany them on a tour of the music festivals of Europe. They duly turned up, stayed at the Savoy and took Erika to a round of concerts and operas in London. There were two sons. When Erica told me about all of this, I predicted that one of them (at least) would want to marry her. I was right and she did.

It was in London that I first became enthusiastic about Scottish dancing, which had been neglected by my education in Scotland. I discovered that the Royal Scottish Country Dance Society had classes in Fetter Lane and a new and passionate pleasure was born for me at once. I agree entirely with a remark by Moray McLaren, which years later I persuaded Robbie Shepherd to add to his essay on dance in a book which I edited, *Scotland: A Concise Cultural History*. McLaren said of Scottish Country dances: 'In its passionate formality, in its blending of abandon and style, in its rhythm of colour and pattern it expresses the Scottish spirit as almost nothing else does.'

I was fortunate in my teachers. John Armstrong was enthusiastic, and amusing, but also demanding in his standards. He had worked for the Sadler Wells Ballet with the choreographer of *Donald of the Burthens*, a ballet based on a Highland tale with Scottish steps and formations. He was assisted by Elma Taylor who was so light on her feet that she seemed to be weightless. After this introduction I took part in, and organised, Scottish dancing wherever I went.

My partner in these dances in London was Celia Sharpe. We had become inseparable since we both left Germany. I had never been very keen on the idea of marriage, but my posting abroad for an unknown number of years was approaching. Celia was persuasive that marriage was the only solution. So we were married in the Crown Court Church of Scotland in Covent Garden on 30th May 1953. The choice of this Church was a compromise. I am not an adherent of any church because I am deeply offended by the idea of accepting as an act of faith a body of doctrine which is highly improbable and for which there is no evidence. If it had to be in a Church then the Church of Scotland was less offensive to me than any other because it was less ornate and ritualistic and, I think, less superstitious. As Walter Scott said in *Rob Roy* the Scots are 'more moved by logic than by rhetoric, and more attracted by acute and argumentative reasoning on doctrinal points, than influenced by enthusiastic appeals to the heart.' There he is talking about religion only, because in many matters we are as susceptible to appeals to the heart as anyone could be. Celia, however, was a member of the Church of England and it was only gradually over the years that I began to realise that this was important to her. I have always found it difficult to believe that intelligent people can take religion seriously. Of course, in the past it was the most important thing in life for many people and, in spite of my scepticism, I have to admit that it still is for some people, even in this secular age.

At the same time, there were social advantages in the general acceptance in the past of the teachings of the Church. It gave people a motive, even it it was only the fear of hell fire, to do their best to follow the dictates of Christian morality. The Kirk in Scotland encouraged a spirit of charity, endeavour and a belief in the virtues of education and hard work. This was a major component in the formation of Scottish character and of Scottish achievement. The spirit is not yet entirely dead, as is the famous phrase, 'I may be an atheist, but I reserve the right to be a Presbyterian atheist'; but can it long survive the removal of the religious impulse behind it?

Celia and I went for a short holiday in France. I had been appointed First Secretary in the Embassy in Warsaw and we left to go there about the middle of June 1953. Travel by sea was then happily still normal in the Diplomatic Service. It was not only a pleasure in itself but it meant that you could take all your luggage and household effects with you. Even to Poland, you could travel by a cargo ship which took a few passengers from Hull to Gdynia. So by this means we set off as a married couple for our first diplomatic post abroad.

CHAPTER 9
Warsaw and La Paz
June 1953 – May 1959

J ust before I left for Warsaw, John Rennie, the Head of Chancery, wrote to welcome me to the post. The only advice which he offered was that I should bring several black ties 'because they seem to wear out so quickly in this place'. As a preparation for life in a town ravaged and devastated by war and occupation, it seemed a little eccentric. John, as I soon discovered before I had been long in Warsaw, had a notably sensible and practical approach to life. If something went wrong with a piece of office machinery, which meant mainly duplicators at that time, he would roll up his sleeves and repair it himself. He would cook the crêpes suzettes at his dinner parties or the entire meal at elaborate picnics in which he specialised. He eventually became Head of MI6.

I suppose his remark about the ties was meant as a warning to expect formal entertaining, even in a place where ordinary life was so impoverished and curtailed. Because of the pressures of the UB, (the secret police), social contact with the population was virtually impossible and even officials were hesitant about accepting invitations from Western embassies. The diplomats responded by entertaining one another. Black tie dinners among the ruins were frequent, and because of the rules of precedence you were liable to find yourself sitting next to the same people quite often. This was not entirely useless because it provided an opportunity for the exchange of ideas and experiences which was quite helpful in the curious circumstances in which we found ourselves. We were living in a police state where people were afraid to speak and where the press and radio (it was before the days of television) were vehicles not of information, but of propaganda. Any scrap of information about what was going on was eagerly accepted.

Poland, and Warsaw in particular, had suffered very heavily during the war, as it had tended to do throughout history as the buffer between Germany and Russia. Both the Germans and the Soviet Union had systematically killed people with any potential for leadership. Like Edward I in Scotland in the fourteenth century, they tried to eradicate a nation. The Soviet army had paused on the right bank of the Vistula to allow the Germans to destroy Warsaw. Some of the most notorious of the German concentration camps were in Poland. The end of the war brought little relief because it meant the imposition of a communist regime under Soviet control which was bitterly resented by the majority of the people. The condition of life was dismal in a devastated country with very little import trade and empty shelves in the shops.

Stalin died in March 1953 about three months before I arrived in Poland. The worst excesses of Stalinism were still evident. Arbitrary arrest was prevalent. Even the former communist leader, Wladyslaw Gomulka, had been dismissed and placed in custody in 1948 because of a speech on the traditions of the Polish labour movement, which was interpreted in Moscow as dangerously nationalistic. He remained in custody while I was in Poland, in a building, so it was widely believed, close to a diplomatic country club just outside Warsaw and close to the Vistula. Country Club may sound rather grand. In fact it was a very basic, unpretentious place run by one of the many Scottish women who had married a Polish soldier, stationed in Scotland during the war. Many of them were living in abject poverty.

Even if, to an extent, we shared the privations of the people, we had one advantage over our colleagues in the other Soviet bloc countries. The Russians had imposed travel restrictions on Western diplomats in Moscow who were not allowed to travel in the country without permission. The West had retaliated and this practice had gradually extended to the other countries, except Poland. There seemed to be a tacit agreement on both sides that Polish diplomats could travel freely in the west and that we could do likewise in Poland. This was something of which we took full advantage and not just for amusement.

A number of us in the western embassies, especially the British, Canadians and Americans, began to make a deliberate practice of touring the country. Maps, guidebooks and town plans were not normally available in Poland where they fell into the category of State secrets. Someone discovered that a *Guide Bleue* of Poland in French had been published just before the war and was still useful, even if the postwar settlement had cut off the eastern territories and added others in the west. Also, because hotels were scarce and poor and because you always had the secret police outside the bedroom door, we took to camping and imported tents, cooking-stoves, sleeping-bags and the like. Especially if you had mentioned your travel plans on the telephone, a black Citroen of the secret police would wait outside your house to accompany you from the start. Strangely enough, however, they always seemed to have left their office desks in the clothes they were wearing and with nothing else.

This lack of sensible preparation by the secret police made it easy to make the journey difficult for them. We felt perfectly entitled to torment or tease them since they were in the habit of treating their victims in a much more savage manner. If we stopped in a village they might take the chance to dash into a shop to buy something to eat. That would be the cue for us to drive off, so that they were faced with a choice between losing the chance of a bite to eat or losing us. One of the Americans developed a technique of stopping to throw an empty tin can down a steep slope. The police obviously felt that they should make sure that it did not contain a message to some dissidents, but the American's car had disappeared down the road long before they had made up their minds.

Tom Carter, the Canadian Chargé d'Affaires, who frequently came with me on these expeditions, arrived once in a village square which was full of people at a market. He began to drive slowly round and round the square. This embarrassed the secret police who were supposed to be invisible, although in their office suits and black Citroens, they could not have been more conspicuous. Soon the whole crowd was laughing at this absurd spectacle. So the police stopped to preserve their dignity. Thereupon Tom drove off down the side street. When they followed, he drove back to the square to repeat the performance. All this is very childish, of course, but in the circumstances perhaps justifiable. Anything which ridiculed or humbled the agents of the police state was worthwhile.

One of my colleagues in the British Embassy, Allan Brooke-Turner, was very scholarly with a passionate interest in art, architecture, history and more or less everything. In a place like Cracow, a town full of medieval treasures and quite unchanged by the war, he would spend hours in strenuous sightseeing. His energy was inexhaustible, but his police escort were reduced to pleading for a rest. John Rennie, who took long country walks in all weathers, exposed the UB who tried to follow him to an even more severe trial of their conscientious devotion to duty. Much of our touring was purely for pleasure. We discovered woods and lakes which were delightful places to camp. At least once, we went to ski at Zakopane in the Tatra. Even here the police state intruded. The top of the runs was close to the border with Czechoslovakia. When low cloud descended, the skiers were rounded up by armed border guards until the sky cleared and they could be sure that no one was going to dash across the border. Similarly, there were elaborate searches of the train at border crossings when we went once to Klosters. These countries of the Soviet bloc were hermetically sealed. It was difficult for residents from outside to get entrance visas. Their own inhabitants were not normally allowed to leave, even for a neighbouring member of the Soviet bloc.

John Rennie had discovered that, as a consequence of the close involvement of Scots in Poland in the distant past, some Scottish families, including the Rennies, had been granted all the privileges of the Polish aristocracy. Whatever these privileges might have been, they had long since disappeared along with the aristocracy. But the grant to the Scots had not been specifically repealed, a fact of which John would from time to time remind Polish officials.

There were very few cars in Poland at this time. You could drive back to Warsaw on a Sunday evening and hardly see another one for miles. The hazards were long horse-drawn carts. Quite often the driver, perhaps after a night's drinking, was fast asleep. The horse was perfectly capable of finding its own way home, but might stray across the road to eat a tempting piece of grass. So the cart, which had no lights, might stretch across the whole road. Rather ominously, the Russians had built several straight roads with reinforced bridges running east to west across the country. They had telephone lines, provided and maintained by Soviet soldiers, across the country as well. Once some of them helped us when our car was stuck in mud. We had a friendly conversation, but they told us that they had never heard of either Scotland or Canada.

Of course, this touring also had a serious purpose. We were able to get a more reliable impression of the conditions of life and the attitudes of the people than we could from the propagandist Warsaw press. When we had eluded our UB followers, we could speak to people in shops and on the streets. My own Polish, which is a difficult language, was never good enough for anything but the most rudimentary exchanges, but some Poles spoke German or French. Marion Pikul of the American Embassy was a great asset because she was of Polish descent and spoke the language like a native.

Everything that we saw or heard made it very obvious that the spirit of the people and their Polish patriotism had survived the devastation of the war and the imposition of a régime which they detested. The only available means of expression left to them was the Catholic Church which they attended in vast numbers with a fervour which was political and nationalist as well as religious. The way of life in the country was Spartan and primitive and had hardly changed for centuries. There were cottages with earth floors which the people shared with the animals. Winters were very cold. It was difficult to see how life could survive in a village where the source of water, a well in the main street, had become a solid block of ice. In spite of the misery and hardship, people made the most of it and struggled on. As in Germany at the end of the war, I was amazed, humbled and encouraged by the invincibility of the human determination to survive.

Broadcasts in Polish by other countries, particularly the BBC World Service, were the only source of information about events in the outside world and even now and again in Poland itself. Listening to them was a criminal offence. In any case, it was usually impossible to hear a word of them in Warsaw and other large cities because the Polish Government jammed them by transmitting an undulating noise on the same frequency. By listening on our travels over the country we found that these jamming transmitters were fairly local in effect, and that the BBC was loud and clear only a few miles from Warsaw. This explained how it was that news broadcast by the BBC was soon widely known in Warsaw. The Poles, with long experience of foreign occupation, were accomplished in the evasion of authority. Farmers bringing potatoes and cabbages to the market brought news as well and it spread with remarkable speed over the whole city. A people with such a spirit cannot be suppressed for long. We supported the BBC by sending them pieces of news, impressions of local conditions and reports about the state of jamming. Perhaps it was the most useful work the Embassy did under those conditions.

There was one Pole who openly maintained contact with the Western Embassies and even with the Western press. This was Alfred

Chlapowski who had been in the RAF during the war and had become a correspondent for a Western news agency (UP, I think) after his return to Poland. All the other Western journalists had gradually been expelled on one pretext or another until he was the only one left. His reports had to be submitted for censorship. When he discovered something the censors were likely to suppress, he told us in the expectation that we would report it to the Foreign Office or the BBC. His most sensational scoop was the arrest of Cardinal Wyszinski, to whom most Poles looked on as the leader of the whole nation as well as of the Church. The event was not unknown to us because Allan Brooke-Turner had attended the service from which the Cardinal had been led away by obvious UB agents. Alfred was bursting with fury and indignation both at the event itself and at his impotence as a journalist to report the biggest scoop of his career, but he was able to give us a detailed account of the circumstances.

The Americans regarded Alfred with extreme suspicion on the grounds that he could not behave with such apparent freedom unless he was employed by the UB to trap and mislead us. We thought that he was a brave and sincere man who took the risk of defying the régime because he detested all its works and was determined to do what he could to expose it. It could not last, of course. Bert Davis of the British Council happened to be with him in his room in the Bristol Hotel, where his door was covered with the mastheads of western newspapers, including *The Scotsman*. The telephone rang and Alfred turned pale. 'I am sorry I must go, I have just been told that Tosia (his wife) has been run over by a car and is in a critical state in hospital.' This was simply a device to get him out to the street, where UB agents were waiting to arrest him.

We did not see Alfred or Tosia again as long as any of us were in Poland. Years later, when the regime had relaxed a little, he was not only released from prison but allowed to travel. To my surprise and pleasure, he turned up in my house, 5 Vincent Square in London, one evening when I had some people in for drinks. A day or two later, a couple of men from the security service called at my office and asked if I could explain why I was receiving visitors from Poland. One of my guests must have reported Alfred's arrival. It was not only in Poland that such things happened.

Bert Davis, whom I have just mentioned, lived with his wife, Mary, and his daughter, Caroline, very close to our suburban flat in Warsaw.

His invariable good humour and the range of his interests and talents were a strong defence against the surrounding gloom and austerity of Warsaw. He had been born in Melrose and was a Honours English graduate of Edinburgh University, a contemporary of Sorley Maclean, Robert Garioch, Norman MacCaig and David Daiches. During the war he had been in the King's Own Scottish Borderers and he had taught at the Royal High School. He had read widely and was especially enthusiastic about the Border ballads, Robert Burns and Walter Scott, and often quoted from them. When required, he would play the piano, conduct a choir or direct a play. The music of Mozart was another of his passions.

Clearly, we were kindred spirits. We had great cracks together about all our shared interests and Bert would remark, 'Man this is great. It is just like being in Edinburgh.' Years later, we met in Edinburgh from time to time when he was working there in the British Council and I was on leave. When I eventually returned to Edinburgh for good in 1980 we were close allies in many ways in the Saltire Society and the Advisory Council for the Arts in Scotland until he died in 1992.

Indeed Celia and I were very fortunate in our friends and colleagues in Warsaw: Allan Brooke-Turner and the charming and utterly dependable Hazel Henderson from Oban, whom he afterwards married; Bert and Mary Davis; and the Canadian Tom Carter and Marie-Louise from the French Embassy, whom he married. These and several more were the central core of a group determined to defy the harshness of the surrounding environment. It used to be the habit of those Soviet-bloc countries to employ voluptuous girls to entice western diplomats into situations which made them vulnerable to blackmail. We were slightly offended that no such attempt was made against us. Perhaps the UB were perspicacious enough to see that we were too content with our own relationships to be susceptible.

When I first arrived in Warsaw, the Ambassador was Sir Francis Shepherd, a man of long and very diverse consular and diplomatic experience who had served in the 1914-18 war. He was gentle, open-minded and immensely likeable. When he was about to retire in May 1954, we decided that this was an event that must be marked appropriately. Chancery, in an old and rambling aristocratic town-house, had a ballroom. So we would have a ball and since Sir Francis was Scottish and about to retire to Aboyne, we would have a piper. We borrowed him from a Scottish regiment in Berlin and he was a real treasure who rose admirably to the occasion. He told us that it took three generations to make a piper and he was the third generation. For the night itself, he wrote a special pipe-tune which he called 'The Ambassador's Ball'. When the BBC Overseas Service took an interest, we thought that it would be prudent to change the title to 'Sir Francis Shepherd's Farewell to Warsaw'.

The same ballroom caused us some problems later when a fire broke out on that floor of the building. It was caused by spontaneous combustion of a heavy wooden beam that supported the floor. As an instance of seventeenth century gerry building, it ran through the channel to the main chimney, in which it had been slowly cooking for centuries.

The successor to Sir Francis was a man of very different character, Sir Andrew Noble, 2nd Baronet of Ardkinglas in Argyll. (Did I not say that the Diplomatic Service was full of Scots?) As soon as he arrived he called a meeting of the entire staff and announced that he had a reforming mission. The problem was that it had come to the notice of the Treasury that members of the staff were making substantial profits when they left Warsaw. Nothing offends the official mind more than officials making money and so it had to stop. We were conscientiously following Polish laws by using the official rate for the Zloty, eleven to the pound, if I remember correctly. Its real value was only a fraction of this. Consequently when departing members of the staff sold their cars, which was the usual practice, they were given a mountain of Zlotys. Translated into sterling at the official rate, it was several times the original cost. Outrage. So Noble introduced elaborate controls. Nobody was to be allowed to sell anything without his permission and he would decide how much of the proceeds they could retain. It did not escape notice, however, that Noble spent some time each day studying the Stock Exchange reports in the *Financial Times* and noting the effect of the fluctuations on his own holdings recorded in a large leather-bound notebook.

Sir Andrew had a son and daughter who used to come swimming with us during the school holidays, in a pool in woods just outside Warsaw. The boy, Iain, later became my predecessor as President of the Saltire Society.

It was the policy of the Foreign Office to keep staff in Soviet-bloc countries for no more than two years, which was apparently considered to be the maximum time that people could be expected to endure the conditions. So in early 1955 Personnel Department wrote to me to say that they were working on a posting for me. They could not yet say where it was, but it was a post which they were sure I would greatly enjoy. In my innocence, I thought they meant Paris. But when the posting finally arrived, it was to a place about which I knew virtually nothing.

So, in due course, we proceeded to La Paz, Bolivia in the leisurely progress, normal at the time, by ship. This was a thoroughly enjoyable experience, a cruise holiday at government expense, calling at La Rochelle, Santander, Bermuda, Havana, Panama, Guayaquil, and Lima. Finally we arrived, after about a month, in Antofagasta in Chile from which we were to take the train to La Paz which lies in the Andes at an altitude of about 12,000 feet. Antofagasta is in a region where it seldom rains, but there was a slight shower on the day when we arrived. This brought people onto the streets to revel in this unusual pleasure. I bought a newspaper and was delighted to find that I could understand most of it, not because I had studied Spanish, but because it was so close to Latin. The hotel, where we had to spend a night or two, did not begin to serve dinner until after nine at night. The guide books had warned us of the hazards of the altitude as we climbed up into the Andes, but said that cylinders of oxygen would be available on the train. When we asked the ticket collector about this, he seemed never to have heard of any such thing.

Arriving by train means a slow and gradual introduction to life at over 12,000 feet, which is 2,000 feet higher than the altitude at which the use of oxygen was compulsory in the wartime RAF. For the first week or two most people feel that they are struggling for breath, and often wake up at night with a feeling that they are being strangled. After a week or two the body begins to adjust and you cease to be conscious of the lack of air, as long as you do nothing too strenuous.

The altitude of La Paz is a most distinctive feature. Almost everything in La Paz is the highest of its kind in the world. Water boils at a much lower temperature. Tennis balls have to have holes in them or they fly out of the court at every stroke. Still, the adaptable human body gradually adjusts and before long most people are living a fairly normal life. We became so adjusted to the altitude that it was the unaccustomed air pressure of Santiago that made us feel sick when we flew there once for a skiing holiday in Chile. When I was on leave in London, the tailor looked puzzled and checked his records. I asked what the trouble was. He said that I was the first customer in his experience whose chest had got bigger instead of his belly. He would not say the same nowadays, I am sorry to say.

La Paz had a primitive ski-lift on a glacier two or three thousand feet above the Altiplano where we often went at weekends. We started a Scottish dancing class and gave demonstrations on appropriate occasions such as St Andrew's night. VS Pritchett, the novelist and short story writer, who was doing a South American tour on behalf of the *New Statesman*, was in our house once when this group was practising. He insisted on joining in with more enthusiasm than natural aptitude. I was a little alarmed. He was new to the altitude and over fifty years old, which seemd a considerable age to me at the time. However in spite of his exertions, all was well and this admirable writer, who in the course of a day had established himself in our affections, survived.

Some people were not so fortunate with the altitude. While we were there one of the staff of the two British-owned railway companies arrived back from leave with a new young bride. She turned blue, collapsed and died only a few weeks later. Usually it was not quite so drastic. After I had been in La Paz for several months, a BBC television producer, Tony de Lotbinièr e, come to make a programme about American aid. As it happened, none of us were available to meet him at the airport, but we sent the Ambassador's car. Later that day the hotel telephoned to say that he was very ill. I found him in such a state that I wrapped him in blankets and took him to the American hospital where they gave him oxygen. He recovered and we brought him to stay in our house which was in a suburb about 1,000 feet below the town.

This was not Tony's only encounter with the peculiarities of Bolivia. He told me that he had been warned to expect three things. The first was that the altitude made you feel as if you were dying and that he had certainly experienced. The second was that La Paz was a lawless place where you were liable to be shot in the streets and someone had been shot in the street below his hotel window as he was gasping for breath in bed. The third was that revolutions happened with monotonous regularity.

I assured him that revolutions were now not so frequent as they had been. It was true that the Army Officers' Club had portraits of about as many Presidents of the Republic as there were years of independence, but that the present government had been in power for three years and seemed likely to survive. Shootings in the streets were, in my experience, mercifully rare, but I would find out what had happened under his window.

What had happened had involved the chief pilot of the Bolivian airline, Lloyd Aéreo Boliviano. The pilots wer e on strike for more pay and the director of the company, who was German, happened to run into the chief pilot outside his office, which was next to the hotel. The director told the chief pilot what he thought of him. Pilots were officers and officers did not go on strike. In the middle of the row, he told his secretary to go to his office and fetch his revolver, which was in the top drawer of his desk. He then calmly shot the chief pilot who fell dead to the ground.

Even in La Paz, this was a bit much and the director was arrested. It was not atypical, though, that he was quietly released a few weeks later without trial or sentence. Something rather similar had happened, many years before, to Tony Ashton, a brother of Frederick Ashton, the choreographer. Tony was one of the longest established British residents and one of the most prosperous importers. During the Chaco war with Paraguay in the 1930s he had imported military equipment for the Army. When Bolivia was defeated, the government, looking for a scapegoat, blamed him for alleged inadequacies in the equipment and he was imprisoned. After a few weeks he asked if he could go home for a bath and he was given a couple of hours. He gradually extended the time of these visits, until he simply did not go back to prison at all and no one seemed to mind. Either the Bolivian authorities are very tolerant and forgiving or, as most people assume, you can get away with anything as long as you pay.

Bolivia, which has been an independent country since 1825, has been unfortunate in its wars. In the War of the Pacific, 1879-84, Chile seized the Bolivian Pacific sea-cost in the region of Antofagasta. In the Chaco war in the 1930s Bolivia had hoped to secure an outlet to the Atlantic through the Paraguay River. That failure meant that Bolivia was deprived of all outlets to the sea. Its heartland is the plateau of the Altiplano which has an average height of 12,000 feet and for most of the year is parched and inhospitable. Cold winds are frequent and the temperature often falls below freezing at night, although the air is clear and dry and days without sunshine are exceptional. It is one of the most inaccessible places in the world and, to those who are not used to it, one of the most unwelcoming. La Paz lies in this region in a deep gorge in the plateau.

In spite of these discouragements, the Altiplano is nevertheless the seat of one of the earliest centres of civilisation in the American continent. It is the homeland of the Incas. There is plenty of evidence still of their achievements in architecture, textiles, gold and ceramics. The elegant reed-boats of Lake Titicaca, the crafts, the music and dance of their descendants show that the same talents and impulses are still alive. These indigenous peoples, the so-called Indians of Bolivia, have preserved their way of life and their languages, mainly Aymara and Quechua, with an impressive determination. The Spanish conquest, all the efforts of the Catholic church to convert them, contemporary technology and commercialism have all failed to make any fundamental change. I speak, of course, of a time, now more than forty years ago, and by now global pressures may have reached even the Altiplano.

The men wear the same nondescript jackets and trousers which you see everywhere in the world, but the dress of the women is distinctive, capes, voluminous skirts with many layers of petticoats. In La Paz and in the Altiplano generally they wear bowler hats. It may sound incongruous, but the hats seem to suit them, and they are at least one concession to foreign influence. Legend has it that in the last century an importer in Argentine, with a large consignment of bowlers on his hands which he could not sell, disposed of them cheaply in Bolivia. In Cochabamba, the hats are more picturesque and reveal an earlier influence. They are in the shape of the helmets of the Spanish Conquistadores.

People everywhere tend to prefer the environment to which they are accustomed, which is just as well for the sake of human diversity and the spread of population over the planet. The residents of the Altiplano are an extreme case because they have what most people would consider better land and a better climate within easy reach. In a report which I wrote at the time I said:

> Bolivia's problem is not merely that the population is insufficient
> (the average density is about 7 to the square mile), largely
> illiterate and content with a primitive life, but that it is in the
> wrong place. The Altiplano has more people than it can support;

the development areas in the east have too few to increase
production on an adequate scale. Plans to correct this by
encouraging movement to the east are opposed by the Indian's
preference for his infertile but traditional home.

This quotation comes from my first published book, *Bolivia, Economic
and Commercial Condition*, (1956) which I was asked by the Board of
Trade to write for their series of Overseas Economic Surveys. It is a
dry and factual account, but at least it achieved the distinction of
inclusion in the footnotes of the entry on Bolivia in the 1967 edition
of the *Encyclopaedia Britannica*.

The Altiplano is not the whole of Bolivia. In the west lies the
massive mountain chain of the Andes with peaks of more than 21,000
feet. On the eastern slopes there are humid, semi-tropical valleys,
known as *Yungas*, which drop down to less than 4,000 feet. Vegetation
there is exuberant and a great variety of semi-tropical fruits grow
readily. None were cultivated systematically at the time I speak of,
except coca, the cocaine plant. Probably for centuries the Indians,
especially the adult men, have been addicted to it, long before drug
addiction became an international problem. They chew the raw leaves
along with wood ash, which apparently releases the effect of the
drug. We used to employ a gardener who kept his supply of leaves
in a tin suspended on a tree. One of our dogs (we had two at the
time), noticing that he ate them with evident satisfaction, grasped an
opportunity to seize some. They had no evident effect on him at all.
The effect of the drug on its human consumers seems to be a
suppression of all appetites and all feelings. Once emergency repairs
had to be made to a dam in the Yungas which was part of a hydro-
electric plant belonging to a Canadian company. The engineer in
charge told me that his Bolivian workers had been able to work non-
stop for two or three days with no sleep and very little food but with a
plentiful supply of coca leaves.

Further east, there is the vast but largely unpopulated Oriente,
70% of the area of the country, tropical and potentially rich, but still
in a state of almost complete neglect. In the course of an afternoon's
drive from La Paz, although there are few roads and they are narrow
and unpaved, you can go through the whole range of climates from
the arctic to the tropical. You start in the temperate La Paz, cross a
mountain pass in the region of permanent ice and snow and then

slowly twist down into the valley, which has thicker and thicker vegetation, until you end up among the parrots and oranges.

Perhaps Personnel Department (it was probably my witty friend Simon Dawbarn) were making a sly joke when they said that they were sending me to a post which I would enjoy, or perhaps they knew both me and Bolivia rather better than you might expect. Whichever it was, they were right. I enjoyed Bolivia so much that I requested a second tour after leave (which had the incidental advantage of long sea trips in both directions). In April 1957 our first child, Alastair, was born. We had agonised whether it was desirable for Celia to stay in La Paz for the birth, but we were assured by all the experts that there would be no problem. Since he has always been healthy and robust, I am happy to say, the experts must have been right. A Church of Scotland minister came from Chile to La Paz for the Christening. He was a Highlander who had known the painter Peploe. When he came into the house his first remark was, 'I see you have one of Sam's paintings'.

I found Bolivia a country of inexhaustible fascination because it was so different from everywhere else. Modern commercialism and communications have imposed a blanket of near uniformity over most of the world. Bolivia in its isolation on its high plateau was an exception. Few visitors penetrated to it. Some that we expected were so discouraged by what they heard about the effects of the altitude that they changed their mind. One visitor who did reach us, and by an improbable route, was Robin Hanbury-Tenison. In 1958 he made the first crossing of South America by land at its widest point, from the coast of Brazil to the coast of Peru. This meant traversing hundreds of miles of wild and often uninhabited country and much of it without roads. Towards the end of the journey he turned up in La Paz with one companion, Richard Mason, both in their twenties, in their battered and travel-stained jeep. They stayed with us for a few days and they, their clothes and their jeep were gradually made presentable.

Bolivia was not only different, it was also a living museum of the past. The indigenous peoples had hardly changed their way of life for centuries. Inca civilisation was accomplished in architecture and many of the arts, but it never invented the wheel or writing. Their successors had still hardly got round to either of these. Some had moved from the llama and the donkey to the motor lorry, but most of them still used only the animals and they had no carts, or even wheelbarrows. Most could neither read nor write. This primitivism does not mean that they were objects of pity, because they could teach us much in the strength and contentment of their community.

The so-called white population were largely the descendants of the Spanish invaders. (The terms white and Indian, imported I suppose from North American practice, are absurd, but they are commonly used and there is no convenient substitute.) They were, of course, much more sophisticated and subject to cosmopolitan influence; but they too had many peculiarities of a past age, somewhere in the early nineteenth century when Bolivia first became an independent country. The rapid change of President in the first hundred years of the country's history were the consequences of internal squabbles within this minority. The government of the MNR, the Movement of National Revolution, which seized power in 1952, was a radical change because it had the support of Indian peasants and mine workers. The leaders, including the President, Victor Paz Estenssoro, were still members of the white minority; but it was a real revolution. Before power had rotated between a small white minority dominated by the mine owners. Now the trade union of miners and the peasants were a powerful political force. The three largest mining companies were nationalised and land reform introduced.

The nineteenth century habits of the white minority were particularly evident on such occasions as the National Day. As part of the celebration, there was a *Te Deum* in the Cathedral. The members of the Government sat in thrones at one side of an aisle, facing the diplomatic corps in similar thrones on the other. At particularly solemn moments in the mass, cadets from the Military College, in toy soldier uniforms with epaulettes and plumed hats, fired a salute with, fortunately, blank ammunition. One year the Papal Nuncio presided and a priest gave an excited commentary over a loudspeaker to the crowd in the Square outside. This was so loud that it upset the dignity of the proceedings inside the Cathedral. At the end, as the clergy left in procession between the two rows of thrones, the Nuncio's secretary, Paul Marcinkus, said to us in an audible aside, 'Just wait until the boss gets his hands on that Jesuit.'

Marcinkus had been brought up in Chicago in a family of poor Lithuanian immigrants. He was a genial, good-humoured, irreverent giant of a man with the physique of a heavyweight boxer. This served him well years later when he was a Bishop and a senior figure in the

Vatican when he escorted the Pope on his travels and could effortlessly clear a passage through any crowd. We all enjoyed his company in La Paz and it was sad, but not altogether surprising, to hear that he was eventually involved in a scandal over the Vatican bank. He had no illusions that the world was other than a very tough place where you had to be ruthless to survive.

It may sound improbable, but British interests were closely involved in the affairs of Bolivia. There were two reasons, tin ore and the railways. Bolivia was second only to Malaya as a producer of tin ore, which was by far its most important economic asset. Until 1942, when America built a smelter for strategic reasons, almost all of Bolivian ore went to a smelter in Liverpool. We continued to take a large share of it. Until the introduction of air services, the only contact which Bolivia had with the outside world was by railways. Two of the most important, which have the shortest routes to ports on the Pacific coast of Chile and Peru and carry the most freight, were British built and British owned. The senior staff were British expatriates. The route from Antofagasta was one by which we arrived in La Paz. The other, the Guaqui-La Paz Railway, connected La Paz with Guaqui on Lake Titicaca, where freight and passengers transferred to steamers on this highest navigable lake in the world. They then continued by rail again to Puno in Peru. One of these steamers, with its brass work still gleaming like new, had been built on the Clyde in the previous century, sailed to Peru and then taken to pieces to be transported and re-assembled on the shore of the lake.

The Antofagasta railway had an elegant royal carriage with a bedroom, sitting room, kitchen and viewing platform. It was said to have been built for a visit by Edward, Prince of Wales, presumably in the 1920s. The company allowed us to use this from time to time so that we could travel the country in style and even give small receptions in it in such places as Cochabamba, the second largest city and a much more attractive place than La Paz, or Sucre, which had been and still was in theory, the capital. Because power had moved away from it, Sucre was even more frozen in the past than other places. In the sixteenth century it had been the residence of the Spanish grandees controlling the extraction of silver from the fabulously rich mine of Potosi and its minting into coinage. Correspondence from the Kingdom of Spain to their Viceroy in Upper Peru lay neatly stacked on open shelves in a building in Sucre. Another had been the headquarters of the Inquisition. The flood of silver from Potosi in the sixteenth century had transformed monetary values in the whole of Europe. Even two centuries later Burns uses the word, Potozi, as a synonym for great wealth.

I mentioned this to one of our most responsive and enthusiastic visitors, John Grierson, the great pioneer of documentary film. He arrived in 1958 by way of Lake Titicaca and the Guaqui railway as part of a tour as president of a South American film festival. He was full of excitement about his journey, 'the most beautiful that he had ever made', and responded in much the same way as I did to the remains of the past greatness and of present resistance to cultural assimilation. We both saw parallels with Scotland. I see from the biography by another friend of mine, Forsyth Hardy, that later in his journey Grierson said in a speech in Montevideo: 'I too come from a modest country, Scotland, and know what it is like to live under the shadow of a great and mighty neighbour.' Grierson was delighted to hear that Burns knew about Potosi. We talked about it and I could see that he was already thinking about working it into a film or television programme.

There was much about Bolivia that was unknown to the outside world because of its remoteness and inaccessibility. Peter Scott, the ornithologist and an artist who specialised in painting birds, was a daring and enterprising character. He had served on destroyers during the war, won an Olympic bronze medal in dinghy sailing and led ornithological expeditions all over the world. He too came to Bolivia and was astonished to discover many previously unknown species of birds. In a sense they were unknown even to the Bolivians because he could not find anyone who seemed to be aware of these species or have any name for them.

I had a similar experience with a parrot, an entrancing creature which I acquired by accident. We had been invited to dinner by a family who had a parrot which I admired. A day or two later my host telephoned to say that he had a parrot for me, a kindness which I obviously had to accept. It was quite small, of two shades of green with a red head. I drove it home, sitting imperiously on the seat beside me, clearly a great deal less apprehensive than I was myself. We lived in a large, modern house with a large garden, lined with trees, in Obrajes, a suburb below the town itself. Already in residence were two dogs and a cat and assorted hens and ducks, all of which we had inherited from our predecessor. Apart from Celia and myself, there was a Bolivian staff of a gardener, a woman cook and two maids, all very merry and cheerful. The human residents were all delighted with the new arrival. One of the dogs, Paddy, and the cat, Hamish, were at first inclined to regard the parrot, Lorito, as prey to be hunted; but not for long. Lorito let them know by a loud and terrifying scream that he would stand no nonsense and they all settled down happily together. In fact, Lorito, kept us all in order. He spent the days in the garden, but was brought in at night when the temperature dropped. If the maid who usually did this was late, Lorito marched to the door and screeched for admittance to the perch where he slept.

When the time came to leave La Paz and return to London, we had become so used to Lorito that we could not leave him behind. The Ministry of Agriculture gave us an import licence and he came to live with us in Vincent Square. This was not a success. He was not used to living in a confined space inside and particularly not in a cage. If he was allowed to roam about in the house, his curiosity led him into all kinds of risks. We decided reluctantly that it was no life for him and I remembered that Edinburgh Zoo had a large parrot house with a garden. They accepted him and Donald Cameron, who was visiting us, agreed to take him there. He told us that when he arrived in Waverley Station early in the morning he had to wait in a queue to show his ticket at the exit to the platform. When he put the cage on the ground, Lorito protested with one of his rare, but penetrating, screams to the evident alarm of the passengers in front. The Zoo wrote to say how grateful they were, particularly as he was of a previously unknown species. There he lived, I think happily, for years. I even had the feeling that he recognised me when I went to see him. That may simply have been his usual friendliness, to men at least. For some reason, he was always a little suspicious of women.

We made two memorable journeys while we were in Bolivia. The first of these was by the Guaqui railway and the Lake Titicaca steamer to the ancient Inca capital of Cuzco and to the even more remarkable, long-lost and secret city of Machu Picchu. Like visiting the Acropolis or the Pyramids, this is a journey which brings you into close touch with an ancient civilisation and one which is some ways even more remote from our experience than those of Greece or Egypt.

The other journey was to a much more recent, but still surprising place, Santa Cruz. This is the fifth largest city of Bolivia. Until a road from Cochabamba was completed with American aid in 1952, it had no ground communication with the rest of the country, although there are rail connections with Brazil and Argentina. It is said to have been founded in the sixteenth century by men approaching from the south-east, tempted by reports of Inca gold. When they saw the vast ranges of the Andes rising in front of them, they decided to go no further. For centuries, Santa Cruz has been isolated even by Bolivian standards. No doubt it has changed radically since the completion of the road; but when we were there, it still reminded you of a wild-west film. Streets were unpaved and men with rifle holsters on their saddles hitched their horses outside the saloons. An enterprising Frenchman had established a restaurant in an unlikely building. There was a pension, where most of the few foreign visitors stayed, which had a pet puma, which the Bolivians called tigers. One evening an American couple looked into the bedroom where their small daughter was sleeping and found the puma in bed beside her.

Tony de Lotbinièr e went to Santa Cruz to shoot some scenes for his film. As he was sitting outside a cafe with his Bolivian cameraman, he remarked that all the children playing at their feet looked remarkably similar. 'Yes, of course,' said the cameraman, 'that's because the priest is the father of all of them. He has the right to spend the first night with women who get married.' Tony, who was a Catholic himself, did not say whether he was shocked or incredulous; but, when he was back in La Paz, he told the story to the American wife of the Minister of Justice. She rushed to the Nuncio and demanded action. 'Oh yes, my dear, it is deplorable,' he agreed, 'but we must be patient. We cannot expect to make sudden changes in long established habits.'

My first ambassador in La Paz, Sir John Garnett Lomax, was an unusual diplomat in that he really preferred horses to people. In fact, that meant he was particularly well suited to the old-fashioned Ruritania style of diplomatic life in La Paz. The Ruritanian veneer concealed a turbulent, even violent, society beneath and that suited Lomax as well, because he was a tough and sturdy character. In World War I he had served in France, Belgium, India and Egypt as a driver in horse-drawn artillery, and he was still at his happiest among horses. He used to ride every morning before breakfast and for two or three hours on Saturday. I went with him on a large black and white horse, called, for that reason, Arlequin. We kept them in the stables of the military college where we suspected that the floors were deep in the accumulated manure of a century. Sometimes army officers borrowed our horses for a ceremonial parade in the centre of town. On one of these occasions, Arlequin, or the officer, disgraced himself because the horse soon came back to the stable without his rider.

In La Paz this fixation with horses had its uses, because it was shared with some influential people, even in the revolutionary government. Some of them now and again rode with us, including the daughter of the President of the Republic. Lomax who was impatient, as were the Bolivians, with the niceties of diplomatic correspondence, liked to boast that he conducted most of his official business on horseback. He once began a dispatch with the notable phrase: 'I normally have the honour to refrain from reporting political developments at this post. . .' When he was about to leave La Paz on retirement in 1956, he wrote to ask the Foreign Office (who pay for the transport of cars) if they would cover the cost of transporting his horse. He had a polite reply which said that the matter had been carefully considered but they were afraid that the days when the Office could pay for transporting horses 'had long since passed'.

His successor, Sir James Thyne Henderson, was a very differ ent character, a kind, considerate and prudent Scottish Borderer from the family who owned the firm which made Pringle jerseys. Lomax had written to him to say that in his experience horses were an essential diplomatic asset in La Paz and so would he like to buy his horse. He agreed, but when he arrived he showed no particular anxiety to visit the stable. After a few days I persuaded him to come with me to see his new acquisition. When the stable door was opened, the horse, full of pent-up energy, shot out, like a shell from a gun, with his hooves striking sparks from the cobbles. That settled it. James never went back to the stables.

Life with the Hendersons was much more placid. They were very kind and generous and soon became very popular. James's wife, Karen, was Danish and passionately devoted to the improvement of the house and garden. She soon transformed both from the rather masculine austerity in which she had found them. This made it particularly disturbing when I noticed a serious structural defect in the house when they were at home on their mid-term leave. The Ambassador's residence was close to my own in Obrajes in a parallel street higher up a slope. Since I was in charge of the Embassy in the absence of the

Ambassador, I looked in from time to time to see that all was well. I noticed cracks in the walls which had not been there before and which, on examination, ran through the house from top to bottom. I knew the architect who had designed the house not very many years before. He came with rather a sceptical air, but as soon as he saw the evidence, he turned very white. Various other experts, including the professor of geology from the university were summoned. Monitors which we placed on the cracks showed that they were widening quite quickly.

The diagnosis was clear. The house was built on a stratum of porous earth which was not very deep. Beneath it was a layer of clay which was impenetrable to water. On the slope above the house there was a water course from which water was percolating over the clay below. Before long, the front of the house would detach itself and float down the hill. The remedy was to divert the water course through the garden to the side of the house and to bind the front of the house to the rear by metal rods, a major and very expensive operation. To their credit, the Department of Works, who were responsible for Government buildings, sent out a couple of experts and the expenditure was authorised and the work put in hand with very little delay.

By this time, the Hendersons were on a ship on the long voyage back to South America. I had the delicate task of sending them a telegram to tell them that the house and garden, on which Karen had lavished so much love and energy, were being reduced to a building site. I made various suggestions for some other place for them to live while all this was going on, but they decided to camp in the rear of the house amid the confusion. Diplomatic life is not all ease and elegance.

In 1959 my tour in La Paz came to an end and on the 4th May I returned to the Foreign Office.

CHAPTER 10
Foreign Office, Havana
May 1959 – April 1964

On my return to the Foreign Office I was appointed at first to the American Department. Henry Hankey, the head, might I think be regarded as an ideal diplomat. Nothing could disturb his good nature, optimism and benevolence and all his instincts were those of the devoted public servant. He had been born to it. His father, Lord Hankey, had been secretary to the Cabinet during World War I. As a young boy, his father had given him the job of keeping a count of the number of guests in the drawing-room of No 10, so that they could be diverted if they reached a number that the floor might not support. (It has been reinforced since then.) He could speak fluently and spontaneously in the language of a diplomatic note or a white paper. 'I think we might say,' he would begin, and the words that followed could be used without alteration in the final text. He had been the official on duty on the night of 2nd September 1939 to await the reply to the British ultimatum to Germany and report next morning to the Cabinet that none had been received. In spite of all this, he was a balanced human being; he painted, was a fine pianist and a keen skier. His wife, Vronwy, was an archaeologist and a classical scholar.

The American Department was unusual in the sense that the worldwide involvement of the United States meant that we might have had to concern ourselves with virtually every diplomatic question that existed. In fact, of course, common sense prevailed and relations with the United States were divided between virtually all other Departments. We had certainly a responsibility to follow internal American developments that might impinge on us, but the main work of the Department was with Latin America, and with Antarctica because of the negotiation of an Antarctic Treaty, of which Henry was regarded as the architect.

As it happened, my arrival in the American Department more or less coincided with significant developments in Cuba, a place with which I was to become familiar. Fidel Castro seized power from the tyrannical and unpopular Fulgenico Batistà in January 1959. Castro's relationship with the United States, who had at first supported him, deteriorated when he began policies of nationalisation and land reform and contacts with the Soviet Union and China. The Americans broke off diplomatic relations with Cuba in January 1961 and in April launched the fiasco of an invasion by Cuban exiles at the Bay of Pigs. This encouraged Castro to claim to be a Marxist-Leninist of long standing and to seek the help of the Soviet Union. Our view was that American impatience and intolerance, not to say, indirect armed intervention, had forced Castro into this position. Efforts to persuade the Americans to show more restraint fell on deaf ears. As they said, it was all very well for us to be so detached; but American companies had suffered from Castro's confiscations and the island was only ninety miles from America. To them, Castro was a very close and direct threat and a dangerous example to the rest of Latin America. They reminded us that in America the Monroe Doctrine (which basically is the belief that the outside world has no right to intervene in the American continent) was as fundamental as the balance of power in Europe was to us. I do not think that any of us at that time imagined that Soviet intervention would go so far and so fast as it did.

After some time, I was moved from the American Department to become the Assistant Head (Political) of United Nations Department. This was the Department responsible for the co-ordination of the instructions to our delegations in the Security Council and the General Assembly and was therefore involved in all the major international crises. It often meant working late into the night and seeking ministerial approval at awkward hours.

For much of this time Alec Douglas-Home was Foreign Secretary. He had a pleasantly relaxed manner and treated officials as friends and colleagues, which is more than you could say for many Conservative ministers. They often seemed to regard us both with suspicion and condescension. I think that they took the phrase, civil servants, (not that we even thought of ourselves as such) rather too literally in the spirit of upstairs downstairs. It was not unknown, at meetings with ministers from other governments and the like, for a Conservative minister to offer them a sherry or a whisky and ignore the officials without whom they would have been helpless. But with Douglas-Home it was quite different. He was always ready to blether about life in the Borders or chat about cricket. (He was said to be the only Cabinet Minister who had played the game in a first-class team, Middlesex, in the 20s). If you tried to telephone him when he was at home at the Hirsel, a crisis seemed to lose its urgency when his butler said, 'I am sorry but his lordship is out on the moors.'

Because I was convinced that Douglas-Home was essentially a decent human being, I was shocked by his last-minute broadcast just before the Scottish devolution referendum of 1979. This was a plea to the Scots to vote No, not because he was against a Scottish Parliament, but to give an opportunity to bring in a better Bill for a stronger Parliament with tax-raising powers. Since Douglas-Home was widely respected in Scotland, this probably contributed greatly to the reduction of the Yes majority to so small a scale that the Thatcher Government shortly afterwards was able to use this as a pretext for rescinding the legislation, so imposing on us a long wait of about twenty years. Many years later, I had a chance to ask him about this when he came to lunch with Alastair Dunnett's 'Guardians' (about which I shall say something in due course). He did not give a very clear answer, but I think that what he said could be interpreted as an apology. I suppose the truth is that he felt that he had to respond to an appeal from Margaret Thatcher to come to the aid of the Party.

One of the dominant themes of the United Nations at this time was 'decolonisation', the process by which colonies became independent. The majority of them had been British and their emancipation proceeded very smoothly with no resistance on the part of the Conservative Government. This was perhaps surprising. It was, after all, not long after Churchill had famously proclaimed, 'I did not become her Majesty's First Minister in order to preside over the dissolution of the British Empire.' Once during the summer so many people were on holiday that I found myself representing the Foreign Office in a meeting about a stage in this process with Iain Macleod and Duncan Sandys, the Colonial and Commonwealth Secretaries. They showed no inclination to resist this emancipation of the remaining colonies. There was a general realisation, even among Conservative Ministers, that British power had so far declined that we could not resist the force of world opinion, including that of the United States, and pressure from the colonies themselves.

Ludovic Kennedy in a television programme once remarked that he had been present as a BBC reporter at scores of handover ceremonies in former British colonies when the Union flag was lowered and the flag of the newly independent country was raised. 'I started to think,' he said. 'If these little places, and some of them very small and very poor, can have self-government, why can't Scotland?' This was a thought that occurred to many people. Scotland with its centuries of experience as an independent country, its own legal and educational systems, its administrative structure, its advanced economy and its educated population, was a far more promising candidate for independence, one might well conclude, than most, and perhaps all, of these former colonies. Ruling circles in England, and even many people in Scotland, have been reluctant to reach this conclusion. Of course English rulers since the early middle ages have imagined that they had a right to aspire to the control of the whole island. The formation of the state of Great Britain accomplished that aspiration, but only in 1707. In the comparatively short period since then, people have become used to thinking of it as the natural and normal state of affairs. This idea has been powerfully reinforced by the propaganda instruments of the British state, which include the monarchy, the film industry and the BBC.

During the whole of this period in London Harold Macmillan was Prime Minister. I had first encountered him in Berlin just after the war. He had an unmistakable air of effortless superiority. He was of Hebridean descent, but had adopted the attitudes of the English aristocracy into which he had married. As Prime Minister, he was one of the last of the Tory grandees and his sense of style and imperturbability influenced the whole Government. I think that he cultivated the performance quite deliberately. When we prepared a guest list for a reception at No. 10 for a State visit of the President of Peru, he minuted that, 'we need to brighten it by the addition of some pretty duchesses and their daughters.' He was determined that Archbishop Makarios would not upstage him at a meeting over Cyprus in Lancaster House. So he arrived early, sat with his back to the entrance and engaged his staff in an animated conversation. Makarios arrived and paused at the door. After a few seconds, long enough to deflate him, Macmillan deigned to notice his arrival. 'Oh Archbishop, how kind of your to join us.' When people in London made a great fuss over the visit of the Soviet astronaut, Yuri Gagarin, Macmillan told the Cabinet, 'Don't worry, it would have been a hundred times worse if they had sent the dog.'

We needed somewhere to live in London and were lucky enough to find a house at 5 Vincent Square, a curiously tranquil place, although it is between Victoria Station and the Houses of Parliament. There is a large green space, the playing fields of Westminster School, in the middle of the Square. When they played there at the weekends you might be on a village green. The house had a basement, which we let, and three other floors, but it was quite small because it was very narrow, only as wide as one room. One of our neighbours was the Labour MP and subsequently Minister, Richard Crossman, who lived at No. 9. Crossman was a highly intelligent man who had written books about Plato and Socrates, had taught philosophy and had been for years assistant editor of the *New Statesman*, as well as a member of the Labour National Executive Committee. The conversation of politicians, especially now in this age of sound-bites and rigid party discipline, tends to be tedious and predictable. They are afraid of departing even by an iota from the party line. Crossman was not like that. He positively revelled in indiscretion. He told me once that the trouble about a party which represented the working class was that people with energy and intelligence were always trying to better themselves and move into the managerial or property-owning classes. 'We are left with the residue and that is an unsatisfactory base for a party or any other organisation.'

We had not been in London long before our second child, Catharine, was born on 17 July 1959 at Eastbourne. Celia had chosen the hospital there in preference to London. Her father had a house, Dragonfield, in a village, Boreham Street, which is not far from Eastbourne and we had taken over a smaller house, Little Dragonfield, which was nextdoor. Celia preferred life in the country and so I began to spend the week in London and then go down to Sussex for the weekends. The obvious course was to dispose of the Vincent Square house, which was a pity and acquire a small flat instead. We found a modern flat with a sitting room, a bedroom, a kitchen and bathroom at 35 Buckingham Gate. It was even closer to the Foreign Office, which was barely five minutes walk through St James's Park.

Since my rowing club days in Edinburgh, I have enjoyed pottering about in boats, either rowing or sailing, but I have never been keen on racing which seemed to me to destroy the essential pleasure of moving about over water without rush or stress. I bought a sailing dinghy and joined the London Corinthian Sailing Club at Hammersmith. I admit that this was not the most stress-free kind of sailing. The current in the Thames was strong, the bridge downstream was too low for the mast and there was a fairly constant traffic of tugs pulling barges.

We continued, of course, with our other old ploys, Scottish dancing, Edinburgh for the Festival, Klosters for skiing. In some years I went to St Moritz instead because of the Army Ski Association which the assistant military attaché in Warsaw had persuaded me to join. It was in St Moritz that I passed the first class test of the Ski Club of Great Britain. It involved, among other things, doing a downhill course at a respectable racing speed.

In St Moritz too, where I went without Celia, I had a number of these brief holiday affairs, once with a passionate French woman and once with an air-hostess, Johanne. When I was back in London, she said in a letter, 'I find it hard to believe that what happened between us is really true. It changed the holiday from one that was very enjoyable to one I shall never forget. I found it so difficult not to talk about you to the others and boast about how marvellous you are.' She was grateful but she could not see me again. She was getting married and had wanted to lose her virginity before that. The reasoning behind this was not obvious but she was attractive, rational and intelligent. In London I had too a delightful relationship with a secretary in the Office, Ann Breingan, an attractive girl with a warm personality and a subtle wit. In May 1960 she was part of the delegation to the Summit meeting in Paris which was broken up by Khruschev over the U-2 incident.

In the summer of 1962 I was at one of the conferences in an Oxford college which the Foreign Office arranges or participates in from time to time. On the final Sunday, David Muirhead, the head of Personnel Department, turned up. He told me that they wanted to send me to Havana as Head of Chancery and Deputy Head of the Post. It would involve promoting me to the rank of Counsellor, the youngest one in the Service.

I still have a letter which the Ambassador, Sir Herbert Marchmont, wrote to me in August. My predecessor, Keith Oakeshott, was leaving in the last days of September, so he hoped that I could arrive in October 'nearer the 15th than the 30th.' He hoped that we should not find it 'too unpleasant a posting. Things at the moment are reasonably calm, but we tend to sit on the edge of our chair wondering what tomorrow will bring even when the tension is only slight.'

We travelled through Washington. The idea was that I should call on the Cuban experts in the State Department, the Pentagon and the CIA for a discussion on the situation in the island. The arrangements for this were in the hands of an old friend, Iain Sutherland. He had been at the Royal High School in Edinburgh, before Aberdeen Grammar School, Aberdeen University and Balliol; but we first met in Paris. He was sent there by the Foreign Office to study Russian among the emigré community at the same time that I was there to improve my French. Both of his parents were painters, DM Sutherland and Dorothy Johnstone, who worked and taught in Aberdeen. He had been First Secretary in Havana from 1959 until he was posted to Washington in 1962 and so was the obvious man to deal with the State Department over Cuban questions. Years later, Iain ended his career as Ambassador to Moscow. He wrote to me shortly before he retired in 1985 to say that he contemplated becoming involved, like me, in Scottish affairs but unfortunately he died before this was possible.

We arrived in Washington about the middle of October to be met by a lugubrious Iain who said that he was embarrassed to say that all of his carefully planned programme of visits had been cancelled by the Americans. They had put a complete embargo on any discussion with him about Cuba. It was apparent that something drastic, some major switch in policy, was about to happen. At all events, we had no alternative but to proceed on our journey by train to Miami. There military preparations were only too evident – ships were visible at sea and airforce planes were accumulating at the airport. We presented ourselves at the KLM desk for a flight to Havana, which turned out to be the last one for many years.

'Were we quite sure that we wanted to fly to Havana? Had we not noticed that something unusual was going on?' I told them that the decision was not in our hands. The only other passenger on the plane was another diplomat returning, reluctantly, to his post. That evening President Kennedy announced in a broadcast that the Soviet Government was installing ballistic missiles with atomic warheads in Cuba and that the American Navy would impose a blockade of the island until they were removed. Marchmont had been right to say that he was sitting on the edge of his chair. We were now at the epicentre of a crisis that involved the risk of a nuclear war.

A welcoming party with our Western colleagues, who were not very numerous, became an inquest into the situation. I think that we felt a bit like the garrison of a besieged town. Several people asked me why we had come. They had no option because they were already here, but we could have had the sense to find some pretext to stay away. There was a general air of despondency, but no sense of panic. After all, we were hardly more exposed than anyone else. A nuclear war would leave few, if any, survivors. I do not suppose that any of us really expected it to come to that. We all believed, I think, that common sense would prevail, because the alternative would have been so catastrophic.

The immediate crisis was resolved quite quickly. Khruschev agreed to remove the missiles and Kennedy to lift the naval blockade. Castro refused to admit UN observers to report the removal of the missiles, but that did not disturb the Americans because their reconnaissance aircraft kept a constant watch on the situation. At the crucial time, however, when the missiles should have been moving to the ports, the ground became invisible from the air because of heavy cloud. We received a somewhat frantic emergency telegram. The hawks in the Pentagon were becoming impatient. Could we provide hard evidence that the Russians were complying with the agreement? This was quite simple. We knew where the missile sites were from the American reconnaissance photographs which were very clear and detailed. I simply drove around them and saw the Russians hard at work. In places they were having problems with missile-trailers in muddy fields but they were clearly doing their best. Convoys of these long, sinister trailers were moving to the port of Matangas and the ships were waiting to receive them. It has been said that my report, by calming nerves in Washington, may have prevented a nuclear war.

A few days after we arrived in Cuba, the Soviet Embassy had their customary reception on 7th November to celebrate the revolution of 1917. My colleagues in the Embassy said that this was an opportunity for me to encounter Fidel Castro and members of his Government. The evening was warm, even in November, and the party was in the garden behind the house. After about a couple of hours, which is more than long enough for any cocktail party, there was still no sign of Fidel or his henchmen. I decided to leave and I was walking through the house to the front door, when there he was walking towards me. He seemed to assume that I was a member of the Soviet Embassy who had been waiting all this time to greet him. He threw his arms around me and began a flowery speech, for which the Spanish language is particularly apt, about the great and happy anniversary, fraternal greetings, long live our revolutions and so forth. When I could get a word in I said, 'Stop, stop, you have got the wrong man.' 'Well, who are you then?' So I told him. He thought this was a great joke and so did I and we laughed together about nothing in particular for some time. He was relaxed, convivial and utterly without pomposity.

Thereafter, we had a friendly, if distant, relationship. I had a red, open sports car which was conspicuous in Havana where most cars were old and large American monsters. Once or twice when I was driving to and from the office I encountered Fidel in one such American car, escorted by another, and he would lean out and wave as he was driven past. When we met at some reception or other he told me more than once how much he admired my car. I began to wonder if I should offer it to him for the sake of good relations between our Governments.

At such events, Che Guevera was sometimes also present. He later became a romantic icon for a whole generation. A poster with his photograph by Alberto Korde became an essential decoration in student bedrooms almost everywhere. In the flesh, he made no impression at all. He was small and insignificant-looking, especially beside Fidel who was more than life size in every sense of the term, bursting with energy, ideas and self-confidence. Che hardly spoke, but Fidel did not give him much of a chance. Perhaps that is why he went off to Bolivia to try to start his own revolution.

Some time after our first meeting Fidel accepted an invitation to lunch in the Ambassador's residence, which was, I think, the first time he had accepted such an invitation from a western Embassy. As usual, we began with drinks in the garden. Conversation was a bit stiff at first, but suddenly the Ambassador's two large and energetic poodles burst upon the scene. They had been shut up to prevent such a disturbance, but someone had opened the door by mistake. Fidel greeted the dogs like long-lost friends and then began a long discourse about dogs, their characteristics and the history of their relationship with human society. The Jesuits who had educated Fidel had evidently made a good job of it. He had an organised and well-stocked mind and an urge to share his knowledge. You could see why making speeches for three hours or so came quite naturally to him, and these speeches too were always coherent and logically constructed. His ego and self-esteem were equally obvious. It would never occur to him that people might not want to stand three or four hours in the sun listening to him. He stayed four hours at this lunch as well and monopolised the conversation, but he held the attention.

Jimmy Hepburn, a Scot who represented the Royal Bank of Canada in Cuba, told me about an incident which shows Fidel's direct, hands-on, method of running his Government. The American and Cuban Governments had reached an agreement under which the Cubans would release the prisoners taken at the Bay of Pigs and the Americans would deliver a large supply of medicines. The two events were to happen as though they were spontaneous and unconnected to avoid an appearance of horse-trading in human beings. Hepburn's bank was involved, because the Cuban Government used it for their financial dealings with western countries. For this reason, they were the only foreign bank which had been allowed to maintain an office in Cuba.

One Saturday afternoon, when this transaction was about to take effect, Hepburn was sitting in his flat and the doorbell rang. There was Castro with two others. 'Hello Jimmy,' he said, 'sorry to trouble you, but we need a quick decision. These two colleagues of mine from the Ministry of Finance and the Central Bank tell me that I am being taken for a ride. We are about to send the Bay of Pigs people to the States, but they tell me that there is no guarantee that the Americans will keep their side of the deal. What do you say about that?'

'No need to worry, Commandante,' (which was the polite form of address) 'the funds have been deposited with my head office and payments made to the suppliers.'

'Right, Jimmy. I know you and I know the Royal Bank. Do you give me your word that I can rely on that absolutely.'

'Yes, certainly.'

'There you are,' said Castro, turning to the two officials. 'That's the way to do business. Find the right man and ask the right questions.'

In July 1963 Graham Greene turned up for a few days to see what had happened to the setting of *Our Man in Havana*. He arrived by air from Mexico City. The only two civilian air services still operating to Cuba were the Mexican service and one from Prague. The Americans had contrived the suspension of all others. Greene told me about his impressions of Mexico. The best way to get under the surface of a strange city, he said is to ask a taxi driver. So he had done that.

'Well, Sènor, it depends what you want and how much you can afford. I know of a place where you drink as much champagne as you like and fuck as many girls as you can manage. But it costs $500. Be realistic, can you drink enough glasses and fuck enough girls to be worth that much?' I should have asked if had found it worthwhile, but I didn't. He told me that brothels were a great source of both insight and comedy.

The British press was full at that time of the Profumo case. Greene said that he was very sorry to be out of London when such interesting things were going on. When he heard that I came from Edinburgh, he told me that he greatly admired Muriel Spark and asked if I thought that her qualities as a novelist were related to her conversion to Catholicism. At another point in the conversation he said, 'It does not matter how a novelist behaves, but he has to be deeply concerned with moral issues.' I said that in Scotland we tended to be obsessed with morality but thought that it was a consequence of our Presbyterianism as in Spark's *Jean Brodie*.

Greene said that he had been in Havana several times when Batista was in power and supported by the Americans. Now they were doing their best to overthrow Castro. Even if Castro was intolerant and dictatorial, he was sure that he was not as barbarious and bloody as Batista. Castro was a refreshing change. The Americans always seem to be on the wrong side. He had enjoyed Batista's Havana before he had heard about the tortures and outrages. It was a place where every indulgence was possible. Now it was much less fun perhaps, but certainly better for the people at large. The whole feel of the place was quite different – the atmosphere was even optimistic, in spite of all the problems.

Greene was on his way to Papa Doc's Haiti, which, by all accounts, was even bloodier than Batista's Cuba. Travelling in such precarious places shows, I think, that Greene had remarkable courage. You would not have guessed that from his appearance. He looked like a gentle and rather diffident and shy academic.

Before I came to Cuba I had experience of communism in Poland and of Latin America in Bolivia. I thought that in Cuba I should find a combination of the worst features of both of them, the intimidation and tedium of one and the inequalities and muddle of the other. I was wrong. Cuba was quite different from both. The shops in Cuba were even emptier than in Poland, but the people were much less depressed. Cuba had been a country, like much of Latin America, with a vast gulf between the rich and the poor. Now most of the rich people had exiled themselves and the régime was creating a new kind of equality. People were still poor but they were beginning to have greater access to such things as education and medical services. Certainly, there were political prisoners. There were people who detested the régime and they were likely to be arrested if they spoke out too indiscreetly. My impression, though, was that more people were in favour of Castro than against him.

The Cubans are a very likeable people, 'contented,' in the Scots phrase, 'wi little and canty wi mair'. Most of them are friendly and relaxed and disposed by nature to music and dance. They are also remarkably honest. Even at this time of severe shortage, I never heard of any theft. You could leave your belongings lying on a beach and be quite sure that they would still be there when you came back from a swim. They enjoy life and do not take such things as political dogma very seriously. A Dutch Marxist was very disconcerted by this. He had come to Cuba to write a book about this new triumph of the cause and had been interviewing many people in the upper reaches of the Government. His conclusion was that none of them had the slightest grasp of Marxist philosophy or even interest in it. I told him that this was not surprising. Faced with American hostility, the régime had needed a powerful friend. They had expressed as much conformist zeal as was necessary to enlist Soviet support.

Since the Americans were doing their best to persuade other governments to sever all links with Cuba, the Cuban Government were naturally well-disposed to those who still maintained diplomatic relations with them. Cuban ministries went out of their way to be friendly and co-operative. They even allowed us to run our own air service. We proposed this partly because of the scarcity of flights but also because of the shortages of food. The Foreign Ministry organised a weekly delivery of food to diplomatic households. You could express preferences, but what you received depended on what was available and that was usually fish and rice. We suggested a weekly chartered flight from the Bahamas which could bring in mail, diplomatic bags, and, more to the point, food and drink. The Cubans agreed and, more surprisingly, all the Western governments agreed to share the cost.

I travelled on this flight when the Americans in the winter of 1963 asked if I could go to Washington to brief them about the situation in Cuba. Shortly after we left Havana, an American fighter flew alarmingly close. I mentioned this to a man in the Pentagon. 'Oh yes,' he said, 'we intercept all flights from Cuba. Our pilots radio back for instructions. They shoot them down if they are not given clearance.'

In Washington, I went the rounds of the Pentagon, CIA and the State Department and in all of them a large group of officials asked me detailed questions. In the final session in the State Department one of their senior people was in the chair. He asked what I thought about the character of Castro, the attitude of the people and the stability of the régime. I knew, of course, that they wanted to hear that he was a ruthless dictator, detested by the great majority of the people, and likely to be overthrown by a popular rising, perhaps with a little discreet support from outside. What I told them was quite different, as will be apparent from what I have written above. In spite of his ruthlessness, Castro was formidable. He had many enemies, but the support of the majority. There were no signs that the régime was likely to collapse. This was met at first with stony silence, broken by the chairman who remarked, 'Well all I can say is that it is a pity he is not on our side.'

This was nearly forty years ago and Castro and his régime are still in place. In March 2001 the State Department published some of their papers of forty years before about Castro's Cuba. One of them was a brief for the President which said of Castro, 'It would be a serious mistake to underestimate this man. He is clearly a strong personality and a born leader of great personal courage and conviction.' At least some people in the State Department had not been blinded by prejudice.

Cuba is a country with wonderful beaches and with coral reefs inhabited by brightly coloured tropical fish. I spent much of my spare time exploring these reefs, diving under the surface with mask and flippers for the first time. The Embassy had a house on a cliff overlooking such a beach some miles from Havana. It was quite a simple place which had been donated to the Embassy and many of the Embassy staff spent weekends there.

My companion on many of these expeditions, more in the sea than out of it, was a secretary from the Embassy, Anthea Perry. She was then about 25 (and I was 43), attractive, with a warm and friendly personality and very athletic. She had trained as a competitive swimmer, played a formidable game of tennis and even, for the first and only time in my life, persuaded me sometimes to play golf in a Club in Havana which had curiously survived the Revolution.

I have always been vulnerable to the charms of women. Quite often I have indulged in delightful affairs about which both of us were discreet to avoid causing pain or embarrassment to others. Three or four times in my life I have been struck by something much more powerful, falling irresistibly in love to the point where prudence, discretion or subterfuge were impossible or superfluous. This was such a case. In a small community like the Embassy, I suppose our attitude to one another was obvious from everything we did or said.

Celia did not like it, of course, but she understood. We even went together to New York to see Anthea off on the French liner, *Normandie*, when she was posted from Havana in the early months of 1964.

That was not the end. I was also posted from Havana not long afterwards. Somehow I contrived to meet Anthea in Naples and sail with her to Athens in a ship which was sailing for her next posting in Israel. I also once visited her in Tel Aviv. These moves, or some of them, reached the ears of Personnel Department of the Foreign Office. I do not think that they seek out information like this, but if it is formally brought to their notice, they apparently feel that they have to react. Anthea's mother made a formal complaint about this married man who had seduced her innocent daughter. I can imagine the terms of it because Anthea gave me one of her mother's letters where she denounced me in the most violent terms. She was clearly one of these fierce, Tory ladies with strong feelings about the sanctity of marriage, and the glories of the monarchy and the British Empire, enough to terrify any bureaucrat.

David Muirhead's response was to tell me that I had been guilty of a 'lack of judgement'. I do not see what judgement had to do with it, but this amounts, apparently, in the vocabulary of the Foreign Office, to strong censure. My friend, Simon Dawbarn, who was the Assistant Head of Personnel Department at the time, said that he was ashamed that the Department took such an attitude of puritanical pomposity. He thought that no other diplomatic service in the world would concern itself with such a matter. At all events, there is little doubt that this was a major setback to my progress up the promotion ladder.

I have no regrets. Anthea and I, although of course with time and separation our feelings cooled, have remained friends. For some years, she sent me wonderfully vivid and spirited letters about her experience in other Embassies. They confirmed, if confirmation was needed, that my infidelities were normal behaviour.

Our man in Havana, 1963

CHAPTER 11

Canadian National Defence College
1964-1965

After Havana my next appointment, which made more sense than might at first appear, was to the Canadian National Defence College in Kingston, Ontario. In a refreshing change from normal diplomatic life, I was to be on Course XVIII which lasted about a year with thirty participants. The majority of them were, of course, Canadian, both fairly senior service officers and civil servants from a variety of ministries. The United Kingdom and the United States each had an officer from the Army, Navy, and Air Force and a diplomat from the Foreign Office and State Department. My British colleagues were Captain Sir Edward Archdale from the navy, Group Captain JS Smith from the RAF and from the army, Brigadier David Tyacke, who became a particular friend. I went alone to Kingston. Celia had decided to stay in Sussex with the children.

David Tyacke, who was Cornish and proud of it, was very different from the conventional idea of an Army officer. He was intelligent, clear-headed and efficient, but also sensitive with a strong sense of social justice. Once he told me that his days in the Indian Army had made him ashamed of his service. 'Do you mean because of the way you treated the Indians?' I asked. 'No, because of the way we treated our own other ranks. Officers had a great deal of luxury, comfort and privilege, clubs, polo, and all the rest of it. Conditions for the men were little better than prison.'

Kingston is a small town on Lake Ontario, about midway between Montreal and Toronto. It has a distinctly Scottish atmosphere. The local explanation is that the houses in the centre were built in stone by Scottish masons. They are said to have been men who worked on the Caledonian Canal and then came to Canada to build the Rideau Canal between Kingston and Ottawa. Kingston is dominated by

military and academic institutions, Queen's University, the Royal
Military College (which is the Canadian Sandhurst), the Staff College,
and if my memory serves , the Army School of Signals. There is also a
prison, known as the Penitentiary. One of our Canadian Army
colleagues, Lt Col Mike Webber, was fond of remarking that he had
been in every institution in Kingston except the Penitentiary – so far.

The Defence College shared an old barracks, which was a
handsome group of buildings on the lakeside, with the Staff College.
We could each have a bedroom there, if we wished, and I did live
there until I found a delightful little house not far away. It was an old
stone building, probably part of a stable block originally, with a kitchen
and sitting room downstairs and a bedroom and bathroom aloft. I say
aloft because the steep and narrow stairs had a rope handrail and felt
very much like a ship.

The Canadians are a warm and welcoming people, particularly in
a small community like Kingston and especially one which is
accustomed to receiving a fluctuating population of students and the
military. In no time at all you are made to feel thoroughly at home
with friends in all directions. The Royal Military College gave us the
use of their ice rink and their sail boats on the lake. Once, when a
group of us were proposing on a free weekend to borrow one of these
boats, I suggested that we should take some food and wine and make
a real excursion of it. The Canadians looked a bit furtive and said that
it would probably be all right, if we were careful. They explained that
it was against the law in Ontario to consume alcohol in daylight in a
public place. This puritanism was also attributed to Scottish influence.
Galpin of the Department of External Affairs had a more elaborate
explanation. He said that in early days in Canada, the towns had to
defend themselves against the excesses of men, such as fur trappers,
miners or lumberjacks, who descended on them to spend their
earnings after weeks in the wilds.

Queen's University, another institution conscious of its Scottish
roots, was also very hospitable and made its library available to us.
When I was doing some research about the reign of James IV, as a
change from preoccupation with nuclear strategy, I had difficulty in
tracing a book. Eventually a young and bright member of the staff
produced it triumphantly. 'It is in a special section,' she said. 'It is
called the Tweedsmuir Collection. I have no idea why.' Such is fame.
John Buchan, as Lord Tweedsmuir and Governor General, had died

163

in Ottawa in 1940 and had evidently left his books to Queen's. Twenty five years later this intelligent Canadian had never heard of him.

I have mentioned nuclear strategy and that was the major theme of the Defence College. For the Canadian Government it was an elaborate and expensive undertaking, but its purpose was to study the problems of a world faced with the prospect of nuclear war and to prepare the next generation of their top officers and officials to cope with them. We had an intensive programme of lectures, discussions, and the drafting of papers in response to set problems about Canadian policy, the North Atlantic Alliance, the United Nations, the Communist Bloc, Warfare and Weapons Systems, Africa, Asia and Latin America. We had tours in a Canadian Air Force plane of about a month across North America, mainly to nuclear installations, and of a month and a half to Europe and Africa. The whole culminated in a month devoted to nuclear strategy. The lecturers were mainly academics from Canadian universities, but also quite frequently ministers of the Canadian Government, who were impressively accessible and articulate.

On the North American Tour, from 17th January to 13th February 1964, we went first to Yellowknife. This is a small mining town, not far south of the Arctic Circle, where they mine gold which promptly then goes underground again in the vaults of the Canadian Central Bank. It was of course cold, so cold indeed that the taxis outside the hotel kept their engines running permanently. During the day, with sunshine and no wind, it was sharp and pleasant. At lunch with the local notables I was sitting next to an official from the Department of Northern Affairs. He told me that he had been in Yellowknife for more than ten years and did not want to leave it. I asked if the climate was not a little trying. 'Well,' he replied, 'it is sometimes too hot in July.'

I felt the full rigour of the Canadian winter in Winnipeg. When we arrived in our hotel there, I noticed from a poster in the hall that a film which I had long wanted to see was on in a local cinema. My colleagues, as was their habit, congregated in one of the bedrooms for drinks. I could not persuade any of them to come to the film, so I went alone. Since I did not know the place, I took a taxi and discovered that the cinema was not far away. At the end of the film, I decided to walk back to the hotel and that was agreeable enough at first. When I turned into a long avenue, in which the hotel stood, I suddenly felt the full force of the icy wind. It cut to the bone and I hardly expected to be able to reach the hotel alive. The survival of the early settlers during their first winters in such a climate is a tribute to human endurance.

After a pleasant visit to Vancouver, we entered the United States and encountered more serious matters. We went to the American Air Force Academy where officers are trained with a passionate rigour beside which Sparta and Prussia would be tame. The cadets are not allowed to have any contact with the outside world for their first month because they have to be weaned, one of the instructors told us, from the effeminate weakness of contemporary society. The classrooms have no windows because the view might distract. All the cadets have to go into the water from the top of an Olympic diving board, whether they can dive or not. When they survive all this, they expect to soar through the skies in jet fighters; but many have a different fate. We encountered some of the graduates in the awesome, but boring, job as custodians of an inter-continental ballistic missile. There they sat, two together, in a hole in the ground waiting for the order to release the monster that could begin the destruction of all life on the planet.

We went to the headquarters of the Air Defence of North America which you reach by bus through a long tunnel which bores into the heart of a mountain. There were rooms fitted with the huge computers which existed at that time. They are connected with radar stations in diverse parts of the globe and supply information to the control centre which is like a theatre, where the controllers, as the audience, sit facing several large screens. For our benefit, they simulated a nuclear attack from the Soviet Union. The screens showed the predicted place of impact and the minutes elapsing, counting down from twenty, until they were due to arrive. If this were to happen in reality, the general on duty would telephone the President and say something like this; 'Mr President, we have information that the Soviets have released two missiles which are due to hit New York and Washington in 18, 17 minutes from now. What are your orders?' He has to decide, within these rapidly elapsing minutes, either to wait or order immediate retaliation. Just a few minutes to determine the fate of the world.

When we were briefed about all this, we were told that this subterranean headquarters had enough food, water and oxygen for the staff to be able to survive for ninety days. Why only ninety days? Because by that time, all life outside would have been extinguished and there would be no point in anyone else trying to stay alive. I asked if, even after a full nuclear exchange between the Soviet Union and the United States, might not some life survive in the southern hemisphere, perhaps in Australia or South America? 'Oh no, no chance,' was the reply. 'They might last a week or so, but soon the whole atmosphere would be radioactive. They would not escape.'

At the headquarters in Norfolk Virginia of the nuclear submarines, we were addressed by a senior officer who might have been a character like Dr Strangelove in a satirical film. He spoke to us in front of a map of the world with a long pointer in his hand. 'Gentlemen, the first point which you must grasp is that in this headquarters we have the capacity to destroy – and I mean destroy – the entire Soviet Union within twenty minutes. Is that understood?' As he spoke he hammered the map with his pointer between each phrase. We were nervous wrecks by the end of it.

Nor was it very reassuring to meet the calmer men who would actually issue the order to fire. It was explained to us that the submarines at sea could receive radio messages, but maintained radio silence to avoid revealing their position. Their missiles were already targeted permanently on objectives in the Soviet Union. If it was decided to release the missiles, the procedure was quite simple. The two officers at the control desk each had a key on a chain round his neck. On an order to fire, they had to obtain the code-word of the day by simultaneously inserting the two keys in locks in front of them. They would then transmit a radio message to the submarine or submarines concerned: 'I have a red emergency message for you,' followed by the code word. That was it. We were told that two officers were necessary as a precaution against the remote possibility that one might act on a mad impulse. But as the lecturer said this, there was only one officer at the desk and the other (presumably, attending to a call of nature) had left his key on the desk.

Our course directors did not ignore conventional warfare. We went, for instance, to the American School of Infantry, which was even tougher than the Air Force Academy. Everything was done at a run. We were all made honorary members of the US Infantry and given a badge, showing a bayonet with the slogan below, 'Follow Me'. That, we were told, was the spirit of the infantry officer (provided he was junior enough, I suppose). 'You do not tell your men what to do; you lead from the front.' In the officers' mess there was a hall with a high wooden ceiling, covered with dollar bills. It was a tradition at mess parties to display you athleticism and courage (for the ceiling was very high and the floor very hard) by climbing up on a human pyramid to add a bill to the collection.

Many of the instructors in this place were Americans from the Southern States whose soft accents and impeccable manners were in curious contradiction to their aggressive doctrines. There was a deliberate frenzy and craziness about it all, but it was craziness of a kind which was infinitely less dangerous than the madness of the nuclear planners. The more you learned about the complex calculations involving the prospect of the instant death of millions, the more it was obvious that the world was teetering on the brink of ultimate catastrophe.

Of course, not all of my time at the Defence College was taken up with such grave questions. I had at first proposed not to have a car because everything in Kingston was within walking distance, but I was persuaded that life in North America without a car is inconceivable. I bought a second-hand red MG sports car and I was able now and again to use it for a weekend skiing in the Laurentians. Once on the return journey I took a route by minor roads and was suddenly startled to see sign posts with such familiar names as Dalkeith, Lasswade and Eskbank. Was I dreaming or back in Scotland?

Erika, whom I mentioned in previous chapters, wrote to me to say that I was in easy reach of her country house in New York State. She knew this because when her husband was a student at Queen's he had come home for the weekends. So, would I come? I did, of course. I knew that she had married a wealthy American, but I had not expected the truly ducal establishment in which I found her. The neighbouring town, Morrisville was named after the family and they owned an enormous tract of the surrounding country. It had, they told me, been awarded to an ancestor in compensation for the destruction of his farmhouse in Manhattan by the redcoats during the war of independence. They still owned a piece of Manhattan as well and another later ancestor had married a heiress with mining properties in Montana. There were several family houses, apart from Erika's, on the estate. Her mother in law lived in the principal one where she had a butler and housemaids, dressed in the sort of uniforms you see in old editions of Mrs Beaton. Erika was quite unspoit by all their wealth and behaved as though it was a commonplace of no great importance. There was a stable with several horses, a staff of grooms and an indoor riding ring. One day we rode for miles, apparently without leaving the family property. She laughed when I told her that I had not known that some people in America lived like dukes in eighteenth century Europe. She confessed that she was having a passionate affair with her tennis coach. 'You were quite right you know in the things you said when you were trying to seduce me in Berlin. I only found that out later, but I wish I had not been so pious and stubborn at the time.' Too late is the saddest phrase in the language.

The Defence College tour to Africa and Europe took us, in our Canadian Air Force plane, to Gibraltar, Abidjan, Accra, Bangui, Dar es Salaam, Aden, Cairo, Rome, Naples, Belgrade, Bonn, Berlin, Paris and London. We left Kingston on 16th March 1965 and returned on 1st May. In most places we had discussions with senior officials, ministers or heads of government. In Abidjan, sitting at dinner between two officials of the Government of the Cote d' Ivoire. I asked about the languages of the country. The reply was emphatic: *'Mais, monsieur, nous faisons partie de la civilisation française.'* There seemed to be rather less satisfaction with the civilisation of the former colonial power in Nkrumah's Ghana. In that country the signs of a one-party, or rather a one-man, state, and lavish government expenditure on the trappings of power were very evident. Nkrumah himself arranged that we should be present to hear him speak in Parliament. This included an attack on some imperialistic misdemeanour. The climax was a quotation, not, he said 'from one of our own papers but from one of the most important British newspapers, the *News of the World.'*

Julius Nyerere, the President of Tanzania, was very different. He was intelligent, civilised, sincere and, as he reminded me, a graduate of Edinburgh University. He even translated plays of Shakespeare into Swahili. I had the impression that his official residence had not changed much since the last British Governor had left it, perhaps it still had the same staff. There was something very familiar about the smell of the furniture polish. Magazines like *Country Life* and *Punch* lay on the coffee tables.

In Cairo the Egyptian colonel who was responsible for our programme had arranged visits to factories and the like. We told him that other countries had such things, but we were much more interested in the temples and pyramids which were unique to Egypt. This struck an instant chord because he revealed that his father had been a professor of archaeology and that he was an enthusiastic amateur himself. We therefore had time for pyramids and museums and had some other such diversions from the serious business of visiting the Aswan Dam. There men in biblical dress on mules worked beside the bulldozers and concrete-mixers. As we were flying back to Cairo on an Illushyn plane of the Egyptian Air Force, one of the officers came back from the cabin to tell us that they were having a little problem with navigation because a sandstorm was preventing them from following the Nile. 'But surely,' one of our Canadian Air Force officers said, 'in a plane like this, you do not need to see the ground.' 'Yes, we have the equipment, but we have not yet learned how to use it.' The storm cleared and we arrived back in Cairo, but the later rapid collapse of the Egyptian Air Force in the Six Days War was not a surprise.

When we arrived in Rome and were met by people from the Canadian Embassy, the first question from our American Military member was, 'say, can you find a decent hamburger in this place?' To my surprise, several of our Canadian Colleagues told me that they had been charged by their wives to buy gloves for them in Rome. Why gloves? Because officers' wives in Canada have to wear them for coffee mornings and tea parties, part of the old-fashioned charm of the country.

In Belgrade Duncan Wilson, an old friend from Berlin and the Foreign Office, was Ambassador. He invited me to dinner with just himself and his wife, Betty. During our stay in Belgrade the Yugoslav army briefed, or indoctrinated, us with enthusiastic efficiency. We were taken to a military museum which began with Turkish atrocities and ended with the apotheosis of Tito. We were left with an uneasy feeling about Serbian militarism. They took us, for instance, to a hill where they said that a solitary Serbian machine gunner had held up an entire German division.

We arrived back in Kingston on 1st May 1965 for the final three months of discussion on global strategy and Canadian defence and foreign policies. The whole course was a illuminating experience and a great privilege, for which the participants had every reason to be grateful to the Canadian Government. I was sorry to hear a year or two ago that they had decided to close the College, although it was for an encouraging reason. They could no longer justify the heavy cost since, with the end of the perceived threat of nuclear war, the College had lost its purpose.

The architect Sir Basil Spence in front of the British Pavilion at Expo '67

CHAPTER 12
Expo '67
1965 -1967

After the Defence College, Personnel Department came up with a
further surprise. I was offered the tempting, but utterly
unexpected, post as Secretary General (which later became Deputy
Commissioner-General) for the British participation in the World
Exhibition in Montreal, Expo '67. From global strategy to show-biz.
The Canadian Government were staging the exhibition as part of the
celebration of the Centennial of Canadian Confederation in 1867. It
was to be a major event with seventy countries participating with
estimates of both costs and numbers of visitors all in millions. The
leading orchestras, theatre, opera and ballet companies of the world
were to take part in an associated arts festival. The British Pavilion was to
be designed by Sir Basil Spence and cost two and a half million pounds;
and the total cost of our participation was much more than that.

I arrived in Montreal with Celia, Alastair and Catharine in October
1965 and until the following July worked from the British Government
Office, at first with only a secretary. As activity increased, I set up my
own office in the Place Ville Marie, a suitably elegant and modern
skyscraper, in July 1966. The staff gradually increased with the arrival
of officials for the Central Office of Information who had been involved
in the planning of the Pavilion in London. One of them was Charles
Burnett from Fraserburgh, a talented designer, an enthusiast for
heraldry, of infinite patience, good nature and robust common sense.
I was delighted to meet him again when I returned to Edinburgh in
the 80s. He is now Ross Herald and Chamberlain of the Duff House
outpost of the National Gallery of Scotland.

We moved to the Pavilion itself in March 1967 and the
Commissioner General, Sir William Oliver, arrived in the same month.
He was an army general who had been the British Commandant in

Berlin (but after my time there) and Chief of the General Staff. Immediately before Montreal, his previous appointment was as High Commissioner in Australia from 1954 to 1966. As you might expect from all of this he was an imposing figure who tended at times to pomposity, but was genial and good-natured for all that. He insisted on a white Rolls Royce as his official car, but this sort of showmanship accorded well with the curious role we were both called upon to play.

For the first eighteen months before Oliver arrived, the job involved working out details of the British participation in liaison with the Canadian organisers and with the representatives of the other participating governments. We were involved with the National Theatre, the Royal Ballet, the British Old Vic, Yehudi Menuhin and the Bath Festival Orchestra, the English Opera Group and the Northern Sinfonia over their part in the World Festival. The inclusion of the Northern Sinfonia was the consequence of a personal appeal to me by the mother of the conductor, Boris Brott. She lived in Montreal where her husband, who looked remarkably like Beethoven, was a Professor of Music. We arranged a number of side shows, a hovercraft, a London bus, a pub and a bookshop.

Our publicity campaign from October 1965 was surprisingly successful. We had a whole succession of events with good photograph opportunities which had wide coverage in the press, radio and television. During the six months or so before the Exhibition opened on 26th April, there was hardly a week without extensive coverage in the press on the British Pavilion, at first only in Montreal, but later across Canada and the United States. We started our publicity before other countries and took advantage of the eagerness of the press for advance news about Expo at a time when it was hard to find.

The French language press in Montreal was particularly friendly to us, perhaps because I always took trouble to use both languages. Yves Margraff said in *Le Devoir* that I practiced '*un bilinguisme parfait, d'une élégance dont pourrait avantaguesement s'inspirer les organismes canadiens, qu'ils soient officiels ou privés*' and in the magazine, *Sept-Jours*, that I directed the British participation with '*une rare efficacité*'.

Although from the beginning the British Pavilion was highly praised by the press, there was some adverse criticism of the design in the architectural journals. Sir Basil Spence was very sensitive to this. We must have spent many hours in which he agonised over it endlessly and I did my best to reassure him. His sensitivity and vulnerability were astonishing in an architect of so solid a reputation. Of course, we also talked about his work elsewhere, including the native town of both of us, Edinburgh. I told him that I thought that the destruction of George Square by the University had been a sad act of vandalism. He agreed, but said that he had not been responsible for the destruction. The library was not a bad building in itself, but it should have been built somewhere else.

I suspect, that at least part of the success of our publicity was due to the charm, wit and miniskirts of our thirty hostesses. Dorothy Rogers, quite independently of any influence on my part, was appointed as their chief. I still have a fat album of press cuttings about Expo, which my efficient office kept for me. The hostesses, including Dorothy, frequently enlivened the photographs. One of them, Joanna Woodman, won the title of Miss Expo '67. They were something of a sensation, not only because they were an effervescent bunch of pretty girls, but because the miniskirt was still new and unexpected and was the hallmark of Carnaby Street, then the height of fashion.

Each participating country had a national day when they were expected to give an open-air show in an arena which held 10,000 people. We had something of a crisis during the preparations because of a probably inevitable clash between Ian Hunter in London and Sean Kenny who was working with us in Montreal. Hunter had been the Director of the Edinburgh Festival and of others in Bath, Brighton, London and Adelaide. He was a little inclined to stand on his dignity. Kenny was a highly successful theatre director and stage designer. He was Irish, unconventional and impulsive. At one point, Hunter sent a letter to Kenny which in effect sacked him from the project. Kenny sent a copy to me with as a covering note: 'This two-faced bastard has the gall to write a letter like this. It makes me sick.' Still, somehow the show went ahead.

Most countries did the expected thing, national dances and so forth. Ours was in the same spirit as the pavillion itself, highly irreverent and more mocking than celebratory. I have a copy of a list of the original requirements of the producer, John Wells, which called for 100 Coldstream guards, 50 sailors, 60 girls, a great variety of vehicles and of animals, including a lion and an elephant. We did not go quite as far as that, but very nearly. The public and the press were delighted. *Le Devoir* said (in English): 'Britannia rules the waves? But no, Britannia waives the rules.' In this, and in other ways, there was no doubt that the two most popular participants were the British and the Czechs, who were then demonstrating the first signs of their emancipation from Soviet control. We had very close relations with them.

During the whole period of the exhibition, from 28th April to 27th October, the main job of Oliver and myself was the welcoming of an endless succession of the sort of visitors who expect, and usually receive, special treatment, unlike the millions in the queues. We had many heads of states and governments, countless ministers, artists and celebrities of all kinds. Most of them made a tour of the Pavilion and then had something to eat or drink with us in a room designed by Basil Spence for this purpose. It looked something like the interior of a large coffin with black walls and ceilings, but was brightened by the presence of an admirable girl, Amanda (and never was a name more appropriate) Mills.

Our first such visitor, in fact only two or three days after the opening, was Haile Selassie, the Emperor of Ethiopia, accompanied, not by a lion, but by an ill-tempered and unhouse-trained dog. The one who caused the most disturbance was General de Gaulle who a day or two after he had called on us made his celebrated *Vive le Québec Libre* speech. He spent only about ten minutes with us, but long enough for him to demonstrate that he had been briefed with some idea of our previous careers. Shortly after he left, someone from the staff telephoned our office to say that a dreadful thing had occurred. The General had lost his fountain pen which was of great sentimental value to him. He had used it to write his memoirs and sign treaties. It had last been seen in the hands of Paul Scott. Now it was true that I had handed him a pen to sign the visitors' book, but it was one which we kept for this purpose. Before I could be informed of this alarming accusation, the French telephoned again with profuse apologies. The pen had been found on the floor of his car.

The Queen and Prince Phillip arrived in the St Lawrence by royal yacht on a day of heavy rain, which made the inspection of the guard of honour something of an ordeal for all concerned. The Prince, like most of our visitors, was clearly intrigued by our hostesses and was a little irritated to be called away for his next engagement. Princess Margaret on another occasion was alarmingly flirtatious on a long, dark escalator in the Pavilion. We had no visits from American Presidents, but from the Presidential wives, Jacqui Kennedy and

Lady Bir d Johnson. They were both opposite to my expectations. Mrs Kennedy was subdued and uncommunicative. Her most frequent remark was 'gosh'. Mrs Johnson was bright, responsive and full of intelligent curiosity. She gave me a pen inscribed with her name, which I still have. Among other American visitors the most startling was the pop pianist, Liberace, who had a large wrist watch in the shape of a grand piano, encrusted with diamonds. He was a more agreeable guest than I expected, anxious to please and more apologetic than demanding. He gave the impression that he too thought that his stage personality was ridiculous. The best conversationalist was J K Galbraith. I reminded him of his remark, which was happy to confirm and elaborate, that the Jews were the only serious competitors to the eminence of the people he prefers to call the Scotch.

British ministers came from time to time. James Callaghan, then Chancellor of the Exchequer, came in September 1966 before the Pavilion was complete. The main purpose of his visit was for a meeting of the Commonwealth Finance Ministers, but he spent the first day on our affairs. They were, after all, costing a lot of government money. I met him at the airport and as we drove into Montreal he asked me to tell him about the situation. He did not appear to take very much interest, but when he was interviewed for the radio later in the day, he made all the appropriate points with accuracy and conviction. Tony Benn, who was then called Anthony Wedgwood Benn, Minister of Technology, came in May 1967. I spent the best part of a day going round the whole exhibition with him. His boyish enthusiasm and energy were inexhaustible and the escorting journalists soon abandoned the pursuit. Edward Heath, whom I had encountered when he was a junior minister in the Foreign Office, veered as usual between pomposity and bonhomie.

Henry Moore came for the installation of his sculpture, 'Locking Piece' on a cold windy day in March. Yehudi and Hephzibah Menuhin and Jacqueline du P ré and the Bath Festival Orchestra spent a week with us in June. Menuhin was full of the joy of life and infinitely patient and helpful. In the same month Margot Fonteyn and Rudolf Nureyev came with the Royal Ballet. They arrived together and we had a long and hilarious conversation in the VIP room, hilarious because of Nureyev who was in sparkling form. He spoke, I suspect as an affectation, a peremptory sort of basic English. 'Girl,' (this to Amanda) 'Man wants drink.' He was eloquent about the hardship inflicted on the dancers by the demands of this North American tour. 'These poor girls are treated like slaves. Their little toes all bleed.'

Laurence Olivier was so protected by his staff at the National Theatre in London that we had great difficulty in breaking through to speak to him. When we at last succeeded, he was the opposite of his minders, extremely friendly and co-operative. He came to Montreal in April to inaugurate the World Festival jointly with Jean-Louis Barrault. He came back in October with his company to end the Festival with *Othello*, *Love for Love* and *A Flea in Her Ear*. His departure from Montreal on one of his visits coincided Alastair's departure, alone, at the end of his school holidays. It was obvious from Alastair's behaviour at the airport that he was unhappy to leave. Olivier evidently noticed. I heard afterwards that he left his first class compartment to come and sit beside Alastair to cheer him up.

Olivier agreed on his first visit to open our British Bookshop, although, he said, he was the worst possible choice because he was illiterate. The shop was run by Louis Melzack who became one of my closest friends in Montreal. He had arrived in Montreal as a penniless immigrant from Eastern Europe and began by selling second-hand books from a barrow in the street. From this he had become the owner of a chain of beautifully designed bookshops. He was even prouder of the fact that his son had not only become a professor at Oxford, but the lover of the English actresses, Helen Mirren.

At that time, an English girl of seventeen, Twiggy, so called because she was so thin that she was almost invisible, was probably the most famous of fashion models. She too turned up in the VIP room with her manager, called, presumably by his own invention, Justin De Villeneune. She was refreshingly natural and unspoilt, although she was followed by crowds of screaming teenagers wherever she went. She was particularly thrilled by the fact that she had flown from New York in a private jet.

It must be apparent from all that I have described that the British participation in Expo '67 represented a strongly English view of Britishness, perhaps in fact it was the last successful manifestation of old-fashioned Britishness, even if it was tempered by Carnaby Street. Naturally, I did my best to introduce a more balanced view. Charles Greville in the *Scottish Daily Mail* of 20th December 1966 reported an interview with me in what they called my 'glass-walled office on the 23rd floor of Montreal's swishest skyscraper'. He said that I was 'campaigning rather shamelessly for Scotland' and had advocated a separate Scottish Pavilion. That was fair comment. I had no control over the contents of the British Pavilion which was designed in London. The best I could do, apart from putting in a word for Scotland when suitable opportunities presented themselves, was to recommend a change in practice in any future events of this kind. I suggested a passage for the final report and I have come across a copy of the draft in my papers.

Britain / *Grande-Bretagne*

In accordance with current policy, our Pavilion was named 'Britain' although 'United Kingdom' is not only constitutionally correct but more familiar to Canadians. This also exposed us to the difficulty of having to name it 'Grande-Bretagne' in French, to distinguish it from Brittany, provoking inevitably the question 'why is the country great in French and not in English?'

More important than the name is the question of general approach and presentation. For simplicity, the contents of the Pavilion assumed that there is, and has been for centuries, a homogeneous, political and cultural unit called 'Britain'. This is, of course, not true and many of our visitors knew it. We had many questions about how Scotland, Wales and Northern Ireland fitted into the general concept. All of the constituent parts of the United Kingdom were represented in the Pavilion, but there was no specific reference to their existence. Particularly in Canada, where Scottish influence especially is so strong, this was a pity. In future exhibitions of the kind, we might have a more interesting and varied as well as more honest approach, if we were to pay more attention to the diversity of the United Kingdom than to a mythical uniformity.

The response of the Central Office of Information was to say that of course I was right, but there was no sign of the recommendation when the final report appeared.

I have to admit, however, that the British Pavilion was extremely popular, with a large queue of people almost all day and every day waiting to get in. It was the virtually unanimous view of both the North American and European press that it was the best among the sixty or so pavilions. Perhaps it was surprising that so many millions of people made the journey to Montreal and were prepared to spend so much time in crowds and in queues. It did not seem to me a very enjoyable occupation. You can learn far more from books than you can from shows of this kind. After all, Governments spend money and effort on their pavilions in order to make propaganda for themselves. I suspect that there is a herd instinct which makes people enjoy crowds and there is a feeling that it must be worth doing, if a lot of other people want to. Basil Spence's design for the building, with a soaring tower and defiant cliffs, seemed to be an evocation of past imperial greatness. To some extent, the interior did the opposite because there was a large element of self-mockery and that perhaps was this reason for its success. Nicholas Taylor, in the *Sunday Times*, for example, remarked that the interior 'explodes into a riot of youthful self-criticism and sexiness'. Perhaps, after all, this pavilion was not so much a celebration of imperial greatness, but a cry of relief that all of that was finished.

Montreal is within easy reach of both ski-ing and sailing. In the winter before the Exhibition opened I went to the Laurentians to ski on most Saturdays and Sundays. For the summer I bought a second-hand sailing boat of the Dragon class and installed her at the Royal St Laurence Yacht Club where there are excellent moorings, club house, garden and swimming pool. The climate of Montreal is one of extremes, hot in summer and very cold in the winter, but the Montrealers have learned how to turn both to advantage.

Towards the end of the Exhibition the Permanent Under-Secretary of the Foreign Office was one of our visitors. 'This has all been a great success,' he said, 'and I am sure that it has been a wonderful experience, but I think that it is time you returned to the normality of diplomacy.' I agreed, but I know that most of the staff felt that Expo had been the high point of their experience and that everything afterwards would be an anti-climax.

While I was in Montreal I was offered the CMG, known to the wags as 'Call Me God', which is given to Counsellors in the Diplomatic Service more or less as a matter of routine. I did not decline, which was a bit feeble, but I arranged for it to be sent by post so that I did not have to go to the Palace.

Bill Oliver wrote to me afterwards to say, 'In my view, the success of the British Pavilion was a large measure due to your tenacity in the twelve to eighteen months before Expo started. And the FO have this in writing.' That was kind of him, but I think that the credit was due to the designers of the interior and to the friendliness and intelligence of the young men and women of our staff.

Rudolf Nureyev and Margot Fonteyn with Paul Scott in the British Pavilion, Expo '67, Montreal

CHAPTER 13
Vienna
1967 – 1971

We left Montreal in December 1967, and after leave arrived in Vienna early in 1968. I was the commercial Counsellor and the deputy head of the Post. The Ambassador, Sir Anthony Rumbold, was a tenth baronet and elegant and aristocratic looking, Eton and Magdalen. You might therefore expect to find him a diplomat of the old school, stuffy, a little pompous, confident of his own importance and somewhat reactionary in his views. Tony was not in the least like that. He was tolerant and open-minded and his own tastes tended towards the avant-garde. Arthur Koestler, of *Darkness at Noon* and *Arrow in the Blue*, was one of his friends who came to stay in the Embassy. He was on very good terms too with Bruno Kreisky, the Social Democrat who became Chancellor of Austria in 1970. Conversation in Rumbold's Embassy covered all subjects, periods and places and was never dull.

In other respects, appointment to the Embassy in Vienna was for me a return with a vengeance to conventional diplomacy, which is probably more at home there than in anywhere else in the world. After all, many of its conventions and rules were established at the Congress of Vienna. As the capital of what had been a great empire and one of the three or four major world powers, Vienna is full of baroque palaces. Government departments and Embassies are mostly housed in such places, and something of their grandeur rubs off on the occupants. At the same time, memories of the Soviet occupation were still recent and Vienna was close to Hungary and Czechoslovakia, then still very much parts of the Soviet Bloc. East-West tensions were never far away. It was an appropriate setting for the Strategic Arms Limitation Talks (SALT) between the Soviet Union and the United States.

Shortly after our arrival Rumbold gave a reception to introduce us to colleagues from the other embassies. I remember one of the Americans saying, 'welcome to the nineteenth century'. There was a sense in which he was right. Vienna had still not recovered from the war and occupation and it was shabby, run-down and depressed. In many ways it was still recognisably the Vienna of the film of Graham Greene's novel, *The Third Man*. This had advantages too, because it still had many of the graces and conveniences of the past, from the grand to the trivial. You came across so many references to the empire of the past, 'K and K' – Kaiserlich and Könlich – royal and imperial, and to the Emperor Franz Josef himself that you half expected to see him in his carriage, driving out of the Hofburg. The director of the great art collection, the Kunsthistoriche Museum, one of my favourite places, complained to me one day at an Embassy reception of the damage that the fashionable stiletto heels were doing to the gallery floors. 'Of course, you would not have that trouble in London,' he said. 'Why not?' 'Because you still have a Queen.'

A multiplicity of small shops and individual craftsmen still survived. When the Shah of Persia wanted to find people who could build him an Imperial coach, he could not find them in London, but he did in Vienna. Similarly, there were men there who were able to repair mediaeval chainmail damaged in the flooding of the River Arno in Florence. I met and became friendly with a man who had been a foreign correspondent or a secret agent in Moscow (a bit of both, I suspect) who had become so paralysed that he could move few parts of his body apart from his head. That did not stop him running the family business from a wheelchair, which he could control, along with a dictaphone, telephone and such like, by movements of his neck. The business had supplied the metal parts of horse harness for the cavalry of the Imperial army. Since there was no longer much demand for such things, they turned with great success to ski-bindings. When I was on leave in Edinburgh, my wrist watch stopped working. I took it to one of our best watch repairers and asked it it could be repaired. They took it away to look at it and came back to say that it could be done, but they had so much work that it would take about a month. I said that I would have to take it back as I was returning to Vienna in a few days. When I got there, I took it to a small, dusty shop inhabited by one old and bent man in the same street as the offices of the Embassy. He took the watch away to his back shop and in about a couple of minutes he came back and handed it to me. 'Can't you fix it?' I asked. 'Oh yes, it is perfectly all right now, it only needed the tightening of a screw.'

Of course, Vienna is one of the great cities of the world, rich in history and civilisation, the City of Mozart, Beethoven, the Strausses and Mahler, of Klimt, Schiele and Kokoschka, of Kraus and Musil and of Sigmund Freud. It is a city of endless drama and fascination. I do not suppose that anyone can visit it without wanting to come back. It is an addiction and one which modifies the personality of anyone who experiences it. It was a great privilege to live there.

Still, like everything else in life, it had its negative side. Tales were rife in the diplomatic community of encounters with intolerance and interference in their private affairs. Mothers were always being stopped in the streets and told that their children were wearing too many or too few clothes. There were more disturbing stories, too, of instances of racial prejudices and extremism of the right. 'We should never forget,' Rumbold once said to me, 'that the father of the charming ski instructor was probably a captain in the SS, and perhaps a guard at a concentration camp.'

The shadow of Naziism and the war was never far away, although the Austrians had been remarkably successful in somehow representing themselves as one of the victims, instead of one of the perpetrators. To some extent, they were partly one and partly the other, although the newsreel coverage of Hitler's arrival in Vienna certainly suggests that there were plenty of enthusiasts to greet him. During one of my periods as Chargé D'Affaires I was invited to attend a celebration of the liberation of a notorious concentration camp, Mauthausen, which is close to Linz. A monument was to be unveiled and survivors from several countries, mainly from eastern Europe were to attend. Some British parachutists had been among the victims. Clearly, I had to attend, but it was an experience which I dreaded because I was afraid that the emotional response would be overwhelming. It had been the scene of brutality beyond belief. Many men had been worked to death in a quarry and shot if they staggered in carrying stones up a steep path. Others, especially Russians, had simply been starved to death. In fact, it was a humbling and deeply moving experience. The survivors, many in their concentration camp clothes, were dignified and restrained. The speeches did not dwell on the horrors of the past, but on a determination that such deeds should not be seen again.

As we were driving to Mauthausen, my driver told me that he had grown up in the village during the war. Many of the atrocities had been perfectly visible, including shootings on the 'stair of death'. One of their neighbours had been a German officer who spent his days in the camp and returned every evening to the bosom of his adoring and apparently perfectly normal and civilised family. That, of course, is one of the paradoxes, that people who seem to be normal and decent, even kind and generous, can also be involved in acts of atrocious brutality. For most of the time that I was in Vienna Kurt Waldheim, afterwards Secretary General of the United Nations, was Foreign Minister. He was a model of courteous and civilised conduct and a thoughtful and attentive host. In 1986 he was elected as President of Austria, but at that time there was a great deal of controversy about his activities as an intelligence officer in Greece and Yugoslavia during the war. It was alleged that he must have known about atrocities for which his commanding general was executed as a war criminal.

When I first arrived in Vienna I stayed in a flat in the centre of the old town which was rented from an English singer in the Opera. For the arrival of Celia and the children I was lucky enough to find a wonderfully dramatic flat. It was a penthouse in a modern building surrounded by a terrace, but it was on the corner of Rotenturm Strasse and the Stephans Platz, immediately opposite the Cathedral. From our terrace you felt that you could almost touch the gargoyles. I used to walk to the Embassy through the old town and the Stadtpark. This flat too was rented from a singer, Peter Alexander, whom I never met, but who was regarded, apparently, as Austria's and the German-speaking world's, answer to Frank Sinatra. He wrote to me politely and sent some of his records.

Vienna as a setting rose admirably to the demands of a State visit in 1969 by the Queen and Duke of Edinburgh. It is a place where nostalgia for the past is palpable and now they had an excuse to put the great imperial palaces to the sort of use for which they were intended. We had dinner in the Hofburg with players from the Vienna Philharmonic playing Mozart in the musicians' gallery. We ate off gold plates and a dinner service which had been a gift from a Tsar of Russia to an Emperor of Austria. There were real wax candles, profusely melting in the gold candelabra. We had a late night reception in Schonbrunn, a luncheon (it could hardly be called lunch) in the Belvedere and a reception for Commonwealth citizens in the Musikverein.

Such an event, of course, needs a lot of preparation and some delicate negotiation with the host government. Officials from the Palace came out from London once or twice to help with this. They had a cautious and circuitous approach to the potentially embarrassing question of the exchange of presents. Eventually, the Austrians revealed that they proposed to give the Queen a replica of the Benvenuto Cellini salt cellar, one of the treasures of the Kunsthistorische Museum. The Palace official, with elaborate circumlocution, let it be understood that Her Majesty would really like a set of the Maissen figures of the horses of the Spanish Riding School. (As a rare privilege, Princess Anne was allowed to ride one of these horses during the visit, and the royal party included the stud farm on their tour.) But when it came to the point, it was the Cellini piece, and a very fine thing indeed, which the Austrians presented. Quite right too.

There was also a little problem over an opera performance. The Palace did not want it in the programme, because the Queen apparently does not like opera. To the Austrians a State visit without a gala opera performance was unthinkable. Here there was a compromise. There would be a night at the opera, but it would be a light piece, *Fledermaus* in fact. After the performance we had the traditional supper party in Sacher's hotel behind the opera house, a place still redolent of tales of wild parties with cavalry officers and gipsy dancers. The stars were brought in to join us at the stage of coffee and liqueurs. A bit condescending, I thought, like a gracious gesture to the servants or tenants. Still the singers were a jovial lot and soon dispelled the restraint. A day or two later, I found myself standing with the Queen during some lull in the proceedings. To make conversation (which is against the rules, I suppose) I made some remark about this episode. 'Oh, yes,' she said, 'these opera singers are really quite human.'

At this time, and perhaps still, there was a tendency to put emphasis on the commercial work of Embassies, that is to say the help which they give to exporters. Partly this is a reflection of Britain's decline from the status of a Great Power. If you no longer have worldwide power and influence, do you need an elaborate structure of diplomatic missions? Do you have to keep in close touch with political developments everywhere so that you can intervene when you see the need? But, if you can say that you are helping the British economy and balance of payments by promoting exports, that is tangible and persuasive. In any case, in matters of major contracts for capital developments, you may well want to make a high level approach to governments and that is the stuff of diplomacy. Even State visits are justified by the argument that they help exports.

In Vienna, I became the head of the post in the absence of the Ambassador, but I was also appointed as Commercial Counsellor and Consul General. There was a consular section in another building which handled that side of things with perfect competence and did not need my intervention. Much of my time was therefore taken up with commercial questions. I had little instinctive interest in such matters. In fact, I have never entirely lost the feeling that selling things for more than you paid for them is a form of cheating. I regard advertising with a mixture of distaste and derision. It was not for such things that I had joined the diplomatic service. Still you have to face reality and it is possible to become interested in almost anything, if you make the effort.

Although Austria had not fully recovered from the war and occupation, it had an economy which was expanding at an increasing speed. In contrast to the British experience at that time, it was a country which enjoyed a high degree of industrial peace; there had been no strike of any consequence since the war. This was partly due to the effective machinery which they had to settle wages and working conditions by a body in which the unions, the employers and the government were all represented. Many Austrians told me that the real reason was that Austria was such a small country that all the people in these meetings knew one another. They had usually been at school together and had a strong sense of common purpose. They agreed in fact with David Hume's belief that small countries are the most satisfactory form of government. I have no doubt that this is true. For the most part it seemed to be that the negative features of Austrian life were a hangover from the days when it was at the head of a large empire; the positive side was the success that it was achieving as a small country, not much larger than Scotland.

Since the Austrian economy was so buoyant, it was an obvious target for export promotion. We had a special office in Vienna to organise a blatant sales promotion, called a British Week, in October 1968. Shops were persuaded to mount displays of British goods and there were the usual gimmickry of the Edinburgh Police Pipe Band, London buses, beefeaters and bobbies. Similar affairs were held on a smaller scale in several towns all over Austria. I see in a cutting from the Board of Trade *Journal* of 12 July 1968, which has survived among my papers, that I am said to have addressed an audience of more than a thousand people at the end of such a week in Dornbirn. There is also a cutting from the *Financial Times* of 28 April 1971 which says that there has been a 'veritable breakthrough in British exports to Austria' and it attributes this in the first instance to 'the useful work performed by the commercial department of the British Embassy'. I also came across a copy of a letter which Geoffrey Knight, the chairman of the British Aircraft Corporation sent in June 1970 to Denis Greenhill, the Permanent Under-Secretary at the Foreign and Commonwealth Office:

> Dear Sir Denis,
> I am sure that, from time to time, you must receive letters from disgruntled businessmen dissatisfied with the services provided by the Posts in various parts of the world.
> I thought, therefore, that you might be cheered to hear from me of the wonderful job that Paul Scott, Chargé d'Affaires in Vienna, has been doing to assist us in promoting the sale of the BAC One-Eleven in Austria. He has done, and is doing, a really magnificent job for us and it is probably no exaggeration to say that, if it were not for him, we would already have lost the competition to the McDonnell-Douglas company of America.
> Yours sincerely,
> Geoffrey Knight

The trouble with this sort of thing is that I fear it suggested to the FCO that I had a particular aptitude for commercial work, which was not in the least my own view of the matter.

I went home to Edinburgh as often as I could, especially during the Festival. In 1970 we went for a short visit to Venice by train from Vienna and my mother came out from Edinburgh to join us. Incredibly, such were the limits of prewar and wartime travel, and I had been occupied elsewhere since then, this was the first time that I had been to Italy. I realised at once that James Boswell was right. It was indeed the 'Land of Felicity! True seat of all elegant delight!'

Sometimes kindred spirits reacted to my paintings by Peploe and Gillies. One of them was Joe Grimond, the former leader of the Liberal

Party. He told me that he too had a collection of Scottish paintings and invited me to come and see them (which I was sorry to say I never managed to do). We talked a lot about Scotland and found that we had many ideas and reactions in common. He said that he had been to Brussels and had talked to senior people in the European Commission. One of them had said that their vision for the future of Scotland was that it should become one of the few remaining wildernesses for the moral and intellectual refreshment of tourists. 'In that case,' Grimond had replied, 'I find that my enthusiasm for British membership has suddenly evaporated.'

Although I enjoyed life in Vienna and the excursions to the ski slopes in the winter and to the castles and churches in the summer, there were times when my hunger for Scotland became almost irresistible. I happened to notice an advertisement in *The Economist* in October 1969 for the job of General Manager of the development corporation of the new town of Cumbernauld. I sent in an application and nominated Basil Spence and James Henderson as referees. Both of them replied that they would be happy to do what they could; but from Cumbernauld I had no response whatever. AG Macdonell in *England, Their England* said that he found after World War I that the ability to direct the fire of a battery of eighteen-pounder guns was not regarded by employers as a useful qualification. I think that they have the same attitude towards diplomacy. The profession on the whole has a bad press. People assume that we pass the time in an endless sequence of receptions, lunch and dinner parties and even balls and are therefore disqualified for the hard grind of real work.

My son, Alastair, was somewhat rebellious in his early years and, in particular refused to thole boarding schools. An attempt to place him in Fettes was a complete failure; he simply ran away. Celia therefore went back to Sussex to look after him while he went to day school. Even so, I had some alarming letters from Celia's father saying he was beyond control. Catharine was no such problem. I am happy to say that both have become model and irreproachable citizens.

Towards the end of 1969 I had a brief and delightful encounter with an uninhibited, vivacious and beautiful girl. Angela Acland, who was working for a time in the Embassy. She would come away for a weekend with only a toothbrush as her luggage. Her next post was Peking from which she wrote some interesting letters. She was a relative of some kind, a cousin I think, of Anthony Acland with whom I shared a room in the Foreign Office and is now the Provost of Eton.

It was also in Vienna that I became involved in one of the major emotional entanglements of my life. Carolyn Sinclair arrived at the Embassy as a Third Secretary in 1970. She was then about 26, as bright as a spring morning and she had beautiful long red hair. Her mind was alert and sparkling, but she was also remarkably efficient in running such humdrum things as her domestic life and her clothes. She had the ability to carry off some very dramatic garments, such as a long yellow cloak. I once went with her to the diplomatic gallery in the Austrian Parliament and was conscious that all the eyes in the chamber were, not on the speaker, but on her. Beneath the surface glitter, she had serious intellectual interests and in many respects we agreed. She was, after all, Scottish and had been at school in Glasgow and Edinburgh University. Conversation with her could be challenging and intense, but it always sharpened and cleared the mind. From the moment when I first met her, I knew that I was enraptured. We were soon spending virtually every evening together. Our association lasted for the next seven years, on both sides of the Atlantic.

Paul Scott with the Duke of Edinburgh during the State Visit to Austria 1969

Not all fun in the diplomatic life – Paul Scott (left) on duty as Sir Peter
Wilkinson presents his credentials as British Ambassador, Vienna, June 1970

CHAPTER 14

Montreal,
International Institute of Strategic Studies,
European Negotiations
1971-1978

O n 9 November 1970 the Ambassador in Vienna had a personal telegram from the Head of Personnel Department which he passed to me. It read,

> Please now tell Paul Scott about promotion and his posting to
> Montreal. You may tell him that this appointment is recognition
> of his high qualities in respect of both political and commercial
> work. In present circumstances Montreal is a demanding post but
> we think that both Paul and his wife have all the attributes to
> make a success of it.

The reasons for this flattery and the reference to 'present circumstances' was obvious enough. I was being asked to take the place of Jasper Cross, the head of the British Government Office in Montreal. He had been kidnapped on 5th October by the FLQ (*Front pour la Liberation de Québec*) and was still in captivity in some unknown place.

Since the organisation which had kidnapped Cross had also held a leading member of the Quebec Government, Pierre Laporte, and had killed him, there was a serious worry about the outcome. Happily, Jasper was released, without physical injury, on 3rd December and in exchange the kidnappers were allowed to fly to Cuba. When I met him in London he seemed to be quite unaffected by what must have been a desperate ordeal.

This whole affair was, of course, a major political crisis in Canada. The Canadian Government were widely criticised for over-reaction by adopting the War Measures Act which imposed martial law in Quebec. Many people who were in favour of the independence of Quebec, but not of the use of violence to obtain it, were held for some time under arrest. Over-reaction was to be expected in a country like Canada, law-abiding and with no tradition of political violence, which was suddenly faced with such a blatant challenge.

I did not arrive in Montreal until May 1971. By that time, the atmosphere seemed again to be perfectly normal. I was to stay in the same house as Jasper Cross which was a large, solid nineteenth century building in Redpath Crescent, overlooking the city and on the edge of the central hill and public park, Mount Royal, which in location, if not shape, reminded me of the Calton Hill and Arthur's Seat in Edinburgh. During his celebrated visit to Montreal in 1967, Charles de Gaulle had stayed in the same street. Concealed electric buttons, to summon the police, had been installed at various hidden spots in the house, and were liable to be pressed by accident. A police car with two policemen were stationed permanently outside. They did not follow me about, for which I was grateful. You might say that they were guarding the house and not me, but I never felt that I was under any threat.

This was not just complacency. It had become apparent that the FLQ was a very small organisation and that there was virtually no support for its methods. Public revulsion against kidnapping or assassination was so strong and so obvious that it was clearly counter-productive and it was highly improbable that anyone would try it again. People went out of their way to welcome me and I had countless messages of apology and regret for what had happened to Jasper Cross. That is not to say that many Quebecers had abandoned their desire for independence. Support for it continued to grow during my four years in Montreal.

The writer Billy Kay remarked recently that an interesting subject of enquiry would be the tendency of Scots to sympathise with national liberation movements in other countries. He mentioned Boswell in Corsica and Byron in Greece, and the Congress Party in India, which was founded by Allan Octavian Hume, the son of an MP for Montrose. Similarly in Quebec, many of us respond to the force of the arguments of the *Parti Québécois*, although of course I was in no position to show any partiality on the question, one way or the other. I was only an interested, but detached and silent observer. One aspect which surprised me was the passionate resistance of many Canadians, probably a majority, in the rest of Canada to any idea of Quebec becoming independent. Canada is a huge country and it would still be huge without Quebec. It would be better to have a contented, independent, but friendly neighbour, than a restless, unhappy province.

That is true of Scotland and England as well, and indeed there are many points of similarity, but also of difference, between the cases of Scotland and Quebec. Scotland, unlike Quebec, is a country with a long history of independence, but Quebec has for a long time had far greater political autonomy than Scotland. That is still true, even after the restitution of a Scottish Parliament, but with limited power, in 1999.

In Quebec the main symbol of a distinct identity, and therefore the major political issue, is the language. Scotland has two distinct languages, Gaelic and Scots, but both have slowly retreated in the face of the encroachment of English. Both of them have a long and distinguished literary history which continues to the present. The French spoken in Quebec has a very different history. In its origin it is provincial French of the seventeenth and eighteenth centuries for speech in overseas territories always tends to be more conservative than in the country of origin. It has also come under the influence of North American English. The result is a speech which is very different from modern metropolitan French, but it has been much more successful than either Gaelic or Scots in surviving as the language of everyday use. It has been derided, even in Quebec, as a vulgar, degenerate dialect, the speech of the poor or uneducated. But there are people, even at times the intellectuals and the teachers, who have taken the same attitude to Scots, in spite of its impressive pedigree. So this is a further point of mutual understanding and sympathy between Scotland and Quebec. In recent years, Quebec French, like Scots, has enjoyed a resurgence in its literary use, particularly for poetry and drama. The plays of Michel Tremblay have been successful in Scotland in translations into Scots by Martin Bowman and Bill Findlay.

In the magazine, *Maclean's* (the Canadian equivalent of the *New Statesman* or *Spectator*) the novelist, Hugh MacLennan published an article in the issue of October 1973, 'Scotland's Fate: Canada's Lesson'. His argument was that Canada was liable to be absorbed by the United

States as Scotland had been by England. In the course of this he said that Scotland had failed 'because she never discovered a single constructive idea that might have made her national survival of value to the rest of mankind.' It was very different in Canada. 'Though few Canadians dare believe it, Canada today may quite possibly be the best-liked nation in the world.'

In fact, I found in Canada that many Canadians shared this idea of their popularity. It comes, I think, from the reaction of foreigners when they discover that they are not American. Great Powers are always unpopular because they tend to throw their weight around and irritate other people by their pretentions. Oddly enough, since MacLennan was discussing the similarities between Scotland and Canada, this is something else which they have in common. Scots often find they are welcomed when people discover they are not English. That is for the same reason, even if England is now a Great Power only in memory.

I felt that I could not let MacLennan, whom I had met and liked, get away with this allegation about Scotland failing to produce 'constructive ideas'. Since I could not as Consul General engage in public controversy, I wrote an open letter to MacLennan under the name of Patrick Paniter. (He was the secretary for Latin correspondence of James IV, whom I was studying at the time.) I argued that Scotland has always been productive of ideas and many of them have been of great use to the rest of the world. This gave me too an opportunity to suggest, as had appeared to me for some time, that the influence of Scotland was strong in Quebec as well as in the rest of Canada.

> When MacLennan heard people say that 'Canada is the Scotland of North America' were they in fact thinking only of Canada's geographical position, with the United States as Canada's England? Were they not also thinking of the enormous Scottish influence in Canada? The history of Canada is full of Scottish names; there were Scotsmen on both sides in the battle on the Plains of Abraham. The fact that the British troops were largely Scottish Highlanders, who spoke Gaelic and some French, but little English, is one of the reasons why Quebec is still French-speaking. It is also the main reason why Quebec folk music and story is more Scottish than French. The barriers of language and religion have concealed the fact that Quebec and Scotland, and therefore Quebec and the rest of Canada, have more in common than they realise.

The magazine published my letter in an abbreviated form and sent the original to MacLennan. He sent me a charming reply, pleading guilty to an ambiguity in his essay, and ending: 'Thank you again for writing for Scotland. It's a country I love. How could I help it?'

Leaving Vienna had meant, of course, leaving Carolyn who stayed there until October 1973. We had no alternative because membership of the Diplomatic Service involved an obligation to go where and when you were sent. It was difficult for both of us, as was obvious from the long and agonised correspondence which then began. I have only Carolyn's side of it, but she wrote letters of three or four pages every two or three days for all the time we were apart and that was most of it during the next seven years. They would make a book by themselves.

I think that it was this experience of imposed separation which turned Carolyn against the diplomatic life, for she had a great hunger for stability and continuity. Almost as soon as she severed our relationship, she transferred to the Treasury and married a steady Home Civil Servant. She was intellectually bold, but physically timid. She would come to the mountains, but nothing would persuade her to put skis on her feet. Walking securely on the paths in the valley was more her style. She appeared to be confident and self-assured, but frustration or criticism, explicit or implied, could create a mood of depression, when she badly needed reassurance. Once when I was reading Hardy's *Jude the Obscure*, I read out a phrase in the preface: 'the slight, pale, "batchelor girl" – the intellectualised, emancipated bundle of nerves.' She wanted to know if I thought that the description applied to her. Well, it did in a way, but at the same time almost always, except in rare crises of emotion, she was the most delightful, entertaining and stimulating of companions.

Somehow or other, we managed during these seven years to have many holidays together in various parts of the world, the north of Italy, Klosters (at least twice), New York State, the Scottish Borders, the Dordogne, usually in pleasant, rented country cottages.

Where, you might ask, was Celia? She had established the pattern of dividing her time between my post and England, either in her father's house in Sussex or our flat in Buckingham Gate in London. The purpose of this, ostensible or real, was to help with the education of Alastair and Catharine.

The first of these holidays with Carolyn, a few months after my posting to Montreal, was memorable for two reasons. First of all it was my introduction, so late in life, to the glories of Italy, apart from the most splendid of them all, Venice, which I had seen before. I met Carolyn in Austria and we drove in her car across the Alps to that whole succession of splendid towns, Verona, Montova, Parma, Bologna, Ravenna, Ferrara, Florence. The historic centres of all of them, and many more which I saw in subsequent years, are visions of the perfection of urban life. As virtually everywhere, the surroundings are a sad mixture of industrial squalor and uninspired architecture, but even that cannot destroy the impact of the heart of these places, with more of beauty to the square yard than anywhere else in the world, one of the greatest accomplishments of human genius.

The second reason why it was memorable was because of the shock when Carolyn told me, almost as soon as we met, and in circumstantial detail, about an affair she was having with an Austrian diplomat who was working in the Ministry. She did not seem to imagine that this would disturb me or make any difference to our relationship and indeed she appeared to take pleasure in lingering over the salacious details. In the long run, it did not make any difference and, of course, I had no right to object. Either about that time, or a little later, I too was having an affair. This was with Yvonne Delaney, a commercial artist working for a Montreal department store, who was very affectionate and as placid as Carolyn was volatile. I do not think that I was honest, or reckless, enough to tell Carolyn about that.

Apart from these activities and the emotional conflicts they engendered, Montreal was full of diverse pleasures, theatres and concert halls and the excitement of a society re-inventing itself, sailing from the Royal St Lawrence Yacht Club in the summer, and skiing in the Laurentians in the winter. I enjoyed the hospitality of the Library of McGill University and took classes in French at the *Université de Montreal*. I gave the occasional lecture, or talk rather, in French or English.

I passed the higher standard Foreign Office examination in French, as I also did at other times in German and Italian. It was the original practice for the Foreign Office to pay an allowance when you passed these examinations, which involved complex translations in both directions, but only while you were in the country concerned.

We had many visitors, private and official. Among the former my very first girlfriend from Edinburgh days, Suzanne Cameron (now Sinclair) and the star of many Saltire Society performances of Scottish verse, Ian Gilmour. From the many official visitors two remain in my mind for quite different reasons, Lord Thorneycroft because of his highly entertaining and indiscrete account of intrigue and back-stabbing in the higher ranks of the Conservative Party, and Norman Wylie, the Lord Advocate at the time, because he brought with him his wife and two officials from the Scottish Office and a thoroughly Edinburgh atmosphere. One of the best conversationalists was Lord Ritchie-Calder, at one time Professor of International Relations at Edinburgh.

In August 1974, when it was about time for me to leave Montreal, the Foreign Office wrote to offer me a sabbatical year as a research associate in the International Institute for Strategic Studies in London. The idea was that I should study and write a paper on the political and administrative aspects of the future of defence organisations in Europe, assuming that there would be a greater degree of European integration and that the United States would eventually play a lesser role within NATO.

As a life of thought, research, and writing has always attracted me, I accepted at once. Also, and I am not sure which of the factors was the more influential, it meant that I should again join Carolyn who had left Vienna for the Foreign Office in October 1973. My secondment for this purpose was formally approved by the Foreign Secretary, and the Director of the Institute, Christopher Bertram, wrote to say that he hoped that I could join them in January 1975.

The offices of the Institute were in Adam Street (so-called after Robert Adam) just off the Strand, near Charing Cross Station. They were therefore within easy walking distance of my flat in Buckingham Gate. The Institute was on quite a small scale with nothing elaborate or pretentious about it, just about half a dozen people with one or two supporting staff in a few rooms. We spent our days partly on research into the written sources and partly in meetings, seminars and the like, with the small group of academics from various universities concerned with strategic questions. There was, for example, an international conference in July at St John's College in Oxford and frequent meetings in the Royal Institute of International Affairs in Chatham House.

In due course, I produced a paper, 'European Co-operation for Defence' which argued that the Soviet Union was as anxious as everyone else to avoid nuclear war, but that there was always a risk of an incident, perhaps between the two Germanies or in Yugoslavia, which one of the super-powers interpreted as a threat to their essential interests. In such a case, it was desirable that fighting should be kept on the conventional level as long as possible to allow the maximum opportunity for second thoughts and negotiation. European conventional forces were inadequate for this purpose. There was therefore a dangerous reliance on tactical nuclear weapons which might prompt a Soviet pre-emptive strike. Since, however, there was a natural reluctance on the part of European governments and taxpayers to increase military expenditure, there was a need for a European defence agency for joint procurement to increase standardisation and economies of scale.

The paper was based on the premise that 'the military posture of the Soviet Union, détente or no détente, is becoming steadily more menacing.' Soviet planners were probably saying the same thing about the American bloc. We have all had an almost miraculous escape from a threat of universal destruction.

I was asked to write a version of the paper, 'Beyond the Eurogroup; new developments in European defence', for publication in the journal of the Royal Institute of International Affairs, *The World Today*. As a consequence, Gordon Lee, the Literary Editor of *The Economist*, got in touch with me to invite me to write book reviews and articles. So began an association with the paper which has continued to the present. For some years, I wrote for them a regular page on Scottish books. Later on, and until now, I have covered the Edinburgh Festival each year. Since I enjoyed book reviewing, especially if your are lucky enough to review books about which you want to read anyway, I began to do them also for *The Scotsman*, under a pseudonym until I retired, and I was one of their reviewers for the Edinburgh Festival Fringe for about thirty years, a strange by-product of a paper on European defence. From about the same time also I started to write reviews, essays and stories for *Blackwood's Magazine*, a publication with a great history, but by then, sadly, in its final phase.

Now that I was back in London, I was able to keep much more closely in touch with events in Scotland. Bert Davis, my kindred spirit from Warsaw, had become the Representative of the British Council in Edinburgh. When he retired from the Council, he became the Organising Secretary of the Saltire Society in May 1974. The Society had been founded in 1936, when Scottish cultural confidence had been at a low ebb, with the intention of stimulating its revival. I had been a member since before the war, and an enthusiastic supporter of its recitals of Scottish poetry and music during many Edinburgh Festivals. I was about to become much more closely involved.

In September 1975 and again in September 1977 the Society held a weekend conference in the University of St Andrews, which I was able to attend. The purpose of the conferences was to review policies affecting the intellectual and cultural life of Scotland and consider what should be done in the new situation where a Scottish Parliament or Assembly was established, which most people then thought was likely to happen in the very near future. The rise in the support of the Scottish National Party in the 1970s seemed to make it inevitable. During the second conference, for which I had written a paper on cultural policy, I suggested that the Saltire Society instead of acting alone in making proposals to the future Scottish Government should try to bring together ideas from organisations of all kinds that were active in the cultural life of Scotland. This proposal was adopted and it was agreed that a committee, with Professor John MacQueen as Convener and Bert Davis as Secretary, should begin the process. They wrote to about 180 organisations, statutory, professional and voluntary. This eventually led to the establishment of the Advisory Council for the Arts in Scotland.

The diplomatic career is a life of constant change. Even if you stay in the normal circuit from embassy to embassy, you still change country, political situation and language every three or four years. In addition, you may be asked to do a great variety of different jobs. The disadvantage of all of this is that that you cannot easily maintain friendships over a long period of time. I have often felt that people who spend a lifetime in the same place, among the friends that they made at school and university, are very fortunate. Diplomats have a great variety of brief acquaintances, but few long-term friends. Still, the frequent change of language and all the rest of it perhaps stimulate the mind and help to keep you intellectually fresh and alert. We liked to think so, in any case.

I now moved from the study of nuclear strategy to the negotiation of international agreements about fishing rights. This next job was concerned with the UK presidency of the European Economic Community in the first half of 1977. The Soviet Union, Poland and East Germany had agreed to come to Brussels to discuss the possibility of entering into agreements with the EEC to permit their fishing fleets to have a share of the fishery in EEC waters. Because of the need to preserve stocks of fish against the pressure of modern methods of fishing, all countries had to accept restrictions. The EEC had a department for this purpose with scientific advisors who studied fluctuations of fish stocks and the safe level of permissible catch to allow them to survive. These negotiations with Eastern European had a political as well as an economic significance. Before this, the Soviet bloc had refused to recognise the existence of the EEC and this was the first time that they had agreed to negotiations, which implied recognition.

Negotiations of this kind were normally conducted by the Commission who were always eager to preserve their prerogatives; but the Soviets also had their sensitivities. They were prepared to negotiate with the representatives of sovereign states with whom they had diplomatic relations, but not with the Commission. As a compromise, it was agreed, or at least understood, that the EEC negotiating team would be headed by a representative of the Government holding the Presidency, supported by those of the other member states and of the Commission. This was sailing into uncharted waters. So there I was, leading a team, which I did not control and none of whom I had so far met, with no staff of my own, no brief and no instructions, and on a subject I knew nothing about. In Whitehall they call it 'playing it by ear' or just muddling through. As sometimes happens in such cases, it all came right in the end, and I had valiant support from everyone concerned in Brussels.

During the whole of this time I stayed in London with frequent sorties to Brussels for meetings. As an Assistant Under Secretary of State in the Foreign and Commonwealth office, I attended the Permanent Under-Secretary's meeting every morning. This brought together the Under-Secretaries, who together controlled departments covering every country in the world. It was an opportunity to hear about the latest crisis and to offer ideas. Some of the problems were internal, including the idiosyncracies and ideas of David Owen, who became Minister of State in the Foreign and Commonwealth Office in 1976 and Foreign Secretary in 1977. I met him only a very few times and he was always perfectly friendly and reasonable. Others seemed to have had a different experience.

David Owen presided over the first formal meeting in Brussels with the Soviet delegation on 16 February 1977, and thereafter left it to me to lead for the Presidency, supported by a spokesman for the Commission. The head of the Soviet delegation was the Minister of Fisheries, Aleksander Ishkov, a shrewd and likeable man. He evidently had a great talent for survival. He was then just over 70 and he had been a Soviet Minister since 1938 when he was first appointed a People's Commissar for the Fish Industry. Many of our informal meetings took place over lunch or dinner in the Soviet Embassy. Ishkov was a genial host who delighted to display masses of caviar and other products of his fishing industry. The spokesman for the Commission was an Irish diplomat, who was born in Glasgow, Eamon Gallagher, who was highly supportive and excellent company.

The first round of negotiations reached rapid agreement on principles. On the third day we were able to issue a joint press release and Ishkov and I held a press conference together. I said that both sides shared a common desire to conserve fish stocks and ensure effective control. Our talks had been held in an excellent atmosphere and it had been a pleasure to work with Ishkov. He replied in similar terms and said that he had a sense of satisfaction at the results achieved. This exchange of amiable remarks did not stop Ishkov making a gentle attempt to prise us away a little from our European partners. After the press conference, he said to me privately that the bilateral relationship between Britain and the Soviet Union on fishing questions had always been eminently satisfactory. He thought that there would still be benefit in bilateral discussion based on this tradition of fruitful co-operation. I said that I hoped that this friendly tradition would continue, but on the British side it must now be within the framework of the Community.

This early stage, which was repeated with the Poles and the East Germans, was the easy bit. Several difficulties lay ahead. In the first place, we had to negotiate the substance of the agreements before we could discuss quantities and licences and there we should have to offer less than the East Europeans would like. Then there were some sensitive areas. There was the preamble, which involved formal recognition by the Soviet Union, East Germany and Poland of the EEC. By just participating, this recognition was clearly implied but signature of a formal treaty was a major step.

Another point was less obvious, but more delicate. There was a clause in the draft, which listed the territories of which the Community was comprised. My instructions were to tell the leaders of the Soviet, Polish and East German delegations that this article 'reflected the position of the Community with regard to Berlin', or, in other words, that we considered that West Berlin was part of the territory of the Community as part of West Germany. Ishkov and the others, of course, resisted, usually with the argument that this point had no place in a fishing agreement and that it should be referred to the Heads of Government of the four occupying powers.

Our own internal procedures were inevitably cumbersome since, in preparation for each step, I had to reach agreement in advance with the Commission and their fishing experts and with the delegations of the other eight member states. Here too the Berlin point was the most sensitive, because our West German colleagues were very nervous about it as a potentially explosive political issue. At one of our dinner parties in the Soviet Embassy they thought that Eamon Gallagher had given too much ground to the Soviet point of view. One of their ministers made a formal complaint to Finn Grundelach, the Vice-President of the Commission but I was able to reassure him that there was no real cause for alarm.

Initially, there had been some doubts within the Commission about the propriety of a Presidency representative leading negotiations on a subject which was within their competency. In fact, it worked perfectly smoothly. Usually there were two spokesmen on our side, myself and the Commission representative, first Gallagher and later Simmonet. When he fell ill, the Commission and the member states asked me to act as sole spokesman. By the time our Presidency ended at the end of June all of the agreements with the Eastern European countries, and one with Norway, were close to conclusion.

Living in London and flying to Brussels only as the negotiations required, I had moved from my flat in Buckingham Gate to join Carolyn in her flat in Pimlico. Since we were both working in the Foreign Office and Carolyn's work took her to Brussels quite frequently as well, we were now more constantly together even than we had been in Vienna. Not only our work, but many of our other interests coincided, many of the same books, films and plays and the same ideas about holidays except skiing, but she was tolerant of that. We had a memorable holiday in a rented cottage in the Dordogne.

The only source of tension in this otherwise idyllic relationship was that Carolyn, with her longing for security and permanence in a constantly changing and impermanent world, wanted me to get a divorce and marry her. Many people, and more at that time than now, would think that this was the normal and proper thing to do in the circumstances.

I consulted lawyers and started to move in that direction but I do not think that I put the pressure and urgency behind it that I might have done. I was pulled in two directions. I was certainly infatuated with Carolyn and delighted in her company, intellectually and physically. Of course, I wanted to be with her as constantly and for as long as possible. On the other hand, I felt a certain obligation to Celia as well. She was, after all, the mother of my children and she had supported me in quite difficult conditions in Poland, Bolivia and Cuba. Also, to my regret, she had moved in recent years to more active identity with the Anglican Church and disapproved strongly of divorce. She would probably resist and I did not want to upset her. Then, marriage between two members of the Diplomatic Service would present its own problem. We could hardly expect to be posted together to the same place. We did talk about what we should do when I retired, when the time came, to Edinburgh, to which I was very anxious to return. That would mean commuting frequently to wherever Carolyn might be. Not so difficult, if it was London. But if it was Tokyo?

The Foreign Office precipitated a decision by raising the question of my next posting and offering me an embassy in South America. I said, for obvious reasons, that I would greatly prefer to stay in Europe. They said that the first early vacancy would be Consul-General in Milan and simultaneously Minister for the North of Italy. This was a very tempting offer, but as it soon became apparent, it did not resolve the problem of my future life with Carolyn.

I left for Milan in the autumn of 1977.

CHAPTER 15
Milan and Thoughts of Scotland
1977 – 1980

M y official residence in Milan was the top floor of a building at
51 Corso Venezia which had been the French Embassy to the
Cisalpine republic during the Napoleonic Wars. A plaque on the wall
outside said that Stendhal, as a young officer, had lived there as a
member of the staff. There was a large terrace with a fish pond and a
pergola. The spacious public rooms had marble floors and finely
moulded ceilings. A corridor lined with bookshelves had ample space
for my books. The office in Via San Paolo had no such pretensions. It
was an adequate, but simple, set of rooms in a modern office block,
not far from the Duomo, which is one of the architectural glories of
Milan. The office and the residence were about ten minutes walk apart
and I used to walk in both directions twice a day with no fuss about
security. Kidnappings and assassinations were prevalent in Italy at that
time but, so far at least, foreign diplomats had not been their target.

I was very conscious of the fact that, deservedly or not, I had been
given a truly enviable job. Carolyn, in a letter in May 1978, described
it as 'fifteen minutes work a day and carte blanche to tour the
splendours of perhaps the most splendid country in Europe.' This
was a wild exaggeration, of course. I had enough work in the office to
keep me fairly fully occupied, although the staff in all departments
were admirable and solved more problems than they created. On the
other hand, it was true that I was free, and indeed required, to travel
all over the north of Italy as far as the southern border of Tuscany. I
had consular posts under my supervision in Genoa, Turin, Florence
and Venice. In Venice the Consulate was a handsome, but manageable,
palazzo on the Grand Canal, adjacent to the Accademia and with its
own elegant motor-boat moored at its landing stage. It was my
responsibility also to establish good relations with the Prefects,

provincial and municipal authorities, university Rectors, business and financial leaders, newspapers editors, and the like over the whole area. They were welcoming and generous and had the habit of presenting me with magnificent volumes about the art and architecture of the area. It is no wonder that in notes for a speech which I made soon after I arrived in Italy, I described it as stimulating, exciting, intoxicating, the product of 2000 years of continuous civilisation and a tangible proof of the indestructibility and genius of the human spirit.

These early months of my stay in Italy were, however, over-shadowed by a crisis in my relationship with Carolyn which finally brought it to an end after seven intense and often deeply happy years. As late as January 1976 she told me in a letter, 'I respect and admire you more than any man I have ever known (or woman, I think). That is really what matters. I also happen to love you.' But the crisis developed over a longer time than I at first realised. When I arrived in London from Montreal, towards the end of 1974, Carolyn, who left Vienna in October 1973, was working in the Foreign Office. I still had my flat in Buckingham Gate, but most of the time I was living with her in her flat in Sutherland Street. From time to time I went back to my own place when, for instance, Alastair had to be in London. Although rationally she understood why I had to, this infuriated Carolyn.

Celia's behaviour was unpredictable. She delayed and made difficulties about a divorce. She was liable to appear and make a scene or telephone the Foreign Office to protest. Carolyn described this as living under a sword of Damocles. The idea of an irrational third person intruding without warning in her life was very frightening. Also, at about this time, Carolyn was becoming increasingly disillusioned with the Diplomatic Service. She was working on what was called political co-operation, the beginning of an attempt to move towards a common foreign policy among the member states of the EEC. One might think that this would be an interesting and agreeable job, with frequent opportunities for meetings with intelligent colleagues in various European capitals. Carolyn began to be impatient with what she described as pointless debates over the wording of a string of platitudes that would have no impact whatever on real events. 'The task,' she said in a letter, 'is not really worth doing.'

She was no doubt wrong about this, because it was the inevitably tentative and cautious start of a process which could, in the end, have important consequences. I think that she was trying to justify a decision, which was gradually forming in her mind, to ask for a transfer to the Home Civil Service. It was part of her search for stability, continuity and security. Increasingly she hated uncertainty and the Diplomatic Service, where you never knew where you might go next, was uncertain in the extreme.

Then there was the difference in our attitudes towards Scotland. I have just been reading Antonia Fraser's introduction to her anthology, *Scottish Love Poems*. She writes of the wealth and passion of Scottish poetry about love, but also says that he has come to the conclusion that 'the strongest passion of all in the Scottish breast is for Scotland itself.' I think that is true of many Scots, including myself, but there are others, and Carolyn tended in that direction, who go to the other extreme.

HJ Paton, who taught philosophy at St Andrew's and Oxford, wrote a book which was a plea for Scottish independence, *The Claim of Scotland*, published in 1967. In it he discusses the English habit of denigrating Scotland: 'If you hold it a blemish to depart from the English norm, you will see many blemishes in Scotland.' I have no doubt that Paton came across many examples of this attitude in Oxford for it has long been prevalent there. He says that many Scots have been affected by it, which is not surprising because they have either been educated in England, or in Scotland to an English pattern, and broadcasting spreads the same influence. Paton says that some Scots, and he is sorry to say especially women, 'become almost venomous in their contempt for Scotland's past and present.' The American sociologist, Michael Hechter, in his *Internal Colonialism* of 1975 discussed the relationship between England and Scotland, Wales and Ireland. His conclusion was that the metropolitan centre denigrated the culture of dependent territories, to undermine their will to resist and used 'peripheral élites' to assist in the process. The Scots who despise Scotland are, consciously or unconsciously, part of this periphery.

This denigration was not a consequence of deliberate government policy, but a natural consequence of the wealth and dominant political power of England. This encouraged among the English an assumption that they were superior to other people and, as Walter Scott said, a conviction that everything English is right and anything which is not English is therefore wrong. The peripheral élites are self-appointed among those whose education, tastes or ambitions incline them to identify themselves with this perceived English superiority.

Carolyn was not an extreme case in rejecting everything Scottish. Sometimes she seemed to be proud of her Scottish roots and her education in Scotland. There were aspects of Scotland which she admired and she liked to go there on holiday. It was only towards the end of our relationship that she made it clear that she did not share my Scottish enthusiasms. She told me afterwards, in a letter to Milan, that it was a visit to Scotland in August 1977 that brought this issue to a head. We had spent a week in a cottage in Perthshire. On the way back to London we were in Edinburgh for the Festival. I introduced her to Donald Cameron and Bert Davis and we went to a concert in the Assembly Rooms in George Street which was a celebration of Hugh MacDiarmid's 85th birthday. He had been in hospital and looked very frail, but he rallied, climbed on to the platform and summoned up all his old fire to deliver a passionate speech on the need for the emancipation of Scotland. For most of the audience, including me, it was a great and inspiring moment. Carolyn and I had to begin the drive to London that evening and we spent the night in the Carfrae Mill Hotel, where as a schoolboy I often went for lunch on Sundays with my grandfather. I noticed that Carolyn was rather subdued and unenthusiastic, but I thought that it was because she was tired. It was only in her letter in the following February that she told me what her feelings had been.

> The week in Perthshire was not a total success. I liked Donald
> and Bert, but I found the intense preoccupation with things
> Scottish oppressive. I hated the MacDiarmid concert. I felt
> keenly that this was not a world I could possibly belong to. But
> it is very much your world – or at least, the world you really
> want to be in.

She was quite right in that last sentence, of course.

In my first few months in Milan she continued to send me long, detailed letters about her thoughts and emotions, her work, the plays and films she saw, the books she read and the people she met. Perhaps she was less than frank about men in her life; but I suppose that was fair enough. Had I told her about Yvonne, for instance? Still, references to a certain Stephen (referred to as S, just as she referred to me as P) began to appear more frequently. Not so much because of this, but from the analysis of her feelings in her letters, the tone of her telephone calls and the postponements of any visit to Italy, it began to appear that she had decided against marriage with me. So I asked her and she replied on 8 January 1978.

> What you want to do is to go and live in your flat in Edinburgh. If you gave this up in order to be with me, I think you would be bound, secretly, to resent it.
>
> The world you want to belong to is not my world. I very much doubt if I would be happy in it. You know my feelings as an emigré Scot; this is a gut reaction which is not subject to argument.
>
> You ask if I have made up my mind not to marry you. I suppose that I very nearly have. I can't pinpoint a single factor as having swayed the balance. I suppose it is a combination of all the difficulties.

And in another letter two days later:

> All the time I keep thinking of our mutual entanglement which has run for so long and now runs so deep that disengagement is very difficult to envisage. I want to retain what we have, the rare degree of understanding or similarity, the lack of forbidden areas. It is very difficult to envisage the relationship on a basis other than a preliminary to marriage. But that step, even if it were feasible, which at present it is not, I no longer feel able to take.

I was able to go to London for a few days in February 1978. Carolyn asked me in a letter to come round to her flat, but at the same time referred to two of the main problems – 'the age difference and your romantic passion for Scotland which I cannot share.' As far as I can remember, this was the only time she mentioned the question of age, of which we had hardly seemed to be conscious. But it was a very real point. She was twenty four years younger than me. Especially to someone so eager for a long and stable relationship, and for companionship in old age, that should have ruled me out from the start.

I did go to the flat, which we had shared for about three years, but she was cold, decisive and unyielding. She was capable of ruthlessness in action as in speech. It was for me a shattering experience. I wrote three poems about it and sent them to her afterwards. She returned them with a letter in which she said that she did not think that they were very good. I was not so sure about that.

All rationalisations aside, I suppose that the old ballad had the truth of the matter:

O waly, waly, but love be bonny
A little time, while it is new;
But when 'tis auld, it waxeth cauld,
And fades away like morning dew.

For Carolyn it faded away before it faded also for me. I have to admit, though, that she was right. Our objectives were incompatible and it was just as well that we broke off when we did. I was liberated at once from an emotional switchback and what Tolstoy calls blissful insanity.

For some months after that encounter in London Carolyn continued to write to me. She apologised several times for the pain she had caused and said that she felt guilty. By November of that same year she wrote to say that she was engaged to Stephen. She sent me an account of her wedding and even a description of her dress. It was in the Church of Scotland in Pont Street, where Celia and I had been married about twenty six years before. So she was clinging to a vestige of Scottishness after all. We congratulated one another on the 'generosity' of our responses to the new situation. She succeeded almost immediately in moving to the Treasury,

I wrote about my letters to her. If she was tempted to throw them away, could I have them back instead? 'There is more of me in them than in anything else,' I wrote. In her reply she said that she must speak to Stephen about them. She would keep the letters unless that upset him, but she would add a codicil to her will for the return of them to me, if she died before me! She seems to have meant this seriously. I have no idea if they still exist and will eventually emerge.

Our correspondence continued for some time, but no longer in its old intensity and volume. The last letter which I had from her was in June 1980. On 17 October of that year I passed through London on my way to a Wilton Park conference. We met for a drink in the downstairs bar of St Stephen's at the end of Whitehall. We talked in the familiar, easy way, almost as though nothing had changed. She was keen to stay in the Treasury, but was worried because they seemed to regard her as a temporary outsider. Since then, I have not heard from her or seen her. I noticed from a newspaper article that at some time during the Thatcher years she was working in the Policy Unit in No 10. I should like to have heard her comments about that. In, I think, 1988 I had to go to London for a television programme and I had noticed that she was by then Director of the Constitutional and Community Policy Directorate in the Home Office. Since I was a spokesman for the SNP and was writing frequently in the press about constitutional questions, I thought that a discussion might be useful to both of us. I telephoned her office and suggested that we might meet for lunch; she declined. About a year later, I went to Vienna for a conference of Europe of the Cultures and found that the organisers had booked me into a new hotel very close to Modena Park, where Carolyn used to live. The coincidence was so unexpected that I wrote to her about how Vienna was, in many respects, still the same, but also very different in its new prosperity. She did not reply.

At Easter 1978, Edward Heath who had lost the leadership of the Conservative Party to Margaret Thatcher in 1975, came to Milan to conduct the European Community Youth Orchestra. He had consulted me about his visit in advance and I invited him to stay with me in Corso Venezia. He was an undemanding guest, although that was not the reputation he had when he had stayed in Embassies as Prime Minister. Most of the time he was rather morose and subdued, but he switched on his geniality and was a transformed character whenever I introduced him to a group of journalists. He made no secret, either in private conversation or at social events, of his contempt and loathing of Margaret Thatcher. At a lunch for British businessmen, he referred in his speech to his Declaration of Perth and said that he was adamantly in favour of a Scottish Parliament and that the constitutional *status quo* was no longer tenable.

Later that month, and it proves that the fairy godmother department works in the Diplomatic Service as well as in the Army, it was agreed that I should spend several weeks in Florence to improve my Italian at a course in the British Institute. I stayed in the comfortable and delightfully old-fashioned Pensione Beacci in the Via Tornabuoni in the heart of the old town. Many of the other guests were art historians or scholars of one kind or another. The bedrooms had bookcases and desks with reading lamps, which are quite rare in Italian hotels. Conversation at dinner tended to reflect this scholarly atmosphere. The place was owned, and presided over with an aristocratic air, by an elderly lady, Lianna Beacci.

This stay in Florence was one of the most fascinating and enlightening experiences. I immersed myself in the Italian Renaissance and spent hours every day in the galleries, churches and palaces of this extraordinary town, forbidding in aspect, but inexhaustibly rich in great works of art. My own personal troubles faded into insignificance.

In May I was invited to a ceremony in the house on the coast at Lerici, on the Gulf of Genoa, where Shelley had been staying at the time of his death by drowning and where his body was buried on the beach in the presence of Byron. The house, which had changed very little since that time, had been run as a Shelley museum, but it had run into financial problems and was about to be sold. Among the guests were the Italian novelist, Mario Soldati, a civilised and pleasant man, and a Scot, Ian Inglis, with whom I at once established a great deal of common ground. He was the son of a Church of Scotland Minister, a graduate in English from Edinburgh University and well read in Scottish literature. For some years he had been living in Italy, at first teaching English at the school for naval cadets in Livorno, Italian at the British Institute in Florence, now English at the University of Pisa. He invited me to come and stay in his farmhouse, Il Gallo, in the hills above a village, San Martino in Freddana, not far from Lucca. It was a truly idyllic and peaceful place, with a wonderful view over wooded hillsides in all directions. There I met his wife, Isabel, from Innerleithen, an attractive woman of infinite patience and resource. As long as I stayed in Italy, and now and again afterwards, I went often to Il Gallo and Ian and Isabel often stayed with me in Milan. Since then, Ian has come many times to Edinburgh, because he is divided between Scotland and Italy. Through them I met many people, also frequent guests at Il Gallo, especially Iseabail Macleod, one of the editors of the various publications of the Scottish National Dictionary, a native Gaelic speaker and a doughty fechter for the Scots tongue. Also through Ian, I met some of the expatriate community in Tuscany, such as Joseph Macleod, a poet and wartime BBC news reader, who lived with his delightful Italian wife in the hills above Florence.

A Twentieth Century Life

Like Ian, he was torn between Italy and Scotland and still kept a flat in Edinburgh. He told me that he loved Edinburgh and spent a month there every summer in his flat in Carlton Terrace. He rarely emerged from it because he wanted to be with his books which were stored there and not in Florence; rather a sad arrangement, it seemed to me.

From the first of January 1979 to the present I have kept a diary, not with daily, but with fairly frequent, entries. I had tried this before many times, but always abandoned the effort after a few days or a few weeks. From now on, I can reinforce my memory and the evidence of letters and other papers with a record made at the time. I see, for instance, that on 8 February 1979 I shared a table at lunch in the house of Ron Robertson, the Consul in Florence, with Charles Wilson and Harold Acton. Wilson was professor of Modern History at Cambridge, seconded at the time to the European University Institute at Florence. Acton was the celebrated author of *Memoirs of an Aesthete*. I asked Wilson about Trevor Roper who had made a curious impression on me when I met him once at a conference in Oxford and who seemed, although he had a house near Abbotsford, to have a fierce dislike of everything Scottish. Wilson said that Roper had always been kind to him personally, but that he was a strange character, so given to controversy that he lost all control over what he was writing and was apparently unconscious of the extent to which he was departing from all reasonable standards of fairness or scholarship. Wilson said that over Christmas he had been reading the diaries of Evelyn Waugh. I said that I was surprised; the extracts that had been published in one of the Sunday supplements suggested that they were a sorry mixture of snobbery and bitchiness. Acton said that he was probably drunk when he wrote them, as he was frequently. He then went on to tell us that he had first met Waugh when he had been asked to call at his club about eleven in the morning. He had been drinking champagne and was already far from sober. I had not known, as perhaps I should, that Waugh and Acton were old friends.

In spite of this, Acton pressed me to visit him in his villa in Florence, La Pietra. This was a magnificent establishment, a renaissance villa, full of fine furniture and Italian old masters. He took me first for a tour of the garden which was magnificent, with a large collection of statues, an open air theatre, a grotto and a view of the Duomo, skilfully framed by trees. As we returned to the house, the butler, who had evidently been waiting behind the door for us, threw it open precisely at the moment when we arrived. Acton had a great air about him, but he was neither arrogant nor pompous. He was elaborately courteous and he had the poshest of the posh accents, which was said to have been copied at one remove from Oscar Wilde.

Acton told me that he was descended from the Acton that Smollett met in Florence. Sure enough I afterwards came across the passage in a letter of 28 January 1765 in Tobias Smollett's *Travels Through France and Italy*, where he is speaking about the Tuscan navy:

> He that now commands the emperor's navy, consisting of a few frigates, is an Englishman, called Acton, who was heretofore captain of a ship in our East India company's service. He has lately embraced the catholic religion, and has been created admiral of Tuscany.

Acton did not mention that this same ancestor was related to Edward Gibbon who in a letter from Rome said that Commodore John Acton was 'in a most melancholy situation', apparently because he had been neglected by all his English friends in consequence of his change of religion.

Harold Acton said that his family had remained in Italy, in service of the government of Tuscany and Naples, since the eighteenth century, but that the sons had always been sent to school in England. He, for instance, had been at Eton and Christ Church. Now they had run out of descendants; he had never married. So what was to happen to the villa, all his pictures, books and other objects when he died? He had offered them, in succession, along with a substantial endowment, to his own college, various other colleges in Oxford and to the University as a whole, as an ideal place for the study of Italian art, literature and thought. They had all declined on the grounds that it was too heavy a responsibility. Acton was scathing in his denunciation of this philistinism (his favourite *bête noir*), timidity and lack of imagination. He now proposed to offer it to an American university instead.

I heard of the next step of this saga years afterwards from an article by Michael Sheridan in *The Spectator* of 13 April 1996. Acton had died two years before this and had indeed left his estate, estimated at between $100 million and $500 million, to New York University. The

213

will was being contested by none other than Lianna Beacci, the presiding genius of the pensione in Via Tornabuoni. It had transpired that she was Harold's half-sister, the offspring of an affair between his father, Arthur, and an Italian secretary. The entire palazzo in Via Tornabuoni had been given by Arthur to his mistress and the other side of the street to the British Institute. The same article gave a very different account of the Actons' connection with Italy. It said that Arthur Acton had arrived in Florence in 1903 with a very wealthy American bride and then bought La Pietra. Harold had told me that his father had bought most of the statues in the gardens at a time when impoverished Italian aristocrats were selling them very cheaply; but he had left me with the impression that the family had lived in La Pietra for centuries. Still, I suppose, it is possible that they had lived in Italy since the eighteenth century, if not in such an aristocratic style. I am sure that Harold would have shuddered at any suggestion that he, or his father, were merely *nouveau riche*.

Among all the wonderful towns of northern Italy, the two which are supreme are Florence and Venice. They are both great creations of the human spirit, but in many ways they are opposites. Florence is classical, austere, masculine; Venice is flamboyant, outrageous, seductive. I have never met anyone who has not immediately succumbed to this seduction, even if the harlot shows obvious sign of age and decay. Most of my friends in Venice were, in various ways, engaged in the ceaseless struggle to preserve this incomparable treasure for future generations. Chief among them was Ashley Clarke, then vice-chairman of the Venice in Peril Fund. He had retired as Ambassador in Rome in 1962 and lived in a delightful house on a quiet canal. I went at least twice with him in the consular motor boat to Torcello to inspect work on the restoration of the mosaics high above the floor of the ancient Cathedral, rebuilt, as the guidebook says, in 1008.

On the first occasion I declined an invitation to climb up on the rickety scaffolding because I was having trouble, even then, with a knee. Next time I had no such excuse. As I climbed up on this trembling structure, so high above the ground that people on the floor looked very small and far away, a scene came into my mind from the film *Don't Look Now*, a film very evocative of the mysterious side of Venice, where exactly such a scaffolding collapsed. But I could not admit to nerves. There was Ashley, nearly twenty years older, scampering about, intent only on a minute examination of these wonderful mosaics.

Another warrior in the cause was an American art historian, Marilyn Perry. She had been involved in the restoration of the very fine Romanesque Church, Santa Maria e Donato in Murano, and had written a guidebook, both on that and on the horses of St Mark's when they went to London for an exhibition in the Royal Academy. She lived in quite a modest flat, but on a top floor with an almost 360⁰ view on the Giudecca, opposite the Redentore. One of my most vivid memories of Venice is when I went there for a party on the night when the delivery of Venice from the plague is celebrated by the building of a bridge of boats, immediately below Marilyn's flat. There were multitudes of fireworks, magnified by their reflection in the water, and music in gondolas, unfortunately modern pop, and not, as it should have been, Vivaldi and Monteverdi. Two other memories: a visit by motorboat to San Lazzaro degli Armeni, where I was ceremoniously welcomed by the Armenian monks, who spoke about Byron as though he had been a recent visitor; another visit to a suitably unostentatious Franciscan monastery, San Francesco del Deserto, where a monk similarly told me about St Francis, as if he had known him personally.

In addition to all my travelling over the north of Italy for my official calls, I was also invited quite often to give lectures. I see from my diary that in 1979 and 1980 I lectured twice in Florence, Venice and Mantova and once in Genoa, Trento, Bologna, Chiavari and, outside my normal area, Bari. The subjects were mainly literary and usually about people who brought Scotland and Italy together, such as Boswell, Robert Adam, Smollett, Byron and Walter Scott. Each year I went to Rome for a conference in the Embassy and stayed very luxuriously in the splendid residence of the Ambassador, the Villa Wolskonsky.

I also remember in particular two conferences of a different kind. The first of these in the summer of 1978 was in Parma. It was called by an association which had been set up to organise a Verdi Festival in Parma, the town where he had spent much of his life. They had invited the directors of all important festivals in Europe to take part and they came from Bregenz, Salzburg, Verona, Prague, Berlin, Dubrovnik, Szeged and Flanders. Edinburgh said that they were sorry that they could not send anyone and asked if I would represent them. This, I did, carefully explaining that I had no official standing in the matter and could speak only as an enthusiastic member of the audience since the first Festival in 1946. I still have my speaking notes. I began by asking why Edinburgh became the site of a major festival and gave these reasons:

> 1. A town of the right size: large enough to have places for performances, hotels, restaurants, etc; but not so large that the festival is swamped; for three weeks each year it dominates the town.
> 2. A town that is a work of art in itself with an individual character, romantic history and distinguished achievement in the arts and intellect.
> 3. A town that has been looking for a role to replace the loss of the Parliament. If it could not be a real political capital, it could still be, as in the period 1750 to 1840, a capital of art and intellect.

My conclusion was that Parma had very similar qualities and would be an ideal location for a festival. The organisers wrote to me afterwards to thank me in very ornate language and to say that if they succeeded, as they expected, in launching a festival, part of the credit would be mine. I imagine that they sent the same letter to all of the speakers.

This event had a fortunate, if incidental, consequence. When I was in Edinburgh for that year's Festival, the Director, Peter Diamond, invited me to a dinner party on the last night to thank me for my part in the Parma conference. It was at this party that I first met Alastair and Dorothy Dunnett, who became staunch friends and allies when I returned to Edinburgh two years later. I happened to mention the page on Scottish books that I was writing at that time for *The Economist*. Alastair said at once that he had noticed that these pages were being written by a kindred spirit and that he was delighted to meet me. While I was still in Milan, Alastair nominated me as a member of the Edinburgh Festival Society, the body which, in theory at least, is responsible for the whole affair.

The second of the two conferences was in Modena in March 1980. It was a celebration of the work of John Grierson, the Scottish pioneer of the documentary film, whom I had met in La Paz. When the organisers came to discuss their plans with me, some months in advance, I said that the one man whom they must include was Forsyth Hardy. He had written a biography of Grierson and was in charge of his archive in Stirling University. They invited him and, among many others, also Edgar Anstey, who was one of Grierson's earliest collaborators. Modena is a small but delightful town and it staged a remarkably lavish and ambitious celebration. There were posters in almost every shop window and banners across the streets. Every meal was a party. They showed some seventy films by, or associated with, Grierson. There was a very comprehensive programme of lectures and discussions and a book about Grierson with reviews of all the films in which he was involved. When he was back in Edinburgh, Hardy wrote an enthusiastic report for *The Scotsman* which ended: 'And so Italy has celebrated the work of a Scottish film pioneer, more thoroughly, I believe, than has yet taken place elsewhere.'

I wrote in my diary for 8th March 1980:

Hardy and Anstey disposed firmly of a doubt that had been troubling me, Allan Massie in a review of Hardy's latest book, *Grierson on Scotland*, had said that Grierson had a reputation for having a reputation, but had only made one film himself. How fair was this? Hardy and Anstey left no room for doubt that Grierson's contribution was decisive in inspiring, arranging and creating with inexhaustible energy.

One night at dinner, I remarked that I had met Grierson in La Paz and that I had been flattered by his asking me during a conversation, if he could take notes. Could I remember any of the points, Hardy asked. Yes, at least one or two. Grierson had been very enthusiastic when I told him that Robert Burns had referred to the silver mines of Potosi, and he had praised a Bolivian film maker. 'It is all in my biography,' said Hardy. Next morning at breakfast he showed me the passage, a very acccurate account of a conversation about twenty five years before.

On 10th May 1979 the London Sinfonetta gave the first performance of a production of Stravinsky's *The Rake's Progress*, for which Christopher Auden wrote the libretto. This was in the Teatro Lirico, but under the auspices of La Scala. David Hockney designed the sets and costumes, which I said in my diary, were fresh and charming. After the performance we had a supper party with Hockney, the conductor, Claudio Abbado, and the producer, John Cox, who had worked on the British Day at Expo '67. Although Hockney wore one red and one yellow tennis shoe, he seemed perfectly sane. He had an attractive and forceful personality which had, by all accounts, worked wonders with the scene painters. Abbado's wife told me that she did not like music. When I asked if that did not cause something of a problem when she was married to a conductor, she replied, 'Not at all; it is not his music that attracts me.'

I met Graham Sutherland twice at openings of his work in Milan in June and November 1979. He was a gentle, modest man, who lived just over the border with France, at Mentone, and had many Italian friends. His wife told me that he refused to have guests because they would interfere with his work; but she thought that this was rather boring. She was an exuberant woman who seemed a bit incongruous, but her pride in him was obvious. Sutherland told me about painting his portrait of Somerset Maugham, which was the first time he had painted a portrait. He said that Maugham had afterwards spread the story that he had sat only because Sutherland had pestered him to agree to it. That, he said, was the precise opposite of the truth. Then Maugham had contrived to have the portrait left to the Tate in a devious way to conceal that was what he had wanted.

The area with which I was concerned, Italy north of Latium and Abruzzo, more or less corresponds with a notional division of Italy into two parts, North and South, a division which exists if only because the majority of Italians think that it does. Italians in the North think of themselves as belonging to the mainstream of European civilisation, enlightened, hard-working and technologically advanced. They think of the people in the South as poor and backward and doomed to remain so because of their lack of energy, determination and ability. They regard them as vastly inferior to themselves and deficient in all the qualities needed for success in the contemporary world. They think of them as a social and economic liability. They see the border between North and South as one between the European heartland and the Mediterranean world, and they place it not far south of Florence. This division has many of the qualities of a myth, but that it also has some reality appears from statistics of every kind from unemployment and income per head to illiteracy and the result of school examinations. The people of the North think of Rome as something apart and not properly belonging to the South, although geographically surrounded by it and strongly infected by Southern attitudes and habits. Of course, there is much that is prejudiced and unfair about this northern attitude. It overlooks, for instance, that the prosperity of the North is sustained by many southern workers in the factories in the North.

As you travel through northern Italy, your first impression is likely to be one of extraordinary prosperity. There is very little outward sign either of political tension or of economic difficulty. From outward appearance at least, I would say that the standard of living seems higher than anywhere else of which I have personal experience, not excluding North America. The Americans may have larger cars and more air conditioning, but the Italians of the North eat better, dress more fashionably and take longer and more frequent holidays. When you go from the North of Italy into Switzerland, you do not have the impression of going from a poorer country to a richer, but of precisely the opposite. It is partly because the Italians, unlike the Swiss, believe in outward show and therefore insist on fashionable clothes and flashy cars, but it is not merely outward show. Every form of expenditure for personal gratification is at a high level. Imports of champagne and whisky per head of the population beat all records. The addiction to the motor car and the weekend in the mountains or at the sea jams the roads every Sunday evening. The town is deserted for the whole of August when the population moves on to the beaches of Italy, except for those who follow the more recent fashion for holidays in exotic places like Siam. The food shops and restaurants are among the best in the world.

If next you go and discuss the situation with a Milanese banker, you will be given a completely different story which seems to bear no relation to your observations. He will give you a very gloomy account of the fundamental weakness and hopeless future of the Italian economy. He will say that the country is living wildly beyond its means, that the labour and social legislation is a weight which the economy cannot bear, that industry is now being driven into bankruptcy and being kept afloat by loans, and that all of these things are building up an accumulated debt which is bound to lead to the complete collapse of the currency. He will probably then admit that he is speaking in orthodox financial terms and with reference to the part of the economy which is susceptible to statistics, that in Italy nothing is quite what it seems and that the Italians will probably continue to display the extraordinary capacity for survival which they have always shown.

It is a commonplace of comment on Italy that it is a poor country. This is repeated by Italian politicians, when it suits them, and by the people at large who are simultaneously enjoying the lavish standard of living I have described. Italy is poor in the sense that it has no mineral resources to speak of, but it is rich in the talent and flair of the people and in the astonishing fertility of the soil, even if much of this is now neglected. It is presumably on these two assets that the astonishing wealth of the past was based. Everywhere in the North of Italy it is impossible to escape the evidence of past wealth. The whole region is packed with towns of staggering artistic and architectural richness, not only Florence and Venice, but others which are smaller and less well-known like Parma, Ferrara or Mantova. Byron said that there were no provincial towns in Italy, only capitals. He was right in the sense (and there are others) that these towns, even the smallest of them, have palaces, cathedrals, theatres and great townhouses which would be the boast of a capital city anywhere else in the world. The talent and energy that created these towns is not dead yet. One of the ways in which it expresses itself is in an unofficial, submerged or secret economy which escapes the statistics. All over the North of Italy there are small successful industries, many of them family concerns, producing goods of high added value which command a ready sale on the world markets. They keep to themselves and evade the more stringent requirements of labour legislation and probably taxation as well. They are the opposite side of the coin from the large bankrupt enterprises and are part of the explanation for the discrepancy between the statistics and the facts.

There are political as well as economic contradictions. Piero Ottone in his book *Come Finirà?* makes the point that the Christian Democrats do not understand the West in general and the capitalist system and the need for profit in particular. They see nothing wrong with the creation of vast enterprises, running at heavy financial loss, with no other purpose than the creation of employment and a reserve of grateful voters. For the same reasons, government departments and agencies are grossly overstaffed. Expense is no object. The Christian Democrats behave as if they believed that wealth could be created by printing banknotes. Hence the despair of the Milanese bankers. This is one of the ways in which the dominant ethos within the Christian Democrat Party is quite alien to the Northern Italian, who is nothing if not economically realistic with a keen sense of the importance of profit. As Ottone also says, nearly all Italians seem to be firmly convinced that their country is badly governed. Everywhere in the north one is told constantly about the ineptitude of Italian politicians and the appalling inadequacies of the administration. There is a curiously detached attitude to the political game as it is played in Rome and it is regarded with little except boredom and distaste.

I began this chapter by speaking of the pleasures of living in Italy, in the words of Boswell again, the land of felicity. This is not only because of its climate and natural beauty and the wealth of the products of the soil in wine, cheeses, fruit and vegetables; it is because of the attitude of the people. Samuel Johnson said that in human life there is little to be enjoyed and much to be endured, but I doubt if anyone feels like that in Italy. The Italian attitude, and it is reflected in the pleasures of their cuisine as well as in the splendours of their art, is that life is there to be enjoyed to the full. That is what makes them so difficult to govern because it is difficult to persuade an Italian to do anything that does not accord with his own pleasure.

Does it also account for the violence which disfigured so much of Italian life? Presumably it does, for much of it is purely criminal and motivated by greed which can reflect an urgent desire for self-satisfaction. This threat of robbery or kidnapping make the wealthy leave their jewellery, fashionable clothes and large cars at home. There is a passage in my diary on 31 July 1979, to the effect that this atmosphere of threat makes some people feel that life in Italy was becoming intolerable and it notes: 'Yesterday a judge was killed who was a close friend of Mario Borg in my office and a professional colleague of his wife.' A Carabinieri General, Dalla Chiesa, who was in charge of dealing with this sort of threat, was a charming and civilized man. Because of his efficiency, he was sent to Sicily for the campaign against the Mafia, but he was assassinated within a few months. There was also the threat of political violence. While I was in Milan, the former Prime Minister, Aldo Moro, was kidnapped by the Red Brigades and then murdered by them on 9 May 1978. A bomb, attributed to rightwing extremists, killed many people in the railway station of Bologna. There were times when the authorities insisted on providing me with an armed guard, but optimistically perhaps, I never felt that I was a particular target.

I often wish that I had known Italy before it was blighted by industrialisation. You might say the same of most countries, but in Italy it is more blatant. The mediaeval centres of many towns survive in their splendour, not only because the wars of the past must have been remarkably undestructive, but also because in the nineteenth century there was no economic impulse to rebuild them. The historic centres survived for the same reason as the town of Sucre in Bolivia. By the time that extensive industrialisation reached Italy, and that was quite late in the twentieth century, people realised that these beautiful places were an asset greatly worth preserving. That did not apply to the surroundings districts and the countryside at large, which have often been reduced to a sordid mess, no better than other parts of Europe.

Of course, in Italy, as everywhere else, part of my mind and attention was in Scotland. My reviewing for *The Economist*, *The Scotsman*, and *Blackwood's* kept me supplied with new Scottish books. I also started to write books of my own. The first of them, which I had started when I was in London, had been suggested to me by Bert Davis. The Saltire Society had published a book, *Blast and Counterblast*, in 1960, edited by J B Cowan, which examined contemporary writings on the Scottish reformation from both sides of the argument. Would I like to produce something similar on the controversies which led to the Union of 1707? This was a subject which had long been of great interest to me and I started to research it in the British Museum and in the National Library of Scotland during my visits to Edinburgh. It soon became apparent to me that the generally accepted view of the nature of the Union, and the way in which it came about, was little better than unionist propaganda.

The Union was not the result of genuine negotiations but a *diktat* by England, determined to secure its northern border by keeping Scotland in political subjection. Nor was it a bargain in which Scotland bartered independence for access to the English and colonial markets. As the Scots expected at the time, the immediate economic consequences of the Union on Scotland were harmful. It took about sixty years for Scotland to recover by its own efforts and by means of new agricultural and industrial methods. The English Government had little difficulty in insisting on their draft Treaty during the talks in London, especially as they had selected the Scottish representatives. They still had to secure the ratification of the Treaty by the Scottish

Parliament. That was a much more difficult problem.

The idea of 'incorporating' Union was repugnant to most of the Scottish people. The Scottish Parliament in 1703 and 1704 in the Act of Security had made a firm declaration of their intention to reassert Scottish independence. This is where the skill, determination and ruthlessness of the English governmental machine came into play. Several tempting inducements to the classes represented in the Scottish Parliament were included in the draft Treaty (including the repayment of the investments in the Darien venture). Bribery was increased. Daniel Defoe and others were employed as English agents and propagandists. Behind it all, as Sir John Clerk of Penicuik wrote at the time, was the implied threat that the alternative was an English invasion and the imposition of worse terms.

All of this, although contrary to the orthodox view, was perfectly apparent from the contemporary documents. Most of them have been published at one time or another and it took no great skill to unearth them. In *1707: the Union of Scotland and England*, I assembled extracts from these documents in what I called in the Introduction 'something between a source book, a narrative and a commentary.' I sent the typescript to the Saltire Society and to Chambers, the publishers, in April 1978. It did finally appear in September of the following year, when Chambers gave launch parties, which I attended, in Edinburgh and London. This was my first published book since my official publication on Bolivia in 1956. I think also that it was probably the most widely reviewed of all my books. Allan Massie in *Blackwood's* said that it was 'invaluable, acute and cogent'. In an article in *The Scotsman* he said that it was characteristic of the Scottish interest in history that Neal Ascherson's review ('lucid and highly revealing') should appear in the centre page and not among the other book reviews. Both the *TLS* and *The Economist* reviewed it, and that is fairly rare for Scottish books.

I do not suppose that this one little book made any great impact on the deeply embedded and quite erroneous view of the nature and origins of the Union, but I think that it did something to open up the debate. Gordon Donaldson, at that time professor of Scottish History in Edinburgh, wrote in *Books in Scotland*, 'If Mr Scott has proved anything it is, above all, that the debates of 1706-07 were not final.' To take only one point, the curious behaviour of the Duke of Hamilton. He posed as the leader of the opposition, but at several crucial points he had betrayed the cause. It was due to him, for instance, that the appointments on both sides for the discussion of the Treaty were left to the Queen (which meant the English Government). Why did he behave like this? Well, there is plenty of evidence that he was in the pay of the English Government but no one, it seems, had previously drawn attention to it.

Bruce Lenman of St Andrews University in his essay in *Why Scottish History Matters* (Saltire Society, 1991) said that 'it was nice to have a conclusive demonstration from Paul Scott of something which everyone had always suspected.' John Gibson spoke to me about this at a PEN lunch in December 1980. He is a retired senior civil servant in the Scottish Office who has written a number of useful books about Jacobitism. He said that his research fully substantiated my account of Hamilton's motives. 'Strange,' he said, 'that it took 250 years for some one to notice it.' I think that it is an indication of the power of the pressure for conformity with the Unionist view that even honest and competent historians have been prepared to turn a blind eye to so much evidence and for so long.

On 23rd May 1979 I had a conversation with André Fontaine, the editor of *Le Monde*, who had come to Milan to give a lecture at the French Institute. He told me that Jean Monet had been startled and disturbed by Lord Perth who had said to him that Scotland would be independent within ten years. I do not know whether Perth had been speaking before or after the Referendum of March 1979. That miserable affair postponed the recovery of the Scottish Parliament by twenty years, but to forecast that devolution would be followed by independence within twenty years is, I think, about right.

Even before *1707* was published, I started work on two other books. The first was a book on Sir Walter Scott, which became *Walter Scott and Scotland*, published by Blackwood's in 1981. The title was a deliberate echo of Edwin Muir's book about Scott, to which I was, in a sense, replying. Again I wanted to argue against some strongly entrenched ideas which I thought were mistaken. A great deal of nonsense is talked and written about Scott, usually by people who seem to have read very little of his work. It is true that he was a Tory, as the term was understood in his own time. It is also true that he was in favour of social stability and distrustful of sudden change; but it is not true that he distorted Scottish history and was an uncritical enthusiast for the Union of 1707. In fact, as I argued in an essay which I wrote for *Blackwood's Magazine* in September 1976, his *Letters of Malachi Malagrowther* were a passionate argument against English interference in Scottish affairs and a defence of the cultural identity of Scotland. It was, I suggested, the first manifesto of modern Scottish nationalism. Also, and it is another point which I thought required to be reasserted, Scott was, as Byron said, 'as nearly thorough good man as man can be.' This shines transparently through Scott's letters and his incomparable *Journal* but it has become fashionable to speak contemptuously of him. The most recent biography by John Sutherland, published in 1995, begins in that style, but it becomes more sympathetic as it proceeds. When Sutherland came to address the Edinburgh Sir Walter Scott Club, I said to him that it seemed to me that he had set out to try to debunk, but that the more he read of Scott, the more he admired him. He agreed.

Reviews of *Walter Scott and Scotland* were generally favourable, although some of the reviewers, such as Douglas Dunn and James Robertson, seemed to be anxious to cling to disapproval of Scott. Claire Lamont in the *Times Literary Supplement* (13 August 1982) was one of the most understanding of my position. The warmest reaction was by Maurice Lindsay, a poet who has himself written so much and so well about Scottish literature:

> What makes this book so rewarding and delightful to read, however, is ultimately not its substance, sound though that may be, but the manner in which Mr Scott's elegant and economical prose brings his great predecessor to life before our very eyes.
>
> (*Scottish Field*, December, 1981)

Whether I have shaken the Unionist view of Scott, I am not so sure. But I think that I have at least introduced a wider understanding of the significance of the Malachi letters.

The next book was a collection of essays which Bert Davis and I edited together, *The Age of MacDiarmid*, which was a phrase I had used in one of my pages on Scottish books in *The Economist* in October 1977. I agreed, in other words with David Murison when he said, 'After MacDiarmid, as after Knox, Scotland will never be the same again.' When MacDiarmid died in September 1978, I happened to be in Edinburgh on my annual visit to the Festival. Bert Davis and I went to Langholm for the funeral, although, I have to admit, funerals are events which I usually avoid. Norman MacCaig, brother poet and old and trusty friend of MacDiarmid, gave an oration (no lesser word will do) at the graveside. It was spontaneous, lyrical, moving and magnificent, but incredibly no recording was made and no text has survived.

Bert and I resolved, on that same evening I think, that we must collect together essays by his contemporaries to record these feelings and ideas about MacDiarmid. We soon assembled an impressive team. It included JK Annand, George Bruce, David Daiches, Norman MacCaig (but only in a short poem, not the oration), Sorley Maclean, Edwin Morgan, Tom Scott, Ian Crichton Smith and several others. I spoke to MacCaig about the book on 1st March 1979, the day of the frustrated Referendum. I was, of course, in Edinburgh at the time. He said that he was perhaps wrong in refusing to contribute, apart from a poem; but he had a strong feeling that he could not put his thoughts about MacDiarmid into writing. He had no record of his funeral address and could not reconstruct it. 'Once in a life-time was enough.' We also failed with that genial reincarnation of Robert Fergusson, Robert Garioch, the poetic voice of twentieth century Edinburgh as Fergusson was of the eighteenth. On another occasion, Sorley Maclean (who we used to call Sam) explained that Garioch and MacDiarmid did not get on together, and MacDiarmid had at one time threatened to take Garioch to court. 'Garioch was not the sort of man to write a hostile piece about anyone. He would rather say nothing.' The book was published by Mainstream in hardback in 1980 and in paperback in 1992.

From the late 70s onwards I have spent as much time as I could seize from other things in writing and much of my reading has been preparation for it. It was not only the books that I have mentioned, but a steady output of essays and book reviews. In my diary for 27 May 1980, when I was on visit to Edinburgh, I wrote:

> We went with my brother to see the boat which he is building at Aberdour. A few years ago, I could not happily face a summer without a boat. Now I think that they take up too much time. Reading and writing have taken a grip of me and I am reluctant to spend much time on anything else. Having started rather late to write, I have to pack a lifetime into the next ten years.

I had, of course, been writing Foreign Office minutes, dispatches, telegrams and what not for years, but what I meant in that entry was writing for publication. And why did I allow myself only ten years? Did I expect to die at the biblical seventy? In fact, I have been lucky enough, so far, to have had an extra very busy decade.

Another remark about writing in the entry for 6 January 1979:

> A curious thing I find about writing; ideas, phrases, new lines of argument seem to jump unbidden into the mind. You don't always have to strive for them; they just arrive and often the best of them. It is almost as if one were writing to the dictation of someone else.

I still find this. Presumably it is our old friend the sub-conscious mind. The brain seems to go on working, even when you are not fully aware of it. It stores up its thoughts like a computer and they come out, when you press the right buttons. Some of my best ideas seem to arrive when I am asleep and I wake up and make notes in case they are forgotten by the morning.

There were, of course, other enthusiasms, skiing for instance. At one time, at the beginning of January 1979, I began to think that my passion for it has lost its edge; but I went next weekend with Alastair to St Moritz and 'the old excitement and delight came back at once'. I went to St Moritz nearly every weekend in the season and took my usual holiday in Klosters. So it has continued.

By 1979 and 1980, I was able to visit Edinburgh two or three times a year. I had to attend to a number of things, apart from the Edinburgh Festival, when I wrote Fringe reviews for *The Scotsman*. I had been searching for a flat and eventually bought one in June 1978 at Drumsheugh Gardens where I have been living very happily for the last twenty years. There were meetings with publishers, and my fellow editor, Bert Davis, over the books. Then a committee of the Saltire Society, with Professor John MacQueen as Convener and Bert as Secretary, was pressing on with the proposal which I had made at the conference in St Andrews in 1977 to see if organisations involved in the cultural life of the country would be interested in the foundation of a joint body to evolve ideas on cultural policy. They consulted about 180 organisations and 82 responded favourably. The Society invited them to a conference on 17 February 1979 which I attended. The conference approved a manifesto and agreed to the formation of an Advisory Council.

During that same visit, I did what I could by writing letters to the press, attending meetings and taking part in radio phone-in programs, to help with the campaign for a Yes vote in the Referendum on a Scottish Parliament on 18 March. My diary for 22 February records a lunch with Harry Reid, then Features Editor of *The Scotsman*. He was confident of a good Yes majority. I had misgivings about the effect of the deliberately unscrupulous and misleading No campaign and the present unpopularity of the Labour Government. In a sense we were both right. It was a Yes majority, but not one which was large enough to satisfy the outrageous 40% requirement (of the electoral roll, not just of those voting) or convincing enough to make Home Rule irresistible.

I tried to help save *Blackwood's Magazine*. In the late 70s David Fletcher had been appointed as editor, the first since the magazine was founded in 1817 who had not been a member of the family. In recent years it had declined from its satirical and literary origins to become largely a vehicle for colonial and military reminiscences, read, it was said, by retired colonels in all quarters of the globe. David had set about giving the magazine new life and vigour and I had become a constant contributor. Suddenly David was sacked and a Blackwood took over. Then when I was in Edinburgh in May 1980, I was told by telephone that they were losing money and had decided to stop publication. I went to see Michael Blackwood and did my best to persuade him that it should not be impossible to set up a trust to raise funds. He agreed to try. I spoke to the Scottish Arts Council and to Alastair Dunnett who tried to enlist the interest of some of his friends who were potentates of newspaper publishing. We failed.

I persuaded Marilyn Perry, the art historian from Venice, to take an interest in the restoration of the Boswell house at Auchinleck, an elegant and not too large eighteenth century building in a fine setting, but now sadly neglected and decayed. She was now the director of an American trust and in charge of funds which are used for such projects all over the world. She came with Bert and me to see the house. I think that she was impressed by what the house had been and could still be, but thought that it was too far gone to be easy to rescue and then to what purpose could it be put? Lord Auchinleck's inscription is still above the door, *quod petis, hic est* – what you seek is here; but within the house was empty and there were holes in the floors and ceilings which threatened to collapse. Other efforts have been made to save the house since then. The Marquis of Bute, who was Chairman of the National Trust for Scotland and a great champion of all such causes, gave his support to one of them. I was delighted to find that there was still a James Boswell of Auchinleck. I gather from the press that in the year 2000, there was a serious prospect of a thorough restoration. Both from its quality and its associations, the house is a treasure which should not be lost.

When I read in my diary about these visits to Edinburgh I am struck by the large number of friends I already, and still, had in my home city. I remarked that I could hardly ever go anywhere in Edinburgh without meeting someone I know. In one day, for instance, by accident or design, I met Anne Smith who had started the *Literary Review* and asked me to write for it, Neal Ascherson who said that he would arrange for me to meet Bernard Crick and Karl Miller when I passed through London (which I duly did), and the tireless Richard Demarco, bubbling with enthusiasm as usual. I often met Stephen Maxwell, then research officer of the SNP. In the Arts Club, I met the cartoonist, Emilio Coia, who embodied in his person the irresistible charm of Italy combined with the easy familiarity of the Glaswegian, Jack Firth, a fine painter in watercolour, and Norman Wilson, who invited me to write a piece for a book which he was editing about Edinburgh. At dinner with Alastair Dunnett, I met John Smith, who later became leader of the Labour Party. He gave me the impression that he would rather practice as an advocate than as a politician. With Joan Lingard I defended the Edinburgh bourgeoisie against the suggestion in her novel, *The Second Flowering of Emily Montjoy*, that they were snobbish, timid, conformist, sexless and impervious to new ideas. Of course there are some people like that, but I do not think that they are a majority. Allan Massie came to lunch in the New Club and stayed for about three hours of constant talk. On 2nd March 1979 I went for the first time to a dinner of the Edinburgh Sir Walter Scott Club. Patricia Maxwell Scott ask ed to meet me and said that she approved of an article that I had written for *The Scotsman* about her ancestor, Sir Walter Scott. She said that it was very balanced and fair and she thought that we must be cousins.

During the 1980 Festival we had a party to launch the MacDiarmid book. Anthony Burgess, who was in Edinburgh to give a lecture, came and said that he regarded MacDiarmid as the greatest poet of the twentieth century. Donald Campbell, a fine dramatist whose work has been deplorably neglected in recent years, spoke about the expressive qualities of the Scots language. An ability to speak it was a great asset, not an impediment as some people seemed to think. He told me that the National Theatre in London had declined his play, *The Widows of Clyth*, on the grounds that it was a Scottish play and therefore not for them. At a poetry reading in a converted kirk Robert Garioch said, 'the kirks used to convert the sinners; now the sinners convert the kirks.' He was a delightful character of high intelligence and literary skill who liked to pose as a simple, unpretentious soul. Of all the readers of their own verse, a very popular activity in the 70s and 80s, I think that Garioch was the most entertaining. He had a particular gift for the unexpected observation and the throwaway line. I noticed at about this time that Sorley Maclean seldom finished a sentence and seemed to lose track of his thoughts. I was afraid that it was a sign of age, but probably, on the contrary, it was because he was being struck by new ideas. He always gave the impression that his mind was working on more than one plane at a time. When Edinburgh University started having an Alumnus of the Year, I proposed that Sorley should be the first. I am glad that they had the good sense to agree. We tried hard for years, through AdCAS and Scottish PEN, to persuade the Nobel committee that Sorley amply deserved the Prize for Literature, but with no success.

It was during 1979 that Laura Fiorentini and I became indispensable to one another. She was an Italian member of the staff of the Consulate-General, who was born in Genoa and had spent some time in New York where her father had worked for an Italian bank. Our acquaintance began when she coached me in conversational Italian for the Foreign Office language examination. We soon discovered that we shared interests and attitudes to a remarkable degree. Italy had enriched my life in many ways, but meeting Laura has been the most important of all to me. With her, the melancholy ballad about the decay of love has not applied. Time has consolidated and not weakened it.

It might be supposed that Italy and Scotland are so different in habits and spirit that the citizens of one would not readily feel at home in the other. Scotland, after all, is a cold, northern land, sometimes harsh as an environment, with people to whom something of the Presbyterian ethos still clings, with its belief in high endeavour, self-restraint and plain living. We are inclined to assume that life is a struggle, a sair trauchle. Italy is part of the warm south, a land of grapes and peaches. The people are exuberant, extrovert and full of the joy of life. Even so, there seems to be a fundamental affinity between the Italians and the Scots and we blend well together. People like Alberto Morrocco and Richard Demarco are both Scottish and Italian.

So it is with Laura and me. She is, as Harry Reid said in a profile, a beautiful Italian lady. For more than twenty years we have had a perfect partnership, delighting in the company of one another and agreeing about nearly everything, with the possible trivial exception of the temperature. She is generous, careful of the interests and feelings of others, bright and helpful, the sort of person that everyone likes. She never questioned my decision not to seek a divorce.

There are Scottish characteristics that appeal strongly to her, the social cohesion, the reliability of people and their seriousness of purpose. From my first sight of Italy, I have admired its zest for life and inexhaustible talent, flair and creativity. Laura came with me to the Edinburgh Festival in 1979. It was her first visit to Scotland, but she felt immediately at home. Years later, in 1992, she was asked by Michael Russell to write an account of her feelings about the place for a book which he was editing, *Edinburgh: A Celebration*. This is what she said:

> It was love at first sight. Arriving in Edinburgh, back in 1979, looking from Soutra hill down at the city skyline in the amazing light of a clear summer dawn, the impression was of total astonishment and fulfilment. I was 'coming home' at last to the place where I have always belonged in my dreams and from the first moment it was as if I have been living here all my life. The enthusiasm and the sheer pleasure of living in this marvellous city have not faded away with the years, and, to this day, they are for me as strong and as deep as ever.
>
> It is difficult to explain why Edinburgh is so congenial to my character. What do I like here that I cannot find elsewhere, not even, I would say, in my own native country? There is the striking architecture; there are the wonderful diverse colours of a

typically northern latitude – rapidly changing skies, golden
summer sunsets, the intense brilliance of the winter light. But,
above all, there is the enjoyment of everyday life. To my mind,
Edinburgh is the perfect place for a civilised existence. Its
compact size means that you can live and work here without
losing your individuality, as is liable to happen in the anonymity,
stress and chaos of a modern, larger metropolis. Although I work
in a predominantly Italian environment, I have made a great
many Scottish friends as well. I think Italians feel particularly at
home here, because of the friendliness of the people and because
they recognise in Edinburgh a capital with deep European roots.

When we went back to Milan after the 1980 Festival, I had only
two more months left of my career as a diplomat because I was due to
retire on my 60th birthday, 7th November. This meant, of course, the
usual pressure of packing and farewell parties, but otherwise life went
on as usual. I went, for instance, to San Sepolcro in early October for
a presentation of a gold medal to Lord Clark, the Kenneth Clark who
was a former Director of the National Gallery and the script writer of
a celebrated history of art for television, *Civilisation*. San Sepolcro is a
small, pleasant town between Florence and Urbino. It was the
birthplace in 1492 of Piero della Francesca and still holds his
Resurrection, which Aldous Huxley said was the most beautiful painting
in the world. The town had decided to honour Clark because, fifty
years ago, he had written the first scholarly book about Piero.

When Clark phoned me a week or two before the event I offered
to meet him and his wife in Florence with my official car and take
them to San Sepolcro. We drove first to Arezzo to see Piero's frescoes
in San Francesco and the Cathedral. Clark was furious about a recent
restoration which had removed large areas of earlier repainting, and
left showing blank spaces. He said that this was purism gone mad,
preferring authenticity to beauty. The old repainting had probably
been close to the original and was certainly preferable to empty space.
At dinner that night with just the three of us in the hotel in San
Sepolcro, Lady Clark was amusing about her experiences during the
war when she was 'in the army'. Kenneth told me that although most
of his life had been in England, he was proud of his Scottish ancestry.
He was a great admirer of Scottish character and achievement, as he
thought he had made clear in *Civilisation*, where he had described

Scotland as a 'force in European civilisation.' He called for whisky so that we could drink a toast to celebrate it.

The ceremony next day was a tremendous show of the kind which only Italy can produce. There was a guard of honour of crossbow men and flag throwers and a concert of music of the fifteenth century. I still have the text of Clark's speech in Italian. Afterwards there was, as always on such occasions, an enormous, delicious and prolonged lunch. During it the director of the municipal library introduced himself to me and asked if I thought that Clark would like to see it. When I looked a little doubtful, he said that they had municipal records back to the time of Piero and many of the earliest printed books, including the first printed Virgil. So, of course, we went and were glad that we did. It was yet another demonstration of the extraordinary stability and continuity of the life of Italian cities.

Almost as my last official act in the Diplomatic Service, I went for some days in mid-October 1980 to attend a conference at what was still called Wilton Park, although confusingly it was now housed in Winton House, near Steyning in west Sussex. Wilton Park, as an institution, was established by the Foreign Office just after the war to re-educate influential Germans in the ways of democracy. It has survived by widening its scope to include participants from all parts of the world to engage in discussion on diverse political, social and economic questions. Throughout my career I have nominated intellectuals, politicians and journalists to take part. For some time the Director had pressed me to come myself. Now, at the last minute, I agreed, tempted by the subject, 'Regional power and ethnic identity in a changing world'. I was curious to see how they would handle the Scottish question.

The group included people from America, Canada, India and several countries in Africa and Europe. Not surprisingly, there was some confusion about the scope of the subject. Some assumed that regions were parts of existing countries and others that they were groupings of countries, such as South-East Asia. Still, on one of the days the focus was on Scotland. Neil MacCormick spoke before lunch. This was the first time I had met him, but I knew that he was an international lawyer of great distinction and a prominent member of the SNP. He was also a man of great friendliness and charm; you might disagree with Neil, but you were bound to like him. The afternoon speaker was Malcom Rifkind, the Conservative MP for Edinburgh Pentlands, and at that time Parliamentary Under-Secretary at the Foreign Office in the Thatcher Government. Both speakers began with a general approach to the subject, but inevitably, at that time and with two such speakers, the Scottish question was inescapable.

Malcolm Rifkind is intelligent and quick-witted and I have no doubt that he was excellent in his former profession as an advocate at the Scottish bar. In fact, he has always seemed to me to approach politics in the same spirit, applying his debating skill to support whichever side he happened to be working for at the time. Before the Referendum, he had been an eloquent advocate for a Scottish Parliament. When he became a member of Thatcher's government, he was equally eloquent against it. This time, he miscalculated his audience, evidently assuming that they were a collection of foreigners who knew nothing about the subject. He began, perhaps by habit, by rehearsing some of his old arguments in favour of the Parliament: Scotland was the only country in the world with its own legal system, but no power to amend its own laws, and so forth. Then, he said, that this whole issue had now been settled because the Scottish people in the Referendum had firmly rejected the whole idea of a Scottish Parliament.

I took him up on this. Had not Churchill said that in the British system, a majority of one was sufficient? Was there not a majority in Scotland for a Parliament? And what about Douglas Home's broadcast asking people to vote No, on the understanding that a Conservative Government would introduce a bill for a Scottish Parliament with strong powers? When was that going to happen? I was supported by two members of the permanent staff. Rifkind wriggled skilfully but he was seen to wriggle. Afterwards his private secretary said that he had never seen a minister treated in public in such a manner by Government servants. I replied, 'did he not deserve it?'

CHAPTER 16
Back in Scotland (1)
The 1980s

On the 7th of November I left Milan and the Diplomatic Service. I do not think that Laura and I ever discussed whether she would come with me to Edinburgh. We both simply assumed that she would. We drove at a leisurely pace, for we now had time, through France, by way of Avignon, Rouen, Versailles and Paris. On 17th November 1980, we arrived in Edinburgh to begin a new life. I wrote in my diary that evening.

> The first day of freedom in Edinburgh. It is a delightful thought that I do not have to try to cram everything into a week or two, but that time stretches ahead for a few years at least.
>
> I had to go to the offices of Lothian Region for a parking permit and was present at a little scene which – I like to think – shows that in Edinburgh we have not yet lost our concern for moral rectitude. A man handed over the counter a 50p piece which he had found on the floor. A woman standing there said that she was afraid that she might have dropped it. 'Please then take it,' said the assistant behind the counter. 'Oh no, I can't do that, because I cannot be absolutely sure that it is mine.'

That entry reflects two of the ideas that were occupying my mind at the time. The first was my pleasure at the thought that I could now devote all my time to my own objectives; but there was still urgency, still a wish to do much in a few remaining years. Secondly, I think that I was a little worried about how Scotland might have changed. To what extent did the old moral and intellectual aspirations still apply? Had we succumbed to the general tendency in the world at large to lower expectations about both of these things?

235

My first experiences were encouraging, as I said in an article in *The Scotsman* on 6th January 1981.

> I have recently come back to live in Edinburgh, after – the arithmetic astounds me – working outside Scotland for nearly 40 years. I am not doing this quite in the spirit of Edward Gibbon, who says in his *Autobiography*, 'I have always cherished a secret wish that the school of my youth might become the retreat of my declining age.' Not quite in this spirit, because I have never lost touch with Edinburgh; I have always thought of it as the natural and proper, as well as the most agreeable, place to live; my time abroad has been a sort of temporary aberration; I have more friends here than anywhere else.

> The other day when I was telling a friend about my satisfaction about living in Edinburgh, she said that every time she came out of her front door she thought how lucky she was just to be here. That is exactly how I feel about Edinburgh. This is not, let me say at once, an uncritical enthusiasm. Just because I enjoy and admire Edinburgh so much, I am hypersensitive about its failings and shortcomings. The destruction of part of it, as, for instance, George Square or David Hume's house in South St David Street, hurt me like an amputation. The blemishes, of which I could give you a long and depressing list, give me a feeling of personal shame.

> Enough of the essential character of the place, both in the buildings and the people, remains to justify the enthusiasm; but I often feel that its survival is precarious. Also, because I have always come back to Edinburgh frequently, if briefly, and because I read *The Scotsman* and most of the magazines even when I am away, I am reasonably in touch with recent events. I know that I have come back at an unhappy and discouraging time. It is sad to think of the change from the optimism and hope of just two or three years ago when the expectation that we were to resume some degree of responsibility for our own affairs invigorated all aspects of Scottish life.

> The swindle of the referendum, for that is what it was, changed all that, for the time being at least. Now we are saddled with a Government, that we did not elect, which, in the service of a simplistic economic theory, is conducting a policy which leads not

only to huge unemployment, but also to long-term economic, educational and social decline. There is certainly enough to be depressed and worried about.

In spite of all this, I have found enormous encouragement in my first few weeks in Edinburgh. The flitting of one's plenishing and effects, moving into a new house, in any country in the world, always throws you on the mercy of all sorts of people. You need the help of plumbers, painters and joiners, who if they are unreliable and inconsiderate, can easily make your life a misery. You have to buy things like curtains and floor-coverings, for which you need help and advice. You have to find out about parking regulations, doctors and dentists, rubbish removals and all the other things which residents take for granted. I have gone through this process more often and in more countries than I want to count.

Usually, even if you are in a privileged position with an office staff to help, it is a frustrating and exasperating business. In Edinburgh it has been, almost a pleasure. Everything has been done with an efficiency and dispatch which exceeds anything that I can remember. Everyone I have approached in private firms, Government offices and everywhere else has been agreeable, friendly and dependable. If they say that they will telephone back, they do, and usually within an hour or two. If they say that they will send something by post, it arrives the next day. If they make an appointment, they keep it. All the people involved were a pleasure to meet and talk to. All give the impression that they are genuinely anxious to help.

You begin to have the feeling that the 'caring society' is more than an empty phrase. Of course, I shall be accused of sentiment-ality and wishful thinking, but such, in sober truth, is my experience. In Scotland, we have for long been too modest about our assets, resources and capabilities. We have been too easily discouraged by such reverses as the Government calmly setting aside the Scotland Act, although, remember (I refer to a Conservative Party leaflet of the time), the Conservatives 'were not against devolution as such but only against that particular scheme.'

We seem now to be accepting unemployment, the squandering of oil revenues, the cuts in education and services, the destruction of the railways in the same attitude of passive despair. This lack of self-confidence is the natural result I suppose, of the absence of responsibility for our own affairs. The truth is that we do not realise our own potential and our own strength. The chief of these is a population full of talented, friendly, kind and well-disposed people. This is something which unfortunately, is much rarer in the world at large than one might suppose! Among all the advantages of Edinburgh, this is the main reason why it is good to be home again. It is also the main reason why we can still have confidence in the future.

I said in a longer essay in the *Scottish Review* of May 1981 that I had never had any doubt that Scotland, and Edinburgh in particular, was where I wanted to live, even if I had spent my whole professional life in other places. At the same time, I was very conscious that there were serious grounds for alarm about the situation in which Scotland found itself.

My attitude to Scotland did not imply contentment with the deplorable state into which the country had sunk. How could it when we were surrounded with blatant evidence of decline and decay, when Scotland compared so unfavourably with our European neighbours in almost every comparable statistic: disease, crime, poverty, unemployment, and when the contrast between the potential and the performance was so pitiful? Of course, world recession at the time, abetted by the policies of Westminster, was making everything worse; but we were suffering from the accumulation of years of government which was irresponsible in every sense of the term.

The more one cares about Scotland, the more these things are painful and impossible to accept. I think that Eric Linklater was right when he said in *The Lion and the Unicorn* in 1935, 'I believe people degenerate when they lose control of their own affairs.' That degeneration has blighted Scotland since Westminster assumed control of almost every aspect of life, beginning gently in the nineteenth century and reaching a drastic degree from about the time of World War I. The Union of 1707 prepared the way for this, of course, but its full effects were delayed for about 200 years. For that period, the Church, education, the law and local administration, all of which the Union left largely in Scottish hands, had more direct effect than central government on people's lives. The degeneration, and the resistance to it, began when that ceased to be true. It leads inevitably to a debilitating sense of inferiority.

It is for this reason that the Referendum of March 1979 was such a disaster. It was disastrous, not only because the hopes and aspirations of a hundred years were once again frustrated, but in the method of the frustration. The No side so conducted their campaign that it became an exercise in mass manipulation, one of the worst aspects of contemporary life, by deliberately playing on the degenerate feeling of inferiority spawned by decades of dependence. They rigged the rules by the 40% requirement, an innovation in British politics where every issue, even the gravest, has always before been settled by simple majority. They avoided rational debate by preventing the distribution of an explanatory leaflet, by obtaining a ban on party political broadcasts and even suppressing a statement by the Church of Scotland of the position affirmed many times by the General Assembly. Instead they used advertising techniques to exploit the instinctive dislike of all government which at that time, after a miserable winter of strikes, was particularly strong. They were ingenious in their confusion of the issues. They claimed, as in Lord Home's broadcast and in the official leaflets of the Conservative Party, to be in favour of more effective devolution, and conveniently forgot about this immediately afterwards.

When I compared the Scotland of 1980 with the Scotland which I had left in 1944 I felt that there was a mixture of both improvement and decline. There had been an obvious rise in the prosperity of a large part of the population. Foreign holidays and the ownership of such things as motor cars, radios, refridgerators and telephones, had been confined to a wealthy minority in the 40s. They were now taken for granted by nearly everyone with a wage-earner in the family. Television was, of course, unknown in the 40s and computers were only beginning to appear in the 80s. I am not sure if all of these things meant that life was becoming more agreeable or, in Sir John Sinclair's phrase, that there was a greater '*quantum* of happiness'.

For one thing a deplorably large number of people were still living in poverty. Drugs and AIDS had brought new miseries and, largely because of the drugs, crime and violence had increased. Certainly, more people had cars, but they blocked the streets and poisoned the atmosphere. More people went to universities, but the cuts in funding put more strain on them and on the increasingly harassed academic staff. Altogether, I am inclined to think that life in the Scotland of my youth was simpler and more Spartan, but, in many ways more satisfying.

Scotland of the 80s had also become more conscious of its

239

distinctiveness and more anxious to preserve it against the pressure for global conformity; but, paradoxically, it had become markedly less distinctively Scottish in practice. These two opposite tendencies were most obvious in language. For both Gaelic and Scots there were more dictionaries, books, scholarly conferences and organisations devoted to their preservation. There were still poets following the lead of Hugh MacDiarmid and Sorley Maclean. On the other hand, there had been a marked decline in the native speakers of both languages. For decades, broadcasting and the cinema had made English and American voices, but few Scottish ones, familiar to everyone. In the Edinburgh of the 1980s, but less so in other parts of the country, I was struck by the rarity of Scottish accents and even greater rarity of Scots vocabulary.

There were other ways in which Scotland had obviously become more Anglicised. Scottish industry used to be largely Scottish owned and controlled and it had been, in Tom Devine's phrase, 'a global economic power.' In the 1980s the heavy industries were close to extinction and such industry as remained was mostly foreign-owned. A similar change was evident even in the shops. Family businesses had disappeared and had been replaced by branches of chains which were also under external ownership and control. It is now a common experience to discover that a service, such as the payment of telephone bills and of insurance policies, had been transferred from a local office to one in England.

I was amazed to discover that Guy Fawkes night, which we used to regard as a celebration of an event in English history which had nothing to do with us, was now being celebrated quite widely in Edinburgh. It was the same with Christmas and all the commercialised nonsense of trees, cards and an orgy of present buying which is now on a massive and absurd scale. Before the war it had hardly been treated at all as a holiday in Scotland – most shops, offices and factories worked normally. By 1980 it had become a compulsory feast – people might complain about it, but they complied. As with language, television is probably the major factor in the change.

When I was working abroad I managed sometimes to come home for Hogmanay. In the company of such stalwarts as Donald Cameron, Charles Johnson (before he went off to be a Sheriff in Glasgow) and Bert Davis we made some memorable visits to the houses of friends and acquaintances. I remember in particular arriving with Bert in the flat of Norman MacCaig where different parties were going on in several rooms and Hugh MacDiarmid had already been put to bed. Such things had not entirely died out in the 1980s, but moving in the middle of a winter's night from house to house is all very well in a village, but a strain in a town, especially as drinking and driving become socially unacceptable. As you get older, the temptation is stronger to stay comfortably at home. More recently Edinburgh and Glasgow, and some other towns as well, have organised massive street parties. These are, no doubt, good fun for the gregarious young; but they do not have the warmth and intimacy of gatherings in the old style round a friendly fireside.

The biggest change of all in the Scotland to which I returned in 1980 was the drastic decline in religious belief and observance. From the Reformation until late in the nineteenth century Scotland was a predominantly Protestant country and the Church of Scotland was the major unifying force with a dominant influence on the attitudes and behaviour of the people. When Sydney Smith, one of the founders of the *Edinburgh Review*, arrived in Edinburgh in 1798 he recorded his first impressions of the Scots in a letter:

> They are very much in earnest in their religion, tho' less so than they were. In England I maintain that (except amongst ladies in the middle class of life) there is no religion at all. The Clergy of England [Smith was one himself] have no more influence over the people at large than the Cheesemongers of England have. In Scotland the Clergy are extremely active in the discharge of their functions, and are from the hold they have on the minds of the people a very important body of men. The common people are extremely conversant with the Scriptures, are really not so much pupils, as formidable critics to their preachers; many of them are well read in controversial divinity. They are perhaps in some points of view the most remarkable nation in the world and no country can afford an example of so much order, morality, economy, and knowledge amongst the lower classes of society. Every nation has its peculiarities, the very improved state of the common people appears to me at present to be the phenomenon of this country.

There is plenty of evidence to support the accuracy of Smith's description at that time. The influence of the Church of Scotland as a unifying force was greatly diminished by the Disruption of 1843 when it split virtually into two separate churches. Most of it eventually came together again, but it was preoccupied with this internal matter for the second half of the nineteenth century when industrialisation was bringing new social problems. At the same period, Catholicism once again became strong in Scotland because of Irish, Polish and Italian immigration. In his *Scottish Journey* first published in 1935, Edwin Muir said that the distinctive national character of Scotland 'is now falling to pieces, for there is no visible and effective power to hold it together.' From the Union to the Disruption the Church of Scotland had been such a power and its General Assembly had been to some extent a substitute for the lost Parliament. It never fully recovered the place in the national life which it lost in 1843.

There were other consequences of the decline in the influence of the Church of Scotland. During the Scottish Renaissance of the 1920s and 30s it was fashionable to condemn the Reformation as a destructive force which had broken Scotland's cultural links with the rest of Europe and discouraged the arts as a distraction from serious spiritual concerns. There is certainly an element of truth in this, even if James Macmillan greatly exaggerated it in his celebrated lecture at the start of the Edinburgh Festival in 1999. On the other hand, the reformed Church fostered other qualities and ideas which have helped to form the Scottish character. They include a strongly democratic conviction that all people have equal rights, a distrust of pretension and privilege, a belief in the virtues of effort and a simple way of life, and in education and the intellect. Many Scots no longer find religion acceptable, because that involves the acceptance of improbable theories without rational evidence, but still accept the attitudes and values which George Davie has called the Democratic Intellect. They are, if you like, Presbyterian Atheists. I am one myself.

In the Scotland of 1944 the influence of the Churches of all persuasions had declined, but it was still visible, most obviously in the observance of Sunday, where most human activity, except going to church, was discouraged. By 1980 the country, which was once highly religious, had become almost entirely secular. The only new churches that were still being built were mosques for the new Islamic community from Pakistan and Bangladesh. You might say that the new secularism was a victory of reason over superstition, except that there were signs that the old religion was being replaced by a new, and more destructive, faith in consumerism and the search for instant, selfish and easy gratification.

In a recent essay by Joyce McMillan about the decline in traditional religion, she condemns 'the ignorance, the contempt, the sneering secularism, the lack of aesthetic awareness, and the failure to acknowledge the positive aspects of all these traditions as part of our civic life.' I agree. There is much that is objectionable in organised religion of all denominations, but in the past it has been a powerful encouragement of desirable attitudes and aspirations. We still have to find a substitute.

In *The Democratic Intellect*, George Davie says that Scottish history has been marked by an 'alternation between catastrophe and renaissance, in which the distinctive national inheritance was more than once brought to the very brink of ruin only to be saved at the last minute by a sudden burst of reviving energy.' We have been going through such a revival almost continuously, with the intervals of the World Wars, since the 1880s. It was then, the age of Stevenson, McTaggart and Geddes, and the start of the Home Rule campaign, that there was talk of a Scottish renaissance. That was asserted with greater confidence and coherence after World War I by Hugh MacDiarmid and the circle around him. Scottish literature, painting and music are now all flourishing.

So why do we have to worry? I think in the first place because awareness of Scottish culture, both in the past and in the present, has not been widespread. Our schools paid little attention to it and television, the chief cultural influence in contemporary society, mostly came from London. The consequence was a feeling of inferiority, the so-called Scottish cringe, and even, as Cairns Craig and others have said, self-hatred. Also, the need for independence had become still more urgent. Even the limited autonomy which the Union of 1707 had left to Scotland was disappearing as the interference of Westminster increased and in 1980 all the signs were that the Thatcher Government would be more centralising than ever. The European organisation was also becoming more powerful and that meant that Scotland had to be accepted as a Member State if our voice was to be heard. If you believed, as I do, that the cultural diversity of Europe is one of its virtues and that Scotland has the capacity to make, as in the past, its own valuable and distinctive contribution, then it was clear that there was an urgent need for action. We required to assert control over our own affairs and to extend awareness and understanding of our cultural identity. I returned to Edinburgh with the determination to use my remaining time and energy to do all I could to help with these two causes. It was as if the whole of my previous experience had been a preparation for this campaign.

There were two ways in which I thought I could help: by writing books, articles and letters to the press; and by taking an active part in the organisations working to these ends. To some extent, I had been doing both while I was still abroad. I had written for the press under a pseudonym and, under my own name, published books. I had long been a member of some of the appropriate organisations, especially the SNP and the Saltire Society. Now at last I could give my undivided attention to these things and try to make up for lost time. Laura helped me in all my activities. From April 1981 she had a part-time job in the Italian Cultural Institute and from May 1984 a full-time one in the Consulate General. This meant, of course, that she had much less time at home, but we both made full use of the evenings and weekends.

Since the 1930s the Saltire Society had published books, organised conferences and performances and award schemes for excellence in many activities from housing design, civil engineering and science to school choirs. It published early Scottish literature at a time when it was not otherwise available, advocated greater attention to Scottish history and literature and languages in the schools and universities and encouraged Scottish music. Maurice Lindsay in his book, *Francis George Scott and the Scottish Renaissance* (1980) said that a measure of the success of the Society 'is the vastly improved state of all these concerns half a century later.' Nigel Tranter once remarked that if more people in Scotland supported the Saltire Society, it would be a much better place.

In anticipation of my return to Edinburgh, I had been elected to the Executive Committee of the Society and I attended my first meeting of it on 29th November, 1980. They asked me to become chairman of the Publications Committee and Ian Gilmour wrote to invite me to join the Festival Committee. I had already in my first three weeks back in Edinburgh been to meetings of the Andrew Fletcher Society and the Scots Language Society.

The number of committees of various organisations of which I became a member soon multiplied. At various times they included, apart from the Saltire Society, the councils and executive committees of the SNP, the Campaign for a Scottish Assembly, the National Trust for Scotland, the Edinburgh Festival, the Scots Language Society, the Association for Scottish Literary Studies, the Campaign for a Scottish National Theatre, the Scottish Centre of International PEN, the Cockburn Association, the Edinburgh Sir Walter Scott Club, the Scottish Centre for Economic and Social Research, the Scottish Poetry Library, the Advisory Council for the Arts in Scotland and the Andrew Fletcher Society. For some of these organisations I have been chairman or president and, at the time of writing, I have been on some of the committees for about twenty years.

Listed together like this it sounds excessive. It might have been an even longer list, because I had to decline many invitations on the grounds that I simply did not have time. Harry Reid in a profile in *The Herald* on 10 Sept 1990 said, 'the sheer scale of Scott's commitment to Scottish causes over the past decade has been awe-inspiring.' Allen Wright in *The Scotsman* said that I had applied to the Scottish cause skills which I had acquired through years of diplomatic experience.

Others were more suspicious. I have been told that Neal Ascherson (who became a friend) had thought when I first appeared on the Edinburgh scene that I was a Government agent. James Halliday in the *Scots Independent* of August 1991 confessed that he had at first cherished 'a furtive feeling of resentment when such talented newcomers appeared to be teaching their grandmothers to suck eggs.' But he generously said that he had been converted by one of my books which was published in 1991, *Towards Independence*, and which he reviewed: 'I now wish, very publicly and most sincerely, to beg his pardon for my doubts and grudges, because he has, in this collection, done the finest service to the national intellectual cause which has appeared, in my judgement, in my lifetime.'

I have sometimes been asked if it was not inconsistent to spend years in the service of the British State and at the same time argue for the removal of Scotland from it. Recently, I did a long interview about Quebec and Scotland with a friendly and unaggressive interviewer from the French service of Radio Canada and he seemed to be genuinely surprised by my personal position. I do not see any inconsistency myself and I was by no means alone in this respect among my colleagues in the Diplomatic Service. In the 1970s, when the recovery of the Scottish Parliament seemed imminent, I was working in the Foreign Office. Several Scots in senior positions agreed that they looked forward eagerly to the day when they could work in a Foreign Ministry in Edinburgh.

Scotland and England since the Union, and indeed since the Union of the Crowns, have functioned as one state in international relations. As long as this continues, Scots who are interested in the subject can work only in the British Foreign Office. We are in a sense working as allies. When Scotland becomes independent again, as I expect, it will be useful for the Scottish Government to be able to call on the service of people with international experience.

My experience as a diplomat has strongly reinforced my desire to see Scotland independent. In the first place, you are made to see very clearly that the only players on the international scene are independent states. They alone are entitled to have their interests and opinions taken into account. They alone are members of the international organisations and the effect of these organisations is to enhance the influence of the smaller countries. Also, in my fairly wide experience of other countries, I have noticed that those where the people most obviously enjoy a satisfying and contented way of life are small, independent states, similar in size and other ways to Scotland. In, say, Norway, Iceland, Finland, Denmark or Austria, the sheer contentment and pleasure which the people derive from their independence is beyond doubt, and so is the good use they have made of it in creating a prosperous and just society. I have often envied their good fortune.

But why, you might ask, did I allow myself to become involved in so many committees on my return to Edinburgh? They were all on bodies which served purposes in which I passionately believed. If you desire the ends, you can hardly refuse to contribute to the means. Then I suppose that there was a general feeling that, as a man recently retired and still in good health, that I must have plenty of spare time and energy, as well as useful accomplishments. John Drummond in his autobiography, *Tainted by Experience*, says, 'the age of the well-off and knowledgeable enthusiast who can afford to donate his time is now largely over.' But, if you are retired you do not need to be well-off. I was not the only one. In the 1994 edition of his *Scotland and Nationalism*, Christopher Harvie spoke of 'the practically full-time work of two retired public servants, Jim Ross and Paul Scott. Political change always tends to imply youth; in Scotland it would never have happened without the impact of energetic oldies.'

Then these committees performed useful functions and, inadvertently, greatly enlarged my circle of like-minded enthusiasts. The publications committee of the Saltire Society, for example, enabled us to bring into print some valuable books and pamphlets which might not have found a commercial publisher. They included RS Silver's epic play, *The Bruce*, which was eventually produced by the Edinburgh Festival, Lord Cooper's *The Scottish Legal Tradition*, Nigel Grant's *The Crisis in Scottish Education*, Gordon Donaldson's *The Auld Alliance*, Derrick McClure's *Why Scots Matters*, and a joint volume by our leading academic historians, *Why Scots History Matters*, the first of our titles to be reprinted in translation in Japan. I had a longstanding desire to see new editions of classic statements of the case for Scottish self-determination: a pamphlet of 1706, in which Andrew Fletcher probably had a hand, *United and Separate Parliaments*, Lockhart of Carnwath's *Memoirs of the Union* and Scott's *Letters of Malachi Malagrowther*. I published the first of these as a Saltire pamphlet, Blackwood's published for me the *Malachi Letters* in 1981 and the Association for Scottish Literary Studies Lockhart's *Memoirs* in 1995. All of these are essential documents in Scottish constitutional history and it is good to have them back in print after a long period of suppression or neglect.

The Saltire festival committee was also very productive. From the beginning of the Edinburgh Festival in 1947 it staged performances of music and poetry to make sure that the arts of Scotland were not entirely excluded. The Society more or less invented the Fringe which has now grown prodigiously. For decades, these Saltire productions every day, and sometimes more than once, for three weeks each year, were directed by Ian Gilmour and his wife Meta Forest. Both were talented and delightful speakers of poetry in Scots. Through their performances thousands of people over the years discovered the pleasures of this great literature from the mediaeval makars onwards.

Poets had always been involved, but I introduced readings by novelists as well. In the early 80s this was unusual, although it has now become familiar in bookshop launches and the Book Festival. William McIlvanney, who was always ready to give valiant support to a Scottish cause, transformed himself into his characters, for he is a natural born actor. Robin Jenkins had a sharp eye for human imperfections and the tragedies of life; but he was like Samuel Johnson's friend who wanted to be a philosopher, 'but cheerfulness

247

was always breaking in.' Jenkins is invincibly genial and his readings were always richly comic. Even so, he told me that he had expected to mellow as be became older, but, in spite of himself, he was getting more and more Swiftian. Allan Massie was efficient and reticent about his own character and feelings. We have long been sparring partners in newspaper controversy over politics, but that did not disturb our friendship and mutual regard.

Among the poets, Robert Garioch was a particular favourite with the audiences, which was natural because he was a thoroughly admirable and likeable character. Perhaps it is a Scottish habit for people of enormous talent to have an air of invincible modesty. RL Stevenson thought of himself as a reincarnation of Robert Fergusson, but I think Garioch was closer to his spirit. With his throwaway manner and his throwaway lines, he was an entrancing performer in reading his own work.

I suggested that the Saltire should put a plaque on Robert Garioch's house. His son, Ian Sutherland (which was also Robert's actual surname) volunteered to finance it from an award which his father had won just before he died. Shortly after this, on the Glasgow train I met Norman MacCaig, who was slightly drunk at the time. He approved of my idea to put Garioch's own dedication on the plaque:

Thae twa-three chuckie-stones
I lay on Scotland's cairn

MacCaig, whom I found an unpredictable and often cantankerous character, said that he admired much of Garioch's poetry but that his translation of Buchanan's plays, which Garioch himself thought his best work was in fact his worst, dull and boring. The plaque was unveiled on 19th April 1983 before a large gathering of the literati. Alexander Scott gave a warm and generous speech. How lucky Edinburgh is to have such poets as Fergusson, Stevenson, Garioch and Sydney Goodsir Smith.

It is one of my regrets that I hardly knew Sydney Goodsir Smith who died in 1975. Bert Davis, who knew all the literary people of the time, was one of his friends and I had brief encounters with him once or twice during my visits to Edinburgh. I had the impression that he was as robust and Rabelaisian as his poetry suggests and he might have been a difficult man to keep up with on a convivial evening. Alex

Scott used to say that Smith's *Under the Eildon Tree* was the finest sequence of love poems in Scots, or any other language, written in the twentieth century. When I told Sydney's widow, Hazel, that George Mackay Br own had said much the same in his autobiography, she replied, 'that's nothing. Alex Scott told me that it is the best long poem about love since Henryson's *Testament of Cresseid*.'

Hugh MacDiarmid I met quite seldom, but I felt that I knew him better because Bert used to share his reminiscences and his letters with me. He was a ruthless controversialist, but a model of consideration and courtesy in his private relations. His letters to Bert always ended with polite greetings to his wife and daughter. On 29th April 1986 Bert, Lester Borley (the director of the National Trust for Scotland) and I went to MacDiarmid's cottage, Brownsbank near Biggar, to visit his widow, Valda. The purpose was to raise the delicate question of how the cottage could be preserved as a memorial to MacDiarmid and as a place of literary pilgrimage, as it were. Valda, who could be fiery and outspoken was on her best behaviour and very welcoming and hospitable. It was soon clear that we were all thinking on similar lines and Valda said that she would keep the cottage as much as possible as it was when Chris was alive. She used a somewhat pungent phrase when Maurice Lindsay's name came up for some reason. She said he was a man with 'one finger in his arse and his mind in neutral.'

I do not know why she felt like this about Maurice, whom I have mentioned several times. In the early days he had been a keen supporter of MacDiarmid and of the Lallans movement. At that time he wrote poetry in Scots. I remember that he appeared with MacDiarmid at a poetry reading in the Saltire Society. Later he turned to English. But so, after all, did MacDiarmid. Maurice said in a partly autobiographical book, *By Yon Bonnie Banks* (1961), that Scotland was indulging in 'national self-destruction' and was unlikely to survive. He concluded the book with this paragraph:

> For me the love affair is over. The fervour, the obsession with Scottishness for its own sake, the strongly emotional response to whatever carried even the faintest Scottish overtone, all these things have faded to a gentle but regretful affection; an affection, however, which, I fancy, will persist to the end of my days.

249

I suppose therefore that Chris and Valda felt that Lindsay was a traitor to the cause. He is also, in a sense, an odd-man-out among Glasgow writers because he is unashamedly middle-class, when most of the others glory in their working-class roots. In fact, Lindsay has continued to do a great deal for the cause of Scottish letters, not only with his own poetry, but with his *History of Scottish Literature*, his *Burns Encyclopedia*, his editorship of the *Scottish Review* and in many other ways. He has been active too in broadcasting, music criticism and conservation. He has always been most friendly and helpful to me personally. In 1997 Lester Borley asked me to contribute an essay to a joint volume, *Dear Maurice*, to commemorate his 80th birthday. I agreed with pleasure and so did more than twenty others. Brownsbank has been preserved, with a succession of writers in residence, but not by the National Trust.

It was also because of Bert Davis that I first met Sorley Maclean. They were old friends because they had first met when they were students in Edinburgh University. Years before I finally came back to Edinburgh in 1980, I was on leave and proposed to tour through the Highlands. Bert suggested that I should call on Sorley and his wife, Renée, in Plockton, where he was the headmaster of the local school. We had an entrancing conversation which we always seemed to resume where we left off, even if there had been an interval of years. He was unmistakably a poet, or rather a bard in an ancient tradition. His conversation was full of metaphysical leaps and his eyes would glow as a fresh idea came into his mind. When he read his poetry in Gaelic, even those who did not understand a word were overwhelmed by the power of its music and by its evident intensity of feeling. Seamus Heaney had a point when he compared Sorley's delivery to the sound of a pibroch, 'coming from a long way off'.

Whenever any Highlander was mentioned Sorley always enquired into their parentage and relations and was pleased when he could relate them to someone he knew. He once told me about William Mathison, 'his twentieth cousin', who he said was a great authority on Gaelic song, but spent too much time on questions of genealogy. He once told Sorley that he was uneasy if he met a Highlander whose genealogy he did not know. I rather think that Sorley felt the same. He often spoke about other poets, Robert Garioch, for instance. He used to visit him in his father's house in Bellevue Road in Edinburgh. His father was a house painter, who also made and played violins. To get to a seat by the fire, you had to navigate past a printing press, violins in various stages of manufacture and associated debris.

Sorley always referred to MacDiarmid by his real name, Chris Grieve. He said that he had always been very fond of him, but their relationship had 'cooled off' for a time because of a disagreement about one of MacDiarmid's longer poems. He was surprised that MacCaig and MacDiarmid were such close friends, especially as MacCaig always refused to write Scots (although he spoke it) and to take up a political position. Even so, Sorley was pretty sure that MacCaig always voted SNP. Sorley said that he was convinced that MacDiarmid was a great poet on the strength of his first two volumes of lyrics. He could not claim to be familiar with the whole of twentieth century European literature, but he would be surprised if there was a greater poet anywhere else in Europe.

Although Sorley was kind and generous to a fault, the exception was the other Gaelic poet, Derick Thomson. The sad fact was that the two finest Gaelic poets of the century could not stand one another. During the Festival in 1984 I ran into Sorley in the University Staff Club, one of his favourite haunts when he was in Edinburgh. He complained about the Saltire Book Award to Thomson the year before and said that the entry about himself in Thomson's *Companion to Gaelic Culture* was scandalous. When I looked this up afterwards I was not quite sure why Sorley objected so strongly. It did say that his 'work in bringing cross-fertilising influences to Gaelic verse is highly important', and that it was 'a rich blend of diverse preoccupations, emotions and intellect, free-thinking and conservatism.'

Perhaps it was the last word which was offensive. Sorley himself did not win the Saltire Award until 1990, but that was only because the Award was for a book published in the previous year and he had not published one since the Award started until *O Choille gu Bearradh* in 1989.

One of Sorley's 'preoccupations' was a feeling of guilt, not only because he did not take part in the Spanish Civil War, as is apparent from his poetry, but also because he did not volunteer for World War II. Like most of us, he waited until he was 'called up'. More than once he explained to me at some length in conversation and in a letter that both of these failures, as he regarded them, were forced on him by the circumstances of his family who needed his financial support. I tried hard to persuade him that he had nothing to be ashamed of and that no one thought the worse of him for not rushing to volunteer; but I think I failed to convince him.

In July 1985 he telephoned in response to my suggestion that he might write an autobiographical essay for a series I had called Saltire Self Portraits. He said that he had alwasy founbd writing difficult, but now his docotr had told him that he must avoidany exertion. Soem months later when Bert an i had a long conversation with him, we arrranged that Bert would tape an interview for the same purpose. Unfortunately for some reason this never happened.

In September 1981 I agreed to be the chairman of a joint committee between the Saltire Society and the Edinburgh Sir Walter Scott Club to plan the commemoration of the 150th anniversary of the death of Scott. This had an unexpected bonus, the discovery of the work of Anne Carrick. I had been told that she had an exhibition in her house in Kelso of her versions of scenes and characters from the *Minstrelsy of the Scottish Border* in what were variously described as costume figures or dolls. I went to see them without any great expectations, but I was immediately captivated. They were delicate creations in fabric, gauze and tinsel which gave visible form to both the supernatural and the martial ballads. I said to Anne that the collection should be kept intact and the ideal place to display them was Smailholm Tower. She agreed at once. It was there that Scott had first encountered the world of the ballads when as a boy he was sent for his health to live in Sandyknowe farm beneath the Tower. Scott himself in the Introduction to the Third Canto of *Marmion* recalls that he had thought the Tower, 'the mightiest work of human power' and how beside it he had been told:

> Of patriot battles, won of old
> By Wallace wight and Bruce the bold;
> And onward still the Scottish Lion bore,
> And still the scatter'd Southron fled before

Historic Scotland (or whatever it was called in those days) had recently restored this gaunt Border keep and replaced the floors, but it had remained an empty shell. I wrote an enthusiastic review in *The Scotsman*, of Anne Carrick's exhibition. Then I went to see Historic Scotland and the Scottish Tourist Board and the whole project fell into shape with remarkable speed. The Saltire Society bought the

The Saltire Book Award panel, December 1990 – Paul Scott, Derick Thomson, Ian Campbell, Douglas Gifford, Angus Calder, Alan Taylor

collection, with the aid of an anonymous donation arranged by Ian Gilmour; the Tourist Board paid for the display cases and Historic Scotland welcomed the opportunity to give a new life and purpose to the Tower. Twenty years later, the exhibition is still in place.

The Saltire Society gave annual Awards, which were of considerable prestige and influence, for a great variety of activities. There was an obvious gap in the absence of any such award for books (although, I discovered afterwards there had been an occasional one in the 1930s and 50s.) I proposed in March 1981 that we should start one and got the usual answer, 'Good idea. Go ahead.' It was easier than I expected to raise the funds because the Royal Bank of Scotland agreed almost at once to sponsor an annual award of £1,000 for the Scottish Book of the Year. Any new book by an author of Scottish descent or living in Scotland, or a book by anyone on a Scottish subject, was eligible. The Awards Panel, of which I was convener for twelve years, included both academic specialists in Scottish literature, such as Ian Campbell, Douglas Gifford and Isobel Murray; the Gaelic poet, Derick Thomson and writers, journalists and critics, such as Angus Calder, Alan Taylor and Joyce McMillan. This was quite a demanding task because it involved finding the time to read a large number of books, which was why, with reluctance, I decided to retire from it in 1994. It took time, but it was a real pleasure, not only from reading the books themselves, but from the fascination of our conversations as we discussed them. The first Award was to Alasdair Gray in 1982 for *Lanark*, which, I think, will be regarded as the greatest Scottish novel of the twentieth century. The Saltire panel were among the first people to recognise its importance. Since then there has been no shortage of worthy winners.

Alasdair Gray is one of the most gentle and delightful of human beings. He is, I have no doubt, a genius, but he is extremely modest and shy. At the launch of *Lanark*, on which he had been working for decades, he disappeared just as he was about to be introduced to the audience. At another event in Edinburgh he simply failed to arrive and apologised profusely afterwards that he had forgotten about it and had gone to the cinema. It is, I think, because of this shyness that he sometimes adopts funny voices and eccentric behaviour to cover up his embarrassment. He is highly talented as both a painter and a writer and, as you quickly discover when you speak to him, formidably well read and full of new ideas. I was happy to discover, for example, that he shared my enthusiasm for the novels of John Galt. In December 1984 he told me, now that he had published his latest short novel and a collection of his short stories, that he thought his writing would 'tail off'; he found painting more relaxing and satisfying than writing, which was more of a strain on the nerves.

It was after this that he embarked on another mammoth task, *The Book of Prefaces*, which eventually appeared in the year 2000. Only a man of Alasdair's vast reading and energy could have produced such a book in less than a lifetime and no one but Alasdair could have designed and illustrated it to make it a work of art as breathtaking as a medieval manuscript. As his publisher's deadline approached, he felt that he was not going to be able to write all the comments himself and so he asked a few friends, including me, if we would help by writing a few of them. He offered to reward us by drawing a portrait sketch which he would give us and reproduce in the book, which I thought a reward beyond price. He could not resist altering our contributions to his own style, which, I fear, introduced some factual errors. He apologised afterwards for this for he is a man of infinite courtesy and generosity of spirit. I see from my diary that he told me in August 1995 that he greatly admired the things which I did and wrote. I replied, of course, that I felt exactly the same way about him. When I went to his flat in Glasgow so that he could draw a portrait sketch for his *Book of Prefaces*, I was delighted to see that his sitting room had several plaques with saltires and quotations from the Declaration of Arbroath.

When David Hume said that the Scots of his day were the most distinguished people for literature in Europe, he was thinking, not of novels and poetry, but of philosophy, history and even (with Adam Smith) of economics. The narrower view of the term, literature, has its origins, I think, in its interpretation by university departments who by their nature have to specialise. The Saltire Society, I am glad to say, takes a wider view. Winners of the Book Award have included David Daiches for his Gifford Lectures, *God and the Poets*, and Duncan MacMillan for *Scottish Art: 1460-1990*.

God and the Poets probably embraces the width of Daiches's erudition more impressively than other of his many books, ranging, as it does, from the Book of Job, the psalms and medieval Hebrew poetry to Edwin Muir and Hugh MacDiarmid. He is a son of the chief Rabbi in Scotland who was descended from a long line of Hebrew scholars. David called his autobiography *Two Worlds* because he was brought up in Edinburgh in orthodox Judaism at home and in the life of Edinburgh outside. He was a contemporary at Edinburgh University of Sorley Maclean and Bert Davis. His PhD at Cambridge was in English translations of the Hebrew bible. He has taught at Chicago University, Cornell, Cambridge and Sussex, and he has written a history of English Literature; but of the two (or in fact many more) worlds, it has been Scotland and Scottish literature that has prevailed. In a talk which David gave to the Scottish Arts Club in 1995 he said that his father had fallen in love with the Scottish Enlightenment when he was at university in Germany and that his appointment to Edinburgh was the pinnacle of his ambition. David said of himself that he was devoted to Scotland and that at an early age he had set himself the ambition of becoming the leading scholar in the field of Scottish literature. That he has certainly achieved.

One of his lectures in the 1950s about Walter Scott has led to a transformation in the critical approach to Scott and found new pleasures, depths and subtleties in the novels. His book on Robert Burns and his *Paradox of Scottish Culture* have stimulated a new understanding both of Burns and of the eighteenth century in Scotland generally. In 1980 he became the Director of the Institute for Advance Studies in the Humanities of Edinburgh University. He was one of the organisers of the important conference on the Scottish Enlightenment in 1986 in which I played a small part. He is one of my predecessors as president of the Saltire Society and he has also been president of the Association for Scottish Literary Studies. He has been a neighbour and friend ever since I came back to Edinburgh in 1980 and every conversation with him has been an intellectual enrichment. Whether people realise it or not, Daiches is one of the creators of the new atmosphere in Scotland.

The biographical note about Hugh MacDiarmid in the Penguin edition of his *Selected Poems* refers to his award of the Fletcher of Saltoun Medal. Alan Bold in his biography, *MacDiarmid*, says that it was awarded by the Edinburgh University Nationalist Club, 'for services to Scotland'. That phrase, no doubt deliberately, recalls a remark about Fletcher made by George Lockhart of Carnwarth in his *Memoirs of the Union*: 'if ever a man proposes to serve and merit well of his country, let him . . . think himself sufficiently applauded and rewarded by obtaining the character of being like Andrew Fletcher of Saltoun.' As far as I could discover, the award had been made only on this single occasion by the University club, but it seemed to me a good idea and I suggested that the Saltire Society should resume it. It was awarded for the first time in 1989, very appropriately, to David Daiches.

Another Saltire activity was the progress, masterminded by Professor John MacQueen and Bert Davis, towards the formation of a representative body to draw up recommendations about cultural policy. A conference in Edinburgh on 17th February 1979 of some eighty organisations had agreed that an Advisory Council for the Arts in Scotland (AdCAS) should be established. The Referendum of March 1979, followed by the subsequent election of a Conservative Government and the repeal of the Scotland Act, was a major reverse. Even so, John MacQueen was given an assurance by Alex Fletcher, a minister in the Scottish Office, that the Government 'would recognize the value of the advice' of the proposed council. A conference to set up the new organisation was held in Saltire House in Atholl Crescent in Edinburgh on 13th June 1981 with Sir Kenneth Alexander in the Chair. Seventy two organisations were represented. They included the National Galleries, the National Library, Scottish Opera, the Scottish Arts Council, the Scottish Chamber Orchestra, theatre companies, local authorities and many voluntary organisations. A constitution was agreed and an Executive Council, of which I was the Convener, was appointed. Among the members were two poets, Alexander Scott and George Bruce, David Daiches, Nigel Grant (Professor of Education at Glasgow University), Ewan Hooper (the Director of the Scottish Theatre Company), Colin Thompson (the Director of the National Galleries), Anne Smith (the founder of the *Literary Review*) and, of course, John MacQueen and Bert Davis.

For nearly twenty years AdCAS drew up proposals and agitated for a diversity of aims, all of which were intended to enrich the cultural and intellectual life of Scotland. (Bert Davis and I edited a Selection of AdCAS Papers, published in 1991.) Some of the objectives have been achieved, such as the autonomy of the Scottish Arts Council and of the funding of Scottish universities, although not by our efforts alone. Others were more particular to AdCAS. One of the first was a recommendation that there was an urgent need for paperback reprints of important Scottish books, because the majority of them were out of print. We had a series of meetings with the Scottish Arts Council and a scheme was drawn up to give financial support to publishers for this purpose. Several of them responded, notably Canongate. They are meeting the need admirably in a well edited and designed series, Canongate Classics, which is gradually including the major works from Barbour's *Bruce* to the present.

Our most sustained campaign has been for a National Theatre. This has been an aspiration in Scotland since early in the twentieth century; but what I trust is the decisive phase was initiated by an AdCAS conference on 30th May 1987. Virtually every theatre in Scotland was represented. The Directors of the National Theatres of Finland and Iceland encouraged us by their example. Writers, theatre directors and actors spoke, many of them, including David Daiches and Tom Fleming, with eloquence and passion. The demand for a National Theatre was urgent and unanimous. Gerry Mulgrew, the Director of the theatre company, Communicado, said that he had been opposed to the idea of a National Theatre but had been converted by the discussion. The Chairman of the Scottish Arts Council, Sir Allan Peacock, who was present, wrote to me afterwards. 'No-one,' he said, 'could fail to be impressed by the strength of the demand for a national theatre.'

In all of these activities of AdCAS Bert Davis, who for years was the Honorary Secretary, was an indispensable supporter and ally. It was a task for which he was admirably qualified with his wide knowledge of music and literature. We had many shared enthusiasms, including Burns and Scott, from both of whom quotations came readily to his lips. Another of his assets was his huge circle of friends and acquaintances in Scotland. His last job with the British Council was as their representative in Scotland which brought him into touch with practitioners in all the arts. His open, friendly and invariably cheerful and optimistic personality meant that he was a man that no one could dislike.

Bert was active in other organisations as well. He was the business manager of the Edinburgh Quartet and was on the Committee of the Demarco Gallery. The latter was an onerous and delicate task. Our dear friend, Ricky Demarco, was an uncontrollable volcano of ideas, enthusiasms and projects. He did more than anyone to transform the artistic atmosphere of Edinburgh by his exhibitions, theatrical programme, conferences and expeditions which brought avant garde artists from the rest of Europe to Edinburgh and enlivened the whole spirit of the place. The trouble was that his boundless enthusiasm refused to accept bureaucratic rules and financial prudence. It was not easy for his committees to produce some semblance of conformity with the rules. I was glad to see that Ricky acknowledged the help which he had from Bert by dedicating the illustrations which he drew for Andrew Lownie's *Literary Companion to Edinburgh* to him as 'his friend and mentor'.

The working party on the National Theatre set up by the conference in May 1987 included some of the leading Scottish actors and theatre directors, Tom Fleming, Gerry Mulgrew, Gerda Stevenson and Joan Knight. Kenneth Ireland, a founder and former director of the Pitlochry Festival Theatre, was very helpful in research and drafting. Joy Hendry, another strong supporter of the AdCAS, is the editor of the literary review, *Chapman*, in which she published a full report of the conference. Diverse expertise was added by Kirstie Adam, Alex Clark, Alex McCrindle, Lesley Hills, Mary Picken and, the tireless advocate for the Scots language, Billy Kay. I was chairman and Bert Davis the secretary. The report was published on 30th May 1987. It made a powerful case which, as Tom Fleming said, was bound to succeed in the end. I leave subsequent developments to the next chapter.

I had been a supporter of the SNP virtually since it was founded in 1934 and I was active in its organisation in Edinburgh University. My membership lapsed when I was abroad with the Army and the Diplomatic Service, but in anticipation of my return to Scotland, I joined again in 1976. This was in the Murrayfield/Cramond Branch, which was the nearest to my mother's house in Blackhall.

I changed to the Edinburgh Branch, which covers the centre of the town, when I moved into my own flat in Drumsheugh Gardens. Incredibly, the Chairman was Frank Yeaman, who had also been chairman of the Branch in Alva Street of which I had been a member in 1939. I began to become known in the party at large, partly by my journalism, books and broadcasting and also by attending and speaking at meetings of the National Council, National Assembly and Conferences because the SNP is a very democratic organisation. In May 1983 I was asked to stand as the candidate of the party in the General Election for the Constituency of Edinburgh East. I enjoyed the campaign because it involved meeting many people with lively conversation, debates on the radio and the like. As in my later experiences of the kind, I had the impression that I was going to do better than in fact was the case, because people on the whole are so friendly and polite that you think that they, and others like them, are going to vote for you. I think that this is common illusion among election candidates. But it was a time when the fortunes of the SNP were at a low ebb. Quite unreasonably, we were blamed for the failure of the 1979 Referendum. That was a Labour policy for which we had campaigned, but on which Labour itself was split and which some of their prominent members, such as Robin Cook and Brian Wilson, had fought on the other side. In a safe Labour seat I had only 5.5% of the vote, which was fairly typical of SNP results in such seats at the time. I was elected as a member of the National Executive Committee of the party at the Conference in September in 1989.

Very soon after my return to Edinburgh I became a member of the National Executive Committee of another organisation formed at that time to work for the recovery of the Scottish Parliament. This was the Campaign for a Scottish Assembly. It consisted of people who were of Labour, Liberal or SNP persuasion or of no party at all. Like me, they refused to accept the result of the 1979 Referendum, in which after all there had been a majority for Yes, as the final rejection of the cause. The intention was to bring together the parties which were on the Yes side and which represented together about 80% of the Scottish electorate. Every opinion poll for years had shown that such a percentage was in favour of constitutional change. It was entirely undemocratic and unacceptable that the Conservative British Government, under Margaret Thatcher, should deny the clear wish of the Scottish people and impose on Scotland policies which they rejected in election after election.

As in all such campaigns, comparatively few people do the actual work of attending committee meetings, producing ideas and putting them into effect. The few included Jim Boyack, Hugh Millar, Greg McCarra, Bob McLean, Alan Lawson, and Allan Armstrong. We could count on the support, passive and at times active, of many people all over Scotland. I always thought that it was wrong that we should be campaigning for an Assembly and not a Parliament. For over a hundred years the objective had been the recovery of the Parliament and the other word had been substituted by civil servants or politicians in Whitehall, anxious, as always, to use vocabulary, like the word Devolution itself, that was designed to lower Scottish expectations. Perhaps they did not know that in Scotland, the term, Assembly, had four centuries of association with the Church. I proposed that we should revert to use of the word, Parliament, at a conference in Edinburgh in March 1981. But it took some years to persuade the Labour Party to agree.

The most valuable ally of the campaign was a magazine, *Radical Scotland*, which Alan Lawson edited from the first issue in February/ March 1983 to the fifty first and final issue in June/July 1991. It was, I think, the best political journal ever published in Scotland. The final editorial said that 'the case for self-government – and for a separate Scottish political and cultural identity – has been accepted in all but the darkest corners of Scotland'; and that events were developing so fast that a bi-monthly magazine could not keep pace. Probably also, Alan was exhausted by this mammoth achievement and wanted to turn his energies in another direction, for *Radical Scotland* was not his only contribution to the cause.

From the beginning of my association with the Campaign for a Scottish Assembly I had argued that we should try to form a representative body, which I at first called a Constituent Assembly, to draw up detailed proposals for the Parliament we wanted. Gordon Wilson had proposed something similar in the House of Commons in 1980. It should not be left to Whitehall. I wrote a paper which was discussed at a meeting of the National Committee in Aberdeen in May 1981. On 8th July Jim Boyack and Hugh Millar came to my flat in Drumsheugh Gardens to discuss the idea and we agreed that we should work to have it adopted as the policy of the Campaign. In March 1982 Colin Boyd (who is now Lord Advocate) telephoned to ask me to introduce my paper at a Conference of the Campaign on the twentieth. It was passed virtually unanimously.

But how was the Constituent Assembly, or Constitutional Convention as we eventually called it, to be achieved? This was gradually elaborated in the meetings of the Executive Committee and in discussion with representatives of the political parties. This was a slow process, but when we had reached the point when we were ready to go ahead, Alan Lawson suggested the appointment of a Constitutional Steering Committee of 'prominent Scots'. He found ideal people for the tasks of chairman and secretary, Sir Robert Grieve and Jim Ross. Bob Grieve, a neighbour and fellow habitué of the Scottish Arts Club, had been Chief Planner in the Scottish Office, Professor of the subject in Glasgow University and Chairman of the Highlands and Islands Development Board. He was also a passionate Scot, addicted to both our mountains and our poetry, which he could recite at length. He was an admirable chairman, stimulating and encouraging, pressing forward, but giving everyone a good chance to speak. Jim Ross has recently retired as a senior civil servant in the Scottish Office where he had dealt with the Scotland Act of 1979. He had remarkable skill in translating the discussion round the table into a lucid and coherent draft which satisfied all of us. Other members of the Committee included Joy Hendry, Nigel Grant, Maxwell Craig, John Henry, Isobel Lindsay, Una Maclean Mackintosh, Neil MacCormick, Judy Steel and Kenyon Wright.

We met frequently between February and July 1988 when the report was published as *A Claim of Right for Scotland* . This was a title I had suggested. I was working on my book on Andrew Fletcher at the time. In it I had discussed the first Claim of Right in 1689, which, like the second one in 1842, was a protest against misgovernment and the historical parallel was obvious.

The committee had been asked to report on 'all aspects of the case' for setting up a Scottish Constitutional Convention as well as on the practical steps necessary. This led us to examine, not only the need for a Scottish Parliament, but the inadequacies of the British

Constitution. It was a subject on which Jim and I, with our personal experience of working within the system, had strong feelings. In the Report I recognise some phrases of my own, including the passages on the cultural consequences of the Union, the excessive powers of British Prime Ministers and a preference for the term, Parliament. Many of the most potent and epigrammatic phrases, worthy of inclusion in a dictionary of quotations, are pure Jim Ross. In the *Observer* of 31 July 1988 Neal Ascherson said that the Report was 'the most penetrating institutional critique of the United Kingdom I have read in this decade.' The editorial in the *New Statesman* of 26 August said that it included 'the most calm, systematic and damning dissection of Britain's highest office.' It also made such a powerful case for constitutional change that it was now irresistible. Fortunately, the Convention did eventually decide to call for a Parliament and this is the name which has now been firmly established. Gordon Wilson afterwards said that this was the Unionists' biggest mistake. He was right. The existence of a Parliament arouses expectations which cannot tolerate for long the trammels of reserved powers.

CHAPTER 17

Back in Scotland (2)
The 1980s continued

Alastair Dunnett was the creator of yet another initiative designed to work towards the recovery of Scottish self-confidence and a Scottish Parliament. This was not intended to be a mass, or even a public, organisation. His idea was to form a small group of people with ideas about the future of Scotland who would hold discussions privately with leading figures in Scottish life to see how much common ground could be established. Essentially, he thought it might be possible to achieve more by the private persuasion of Government ministers than by public pressure. With almost anyone else in charge, this would have been a hopelessly optimistic venture, but Alastair was uniquely well placed to give the lead.

He had been editor of *The Scotsman* from 1956 to 1972 and had made the paper an eloquent advocate for Home Rule. In the early 1980s he was Chairman of Thomson Scottish Petroleum with an office and boardroom, provided with an excellent catering staff, in Charlotte Square. Alastair knew virtually everyone of any importance in Scotland and I think that everyone who met him at once liked and respected him. He was wonderful company, full of ideas and anecdotes, and invariably cheerful, optimistic and determined to give Scotland a chance to realise its full potential. It soon became apparent that no one, no matter how important, was likely to refuse an invitation from Alastair to join him for lunch and a discussion with his group.

His first step was to send a letter on 6 February 1981 to about half a dozen people, including me, to see if we would be interested. The object, he said, was to find a way 'within the British context . . . to remedy the dwindling reality of Scotland'. He proposed to set up a group to be called (although he came close to apologising for his daring) the 'Guardians', a title resonant of response to crises in the

Scottish past. He enclosed a paper which he said had been drawn up by one or two people who were 'concerned with the condition of Scotland and with the obvious gap which exists between what Scotland is now and what she might become. They see the lights of Scottish individuality going out one by one.' They thought that the 'basic requirements . . . would include a non-separatist, pro-monarchical trend towards a British federal arrangement'. They also spoke of the need as a priority to work towards the restoration and retention of the British name.

Of course there was a good deal in this paper, especially the phrases just quoted, that I thought misguided. At the same time, private discussions with political and other leaders to seek progress towards self-government might help to extract us from the despondency to which Scotland had been reduced by the blatant manipulation of the 1979 Referendum. The following was my reply on 10th February 1981 to Alastair's letter. I quote it in full because it summarises my views on these constitutional issues:

> Thank you very much for your letter of 6th February. I am, of course, very interested in your proposal and entirely agree about the need 'to remedy the dwindling reality of Scotland'. I should be delighted to take part in a discussion on the basis you suggest at any time. Thank you for including me.
>
> I think that it is common ground among those who are concerned about these matters that the essential and urgent thing is for Scotland to achieve more control over her own affairs. Disagreement arises over the degree. My own view is that even a small step – like the Scotland Act – would be better than nothing at all; but we need more and not less. The discussion at the time of the Referendum showed, I think, that the weakness of the Act was that it did not go far enough. We need control over economic affairs, revenue raising powers and an independent voice externally, especially in Brussels. Logically, I think that it is difficult to stop short of the conclusion that Scotland needs as much independence as, say, Denmark or Luxembourg.
>
> It follows from this view that there are one or two points in your draft which I, personally, would put rather differently. Take the reference to the SNP on the first page. It seems to me that the real 'separatism' is the present state of affairs which cuts Scotland off

from the rest of the world, dumb and invisible. Also it is only votes for the SNP which put the Scottish question on the political agenda.

On page 2, the draft mentions monarchism and federalism. I think that monarchism is little more than a picturesque survival, devoid of political reality. I seen no advantage in making an issue of it. Federalism comes up against the problems of the disparity of scale between Scotland and England and the absence of any serious interest in it in England.

Finally the point about the 'British name' on page 3. Only the Scots have ever understood, or cared about, the distinction between English and British. We tried hard for 200 years. I don't see much point in trying to make it a priority now.

But I am sure that there is a great deal of common ground between us. As Eric Linklater put it in 1935, 'I believe people degenerate when they lose control of their own affairs'. That is the basic issue. If we can settle that, the relationship with England and the rest of the EEC will be healthier as well.

As I said at the beginning, I should be very happy to continue the discussion. I hope that we can meet soon.

I do not know who took part in the drafting of Alastair's paper or the extent to which these references to non-separatism. monarchism, federalism and the British name represented Alastair's own view at that time. He never made an issue of any of them during all our discussions, and we did not disagree on any point of importance. Over the next few years he moved steadily towards the views of the SNP. In the summer of 1996 he wrote to Alex Salmond to say that he was now firmly in favour of independence. Shortly afterwards I asked him to lunch in the Scottish Arts Club to meet Alex and his wife, Moira. We had a lively conversation and an enthusiastic meeting of minds. Alastair telephoned me a day or two later to say that he was very impressed by Alex and Moira and that he was surprised that Alex was 'so witty and entertaining'.

In forming his Guardians, Alastair had arrived at a group of about ten people of diverse interests. Membership fluctuated a bit, but frequent attenders included, in no particular order, the following. There was James Adam, a journalist colleague of Alastair, one of his oldest friends and, like most of the group, a fervent Scot. He wrote satirical verse in Scots and taught himself Gaelic, which, as I know from my own efforts, is a considerable feat. Sir Charles Fraser, a lawyer and Purse Bearer to the Lord High Commissioner, was on the boards of many companies. He is a generous and open-minded man who, as he said himself, is unlike most businessmen in taking a keen interest in literature and the arts. Sir Iain Noble is a merchant banker, whose father was the British Ambassador when I was in Warsaw. He was my immediate predecessor as President of the Saltire Society. He is a strong supporter of the Gaelic cause and one of the founders of the Gaelic College, Sabhal Mor Ostaig. Thomas Johnston was Professor of Economics and Vice-Chancellor of Heriot-Watt University and President of the Royal Society of Edinburgh. Lord Birsay was Chairman of the Scottish Land Court, active in many causes and a valiant campaigner for the Scots language.

For the rest of the decade, the Guardians had a series of discussions over lunch with politicians, church leaders, businessmen and academics. We had a discussion about the Labour Party attitude with John Smith in November 1981. He was not yet Party Leader, but he had been Minister in charge of the Scotland Act in the 1970s. He said that Home Rule was an urgent necessity because the Scottish Office was out of control politically. Scotland was going downhill and would disappear unless action was taken. Whitehall departments had been ferocious in defending their areas of power. An all-party initiative was needed, but a difficulty was that the Labour Party was so hostile to the SNP, who poached on their preserves, that they were unable or unwilling to campaign along with them. When I asked if the Campaign for a Scottish Assembly was not an all-party body already in being, Smith said that the Labour Party regarded it as an SNP front.

The accuracy of John Smith's prediction was evident from Labour's response to our attempt to enlist the political parties in the discussion. The CSA called a conference for this purpose in a hotel in Edinburgh on 9th July 1983. All of the parties, except the Conservatives and Labour, sent representatives, although the Labour MP, Denis Canavan, attended 'in a personal capacity'. Gordon Wilson and Winnie Ewing came from the SNP and Russell Johnston from the Liberals. The party representatives all said that they welcomed the initiative of the CSA and urged us to continue our efforts to widen the area of agreement. Our failure to persuade Labour to participate officially was disappointing. I wrote at the time that they seemed to me convinced that co-operation would tend to weaken their dominant role in Scotland.

In the end, however, it was the SNP, and not Labour, who refused to take part in the Convention. The whole atmosphere was changed by a by-election in Govan in November 1988, which Jim Sillars won by 3,500 votes in a seat previously held by Labour with a majority of 19,000. This had effects both on Labour and the SNP. It convinced Labour that they had to do more to try to outflank the SNP on the Home Rule issue. Within the SNP it greatly enhanced the influence of Sillars, a powerful orator and a formidable campaigner. Possibly also the Govan victory encouraged the view that independence was achievable though the ballot box, without the intermediate stage of a devolutionary Parliament. At all events, the SNP decided to withdraw. I did my best to resist this in several long phone calls to Gordon Wilson, then leader of the party. Alex Salmond, in his memoirs, attributes the withdrawal to Sillars: 'He directed the over-hasty exit from the Constitutional Convention in 1989 and flung away the political initiative gained from his victory in the Govan by-election.' Sillars was not alone. Wilson, who is a man of integrity, generosity of spirit and strong views of his own, was adamant that withdrawal was the best policy.

It was certainly not an easy question for the SNP. Labour, on their own admission, were undertaking a policy of so-called devolution, not to move towards independence, but to prevent it. Both Labour and the Liberals said that their policy and the purpose of their Convention was to strengthen the Union. George Robertson, as Labour Shadow Secretary of State, said that 'devolution would kill the SNP stone dead.' The SNP had bitter memories of 1979 when they had campaigned for a Labour measure and had been blamed when it failed.

The irony is that the Constitutional Convention, an idea which I had persuaded the CSA to adopt, did lead to a Scottish Parliament and that in the Referendum of 1997 the SNP campaigned, along with Labour and Liberals, to achieve it. The circumstances had changed since 1989 when it was not clear where a Convention dominated by Labour would lead. In 1997 there was a clear commitment to establish a Scottish Parliament which, although it was hampered by a long list of powers reserved to Westminster, could begin the process of restoring Scotland to the world. I do not think that all the effort which I had put into the CSA had been useless.

Before that meeting with John Smith, Alec Douglas-Home came on 12th October 1981, armed with several pages of hand-written notes. It was brave of him to come at all and we were a little surprised that he had accepted the invitation. He was, after all, widely regarded as the leading villain in the deception of the 1979 Referendum. He was a former Conservative Prime Minister who was highly regarded and trusted by many people in Scotland, and not only because of residual deference to the head of an old Border family.

In the Foreign Office I had many encounters with him when he was Foreign Secretary. He had always struck me as a thoroughly decent, straightforward, kindly man who, unlike most of his Conservative colleagues, was quite free of the arrogance of office. He also gave the impression that he was a patriotic Scot, who, if like the rest of his class anglicised by his education, was genuinely concerned over the well-being and future of Scotland. Many people in Scotland believed that Home had deliberately exploited his reputation to mislead the voters. A few days before the vote on the Referendum he spoke on television to urge a No vote, on the grounds that this would give a Conservative Government an opportunity to introduce a better bill for an Assembly with stronger powers. In fact, of course, Margaret Thatcher, when she became Prime Minister soon after this, repealed the Scotland Act and then for years refused to do anything at all about constitutional change.

I have always been puzzled by this episode. It was difficult to believe that the Douglas Home I knew could be capable of an act which seemed to be so blatantly unscrupulous and dishonest. I can only suppose that he had been manipulated and misled by Margaret Thatcher, that she had appealed to his Tory loyalty to make the broadcast with some vague understanding, which she did not honour, and perhaps never intended to honour.

At the Guardians' lunch, Home began by saying that even without a Parliament or Assembly there were several opportunities for the development and expression of a Scottish point of view, such as COSLA and the ministers in the Scottish Office. In the past, personalities had emerged to give a lead, but that no longer seemed to be true. He was still in favour of devolution, but there was no consensus and progress towards it would have to wait, probably for the Parliament after the next one.

Iain Noble reacted very firmly and effectively to this. The Scottish people had made it abundantly clear for years that they wanted a measure of Home Rule. To disregard that, to keep on saying wait for some eventuality in the future, was a denial of democracy that was quite unacceptable. I asked Home what he meant by an absence of consensus when all political parties, except at the moment the Conservatives, had committed themselves to Home Rule. He said that he meant a lack of agreement among members of both Houses. In that case, I asked, would it not be a good idea to see if the work of detailed discussion and the search for a consensus could be undertaken in Scotland where it properly belonged? An agreed text could then be offered to Parliament for approval. Home more or less indicated assent to this and said that his report of some twelve years earlier might still offer a useful basis. I told him, and he joined in the general laughter, that the Conservative Party office in Atholl Crescent had denied all knowledge of this document and of Heath's 'Declaration of Perth'.

I suggested, with support from others, that it might even be in the interest of the Conservative Party to come back into the mainstream on this issue. In view of his broadcast just before the vote on the Referendum (which had again been mentioned in a *Scotsman* leader only a couple of weeks before our lunch) he was the obvious man to give a lead. Home said that he would speak to Mrs Thatcher. I wonder if he did. The conversation would have been interesting.

When David Steel came to a Guardians' lunch he assured us that the Alliance (as the association between the Liberals as the SDP was then called) would give priority in their programme for constitutional reforms to a Scottish Parliament and to proportional representation. Cardinal Gray, the most genial of prelates, told us that he was a perfervid Scot and strongly in favour of Home Rule. He said that he had taken great care in briefing the Pope for his visit to Scotland to make sure that he understood Scotland's long history as a distinct and special daughter of the Papacy and of the important role of the Church in support of resistance to English invasions. He gave us copies of a pamphlet produced for this purpose. It was, no doubt, in consequence of the Cardinal's briefing that the Pope showed in his speeches in Scotland an appreciative awareness of Scottish nationhood.

Robin Duthie, an industrialist and, among may other things, Chairman of the Scottish Development Agency, did his best to persuade us that all was well without need of constitutional change. His main argument against a Scottish Parliament was the old chestnut of fear of domination by Red Clydeside. Winnie Ewing told us that she had found a much warmer response, both to herself and to Scottish aspirations, in the European Parliament than at Westminster. She encouraged us all by her enthusiastic optimism. Another engagement unfortunately took me away from the meeting with Donald Dewar before the solid discussion began, but I was told afterwards that nothing new or unexpected had emerged.

Lord (Jock) Camer on said that Scottish Home Rule was an idea 'which would not lie down'. Big countries were like dinosaurs – the brain is too far away from the tail. Scotland had a role to play in Europe – it looked across the sea to countries that were never enemies and had languages that were akin. England looked across the Channel to her historic enemy.

If only because as Secretary of State for Scotland he was in a position to act as well as speak, the meeting with George Younger on 5 November 1984 was the most significant of them all. It was one of the longest and the most detailed. From the beginning, he gave a very different impression from the wholly negative one which he was giving in his public speeches, where he repeatedly asserted that any idea of Home Rule was a 'dead duck'. He said that he was concerned that 'Scotland should feel contented with the relationship with the United Kingdom' but he also wanted 'Scotland to do things in her own way whenever that was possible'. When we pressed him about what this meant, in constitutional terms, he said that he was in favour of a federal arrangement. Much more effort would have to be made in England because the English attitude to Scotland, and to the constitutional question, 'varied from downright hostility to complete indifference'. He thought that there was a need for a new effort to work out fresh proposals.

Perhaps all of this was no more than an excuse for doing nothing and a sop to keep the natives quiet for the time being. Still, he had given me an opportunity in his opening remarks to raise some of the matters on which the Advisory Council for the Arts in Scotland (AdCAS) had been agitating. We went through them and on each of the following he said he agreed:

1. Separate arrangements for the funding of the Scottish Universities.
2. A distinct charter for the Scottish Arts Council under the Scottish Office.
3. The consolidation of the Scottish Theatre Company to form

the Scottish National Theatre (Younger said that this was 'a
splendid idea').
4. Official recognition and support for the Scots language as well
as Gaelic.

George Younger was well known for his charm and skill in
disarming petitioners. It is said that many protesters have left a
meeting with him in such a warm glow from the pleasure of his
conversation that it is only some time later that they realise that he
had not conceded any of their demands. Were we victims of the same
technique? Well, it is true that the Conservative Government made
no move towards 'working out fresh proposals' on the constitutional
issue and declined to take part in the Constitutional Convention which
offered a way forward. Also, the Scottish Theatre Company was allowed
to collapse because of inadequate support from the Scottish Arts
Council. On the other hand, Scots was given a little recognition and
support (but much less than Gaelic) and new proposals for the status
and funding of the Scottish Universities and of the Scottish Arts
Council were in fact carried out under the Conservatives. I have no
idea to what extent the discussions with the Guardians contributed to
that result.

Alastair Dunnett was so encouraged by the meeting with Younger
that he felt that we had reached the point where we should now try to
draw our conclusions together and perhaps publish them in a joint
volume. He called us together for an extended session over a weekend
in March 1985 in a delightful and peaceful place, the Crinan Hotel
on the bank of the Crinan Canal. Angus Grossart was asked to lead on
a session on Edinburgh as a major financial centre, Robert Grieve on
the constitution, Hugh Hunter-Gordon and James Adam on the
projection of Scotland abroad and myself on the arts, culture and
education. We had an agreeable and constructive weekend. But the
response to Alastair's request for contributions to a book was another
matter. Many people were willing to talk in private, but reluctant to
reveal their ideas in public. Only two or three people produced
anything at all. The *Glasgow Herald* eventually published most of my
own piece in June 1987. This was reprinted in my book *Towards
Independence* in 1991 and the previously omitted part in *Still in Bed
with an Elephant* in 1998.

The failure of nerve, or excessive prudence, on the part of the potential contributors to the book was one reason for Alastair's decision to wind up the Guardians in June 1990. But with his retirement from Thomson Scottish Petroleum he had in any case lost the support of the staff in Charlotte Square. In his letter about this decision, he said that it had been a real achievement to have attracted so many of the leaders of Scottish affairs to frank, if private, discussions, and said that he thought that 'it was all worth doing'. I am sure that he was right about that.

At the same time, I was a member of many other groups or organisations that aimed at the constitutional and cultural enhancement of Scotland. Sir John Brotherston, who had just retired as the Chief Medical Officer in the Scottish Office, formed an informal group who met to discuss the future Scottish constitution and how it should be achieved. In February 1982 Maurice Lindsay wrote to invite me to join the 1970 Club as the representative of the Saltire Society. 1970 was the European Conservation Year and the activities connected with it in Scotland brought together the directors of many organisations and the heads of some departments in the Scottish Office. They found this cooperation so useful and agreeable that they decided to continue it as a dining club and to invite speakers involved in some aspect of conservation. It has continued to the present. Since membership is related to the appointment it changes as people retire or are replaced. The retired members formed in 1986 a former-members club which is run in much in the same way. In due course I graduated from one to the other.

I am indebted to these two clubs for many pleasant evenings in interesting company and for the friendship of people I might not otherwise have met. They include several directors of the National Trust for Scotland, Sir Jamie Stormonth Darling, Lester Borley and Douglas Dow; the Regius Keeper of the Royal Botanic Gardens in Edinburgh, Douglas Henderson; the director of the Royal Zoological Society in Scotland (and now Chairman of the National Trust) Roger Wheater; the director of the Nature Conservancy Council and enthusiastic polymath, John Morton Boyd; the director of the Scottish Tourist Board, Tom Band; another polymath, Sandy Fenton, who has not only been at various times assistant editor of the *Scottish National Dictionary*, the director of the National Museum of Antiquities and the School of Scottish Studies, but translates poetry from the

Hungarian into Scots; many civil servants from the Scottish Office who do credit to the service and have taken to writing history in their retirement, Bill Scott, John Gibson and Ronnie Cramond. There are many others. They prove that the Edinburgh tradition of clubs for enlightened conversation over a convivial dinner is alive and well.

The high point of many memorable 1970 Club events was a weekend in the island of Rum in 1985, organised by Morton Boyd to celebrate his retirement as Director of the Nature Conservancy Council. He was, so to speak the laird of the island, since his Council had bought the whole place, lock, stock and barrel, family photographs and letters included, from the widow of the former proprietor. He was George Bullough, the son of a Lancashire industrialist, who bought the island in 1888, and was evidently a man of enormous wealth. His son built Kinloch Castle, a compromise between an Italian villa and a Scottish baronial keep. He toured the world in what was evidently a private miniature cruise liner and brought back Chinese vases, lion skins and other exotic curiosities for the decoration of the house. There are also said to have been live turtles and alligators in heated tanks and birds of paradise in the greenhouse. From Europe he collected four-poster beds and stained glass. He had the latest technology in a mechanical organ of great power and percussion and brass effects as well as showers which squirted water at the bather from all directions. In the ballroom there was a minstrels' gallery to hold the band from the ship, and in the dining room a table, which could hold about forty people, also from the ship. Apart from the oriental livestock, all of this was still in full working order when we stayed in the castle. On the west side of the island, Bullough had constructed a miniature acropolis, surmounted by a stone cross, for his own interment. There were relics of an earlier attempt at mausoleum in the form of slabs of mosaic embedded in the hillsides. It is said that Bullough had showed off his future place of rest to a visiting artist who had hesitated and said, 'It reminds me of something. Oh yes. The gentlemens' lavatory in Victoria Station.' Bullough immediately ordered it to be demolished by explosives.

During this weekend, we had Sir William Kerr Fraser, then the Permanent Under Secretary at the Scottish Office, as our guest and speaker. He writes comic verse with fluency and wit and both he and his wife, Marion, are as charming as they are accomplished. In 1990, after he had left the Scottish Office and became the Principal of

Glasgow University, he told me that he was glad to have left the Office, 'which the bigot Michael Forsyth had made a very unhappy place,' but he found academics much more difficult to manage than civil servants. We toured the island and saw the splendid wild horses and the sea-eagles which the Nature Conservancy Council were re-introducing. We also saw otters at play in the sea at a place named, in Gaelic, the point of the otters; but no one was reintroducing the long departed Gaelic-speaking inhabitants.

Perhaps this is the place to mention clubs of the London kind, which are really glorified restaurants which are restricted to members and their guests, but are comfortable and convenient places where you can meet people or read the magazines and newspapers. In London I had joined the Travellers', just across St James Park from the Foreign Office, to which it serves as a canteen for lunch. It also has a handsome and well-stocked library. The Travellers' had given me reciprocal rights to the New Club in Edinburgh, which is new in the same sense as the New Town; it was founded in 1787. Lockhart tells us that Walter Scott was elected a member 'by acclamation' at the time of his financial problems in 1826. I decided that I would seek membership when I returned to Edinburgh in 1980 and I was proposed by a friend of Suzanne Sinclair. It has a splendid site on Princes Street with a superb view towards Edinburgh Castle, a fine collection of prints and paintings of Edinburgh, a useful library, good cooking, a swimming pool and handsome and comfortable rooms. It is regarded as the preserve of the Edinburgh establishment and the press likes to describe it as a nefarious den of plot and intrigues. The membership are largely advocates, judges, senior civil servants, bankers, insurance brokers and the like. I have seen no signs of intrigue. It is a place which embraces you in a warm secure atmosphere, with a solicitous staff and no one disturbs you. For some years, Bert and I used to have lunch week and week about in the New Club (where he was not a member) and the Scottish Arts Club (where I was not). Eventually I joined the Arts Club as well because it provided a complete change from the other place. The food and the view were not as good; but it is spontaneously sociable. The members like to talk to one another and there are quite often evening events with interesting speakers. Among the regulars are Colin Bell, infinitely knowledgeable and courteous as a radio presenter, but somewhat sharper in private conversation;

Martin Huggins who directed the Edinburgh School of English with style and wit; Jack Firth, an accomplished painter and a brilliant commentator on the paintings of others; Shand Hutchinson who gave energetic support to the campaign to save the Portrait Gallery. Bob Grieve, whose death was a sad loss, was another always genial and welcoming presence. For most of the 80s and 90s I was also a member of the University Staff Club in Chambers Street. It was a very useful haven, close to the National Library, the Museum, University, Festival Theatre and James Thin's bookshop. You often ran into people such as Sorley Maclean or Geoffrey Barrow. Towards the end of the 90s it declined because the new generation of hard-pressed academics no longer had the leisure to linger and talk and it was eventually closed. I still feel rather homeless in that part of Edinburgh.

Even before I returned to Edinburgh in 1980 I had joined a number of Scottish organisations in addition to the SNP and the Saltire Society. When I was in London in 1976 someone (I think at a meeting of the London branch of the Saltire Society) had told me about the Association for Scottish Literary Studies. I joined at once because I have always been an enthusiastic reader of Scottish literature from the mediaeval makars to the poets of the twentieth century. I think that it is natural that the literature of one's own country evokes a more direct response than any other. This Association, through its publications and its conferences, has contributed enormously to the great increase in academic interest in Scottish literature and languages, both in Scotland and in other countries, particularly in Canada and the United States. Through its annual volume of new writing, which was originally proposed by Alexander Scott, its influence extends beyond the past and the academic to the present and its conferences for school teachers have helped to dispel the shameful neglect of Scottish literature in the schools.

I became a member of the Council of the Association in 1982 and have stayed on it ever since. There I have met many admirable colleagues – David Daiches, whom I have already mentioned; Tom Crawford who has written excellent books on Burns and Scott and has worked for years on the Boswell papers in Yale; David Hewitt, the general editor of the Edinburgh Edition of the Waverley Novels and who displayed as Treasurer of the Association an unexpected mastery of finance; Derrick McClure, an eloquent champion of the Scots language; Alexander Scott, another enthusiast for the language and literature and also an accomplished poet and dramatist; Ian Campbell, a man of inexhaustible benevolence and helpfulness, is one of the editors of the complete edition of the Carlyle letters and one of my successors as Convenor of the Saltire Book Award panel.

Another society of which I have long been a member is the Scots Language Society, which was originally, and I think more appropriately, called the Lallans Society. Towards the language my feelings are the same as towards Scottish literature, most of the best of which is in Scots. I have never had the good fortune to live in an entirely, or even a predominantly, Scots-speaking environment, but somehow I have an immediate and warm response to it and I am more often moved by poetry in Scots than by any in another language. I do not often attempt to write poetry, but when I do I find that it comes to my mind in Scots.

So when Alex Scott proposed me for the committee at the AGM of the Society in April 1981, I could not refuse. He was inspiring as president, energetic, widely read, eloquent and witty. It is a reproach to Glasgow University that he was never made Professor of Scottish Literature, a post for which he was so well equipped and for which the time had come. Alex was an outspoken Aberdonian who was an officer in the Gordon Highlanders during the war. He was wounded in Normandy and awarded the MC. Some people were offended by his blunt remarks for he did not suffer fools willingly or in silence. He once told me that MacDiarmid was 'quite literally certifiably insane'. Tessa Ransford and Joy Hendry were furious when he replied to a remark about Scottish women poets by the question, 'are there any?' but then I am sure he was teasing. He died in 1989 and David Robb's edition of his *Collected Poems* is a book which has given me great pleasure.

The Scots Language Society has not had as much success, so far, as the Gaelic campaign in obtaining recognition and support from the Government. Scots is spoken and understood by more people than Gaelic. It has an even more substantial and impressive literature. Like Gaelic, it is a language which has been retreating under attack for about three centuries by the schools and, more recently and more powerfully, by the broadcasters. And, like Gaelic, it is a language which will not survive, if we do not preserve it ourselves. Like most languages, Scots has the capacity to express more vividly than any other the feelings of those who grow up in the place where it has acquired a multiplicity of intimate and powerful associations. It is for that reason that it is such an effective medium for poetry and song and for dialogue in novels and on the stage.

With all these attributes, why is it that successive governments have not been prepared to give similar support to Scots as to Gaelic? I think that there are two reasons. The first is that Scots and English share a common origin. They are closely related and have much vocabulary in common. For that reason it is easy for its detractors to represent it as merely bad English which should be avoided by all educated people. The second reason is connected with the first. Since 1603, when James VI flitted to London, Scotland was deprived of a Scots-speaking royal court and source of power and patronage. Everyone with political, social or economic ambitions had to look to London and learn to speak English. The prestige of that language was also enhanced by the adoption in Scotland of the Authorised Version of the Bible. Since English was now the language of ambition, the schools felt obliged to teach it. People were encouraged to despise and avoid Scots and the snobbery, which this inculcated, is still a powerful force. Generations of Scots have been taught that their mother tongue is not acceptable in good company and they have been reduced in consequence to inarticulacy and an inferiority complex.

Of course, the English language is an asset in the modern world. Largely because of the Americans, as David Hume predicted, it has become the major means of international communication. No one would propose that Scottish schools should cease to teach it; but there is no reasons why we should not have both. That would be an asset, not a liability. As John Galt said, and amply proved in his novels, it is a great advantage to have at your disposal the extended vocabulary of the two languages, especially as they overlap and work well together. We should cultivate this bilingualism, which enriches self-expression and makes the acquisition of other languages easier. There is much in the vocabulary and phonology of Scots which has affinities with other European languages. To some extent, bilingualism already exists. Many people tend to write and read in English and speak in Scots. We have to improve the status of Scots by removing the snobbish and ignorant rejection of it. The schools and the broadcasters, who encouraged that attitude in the past, could be the most effective forces to encourage a more enlightened understanding.

We should follow the example of German-speaking Switzerland, a place with which I am familiar. There both German German and

Swiss German exist happily together. The former is usual in writing and in communication with foreigners; the latter for most conversations. Both are used, with more or less equal frequency, in broadcasting. People use and enjoy both languages without any snobbish inhibition. I am not sure how much success the Scots Language Society has had in improving the status, appreciation and use of Scots. There has, so far, been no spectacular breakthrough but there has been a steady increase in recognition of the importance of the language. The Society's main contribution has been through the publication of the periodical, *Lallans*, which has printed much fine work both in prose and verse. It is a reflection of the importance of verse in sustaining the language that most of the editors have been accomplished poets, JK Annand, William Neill, Neil MacCallum and David Purves.

I was also a colleague of Alex Scott on the Editorial Board of the *Scottish Review*, which Maurice Lindsay asked me to join in September 1981. William Wolfe did the same for the committee of his Heritage Group. I was in these first months elected to several other committees, such as those of the Cockburn Association, (which exists to protect the amenity of Edinburgh and is the oldest organisation of its kind in the world) and of the Edinburgh Sir Walter Scott Club. I represented the Saltire Society on the Council of the National Trust for Scotland, which was an agreeable task because it gave me an insight into the working of an organisation of which I had long been a member and whose objectives I thoroughly approved.

At a party which Allan Massie gave in his house in Edinburgh in July 1981 Harry Reid, then of the *Sunday Standard*, but soon to become editor of *The Herald*, went around telling everyone that I should be made editor of *The Scotsman*. Perhaps this was an ironic comment on the diversity of my activities. If I was doing everything else, why not this job as well? But he seemed to approve of the diversity. He told me some years later that he was amazed at the range of my activities and that I was 'a credit to Scotland and an inspiration to all of us.' On another occasion some years later, when he came to dinner in the New Club with his wife, Julie Davidson, in November 1989, Harry said that I was unusual in 'combining the radical and the patrician'. The idea that I was patrician surprised me, but I suppose being a former diplomat and a member of the New Club is likely to give rise to that impression. Perhaps it was for the same reason that Julie once described me in an article in *The Scotsman* as 'enigmatic'. At that time I said to Bert that on the contrary I was perfectly straightforward. 'That is what everyone thinks about himself,' Bert said.

In May 1982 Tessa Ransford asked me to come to a meeting to discuss the establishment of a Scottish Poetry Library. Alan Taylor and Tom Fenton were also there. At subsequent meetings we were joined by Angus Calder, Dolinna MacLennan, Ian Campbell and Cairns Craig. One of the first points to be decided, as so often, was whether the Library should be in Edinburgh, for which I argued, or Glasgow, supported by Angus Calder. Eventually, we were able to launch the project on 24 November 1982 at a public meeting in one of the large lecture theatres of Edinburgh University, at which I took the chair, and to make a case for funding by the Scottish Arts Council. The Library was opened in Tweedale Court, off the High Street of Edinburgh, in 1984. It moved to more spacious and specially designed premises further down the High Street in June 1999. This very real achievement, and valuable addition to the literary assets of Scotland, was entirely due to the single-minded determination and drive of Tessa Ransford. She may look like a slight and gentle woman, but she has a will to defy all obstacles.

I was involved in a number of other campaigns. One, which I took up through AdCAS, was to oppose a proposal to demolish a handsome theatre in Dunfermline, known as the Opera House. This was ultimately referred to the Secretary of State, at that time Malcolm Rifkind. By his personal decision, and against the advice of his officials (so one of them informed me), he authorised the demolition. I remarked in my diary, 'Nothing good is to be expected from this Government.'

That could be applied to the other campaigns as well. An important one was an attempt to stop what amounted to the theft of the Trustee Savings Bank from the depositors who owned it. It had been established in 1810 at Ruthwell in Dumfriesshire by the local minister, Henry Duncan, as the first savings bank of its kind in the world. The idea was to encourage thrift among the poor by providing a bank owned by the depositors and run in their interests alone. Branches rapidly spread over the whole of Scotland. I inherited an interest because my mother had built up an account in our joint names. The proposal to convert the TSB into a profit-making company was, I think, the first act of 'demutualisation', a process which has been accomplished in building societies and insurance companies by the temptation of financial handouts to the mutual owners. The subtlety of that approach had not yet been devised in the TSB case, where the depositors were not offered any compensation for the loss of their property. As always, the campaign was run by a handful of people. Jim Ross, who later drafted *A Claim of Right* was chairman, I was Vice Chairman and Robin Bennett, a Solicitor from Cupar in Fife, was secretary and treasurer. We succeeded in making an impact at the AGM of the Bank in Glasgow. Jim Ross, at his own financial risk, then took the issue to the Court of Session where we were ably represented by William Prosser, then Dean of the Faculty of Advocates. Lord Davidson's judgement on 12 November 1985 was entirely in our favour. He ruled that the bank belonged to the depositors and that its sale by the management to shareholders would be expropriation without compensation. We had a happy celebration in my flat in Drumsheugh Gardens and on 31 December Jim was very appropriately voted Scot of the Year by the listeners to Radio Scotland. This annual vote was a useful means of expressing public feeling and the recognition of achievement, which the BBC in Scotland have unfortunately now abandoned. Perhaps its potential for the embarrassment of the Establishment was too much. There was another example when the vote went to Hamish Henderson, the great collector, elucidator and creator of folk song, after he had publicly rejected the offer of an OBE.

We lost in the end. The bank appealed to the House of Lords, a procedure of doubtful legality under the Treaty of Union. They upheld that other act of highly doubtful legality, the confiscation of the rights of the depositors.

Joan Lingard, another friend from PEN, is an accomplished novelist as well as a woman of charm and sound sense. She called a meeting of writers in December 1983 to plan a campaign of Writers Against the Bomb, that is against the outrage and hazard of submarines with nuclear weapons, based on the Clyde. Some thirty writers from all over Scotland attended and others wrote in support. JB Pick and I were asked to draft a leaflet, which we did. For the next few years we produced leaflets and some very striking posters. I do not know how much effect they had on public opinion, which in Scotland was mostly in agreement with us in any case. They certainly had no visible effect on the determination of British Governments, Conservative and

Labour, to maintain and increase nuclear weapons and station them in Scotland, close to our largest centre of population. They made it certain that the central belt of Scotland would have been one of the first targets if there had been a nuclear war between the super powers. Now that the Soviet Union has dissolved, and there is no longer so great a risk of that sort of war, the issue is less urgent. But it also means that there is now even less of a case for the continuation of these obscene, hazardous and expensive weapons. The sooner they are removed and destroyed, the better; but it looks as if we shall have to wait for independence before that can be achieved.

Apart from these other activities, I also, as is my habit, took classes in the University. In October 1982 I was accepted as a postgraduate student in Edinburgh University for the degree of MSc, which was transferred in May 1983 to MLitt, in Scottish Literature. On the side, as it were, I took the first ordinary class in Humanity, that is to say Latin, returning to my academic roots. I have always been fond of the grandeur and logicality of Latin, compared to which, Walter Scott said, other languages are merely the scraps of speech. It was gratifying to get 85% in the examination at the end of the year. 'The High School will be proud of you,' said Bill Brown, a friend of mine on the staff of the National Library. On Scottish Literature, Ian Campbell pressed me to put in for a PhD; but with all the other things I had to do, I decided to go for the MLitt which required a shorter thesis. My subject was John Galt, a novelist for whom I have an unbounded enthusiasm. I had already written a book on him for the Scottish Writers Series (published in 1985) and, since I had little to add to that, asked if it could be accepted as my thesis. This required the approval of the Head of the Department, Professor WW Robson. He was good enough to agree and to say, in his letter of 25th September 1986, that my book was 'obviously the distinguished work of a mature critic'. I graduated MLitt, *in absentia*, in July 1987.

Also within the University, I was on two committees for some time. The first of these was the Business Committee of the General Council, which is a device to enable the graduates (although, of course, very few take the trouble) to keep in touch with the policy of the University and offer their opinions when they wish. I was sensible enough to decline an invitation to stand for the chairmanship. The other committee, with Lord Clyde as chairman, was set up to try raise funds for the establishment of a Chair in Scottish Literature, which scandalously did not exist. We failed.

Outside the University, I was also studying Gaelic in which Laura joined me. We both felt that it was absurd to live in Scotland without some knowledge of our other ancient language. Without it, you are a stranger in your own country, unable to follow a wonderful body of song, or even to understand, or pronounce, place names on the map. We have used various means, a BBC series, *Can Seo*, a correspondence course, classes with Ronald Black at Telford College and a Scottish Television series *Speaking our Language*. We took the Scottish Certificate examinations, on the ordinary level in 1983 (when I got a 'B') and on higher level in 1985 ('C'). I am still far from content with my halting ability in the language, which is the most difficult that I have tried to learn, or is that merely the effect of age?

Black wrote on one of Laura's Gaelic essays that she clearly had an instinct for the language, probably because of her bilingualism. In fact, her bilingualism in English and Italian is so good that we generally converse in English. Scots is not a problem for her either. In consequence, my Italian, which might have been consolidated by practice, has unfortunately deteriorated through lack of use.

The Edinburgh International Festival has been a central event in my life each year since it started in 1947, but especially since I came bank to Edinburgh in November 1980. Already, thanks to Alastair Dunnett, I had become a member of the Festival Society in June of that year. This consisted partly of councillors from the Edinburgh Council (at that time also of Lothian Region which no longer exists) and of other invited people up to a maximum of 200. It has since become more open in its membership. Their function is similar to that of the shareholders of a company. They (or those of them who choose to come) meet once a year to hear a report by the Festival Director on the previous Festival and on the plans for the next one. Usually the subsequent discussion is brief and undemanding. From the members of this body a Council of about twenty is elected which meets four or five times a year to discuss the affairs of the Festival in more detail. Generally speaking however, the content of the programme is left to the Director. I was elected to this Council for three years in 1984 but I soon found that its proceedings gave very little opportunity to influence artistic policy.

Now it has become a commonplace to say that the purpose of the Festival is to show the best of the culture of the world to Scotland and of Scotland to the world. In the early 1980s, however, the second part of this proposition tended to be forgotten. This had been so in the early years of the Festival as well, which was why the Saltire Society had done its best to give a Scottish content to the Fringe. In October 1982 I wrote a letter on behalf of AdCAS to argue the case for a greater Scottish contribution to the Festival and to make some suggestions on the form which that might take. When John Drummond was Director, as he was from 1978 to 1983, such ideas fell on deaf ears. He was a man of many admirable qualities, full of self-confidence, irresistibly fluent and very knowledgeable about music; but, although his father was a Scottish sea-captain from Glasgow, he had been brought up entirely in England and regarded any reference to Scotland as deplorably parochial.

In May 1981 I wrote to Drummond from the Saltire Society to suggest that the 1982 Festival programme should include something to acknowledge the 150th anniversary of the death of Sir Walter Scott. Drummond declined to take any interest, but after I had enlisted the support of the Lord Provost, Tom Morgan, he eventually agreed to include a lecture about the operas based on one of Scott's novels. After he left Edinburgh I did not see Drummond again until seventeen years later when he came to speak about his autobiography at the Book Festival in August 2000. I was astonished to discover that he recognised me at once and remembered both my name and my connection with the Saltire Society. I must have made a bigger impression than I had realised. I imagine that he thought I was an infernal nuisance.

Drummond's successor, Frank Dunlop, took a very different attitude on these matters. He was in fact the opposite in almost every respect – more interested in drama than in music, about which he knew very little; populist and not patrician; more inclined to welcome healthy vulgarity, than fear, like Drummond, the collapse of all civilised standards. He welcomed my ideas on Scottish matters, included the Saltire events in St Cecilia's Hall in the official programme, asked me to write programme notes for one or two of the drama productions, included performance of RS Silver's play, *The Bruce*, took a very active part in our campaign for a National Theatre, and after all that, said that I was a good influence on him. I think that he was a good influence on the Festival. If it had been in danger of becoming too staid and conventional, Frank put an end to all that.

Frank Dunlop attended a meeting of the working party for a National Theatre on 7th December 1988. He spoke out very strongly against any idea of watering down our original proposals, that is to say against anything less than a company with its own theatre. 'It was tragic for Scotland that this sort of thing happened so often. We shall not achieve anything unless we aim high.' My instincts about all of this were the same as his. After the meeting I drove him to his flat on the Mound. He was bitter about the way in which the Festival was being treated financially and he was doubtful if it could survive much longer. Edinburgh had the capacity to become a world capital of intellect and art, but there were too many people in authority whose outlook was provincial and who were prepared to be dominated by London.

Frank had indeed a very hard time, as John Drummond says in his autobiography, in dealing with a new Labour administration in the city. Many of the Councillors seemed to have no conception of the importance of the Festival and to distrust it as something middle class and élitist, which should be opposed at every opportunity. Frank was eventually able to persuade many of them that there was nothing exclusive about his vision of the Festival. We were fortunate to have a Director with his patience and endurance; many other people would have given up in disgust. He eventually left after eight years in 1991.

Dunlop's inclusion of the Saltire productions in the official Festival programme made an enormous difference. It relieved the Society from the responsibilities of publicity and the selling of tickets, and more importantly, it gave us full houses for every performance. I wrote scripts on such subjects as love poetry and song, Edinburgh from the earliest times to the present, the Scottish Enlightenment, Robert Fergusson and Robert Garioch. All of them consisted of poems, prose extracts, songs and fiddle music, linked with a connecting commentary which I sometimes read myself. One of the pleasures of these programmes from my own point of view was the collaboration with the performers. We had excellent and intelligent actors, who could extract the full force of meaning from any passage, such as Tom Fleming, Edith Macarthur, John Shedden and James Cairncross. Kirsty Wark read for us with the same professionalism that afterwards made her an outstanding television presenter where she combines charm with penetrating interrogation. Among singers, we had Bill McCue, Jean Redpath, Patricia MacMahon, Anne Lorne Gillies, R od Paterson and Andy Hunter. All delightful as people as well as powerful ambassadors for Scottish song. We had two of the must erudite and skilful fiddlers, Ron Gonella and Alastair Hardie. Isobel Mieras, another passionate advocate of Scottish song, not only sang and played the clarsach, but invariably gave wise advice on the direction of the programmes. George Bruce helped with this as well, drawing on his long experience as a BBC producer.

I had a good deal of pleasure in working with George Bruce on an anthology of Scottish letters of all periods, published in 1986 as *The Scottish Postbag*. This was an idea that had been suggested to the Saltire Society by Martin Cummins of the Scottish Post Office Board. George and I, after Maurice Lindsay had declined our original proposal that he should be the editor, engaged for several months in a happy treasure hunt for letters which said something interesting and said it with eloquence and wit. In the end all the great names from Wallace to Sorley Maclean were included, and I think that the book is a good introduction to Scottish history and literature. As I write this, George and I have embarked on a new edition and are looking for suitable letters from the last twenty years. George is an inspiration to all of us. Who else has held a party to celebrate simultaneously his ninetieth birthday and the launch of his latest collection of poetry? That collection, moreover, won the Saltire Award as the Scottish Book of the Year.

Brian McMaster, who became Director of the Edinburgh Festival in 1992, was in many ways the precise opposite from his predecessor, Frank Dunlop. Unlike Frank, he had much more sensitive feel for music and ballet than for drama. Frank was a natural showman who revelled in publicity; but Brian was restrained and reticent. When the Lady Provost, Eleanor McLaughlin, held a press conference to announce his appointment she introduced him and gave an account of his previous career. She then turned to him and asked if he would like to say a few words. His reply was 'not really', and he said very little more in response to questions. During the Festival, he gradually abandoned the press conferences with the directors and stars of the participating companies. None of this meant that he has been unassertive in his management of the Festival. On the contrary, he has refused to include any item which he has not chosen personally.

This meant that he dropped the Saltire Society programmes from the beginning of his reign, which I think was a pity. When he first took over the job, he said that he proposed to have a production of *The Thrie Estaitis* every two or three years as an element of continuity like *Everyman* in Salzburg. So far, all he has done in this respect, has been in one year a modern imitation or parody. I remind him of this gently from time to time. On the other hand McMaster has made a valuable contribution to the Scottish presence in the Festival. At an early stage I remarked to him that I thought that Scottish song, one of our major achievements, should always form part of the Festival programme. At the time, this seemed to surprise him, but before long he mounted a series of performances exploring the riches of the Greig-Duncan collection and he was since done the same to Burns' contribution to James Johnson's Musical Museum, and also in other years for the music of the fiddle, the clarsach and the pipes.

One of the disadvantages of life in the Diplomatic Service is that it produces an unsettled upbringing for children, who have to move from country to country and usually to go to boarding school. When you are home, you are in London. This means that they grow up with little experience of Scotland and the people they meet and marry are unlikely to be Scottish and that often determines where they stay. So it has been with Alastair and Catharine. I have, unfortunately, seen far too little of either of them; but both are well established in a way that suits them. At the end of 1983 Alastair and Catharine spent some time with us in Edinburgh, and were later joined by Alastair's girl friend, Patta Villiers, as prelude to what seemed to me a dangerous and adventurous journey. This was to drive by Landrover to the Sudan across the Sahara desert. I arranged for them to be interviewed by the BBC who asked them to report on their progress. Alastair and Patta were going to work for a relief organisation in the Sudan. Catharine was going for a last fling before she settled down to married life. Both Alastair and Catharine married in 1986 at very grand, and very English, weddings, Alastair to Patta, and Catharine to Robin Howard, a barrister. Since then, Alastair has become a recognised expert in assistance to countries which are being ravaged by war or natural disaster. He and Patta have spent many years abroad, usually in Africa. but also in the Middle East, the Balkans and Indochina. They also have a base in Sussex where Patta works in Brighton

University. Catharine has been bringing up three energetic boys; but somehow finds time to work at garden designs and even to compile the index for my book on Andrew Fletcher.

I started to work on this book about Fletcher in 1987. It was the consequence of a suggestion by John Hulbert, the Secretary of the Andrew Fletcher Society, that I should write a biography. I was very willing to do this because I have been interested in Fletcher since I read WC Mackenzie's book about him, published in 1935, while I was still at school. As soon as I started on my research, I discovered that most of the papers about this particular Fletcher were missing from the family papers in the National Library of Scotland. This is almost certainly because James Boswell sent them, as he had promised, to Rousseau, who had proposed to write a biography. On the other hand, there was a great detail of available information about the debates in the Scottish Parliament from 1703-1707 in the form of diaries and letters to supplement the laconic official record.

Fletcher's defence of Scottish independence in that Parliament was the most important work of his life and the subject of most of his published writing. Historians have generally given an inadequate and misleading account of this Parliament and particularly of Fletcher's role in it. I think that this is probably because they have relied too much on Daniel Defoe's *History of the Union*. He was, after all, employed by the English government as an agent and propagandist. He dealt with Fletcher as the most formidable spokesman on the other side, by the simple, but effective, expedient of not mentioning him at all.

The contemporary papers, for many of the participants wrote intelligent and informative letters, left me in no doubt that the comfortable view of the Union, widely accepted since about the middle of the nineteenth century, was without foundation. This is the theory that the Union was a genuine and enlightened negotiation in which the Scots accepted the loss of their Parliament in exchange for access to the English and colonial markets and, a modern gloss, the protection of English naval power. In fact, as I explain in *Andrew Fletcher and the Treaty of Union*, it was not a real negotiation at all. Both teams were appointed by the English government and the Scottish teams consisted, with one exception, of office holders appointed, paid and instructed by that government. The exception was George Lockhart of Carnwath, whose *Memoirs* of the affair are an important source and one of the liveliest books of its kind. After some years of effort, I persuaded the Association for Scottish Literary Studies to publish an edition with my introduction as the annual volume in 1995.

The Scottish Parliament in 1703 and again in 1704, under the inspiration of Andrew Fletcher, had passed an Act of Security which amounted to a declaration of independence. It provided that on the death of Queen Anne, either the Scottish Parliament would choose a different monarch from England or that all royal power would be transferred from the monarch to the Parliament. Since 1603 when James VI flitted to London, England had controlled foreign and defence policy for Scotland as well as England and made all important state appointments, including the members of the Scottish government, by the exercise of the royal prerogative. This semi-dependence had been disastrous for Scotland and it was from this that the Scottish Parliament proposed to escape.

England regarded this as a threat to her vital interest. She was almost constantly at war with France and was not prepared to tolerate an independent Scotland, the traditional ally of France, on her northern border. The political 'incorporation' of Scotland was the answer and this was achieved by a sophisticated and skilful blend of propaganda, intimidation, bribery and an ingenious appeal in the text of the Treaty of Union itself to the self-interest of the classes, a small minority of the population, who were then represented in the Scottish Parliament. Sir John Clerk of Penicuik was responsible in the Scottish government for the question of foreign trade. In his justification of his support of the Union, he did not claim that it benefited Scottish trade, and in fact its economic consequences were harmful for the next sixty years or so. His explanation was blunt. The alternative to the Union was an English invasion and the imposition of worse terms.

Another book, or rather pamphlet, which I wrote at about this time was *In Bed with an Elephant*, first published by the Saltire Society in 1985. This was an expanded version of a paper which Ian Campbell invited me to give to post-graduate students of Scottish literature at Edinburgh University. The title became one of the currencies of debate about the Scottish situation. I had borrowed it from Pierre Trudeau, who had used it in a speech about Canada's relationship with the United States. He had compared that to a man sharing a bed with an elephant, an experience which is likely to be very uncomfortable or even destructive, even if the elephant has no hostile intentions. Such,

I argued, had been the consequences for Scotland of sharing an island with England.

I have already mentioned Scottish PEN, of which Laura was persuaded by Jim Ford in 1986 to become secretary and treasurer. In 1987 we went for the first time to one of the International PEN Congresses which in that year was in Lugano. By this time I had become a Vice-President of the Scottish Centre and Derry Jeffares, the President, and I were the two Scottish delegates. I had drawn up in advance a draft resolution, very much in line with the *In Bed with an Elephant* theme about the need to defend the languages of smaller countries and linguistic groups from the pressure from their larger neighbours. One of the main activities of International PEN was to defend the right of freedom of expression and to help writers persecuted or imprisoned because of their opinions. The resolution proposed that we should similarly defend the rights of languages and that one of the standing committees should be charged with this responsibility. Although we had not been in touch in advance, the Catalans proposed a very similar resolution. We combined the two and the Lanque D' Oc Centre added their support. The proposal met with general approval and similar ideas were expressed in the literary sessions by Czeslaw Milosz, Lassi Nummi and Alain Bosquet. The resolution was passed unanimously with only one centre, England, abstaining. Following this resolution, most of the work has been led by the Catalans who had the full support of their Government. I was a member of the relevant committee which met during the annual congresses and at special meetings at such places as Valencia and Pamplona. This eventually led to the approval of the Universal Declaration of Linguistic Rights, signed by representatives of PEN Centres and other organisations from more than ninety countries in Barcelona in 1996. The Scottish Centre was represented by Joy Hendry, Laura and myself. The intention is that UNESCO, who supported the venture, will endeavour to make the Declaration the basis of an inter-governmental agreement. I am sure that many governments will resist, because most of them are firm upholders of a linguistic monopoly in their own territory.

I had joined the Edinburgh Sir Walter Scott Club in 1976 while I was still abroad. Its main activity, apart from running an essay competition for Edinburgh schools, was the annual dinner, a major event of the social calendar. Laura and I have been at these dinners, with only one exception, since 1980. A year or two later I joined the Council of the Club and later became Chairman for a few years. It has been the habit of the Club at the dinners to have a toast to the armed forces as well as those to Sir Walter and the City of Edinburgh. The forces toast was probably a relic of the war; but with a reply from an admiral or general, it had tended to become a jingoistic affair reminiscent of a Tory party rally. I persuaded the Council that it should be replaced with a toast each year to something that was part of Scott's life, such as the High School, the University or the Faculty of Advocates. We also expanded our activities to include two lectures a year, a trip to places associated with Scott and now and then a party at Abbotsford where Meta and Ian Gilmour gave readings or Rod Paterson sang. At these events Patricia and Jean Maxwell Scott worthily car ried on the hospitable traditions of the house. I am sure that Sir Walter himself would have found the evenings familiar and congenial.

Although Muriel Spark lives in Umbria, I have been in touch with her several times, usually in connection with Scottish PEN, the Saltire Society or the Edinburgh Sir Walter Scott Club. She intended to speak at various times to all three, Saltire when she won the Book Award, the Scott Club on its anniversary and Scottish PEN to receive honorary membership. In the event she was prevented by illness and other complications from coming to all but the last of these. In her speech to Scottish PEN she said that from 'her experience as a woman of Scottish background' she believed that 'the principles of PEN are especially natural to the Scottish character, with its independent-mindedness, its will to sincerity in public affairs, its sense of our being unquestionably born free.' She was much less forbidding than her reputation suggested and in fact was very warm and friendly. Although she has spent most of her life abroad, something of Edinburgh clings to her still. After all, did she not say that 'nevertheless' was the word most expressive of the Edinburgh spirit? She spoke warmly of her school days in Edinburgh and said that the Border ballads had been her favourite reading and that Walter Scott had given her a sense of history. She approved of my book about him.

On 4 December 1988 Elizabeth Irons, the Secretary of the Dundee University branch of the Federation of Student Nationalists, wrote to invite me to stand as their candidate in the next Rectorial election. I accepted at once. Like many people in Scotland, I have always valued the institution in the four ancient universities and in Dundee of Rectors, elected by the students, as something more than a picturesque mediaeval survival. It gives an elected representative of the students a voice on the University Court, which is the governing body of the University. In the ancient universities, but not Dundee, the Rector chairs the meetings of the Court. It is also an opportunity for the students to express their political convictions. Students, with their healthy scepticism of the establishment, sometime elect people, such as pop stars, who are not very suitable and unlikely to take the office seriously. In the past they were quite often figureheads such as Prime Ministers.

Elizabeth Irons, is the daughter of Norman and Anne Irons, who as the first SNP Lord and Lady Provosts of Edinburgh gave a new style and distinction to these offices. As soon as I met Elizabeth, I knew that my election campaign was in good hands, with her effervescent personality and an instinct for organisation and leadership. I was duly elected in February 1989 and the period of office was for three years. I had many letters of congratulations, including some from people that I had never met.

My first duty was to give a rectorial address when I was installed on 24 April 1989. The *Glasgow Herald* (as it was then called) to my surprise devoted a substantial first leader to the subject under the heading, 'Significant rectorial address'. Christopher Harvie telephoned from Germany to say that it was probably the first time since Carlyle that so much attention had been paid to a rectorial address. I said what about Barrie and Compton Mackenzie? The following are some extracts:

> Tonight the Earl of Dalhousie will install Mr Paul Scott as rector of Dundee University. The occasion will be traditional in that it will combine elements of knockabout students fun – the rectorial 'drag' round the streets of Dundee – and elements of pomp and circumstance – the Bedellus, the Chancellor, the mace, the gowns, the formal robing and disrobing, and so on. But the occasion will be unusual in that Mr Scott intends to use it to make what promises to be a highly significant and controversial rectorial address. He will not just attack the Government's record

on Higher education in Scotland. There would indeed, be
nothing unusual in that; many other public figures have already
done so, with vehemence and anger. What will be different about
his address is that he will attack the underlying philosophy of the
Government from an unashamedly intellectual, and Scottish,
standpoint. Mr Scott will be playing for big stakes; he will be
seeking a new Scottish ideology, potent and popular enough to
take on Thatcherism, and see it off. It is the very loftiness of his
claims, of his aspirations, that will set his speech apart.

Mr Scott is a former career diplomat who left the Foreign
Service in 1980. Since then he has been active in many Scottish
causes. He has also written books on the Act of Union, on Sir
Walter Scott and on John Galt. He is a member of the SNP and
his address will be aggressively nationalistic in tone. He will
conclude it by demanding an independent Scottish Parliament,
by invoking the spirit of Govan. Yet the tone of his address will
be very different from any speech given by Mr Jim Sillars MP, the
victor of Govan.

Mr Scott will attack the Government for its 'barbarism', for its
'totalitarian tendencies', for its 'contempt towards Scottish
opinion', for its 'intellectual pollution' and 'intellectual
vandalism', for its ideology which is 'socially divisive and morally
repugnant'. This kind of thing has of course all been said before,
if perhaps with less eloquence or less force; but Mr Scott in
indicting the Government, is also seeking to move the debate
onto higher ground. He will, in effect, be calling for a new
Scottish Enlightenment. This is portentous stuff.

In this context, it has to be said that the SNP is fortunate to
have someone as experienced, articulate and thoughtful as Paul
Scott to help it to reappraise its policies and to build a new
framework, to give the party intellectual shape and conviction.
Mr Scott's stirring performance at Dundee's Bonar Hall this
evening will signal the way ahead for the Nationalists. Let us
hope that they and not just the students and academics in one of
our beleaguered universities are listening.

The full text of the address was published by the University, with the
title 'The Thinking Nation', and it was reprinted in my book, *Towards
Independence: Essays on Scotland*.

Of course, I have not been alone in calling for a new Scottish Enlightenment. You could say that the Saltire Society set itself this objective when it was founded in 1936 to 'restore the country to its proper place as a creative force in European Civilisation as it was in the eighteenth century'. That earlier enlightenment, all over Europe, aimed at freeing human thought from the shackles of religious superstition. Now the shackles are different, but even more dangerous: greed, commercialism, advertising and propaganda, trivialisation and the wilful denial of all intellectual and artistic standards.

I greatly enjoyed my three years as Rector of Dundee University both in participation in the decision of the University Court and in my relations with the students. Staff and students together were a coherent community which remained cheerful and optimistic, despite the pressures and problems inflicted on the university by a government whose chief objective seemed to be the reduction of expenditure.

Many people told me that morale had been low under a previous Principal, who was apparently arrogant and dictatorial. It was quite different with his successor, Michael Hamlyn. He was open-minded, sympathetic and fair. They were well served too by the University Secretary, Bob Seaton, who always seemed to be unhurried and untroubled. At one meetings of the Court I suggested that they should reverse their earlier opposition to the separate funding of the Scottish Universities and was happy to find that this met with more or less unanimous approval.

With my four colleagues from the ancient universities we formed a group to campaign jointly on such matters on student grants, university funding and the defence of the right to chair university courts. We usually met in the office of Muriel Gray who had become Rector of Edinburgh University with, like me, the support of the SNP. She is well known of course from her television programmes. Her appearance is as striking as her opinions. She detests all cant and pretension and is splendidly frank, irreverent and quick-witted. Pat Kane of Glasgow, also an SNP supporter, is an intellectual and rock musician, which is an interesting combination. Willis Pickard of Aberdeen is an old friend of mine from his days as features editor of *The Scotsman* and subsequently editor of the *Times Educational Supplement (Scotland)*. He is a liberal and a man of sound common sense and dependability. Pickard was succeeded by Colin Bell of the BBC, another SNP adherent. Nicholas Parsons of St Andrews was one of these rectors apparently chosen because of his presentation of popular, but deplorable, television programmes, but he treated his rectorial responsibilities more seriously than we expected.

In May 1990 Michael Hamlyn asked me as Rector to accompany him to the Standing Conference on the Scottish Universities, an annual meeting of the Principals. This was the first time that Rectors had been invited, or at least the three·of us from Dundee, Edinburgh and Glasgow. We met at the Barn, a small eighteenth century country house with a large twentieth century extension, near Edzell. The surrounding Angus countryside is delightful. The house had been left to the Scottish Universities for reading parties and the like by a man who had made a large fortune in coal mining in Ayrshire and in iron and steel in Motherwell. Muriel Gray came from Edinburgh. For some reason Pat Kane of Glasgow University (for whom Muriel and I had campaigned in March) did not appear. It was a great pity that George McNicol, the Principal of Aberdeen, did not invite his Rector, Willis Pickard. Willis had been editor for about ten years of the *Times Educational Supplement, Scotland*. He has a wide knowledge of Scottish education and of politics and affairs generally and could have made a useful contribution to the debate.

The discussion was opened with prepared statements by Kerr Fraser of Glasgow and James Munn of Strathclyde. Both emphasised the distinctiveness of Scottish higher education. Among the Principals, Graham Hills made the most robust statement. He said that there was no doubt that Scotland was a nation, but the universities had failed to become rallying points for national self-expression. There was no benefit to be gained from the British system, but a lot to be gained by greater autonomy. I agreed with him. I suggested that the universities should make a conscious effort to be more Scottish, and also more European and international. This was not inconsistent because the Scottish tradition had always been open to international influence. A more deliberately Scottish policy would build on the social and intellectual advantages of the tradition of the democratic intellect and would strengthen the links between the universities and the community in which they exist. At the time of the 1979 Referendum, the Scottish Universities had opposed the restoration of the Scottish Parliament and the separate funding, and therefore the autonomy, of the universities themselves. It was now generally realised that this had been a mistake. In 1985 the report of the Scottish Tertiary

Muriel Gray, Pat Kane and Paul Scott during Kane's Rectorial campaign, Glasgow University, March 1990

Education Advisory Council (STEAC) had recommended that a separate body should be set up for the planning and funding of higher education in Scotland. I suggested that universities should now support that recommendation.

There was no serious dispute in the meeting about any of these arguments. George McNicol proposed that each university should act separately. Struther Arnold of St Andrews said nothing. Kerr Fraser said that unfortunately there was a lack of unanimity among the Principals even on the extent to which they should act together as a group. No clear decision was taken. In fact, the STEAC recommendation for a Scottish funding body was carried out.

By this time I think that I was reasonably well known within the SNP because of my books, articles and broadcasts and speeches at national council and national conferences; but more so after the publicity over the Dundee rectorial. It was probably for this reason that Neil MacCallum wrote to me in July 1989 to ask me to accept nomination as a vice-president of the party. In November, Gordon Wilson, who was the leader of the party, appointed me as party spokesmen on higher education. So, at the not so tender age of sixty nine, was to begin a decade in which I was very much involved in political affairs.

The Cabinet that never was. SNP members (left to right) George Leslie, John Swinney, Jim Sillars, Andrew Welsh, Margaret Ewing, Alex Salmond, Winnie Ewing, Rob Gibson, Dick Douglas, Paul Scott, Neil MacCormick and Neil Kay

CHAPTER 18

Back in Scotland (3)
The 1990s and after

In December 1988 Alex Salmond had asked me to join the board of the Scottish Centre for Economic and Social Research of which he was chairman. This was a think tank, allied to, but not part of, the SNP. Over the next few years it published a number of papers by such people as Robin Angus, George Rosie, James Mitchell, Christopher Harvie and Neal Ascherson. They included an AdCAS paper, 'Scottish Education: A Declaration of Principles' and one by me 'Cultural Independence', afterwards reprinted in my book, *Defoe in Edinburgh and Other Papers*. When Alex became party leader, I took over as chairman.

The paper on education was a response to the policies that the Conservatives were applying to Scotland, particularly when Michael Forsyth was Secretary of State. To many of us they seemed to be an attack on aspects of the Scottish educational system which were valuable and should be upheld. On behalf of AdCAS, I suggested in November 1988 to a number of people that we might meet to see if we could draw up a short but authoritative statement of the essential characteristics of Scottish education, an attempt, if you like, to define the Democratic Intellect. This letter went to George Davie, David Daiches, Sir Kenneth Alexander (formerly Principal of Stirling University and President of the Saltire Society), Anne Lorne Gillies (one of our best singers of Gaelic and Scots songs and actively engaged in Gaelic education), Willis Pickard (the editor of the *Times Educational Supplement, Scotland*), Fred Forrester (an official of the Educational Institute of Scotland), Nigel Grant (Professor of Education at Glasgow University), Andrew Macpherson (Director of the Centre for Educational Sociology of Edinburgh University), Joy Hendry (the editor of *Chapman* magazine and a former teacher) and other people engaged in education at all levels. Almost all of them accepted although one or two declined on the grounds either that they were too busy or that they felt that participation would be incompatible with their official position.

Nigel Grant acted as secretary of the group and as drafter of the paper. He produced a powerful and well-argued document that described the qualities to which Scottish education had traditionally aspired. It ended by rejecting Michael Forsyth's policies as 'philosophically incoherent and morally repellent', and called for democratic Scottish control of Scottish education. When the paper was launched on 2 May 1989, it was widely reported and generally welcomed by the Scottish press. I think that it increased awareness of the importance of the issues at stake in educational policy and practice.

I was closely involved with the SNP throughout the 1990s. During the summer of 1990 Alex Salmond telephoned me to ask if I thought he should stand for election as convener (which means in effect the leader) of the party. I had not the slightest hesitation in urging him to do so. As he demonstrated time and again during the next ten years or so, no one in Scottish, or British, politics could compete with him in debate. His quick intelligence and wit, retentive memory and absolute sincerity and decency give him almost all the political virtues. Geoffrey Barrow, who taught Alex Scottish history at St Andrew's University, once told me that Alex had been his 'star student' and that it was obvious that 'he was going places'. Moira, his wife, is a great asset as well. She is invariably cheerful, optimistic, welcoming and friendly, but determined to stay in the background. She never speaks to the press or appears on a political platform but it is apparent to everyone who has met her that Alex could not have a more sustaining ally.

Given all this, and Alex's natural gifts as a brilliant performer on television, why do I qualify his political virtues with 'almost all'? When you see him in debate, or television, or canvassing a street in an election, it is difficult to believe that he is hampered a little by shyness. That however is my impression and other people have told me that they feel the same. It makes for a certain awkwardness, or lack of spontaneous warmth, in his dealings with his immediate colleagues. This failing, if failing it is, has not detracted from the heroic contribution which Alex has made to the party and to the Scottish cause. He has transformed the political situation in Scotland by strengthening and consolidating the appeal of the SNP and by his contribution to the success of the 1997 Referendum. That led to the recovery of the Scottish Parliament and independence is now unlikely to be delayed much longer.

Alex was elected as convener of the party at the annual conference in September 1990 in Perth. At the same conference I was again elected to the National Executive Committee and was elected each year until 1997. I was also elected as vice-president of the party in 1992, a post for which Alex asked me to stand. Again I was re-elected until 1997. Since then I have been elected each year as a member of the National Council. From 1989 to 1999 I was the party spokesman and shadow minister for, at various times, education, the arts and broadcasting, and constitutional and international affairs.

Before some of the major public debates with other party leaders, Alex held rehearsals where three of us, including at various times Jim Sillars, John Swinney and Alastair Morgan, acted as the opponents. Alex once said that we did the job more effectively that any of them could have done it for themselves. Two of the most dramatic of these debates were the one which filled the Usher Hall on 8th January 1992 and the head to head between Alex and the hapless George Robertson in the Royal High School Hall in February 1995. In all of them Alex was the clear winner because none of the other contestants could keep pace with his speed of thought or dexterity of language. In the Usher Hall, the response to Alex was so evident that some press reports suggested that the SNP had packed the audience, but it consisted in fact of people who had applied spontaneously to *The Scotsman* for tickets. These debates probably did more than almost anything else to establish the SNP as one of the two major forces in Scottish politics.

Until the election of the Scottish Parliament, the only full-time politicians in the party were the Westminster MPs who were generally either in London or in their constituencies. I was living in Drumsheugh Gardens within five minutes walk of the party HQ in North Charlotte Street. This meant that I was very often called upon to represent the party leader in social engagements, to meet visiting delegations of diverse kinds and to give interviews to foreign journalists of press, radio or television. I was, also, of course, responsible for press releases and press conferences on subjects within my own portfolio. Alex told me that many people had praised my 'work rate'. In June 1991 he asked me to stand in Eastwood at the next General Election, which was in April in the following year. Since this was regarded at the time as the safest Tory seat in Scotland, it was a forlorn hope. I did not mind that; although I should like to have scored a victory for the party, I had no desire to go to Westminster. Once again, I enjoyed the campaign with the opportunities for debate and many interesting conversations with voters. It was this experience which persuaded me to write *Scotland in Europe: A Dialogue with a Sceptical Friend*, the friend being an amalgam of many of the voters of Eastwood.

All of those activities meant I appeared quite frequently in the newspapers and on radio and television. This led to profiles in the press. One by Harry Reid in what was then still called the *Glasgow Herald* of 6 September 1990, described me as the ' most confident, clever and charismatic of nationalists'. Another in *Scotland on Sunday* of 12 January 1992 said that I was 'in a position of some power' but seemed to find it strange that this could be said of a man who was so 'bookish'. It quoted a colleague (whom it did not name): 'Paul should have been alive in late eighteenth century Edinburgh at the time of the Scottish Enlightenment, with his air of a learned gentleman dabbling in literature, letters and affairs of state.' The conclusion was: 'It is Scott's longer view and keen sense of history which is his and his party's asset'. In his book, *The Battle For Scotland*, Andrew Marr referred to me as 'the intellectual elder statesman of the Scottish National Party'. If so, I am afraid that I have, like many others, become an elder statesman, without ever having the chance to be a practising one.

My work for the party meant that I had to try to reduce my other commitments. With some regrets I decided to resign in 1993 as convener of the Saltire Society's Book Awards panel and to resist suggestions that I should stay on as a member. There were two reasons for my regrets. I felt some personal responsibility because I started the awards in the early 1980s. (It was only later that I discovered that there had been a similar award in the 1930s and for two years in the 1950s). Secondly, the discussions round the table at the meetings of the panel were always fascinating, the best conversation in Edinburgh as somebody said. Still, the obligation to read a large number of new books, in addition to all my reading for other purposes, was a heavy demand on my time which I could no longer manage. I am delighted that the Awards continue to flourish as an important element in Scottish literary life.

From 1991 onwards I did my best to find someone who was prepared to take my place after ten years as convener of AdCAS. In this I failed. In fact, in all the organisations in which I am involved, with the possible exception of the SNP, I have noticed that it has become increasingly difficult to find people who are prepared to spend time and effort in unpaid work. There are many conveners, secretaries and treasurers of organisations who stay in the post for years longer than they would like, simply because no one can be found to take over. I do not know why this has happened. Partly perhaps, it is because everyone seems to have less and not more leisure, in spite of computers, mobile telephones and the other devices which are supposed to save time. People have become more competitive, insecure, acquisitive, greedy and grasping for more money than they really need. It is a tendency which Thatcherism encouraged, even if it did not create it.

Towards the end of the 1980s I wrote a paper for the Saltire Society on targets for the 1990s which was approved by the Council of the Society and copies sent to the leaders of the political parties. Its first objective was autonomy for Scottish cultural institutions, especially a funding and planning council for higher education, the Scottish Arts Council and a Scottish Broadcasting Corporation and an authority for independent broadcasting. So far, there had been no progress over broadcasting; rather the reverse, because, unreasonably, it was reserved to Westminster under the Devolution Act. The other two, which are significant steps, both came into effect under a Conservative Government which firmly resisted constitutional change. In spite of this, they evidently felt that they had to make some concessions to the pressure of Scottish opinion in favour of autonomy.

One of the other points in this Saltire document was, of course, the National Theatre. Here progress has been much slower, and that mainly because of the resistance of the Scottish Arts Council. In May 1986 Willis Pickard, who was on the governing body of the Scottish Arts Council at the time, told me that the atmosphere within the Council was unfriendly to Scottish work for the theatre. Both the chairman of the drama committee and the head of department were, he said, anti-Scottish. Their treatment of the Scottish Theatre Company and of Theatre Alba had been scandalous. That he was right was very obvious from the Council's manipulations over the next fifteen years.

The determined opposition of the Scottish Arts Council to the idea of a Scottish National Theatre over this period was surprising. At an earlier stage, a National Theatre had been one of their objectives. In 1971 they announced that they proposed, along with the board of the Royal Lyceum Theatre, to establish a Scottish Theatre Company, 'comparable to Scottish Opera and Scottish Ballet, to provide an international repertoire of drama at the highest standard', and to 'explore Scottish traditions'. This amounts to a good description of a national theatre. When the Scottish Theatre Company (STC) was eventually established ten years later, it was set the impossible task, especially on its very limited funding, of combining a repertory role with touring to the large-capacity commercial theatres. The STC had a notable success in Warsaw in 1986 when Tom Fleming's production of *The Thrie Estaitis* won the Roman Szlydowski Prize. Even so, the company was already under severe financial stress when AdCAS held its National Theatre conference on 30 May 1987.

The Working Party set up by the conference published a report on 30 November 1987 which was sent to the Secretary of State for Scotland and the Scottish Arts Council. Its first recommendation was that the Scottish Theatre Company should be recognised as the nucleus of a National Theatre and that it should be given full support and kept in operation until it could be developed step by step into the National Theatre. Almost immediately afterwards, the Scottish Arts Council allowed the STC to collapse through lack of funding. This was a serious setback but we did not allow that to discourage us from our campaign. The AdCAS committee transformed itself into a campaigning, but quite small, group with a rotating chairmanship which usually met in the Netherbow Theatre in the High Street of Edinburgh. The director of the theatre, Donald Smith, has given valiant support to the campaign. We published another report, *International Excellence: A National Theatre for Scotland* in June 1990.

Between the spring of 1991 and September 1992 the Scottish Arts Council, responding to an initiative by the UK Minister for the Arts, undertook an investigation into the general situation of all the arts in Scotland. They invited comments from individuals and organisations and held public meetings. One of these on drama was held in Stirling on 23 October 1991. The discussion paper, which they circulated in advance, barely mentioned the idea of a National Theatre. I wrote to complain and in response they produced some photocopies of pages of the AdCAS report. At the meeting itself, I had taken care to have some friends with me, Bert, Joy Hendry, Ian Montgomerie and David Purves (whose *Princess and the Puddock* is one of the classics of the contemporary Scottish theatre). In a working group to discuss the National Theatre I think that we won the argument. They took a vote in which 14 were for the National Theatre and 5 against, of whom 4 were theatre managers who were worried that they might lose their subsidy if they offended the Scottish Arts Council. That particular worry has been one of the factors in the entire discussion.

At the end of the Scottish Arts Council enquiry, they commissioned Joyce McMillan to write a report, which was published in 1993. This was a document of over a hundred pages which covered all the arts. The section on drama began: 'The growing confidence in Scotland's indigenous cultural inheritance is also reflected in a strong campaign for a Scottish national theatre.' It went on to rehearse the arguments on both sides very fairly. Joyce McMillan's conclusion was: 'It is generally agreed, however – even by those who have some reservations about the idea of a national theatre – that there is a need for an institution whose remit is to preserve, develop and promote the Scottish dramatic repertoire.' This was, in effect, an endorsement of the essential core of our case by the Arts Council's own enquiry. They clearly had to take some action. We gave them encouragement by the publication in 1994 of a pamphlet, edited by Donald Smith, *The Scottish Stage: A National Theatre for Scotland*, which included a list of some two hundred plays which should be considered for the repertoire.

The response of the Scottish Arts Council was to commission a feasibility study by a firm of consultants, and after a year or two, yet another one. They seemed to hope that we might all be bored into submission and lose interest. We did not, of course, because Scotland certainly needs and deserves a National Theatre. Decisive action had to await the recall of the Scottish Parliament.

I said that the opposition of the Scottish Arts Council was surprising. As Joyce McMillan says in her report, and as I had been arguing for years, 'it is absurd for Scotland, which has little indigenous tradition in ballet and opera, to support major national companies in these areas, while having no national theatre to protect and express our much richer inheritance of Scots drama and theatrical tradition.' Part of the reason for the opposition may well be, as Willis Pickard suggested, a certain lack of enthusiasm for the Scottish tradition on the part of key figures within the Council. Another might be the difficulties which they have had with the existing national companies for opera and ballet. They are too important to be regulated and dismissed at will like the smaller clients of the Council. The major share of funding which the national companies need distorts the balance of the Council's calculations. It would probably be better for all national companies, like the National Library, Galleries and Museums, to be funded directly by the Scottish Executive, (which is the irritating and demeaning name by which we are supposed to refer to the Scottish Government).

While all this was going on, Bert became seriously ill. At least he had the comfort of being nursed with solicitude by his second wife, Margaret, in their comfortable flat in Blacket Place. He died on 2nd July 1992. George Bruce, David Daiches, Sorley Maclean, Alberto Morrocco and I all spoke at his funeral. His death was for me an irreplaceable loss. He supported me in AdCAS and many other activities and campaigns. For instance, he helped me to compare the texts of the pirated and the official editions of the Lockhart of Carnwath's *Memoirs* for the edition I was preparing for the annual volume of the Association for Scottish Literary Studies. Apart from all of that, his wit, good humour and well-stocked mind made his conversation a constant delight. Our lunches together, week by week, were one of my chief pleasures. He was engaged also in many other ploys in which I was not involved, such as his business management of the Edinburgh Quartet. He was an important, if largely uncelebrated, force for good in the cultural life of Scotland. His range of friends was enormous, as was always evident in the splendid parties which Margaret arranged for our joint birthdays (because they were at about the same date). On such occasions, people like David Daiches would propose a toast and Ronald Stevenson write, and play, a piece of music written specially for the event.

This was not my only loss. The worst thing about age is the death of friends. This became a veritable devastation in the 90s. Within three years, from 1995 to 1998, almost a whole era of Scottish poets died, Tom Scott, Alexander Scott, Norman MacCaig, George Mackay Brown, Sorley Maclean and Iain Crichton Smith; Jim Annand died two years earlier and Naomi Mitchison in 1999. I never met Mackay Brown and Tom Scott only once, but the others were all among my friends. Many of the other people that I have mentioned in these pages died in the same period, Robert Grieve, Jock Cameron, Alastair Dunnett, Bob Silver, Morton Boyd, Kenneth Ireland, Alex McCrindle, Patricia Maxwell Scott, Basil Skinner, Alberto Morrocco and Emilio Coia. Forsyth Hardy died in 1984.

There were many others whom I may not have mentioned but whose death was a sad deprivation: Allen Wright, for years the arts editor of *The Scotsman*, a walking encyclopaedia on the history of the Scottish theatre, a firm ally in the cause of the National Theatre and the mastermind of his newspaper's reviews of the Festival; W Gor don Smith whose plays on the Fringe, usually with Russell Hunter as the star, were one of the highlights of many Festivals; Alexander Law who awakened my interest, as a master in the High School, in Ramsay and Fergusson, and who was still as enthusiastic as ever when I met him again in the Friends of Edinburgh University Library when I came back to Edinburgh in 1980. There were two particular losses among my colleagues in the SNP – Robert McIntyre who had been our first MP and who wrote repeatedly to congratulate me on my latest book; and Allan Macartney, deputy leader and MEP and a tireless and highly rational and civilised worker for Scottish independence. Then David Murison whom I had not seen for years because he went back to live in his native Fraserburgh, but in the past I used always to call on him when I was on leave and he was working at his desk in George Square on the *Scottish National Dictionary*. He was of such invincible modesty that he failed to turn up at a dinner in his honour, but he was as full of quips and cracks as he was of learning. Scottish PEN gave lunches in honour of Nigel Tranter on his 80th and 90th birthdays at the Open Arms in Dirleton. He was in sparkling form at both, but he died shortly after the second of them. There are many others, but this is a melancholy subject. For many of these people it is still a pain to realise that I can no longer pick up the phone and speak to them. In my diary on 20 June 1997, I said that I was beginning to wonder if soon any of my friends and allies would be left: 'it is the end of a generation and it is more or less my own generation.' Even as I write this, the death of Jimmy Shand is announced. I knew him only through his recordings and broadcasts, and it was through them that he gave many thousands of people a life-long passion for Scottish dance music.

But the loss of friends is one of the consequences of living into old age. Another is loss of health and faculties. I have been fortunate in remaining reasonably healthy. Although my back and one of my knees have given me trouble from time to time, this is not enough, so far, to stop me skiing.

My main holiday, nearly every year since 1950, and with Laura since 1980, has been to Klosters in eastern Switzerland, at first for a month when Laura was not working full-time in the Italian Consulate, and more recently for three weeks. For the last twenty years we have stayed there in the same place, a real home from home, in a small flat rented from Frau Crameri. Probably my skiing has declined in speed or dash, and I am less inclined to go off on my own in search of untracked powder; but I think it is still quite competent. Laura's skiing has steadily improved. For many years this was the only long holiday we took, although we had the occasional weekend in the Borders or Perthshire or such places as Paris, Dublin or Amsterdam, and we went now and again to Italy for a week or so.

The more earnest topic of age is a subject much discussed by that celebrated pupil of George Buchanan, Michel de Montaigne. I suppose that I agree with him when he says, 'We must cling tooth and claw to the use of the pleasures of this life which the advancing years, one after another, rip from out grasp.' On the other hand, he also says that it is a happy contrivance of nature that age gradually deprives us of our pleasures so that death is no great loss when it arrives. Some of the things which I have given up I do not much regret. That includes sailing, which surprises me when I think how devoted I used to be to it. The loss of Scottish dancing I do very much regret, especially as Laura complains that it deprives her of a partner. It is one thing which my left knee simply refuses to tolerate. I do notice in the last few years that I tire more easily and it often seems a greater pleasure to stay at home than go out, no matter how tempting the event.

Another thing which Montaigne did say on this subject was that he did not agree with 'the ancient who said that he was obliged to the passing years for freeing him from sensual pleasures.' I think that this ancient had a point; the decline in the urgency of sexual desire does have positive advantages. Indeed Montaigne says of it: 'Everywhere else you can preserve some decency; all other activities accept the rules of propriety; this other one can only be thought of as flawed or ridiculous.' You might dispute all of that, but one thing is certain. There are times in life when it takes up so much time and energy that you have little left over for anything else. To escape from that is liberating; but perhaps the pleasure is greater just because the need is less demanding.

Let me quote Montaigne just once more, as the thought is not entirely without connection to the last one. He says that it is impossible to describe what comfort and pleasure he derives from his books and how much succour they bring to his life. 'They are,' he says, 'the best protection which I have found for our human journey.' I said something very similar in the first chapter of this book and I feel it even more strongly towards its end.

You live for years in the happy illusion that you and all your friends will live for ever, but as you get older you come, with increasing frequency, against the harsh reality. My mother died on 5th April 1981 and my brother on 28th April 1986. Both of them were people on whom I could utterly depend. They were undemanding, but always ready to help. Without them the world became a lonelier place.

Another campaign, which this time, unusually, was rapidly and completely successful, was to prevent the closure of the Scottish National Portrait Gallery. Duncan Thomson, the Keeper of the Gallery, had warned me in January 1988 that there was a serious risk that it might be closed. In 1991 and 1992 there were many rumours and speculations in the press that the Trustees of the National Galleries were considering plans for a new National Gallery of Scottish Art, on the grounds that there was not enough space in the existing galleries for the Scottish collection. The general conclusion of the debate in the newspapers was that Scottish paintings should continue to be displayed in their international context and not in isolation. Duncan MacMillan said that a National Gallery without the Scottish collection would be a National Gallery of nowhere.

In 1992 the rumours began to take a more alarming turn, that the plans for the new gallery would involve the closure of the Portrait Gallery as a source of both pictures and funds. Like most people, I found this very difficult to believe. The Portrait Gallery was one of the best of its kind in the world. It was quite different from an art gallery, because it was concerned more with the sitters than the painters. The purpose was to give life to Scottish history and achievement, and deepen our understanding, by showing us what the principal characters looked like. It did this so well that very many people in Scotland feel warm affection and respect for it, as subsequent events demonstrated. Surely it could not be seriously proposed that it should be closed and its collection included in a gallery which had a completely different purpose. James Holloway, who succeeded Duncan Thomson as Keeper of the Portrait Gallery, told me that he had said to Timothy Clifford, the Director of the National Galleries, that it was the most important to Scotland of all the National Galleries because it embodied and represented Scottish achievement of all kinds. 'You have been here too long,' Timothy replied.

The happy illusion that the Portrait Gallery was safe was shattered in January 1993. Nigel McIsaac, (a watercolourist, a member of the Scottish Arts Club and a former arts master at the Royal High School) wrote to me, and to the Saltire Society and the Arts Club, to draw attention to an article by Timothy Clifford. He described the proposal for a new Scottish Gallery of Art and History which would 'subsume all existing material in the Scottish National Portrait Gallery.' The rumours were right after all.

AdCAS discussed this alarming development early in January and approved a letter which I sent to Angus Grossart, the Chairman of the Trustees of the National Galleries, with copies to the press. I pointed out that the Portrait Gallery had been a private gift to the nation for a specific purpose and questioned whether anyone had the right to dispose of its assets for any other purpose. I said that the closure of the Gallery would be 'an act of cultural barbarism' and 'would destroy one of the most valuable and interesting of our Scottish institutions.' We asked for an assurance that whatever steps were taken over a gallery of Scottish art, the Portrait Gallery would be maintained intact. Angus Grossart, who has been a friend since we met through Alastair Dunnett's Guardians, replied politely to this and subsequent letters but he gave me no assurance. AdCAS, the Saltire Society and other organisations, as well as many influential people, kept up a campaign in defence of the Portrait Gallery. At last, the Trustees made an announcement on 30th November, St Andrew's Day, 1993. They said that they would establish a new Gallery of Scottish Art in Kelvingrove Park in Glasgow and they would for this purpose close the Portrait Gallery and transfer the contents to the new Gallery.

Few recent events in Scotland have produced such a passionate reaction. Some people in Glasgow welcomed the proposal as yet another victory over Edinburgh, like the National Orchestra, the Opera and Ballet Companies, the Garden Festival and the City of Culture.

The headline in *The Herald* was 'Pessimism turns to picture of joy' and beneath it, Keith Bruce said that the news was 'all the sweeter because victory over Edinburgh's bid was so unexpected.' Even so, some influential Glasgow voices, such as Alasdair Gray and Elspeth King, spoke out against the closure of the Portrait Gallery and the proposal for a gallery of Scottish art in isolation.

The fury and indignation which then broke out against the proposal had almost nothing to do with simple east–west rivalry. Evidently, very many people felt passionately about the Portrait Gallery, perhaps because it is such an embodiment of the Scottish identity that an attack on it is an attack on the identity itself. Letters of protest dominated the letters page of *The Scotsman* for weeks and the Saltire Society received more letters on this subject, than on any other in its entire history. People of all kinds joined in this protest, including the Conservative ministers, Malcolm Rifkind and Lord Douglas Hamilton, as well as the Countess of Rosebery (a former Trustee of the National Galleries), Ludovic Kennedy and Sir Steven Runciman. In 1854 Thomas Carlyle wrote to David Laing about his proposal for a portrait gallery which, he said, would become one of our 'most popular and cherished National Possessions'. About a 150 years later, the popular reaction to the threat of closure was a convincing demonstration that he was right.

I called a meeting in the Saltire Society of the organisations which had joined in the original AdCAS protest. We formed a 'Save the Portrait Gallery' committee, although we knew that the wider issue of the well-being of the National Galleries as a whole was at stake. Basil Skinner (a former Keeper of the Portrait Gallery), Duncan MacMillan (the leading authority on the history of Scottish Art), Lady Rosebery and Shand Hutchison (the President of the Scottish Arts Club) were all members of this committee. We decided to call a public meeting to discuss the whole issue and invited the trustees to take part. They declined, but Timothy Clifford and Julian Spalding agreed to present the case for the proposals. Basil Skinner, Duncan MacMillan, George Rosie, Alasdair Gray and Lord Perth (who was to open a debate on the subject in the House of Lords) all agreed to speak and I was to take the chair.

We had intended to hold the meeting in the Talbot Rice Gallery of Edinburgh University, but as the signs of public concern steadily grew more obvious, we accepted the offer of the Edinburgh College of Art to provide a large lecture theatre with facilities to transmit the proceedings to any overflow in the corridors and central hall of the building. All of this was needed. Over 1,000 people came on a cold and wet winter evening, 18th Jan 1994. They were probably the most remarkable crowd ever to assemble for a demonstration in Edinburgh. They were remarkable both for their diversity – earls and law lords rubbed shoulders with civil servants, businessmen, painters, students and people of all descriptions – but also for their demeanour. They listened politely to Clifford and Spalding, but their firm determination to preserve the Portrait Gallery was never in doubt. Only one speaker from the floor suggested that it was merely a matter of east-west rivalry and the meeting bristled with disapproval. The atmosphere was electric. You felt that no one could resist such a formidable expression of public resolve. A resolution was passed unanimously calling on the Secretary of State to reject the proposals and on the Trustees either to reopen the question on the basis of public consultation or to resign. Presiding over this meeting was one of the most exciting and satisfying events of my entire career.

I was fairly sure that this meeting alone had removed any risk that the Portrait Gallery would be closed. So it proved. There were face-saving manoeuvres by the Trustees and, on behalf of the Saltire Society, I wrote again to them and to Ian Lang, then Secretary of State. The coup de grâce was administered by Lang on 9th May, 1994. He issued a statement in which he said that he was not prepared to support the proposals of the Trustees for a gallery of Scottish art or to approve the transfer of the collection from the Portrait Gallery. He was prepared to look at a proposal for a new gallery provided that 'wide and open consultation' showed that it 'commands broad public support'. Our victory was complete. The Trustees made one or two proposals for a new gallery in Glasgow, and made a show of public consultation. The original proposal had depended on using the money that would have been saved by the closure of the Portrait Gallery and they were unable to find an adequate alternative source. The whole idea was quietly abandoned.

This idea had been evolved by the Trustees, especially their Chairman, Angus Grossart, and by the Director, Timothy Clifford. The senior staff of the National Galleries had not been consulted and most, if not all, of them were opposed to it. Both Grossart and Clifford remained on perfectly friendly and courteous terms towards me throughout, although I do not know what they thought privately. At one point, Angus invited me to a private talk to try to persuade me of the virtues of the proposal in his handsome office in Queen Street, where he has an interesting collection of pictures. When I met him a year or two later at a launch of a book by Michael Shea, he greeted me as, 'my favourite author, but my most determined opponent.' Timothy congratulated me on the 'brilliance' of my campaign. The truth was that the campaign was genuinely spontaneous. It was good to discover that public opinion could still make quangos and the Government dance to its tune.

My diary on 16 July 1992 records discussions with a number of publishers about the various stages which some of my books had reached. I saw the dust jacket for *Andrew Fletcher and the Treaty of Union*. It was published on 12th August and David Daiches spoke at the launch in the National Library. On the day before we launched the paperback edition of *The Age of MacDiarmid* in his house, Brownsbank, on the one hundredth anniversary of his birth. I had been hoping, against probability that Bert, who worked on this book with me, would have lived to be there.

With Stephanie Wolfe Mur ray of Canongate Books I discussed the title of the book which appeared some time later as *Scotland in Europe: A Dialogue with a Sceptical Friend*. I wrote to Bill Campbell of Mainstream Publishing to propose a *Concise Cultural History of Scotland*, to which the outstanding experts in each discipline would contribute. I had completed my introduction to an edition of Lockhart of Carnwarth's *Memoirs* and I handed over to John Tuckwell the typescript of *Defoe in Edinburgh and Other Papers*, which was another collection of my essays, articles, lectures and the like.

The Association for Scottish Literary Studies publish only one volume a year and the edition of Lockhart's *Memoirs*, which I had advocated for years, had to wait until 1995 when it appeared with the title, *Scotland's Ruine*, (a phrase and spelling, which Lockhart uses to describe the Union). David Szechi, who had edited Lockhart's letters, did the editorial work on the text and provided the notes. I wrote the Introduction and the comparison of the versions in the two earlier editions. There had been no edition since 1817. This is a scandalous neglect which I was delighted to remedy. Lockhart's book is not only one of the liveliest historical memoirs in our literature, but one of the best sources of the events leading up to the Union. He was involved as a member of the Scottish Parliament and as one of the Commissioners sent to London to negotiate, and rather receive, the Treaty. The reader is left in no doubt about Lockhart's views in favour of Scottish independence and the Stewart line; but the account of the facts cannot be faulted. Walter Scott clearly relied on Lockhart for his account of the affair in his *Tales of a Grandfather*. When Byron, towards the end of his life, was looking for an oppressed nation to liberate he wrote to James Murray to ask for a copy of Lockhart's book. We do not know if he received it. If he did he might have decided to liberate Scotland instead of Greece. So it is a fascinating and important book. Its virtual suppression for nearly two hundred years shows, I think, the anxiety of people generally in the age of Empire to see the Union in a favourable light. As I said in the Introduction, 'If you wanted to conceal the facts and maintain that the Union was an act of enlightened statesmanship, then you certainly did not want to encourage people to read Lockhart.'

Shortly after the edition appeared, I met George Davie at a University reception. He said that he had been reading *Scotland's Ruine* and was delighted that I had succeeded in getting it into print. 'You are doing great things for Scotland,' he said. 'It will be recorded in our history.' I remarked in my diary, 'a small footnote, perhaps.'

In my books on Walter Scott and on Fletcher I had challenged conventional and firmly established opinion. In the case of Scott, it was the belief that he was an enthusiast for the 1707 Union. You have only to read in *Letters of Malachi Malagrowther*, or the chapter on the Union in *Tales of a Grandfather*, to see how far that is from the truth. The conventional belief is that the Union was a freely negotiated bargain in which the Scots deliberately exchanged their independence for access to the English and colonial markets. Both are little better than Unionist propaganda, but they have been so strongly expressed for so long that it is very difficult to eradicate them. They are constantly repeated so that I feel that I have to keep on arguing against them. For instance. When I went to London in 1998 to take part in a television programme on the Union for BBC2 I found that both the presenter, Mark Urban, and the other protagonist, Michael Gove of *The Times*, repeated the old myths as if they were unquestionable certainties. This moved me to write *The Boosted Advantages*, which considered the whole question of the effect of the Union on Scotland.

I was elected as President of Scottish PEN in June 1992 and Laura had been secretary and treasurer since 1986. These PEN appointments were by no means sinecures. They became one of the chief preoccupations and demands on the time of both Laura and myself for the next five years. This was because the Scottish branch had taken a decision to offer to act as hosts for an International Congress in Scotland in August 1997. We knew, of course, that this was a formidable commitment, both in administration and in finance. PEN had grown, especially since the end of the Cold War, to become an organisation with centres in about two hundred countries. Each of them was entitled to send two delegates to a Congress, and the host country had to provide, and pay for, their accommodation as well as provide social and literary events for them and all the other PEN members who might attend. Scottish PEN had very little money in reserve and we calculated that we had to raise about £60,000.

You might think that no rational group of people would volunteer to accept such an obligation. We thought it was time for Scotland again to act as the host country (the previous time was in 1950) and an International Congress would make an influential group of people in most countries in the world more aware of Scotland and its literature and give our own writers opportunities to make international contacts. At the end of our term of office, Laura and I were both asked, and we agreed, to continue until after the Congress. We had valiant support from other members of the Committee, particularly Simon Berry and Mary Baxter.

The first requirement was to raise the necessary funds. At quite an early stage the Scottish Arts Council decided to grant £10,000 and Lothian and Edinburgh Enterprise to lend us £7,000, returnable only if our books balanced at the end. Later, as a result of good deal of effort on our part, other sponsors contributed about £5,000, which included a Glenfiddich Award of £2,000. Our main hope was UNESCO which had contributed about £16,000 to previous PEN congresses. For the year in question they were promoting an international seminar on the cultural identity of women, which was to form part of our programme, and providing about the same amount for that purpose. There was some doubt whether they would also manage the usual subsidy towards the other expenses of the Congress. This meant that we had to budget on the assumption that it would not be available and we therefore had a constant struggle to keep costs down and do all we could to raise funds by our own efforts. In the end UNESCO was generous and we ended with a favourable balance. We were able to repay the LEEL loan, which probably surprised them.

The next question, was it to be in Edinburgh or Glasgow, is always, unfortunately, a fruitful source of argument. I had no doubt that Edinburgh was the obvious place; but Glasgow, for reasons which are obscure to the rest of us, stimulates a fierce loyalty in its citizens. Two of them were indispensable members of our committee. In the end, Edinburgh offered a range of locations which Glasgow could not match. The city agreed that we could use the Royal High School building with its handsome Hall (then still expected to become the debating chamber of the Scottish Parliament) for the assembly of delegates. The Secretary of State would give the opening reception in the Signet Library and the Lord President of the Court of Session (moved, he said, by the thought that Boswell, Walter Scott and Stevenson had all been members of the Faculty of Advocates) would allow us to hold the final party in the old Parliament Hall. The National Library would give a reception and lend some of its treasures for an exhibition in the City Arts Centre. Several organisations, including the Saltire Society and the Scott and Stevenson Clubs, agreed to give receptions. Some of the literary discussions would form part of the programme of the Edinburgh Book Festival, and our delegates and visitors could stay on for all the other Edinburgh Festivals which would have already started or follow immediately afterwards. We compromised with the Glasgow lobby by including a visit there for a day of receptions and events.

One consequence of our prudent control of expenditure was to arrange accommodation for the delegates, and other visitors if they wished, in Pollock Halls, student residences at the foot of Arthur's Seat and with a dramatic view of its summit and its cliffs. We were taking a risk. Previous Congresses were usually based in one or more of the best hotels in the place. Would we have a deluge of complaints or a rebellion? Not at all. From the beginning our visitors delighted in the situation and the relaxed atmosphere of the place. They even seemed to enjoy the food. The bookings were handled on our behalf with impeccable efficiency by a department of Edinburgh University, called Unived.

We had another reason for apprehension. International PEN was going through an internal crisis, and the Congress of the previous year, in Guadalajara in Mexico, had ended in a very acrimonious mood. The nominee for International President, the Romanian poet, Ana Blandiana, withdrew because some delegations had criticised the way in which her nomination had been handled. This was part of a campaign against the International Secretary, Alexandre Blokh, who held the office for several years. Apart from his writing, he was an experienced international official who was quick thinking and efficient, and fluent in French, English and Russian. He had been of great service to PEN in establishing the relationship with UNESCO and in helping to establish new centres in the countries of the Soviet Union as it broke up into its component parts. The trouble was that several PEN centres felt that he had become too dictatorial. They wanted to replace him and to change the rules to give more power to an elected committee and less to a new International Secretary. At Guadalajara the International President, Ronald Harwood, agreed to stay on for one more year, but said that he would definitely retire at Edinburgh, where those difficulties would have to be resolved. Several Centres wrote to me in advance to say that they were afraid that we were going to have a very difficult Congress.

In the event, the whole Congress was not only untroubled but was, I think, positively enjoyed by the 400 or so participants from well over one hundred countries. So, at least, many of them tell me when I meet them again even years afterwards. At the opening ceremony, there were speeches by the Scottish novelist William McIlvanney, and one from Martinique, Edouard Glissant, and by the Lord Provost, Eric Milligan, and a Minister from the Scottish Office, Malcolm Chisholm. All of these were well received and set the tone from the start.

The French Consul General handed over an award for the French Government to Alexandre Blokh, which helped to sooth his injured feelings. As President of the Congress, I took the risk of expressing the hope that our discussions would reflect the atmosphere of enlightened Edinburgh. During the assemblies of delegates, Blokh was re-elected for a year, by a good majority, but it was also decided to elect a committee to consider a successor and the revision of the rules. The Mexican poet, Homero Aridjis, was elected International President out of several candidates. He asked me to chair the final day of the assembly on the grounds that he was not yet familiar enough with the procedures and the issues.

The PEN Congress had an incidental result and, in a sense, a permanent memorial. I had several meetings with Herbert Coutts, the Director of Galleries and Museums of the City of Edinburgh, about the exhibition in the City Art Centre. He told me that he would like to establish something like Poets' Corner in Westminster Abbey in the area around the Writers' Museum, with stones bearing the name and dates of Scottish writers and a quotation. I suggested, and it was agreed, that it should be called Makars' Court. There was funding for the initial twelve. I chose them from all of our four languages and from all periods. We had hoped that all twelve would be ready in time for the PEN Congress. In fact, only the stone of John Barbour was ready in time and that was unveiled by Ronald Harwood to mark the opening of the Congress. The first twelve are only the beginning. It is intended that Makars' Court should continue and that the Saltire Society will adjudicate future proposals for inclusion.

In January 1998 Scottish PEN held a party in the Scottish Arts Club to present Laura and me with a silver quaich, purchased with a collection of £500 from the membership, in recognition of our work on the Congress. David Daiches wrote two poems for the occasion in which, quite rightly, he praised the diligence, zeal and kindness of Laura. Her work as both Secretary and Treasurer of such a complex event, in addition to her full time job in the Italian Consulate-General, was truly heroic. David paid me the ultimate compliment of saying that I was almost the incarnation of Andrew Fletcher. Of course, others did an enormous amount of work as well. Mary Baxter managed, in particular, the intricacies of the UNESCO seminar on the position of women with speakers, some of whom were troublesome, from all over the world. Simon Berry dealt skilfully with our public relations and it was due to him that we had a very striking poster and a handsome volume of the programme. For the design of the poster, we organised a competition in the Scottish Art Colleges. It was won by Andrew Stoneman of the Glasgow College. Peter France was invaluable in ensuring that we maintained an appropriate balance between the French and English languages, the two in which PEN has, so far, operated.

The rest of the first twelve stones in Makars' Court were not ready until the summer of 1998. Iain Crichton Smith made the main speech at the formal opening on 4th August. This was only about a month before he died in September, but he seemed to be in his usual cheerful and effervescent form. He had many struggles in his life – the discrimination against his native Gaelic, the repressions of the Free Kirk, his own mental illness. He triumphed over all of them and could not avoid seeing the funny side, even in things which he detested. No one laughed so much about his own weaknesses and misfortunes and he turned them all into the substance of his poetry, novels and short stories in Gaelic and English. He was hilarious in his description of himself as small boy in Lewis finding only novels about English public schools in his own school library and wondering whether such an improbable world could really exist. At the launch of the first two volumes of the Carcanet edition of MacDiarmaid in August 1992, he said that MacDiarmid was an undoubted genius who set out to recreate a nation and that one of his great qualities was that he was afraid of nobody, because he was free from the constraints of a bourgeois profession. Smith was right on both counts. MacDiarmid was not alone in restoring the political and cultural self-confidence of Scotland, in the 'Age of MacDiarmid', but his was the most effective voice. And I am sure that it is true that all the bourgeois professions greatly inhibit the freedom of speech of their practitioners.

At about this time, I was asked by Hugh Andrew of Canongate Books to edit a collection of texts from early times to the present to show the development of the Scottish national consciousness and of constitutional ideas. The result was *Scotland, An Unwon Cause*, (published in 1997). The title was based on a remark in a letter by John Steinbeck in which he said that Scotland was not a lost cause, but one still to be won. That seemed to me a good description of the situation. The book contained official documents and passages from literature, connected by a commentary. I was pleased to see from his footnotes that Norman Davies had made good use of it in writing *The Isles*, a book calculated to destroy for ever the bad old habit of regarding English and British history as synonymous. I think that anyone who reads *The Scottish Postbag*, the *Concise Cultural History* and *An Unwon Cause* will have a pretty good idea of the general course, spirit and achievement of Scotland.

The Edinburgh International Book Festival was established in 1983, at first every second year until, growing in importance and confidence, it became annual in 1998. It has become one of the most lively and interesting events in the life of Edinburgh, with readings, interviews and debates with a great diversity of writers on every conceivable subject. I once described it in a newspaper as a new Edinburgh Enlightenment in itself and I think that is a fair description. From the beginning, I have taken part either talking about my own books, interviewing other writers or participating in debates on many subjects, but especially the Scottish situation, with such people as William McIlvanney, Allan Massie, David Daiches, David McCrone, Cairns Craig, Lindsay Patterson and Charles Kennedy. In 1999 I gave the first of the International PEN lectures. At these debates in the Book Festival and in print Allan Massie and I have frequently been on opposite sides. Massie is an admirable novelist and a prolific columnist who is well-informed on an astonishing rage of subjects. He said in one of his columns that although I am an enthusiast for Scots, I always write English 'with elegance and lucidity'.

In the autumn of 1992 Nigel Bruce wrote to the Saltire Society to propose that there should be a suitable memorial to David Hume in Edinburgh. I was entirely in favour and, as is usual, in such cases, I was asked to convene a committee to take it forward. This eventually led to the unveiling by Sir Stewart Sutherland, Principal of Edinburgh University, on 30th November 1997, of a powerful bronze statue by Alexander Stoddart. He had impressed the selection panel, who had to choose between proposals from a number of Scottish sculptors, both by his preliminary model and by his enthusiasm and the force of his ideas. He was insistent that his Hume should wear a toga, and not eighteenth century dress, to emphasise his timelessness and his relationship with classical tradition. At first this caused some surprise, but I think that the statue has already become a cherished and familiar part of the Edinburgh scene. At the unveiling I said that the statue was 'one of the most ambitious undertakings of the Saltire Society and one of the most conspicuous and enduring'. It cost over £100,000 which we raised partly by public contributions and by the sponsorship of the Bank of Scotland, the Scottish Arts Council National Lottery Fund and the Faculty of Advocates.

Although St Andrew's Day had for some time been intended for the formal unveiling, the City asked us if the statue could be placed on its plinth at a prominent site in the High Street in time for a meeting of the Commonwealth Heads of Government at the end of October. This was done at first light, to avoid the traffic, on the 21st. It was a suitably dramatic conclusion to five years of effort at which all the leading players took part, Sandy Stoddart, Brian Caster (an appropriate name) of the Powderhall Foundry who had cast the statue, and the members of the committee.

In December 1993 I was given the Andrew Fletcher of Saltoun Award by the Saltire Society 'for services to Scotland'. I was especially pleased that the award took the form (as I had requested) of a caricature sketch of myself by Emilio Coia. Emilio and Alberto Morrocco were artists of Italian descent who spent their lives in Scotland and enriched the lives of all who met them by the warmth of their personalities and exuberant good nature. I said in my diary that the world always seemed a happier place when Alberto came into the room. The same was true of Emilio who for years sketched for *The Scotsman* all the leading performers in the Edinburgh Festival. David Daiches, the President of the Society, made the presentation and, I wrote in my diary, 'was typically generous in his remarks'. He spoke of his admiration and affection, of my activity and energy in all aspects of Scottish culture, the insights of my literary criticism and understanding of the political and social background. I was elected President of the Society in 1996, and in the same year gave the annual address as President of the Edinburgh Sir Walter Scott Club.

These events went on against the background of the Scottish political situation and the advance towards the recovery of the Scottish Parliament. During the whole of the decade the SNP increased in strength both in its internal organisation and in the country at large. This was hardly reflected in the results of the General Elections in 1992 and 1997. The reason was obvious enough. The Tory Governments, especially under Margaret Thatcher, were detested by most people in Scotland. Their first political objective was to remove the Tories from office and votes for Labour seemed to be the most likely way to achieve that result. Paradoxically, disapproval of the Tories therefore increased both the desire for Scottish autonomy and support for Labour. In the recent past, the Labour Party in Scotland had tended to be more in favour of British centralism than of Scottish Home Rule. In 1974 the Scottish Executive of the Labour Party rejected any idea of devolution and had to be called to order by the leadership in London, who saw it as a necessary defence against the advance of the SNP. During the Referendum campaign in 1979, many Labour supporters (such as Robin Cook and Brian Wilson who are now British ministers) campaigned for a No vote.

The experience of long years of Tory rule has probably influenced members of the Labour Party to support a Scottish Parliament for its own sake, and not merely as a tactic against the SNP. Certainly, by the last years of this period the Labour Party was so firmly committed to a Scottish Parliament that they could not fail to introduce a bill for the purpose when they achieved power. Labour leaders, such as John Smith, repeatedly said that it was the settled will of the Scottish people, unfinished business, and that there was no need for another referendum. There was a sudden reversal of policy in June 1996 when the new leader, Tony Blair, announced that there was, after all, to be a referendum and not one, but two, questions: Do you want a Scottish Parliament and do you want it to have tax-raising powers? To many people, this looked like an attempt to wriggle out of the commitment, particularly the second question, which looked as if it was designed to invite the answer, No.

During the whole of this period, the Scottish press, most of which is stubbornly opposed to the SNP, has tried hard to depict the party as badly split between what they call the 'fundamentalists' who insist on independence, nothing less, and the 'moderates' who are prepared to accept devolution as a step in the right direction. It is true that there are members of the Scottish National Party who have bitter memories of 1979. The SNP then campaigned vigorously in favour of a Labour policy towards which many Labour people were opposed and for which most of the party did very little. The SNP was then blamed for the comparative failure of the Referendum and its support, in consequence, declined for years. With such a memory, it would be perfectly natural to conclude that we should never again work for a Labour policy, which was designed in any case to outflank us. This feeling certainly existed and it was eloquently expressed by Gordon Wilson, a man of unquestionable wisdom and sincerity, who was SNP leader in 1979. But there was no serious division in the party. The objective of the party was to achieve independence, or in other words, the same status and the same rights as any other member state of the European Union. The restoration of a Scottish Parliament would be a decisive step in that direction and the party would do all that it could to help to bring that about. We would therefore, in spite of the experience of 1979, campaign again for the second referendum.

This Referendum was a resounding success. It was held on 11 September 1997. Either by accident, or by contrivance by someone

The three party leaders, Jim Wallace, Donald Dewar
and Alex Salmond after receiving the Andrew Fletcher Award
for their part in the 1997 Referendum, June 1998

with a feel for history, this was 700 years to the day since Wallace's defeat of the English army at Stirling Brig. 74.3% voted Yes to a Parliament, and 63.5% to the tax question. As Alex Salmond said at the time, this changed everything. There was now no doubt that the Scottish Parliament would be restored. Even the Conservatives, who had resisted for years, now accepted the popular will. The success would not have been possible without the co-operation of the three parties, Labour, Liberal Democrats, and, particularly, the SNP. Alex Salmond virtually led the joint campaign and even Labour welcomed the support of Sean Connery, a long-term supporter of the SNP. That did not stop them, shortly afterwards, vetoing his knighthood that the former Conservative Government had approved.

In recognition of this service to Scotland performed by the three parties, the Saltire Society decided to offer the Andrew Fletcher Award jointly to the three leaders. Alex Salmond and Jim Wallace accepted at once but Donald Dewar hesitated for some weeks, presumably because Labour were now anxious to play down the co-operation between the parties and to claim all the credit for themselves. Still, the Award ceremony, in the Raeburn Room of Edinburgh University in June 1998, was a happy event. We gave each of them an engraved rose bowl and each of them made a speech, in which they were enthusiastic both about the Parliament and the Saltire Society and its objectives. I remarked in my diary that we must hold them to that.

In the run-up to the first elections for the new Parliament, AdCAS considered its future. In one sense, it now had improved opportunities because the Parliament would have the power to enact many of the objectives for which we had campaigned, except on broadcasting which, paradoxically and disgracefully, was still a reserved power. On the other hand, it was already obvious that there would be a multiplicity of lobbying organisations and that each art form, or even many individual companies, would want to have their own. There was the added complication that I had been trying for years to hand over the convenorship, but we had found no one willing to accept.

We held the final AdCAS conference in the New Senate Hall of Edinburgh University on 24th January 1998. The hall was full and it included such people as Timothy Clifford and Lester Borley, both of whom took part in the debates. My own paper, 'The Cringe is the Enemy', ended with a summary of the immediate objectives:

> 1. The most urgent of all is real autonomy for BBC Scotland and
> the creation of a Scottish Broadcasting Authority.
> 2. The schools should be encouraged to give adequate attention
> to Scottish history, especially cultural history, languages,
> literature, ideas and social and economic conditions. Their aim
> should be to cultivate an intelligent awareness of these things
> and to make their pupils feel at home in Scotland.
> 3. The recommendations of the Universal Declaration of
> Linguistic Rights should be applied to Gaelic and Scots.
> 4. A Scottish National Theatre should be funded, along with the
> other national companies, directly by a Ministry for the Arts.
> 5. We should follow the example of the Irish Republic in the
> encouragement of our traditional music and dance as a great
> national asset. A school for them should be established,
> preferably in a restored Linlithgow Palace.
> 6. An agency to foster cultural exchange between Scotland and
> other countries should be established.

None of them has been achieved so far, although there has been progress towards most of them. The conference ended with a unanimous vote that a similar organisation to AdCAS should continue. In subsequent committee meetings several of the most active members, particularly Lorne Boswell of Equity and Donald Smith of the Netherbow, were in favour of a much looser organisation. It was finally decided in January 1999 that we would not join the crush of lobbying bodies, but would organise conferences from time to time as the need arose and would operate, not as a separate body, but through the Saltire Society.

I was also faced with my own decision whether to put my name forward as a candidate for the Parliament. Naomi Mitchison in her wartime diary, *Among You Taking Notes*, wrote on 13th November 1941 that she 'felt the most passionate and disconcerting longing to be a member of the first Scots Parliament under the New Order.' I know that many people felt the same and I certainly did. After all, I had thought about the Parliament, written about it and argued for it, for most of my life. To be a member of it, would have been a highly satisfying culmination, and an opportunity to work for the improvement of the quality of life in Scotland. At the same time, although I was reasonably fit and I think mentally active, the fact was that I was long past the age at which most people retire. Should I leave it to a younger generation? I put the question to both Gordon Wilson and Alex Salmond. Both encouraged me to stand. At the selection meeting, no one raised the question of my age and I was included in the list of approved candidates.

The next step was the Election itself. For this, unlike Westminster, there were two kinds of member. In each constituency a member was to be elected 'first-past-the post', as at Westminster. In addition, there were to be list members for areas of the country elected from party lists, approximately in proportion to the remaining votes. The purpose of this, in addition to an approximation to proportional representation, was to prevent any party winning a majority of seats, and therefore power, on a minority of votes. This happens frequently at Westminster and is almost unavoidable in that system when there are more than two substantial parties. In the Scottish case, there was a strong suspicion that Labour agreed to this system to make it more difficult for the SNP to achieve a majority of seats, and therefore independence. Indeed some of their leaders admitted as much.

I failed to achieve nomination for any of the Edinburgh seats, but I was included in the possibles for the list for the Lothians. There were fifteen of us and we were asked to appear for a hustings meeting, before about 200 constituency representatives, in the Stakis Hotel at

Edinburgh airport in January 1999. We each made a speech of four minutes, followed by three minutes of questions. I said in my diary that it was conducted very efficiently and that the atmosphere was warm, friendly and welcoming. We had to wait a few days for the results of the vote. I emerged in the fifth place, after Margo Macdonald, Kenny MacAskill, Fiona Hyslop and Anne Dana.

This meant that I had a very good theoretical chance of election. One of the people who telephoned to congratulate me said that it would need 31.8% of the vote in the Lothians and at that time *The Herald* System 3 poll put us at 38% over the whole country. An article in *The Scotsman* mentioned me among candidates who were likely to be elected and for a time, even after the Election, many people spoke to me on the assumption that it had happened. If I had been elected, I should have been the oldest member and would therefore have taken the chair at the opening session and made the first speech. George Reid telephoned me to say that it would be wonderful if I had that opportunity. Tom Nairn sent me a copy of his latest book, *Faces of Nationalism*, with an inscription on the fly-leaf: 'Put Seafield right at last! With gratitute and respect, Tom.' Alex Salmond said much the same. So did Winnie Ewing who, in the event, did the job admirably with the memorable remark at the opening session: 'The Scottish Parliament, adjourned on 25th March 1707, is hereby reconvened.'

In the months which led up to the election on 6th May 1999 Labour displaced the SNP as the party leading in the polls and steadily increased its lead. Several reasons have been suggested for this. First of all, the SNP proposed to reject the Labour proposal to cut Income Tax by one penny in the pound. It has become conventional wisdom since the defeat of Labour in 1992 that parties can only win elections by promising to cut tax. But income tax is the fairest form of taxation and there is a clear need for increased revenues to improve the deplorable standards, which are well below those of our neighbours in western Europe, of health services, education, housing and pensions.

Then there was the question of the NATO bombing of Serbia which began in March 1999, two months before the polling day. At the time I was the deputy to George Reid as party spokesman on international affairs. I telephoned him when the bombing started to say that I had very serious misgivings about it. He said that his reaction was the same but he felt that we should not say anything immediately that might appear to undermine British troops while they were in action. He read to me a cautious statement which expressed reservations in a very low key. I accepted it. A few days later it became apparent that the NATO bombing was having precisely the opposite effect from the one intended. So far from protecting the Albanian population of Kosovo, it had provoked and facilitated their wholesale expulsion. The bombing from a great height of a defenceless people on the ground was in any case morally repugnant. George said that he agreed and would relay our views to Alex Salmond who was to make a television broadcast that evening for the 6pm news. Alex denounced the bombing as an act of 'dubious legality and unpardonable folly.'

I do not know if he had been influenced by my conversation with George but he was certainly right. I think that most people would now agree, but the effect on the electorate at the time is difficult to judge. On 7th April I shared a platform with Tam Dalyell, the Labour MP, in a 'Stop the Bombing' meeting, where opposition to it was clearly very strong but that may have been untypical. Although Tam has always been the most determined of Labour opponents of a Scottish Parliament, I have had a friendly relationship with him since I met him when he came on a parliamentary delegation to Montreal. He is like a dog with a bone when he gets his teeth into an issue but his sincerity is obvious.

In the Election campaign, the Labour Party conducted an alarmist, unscrupulous and dishonest assault on the SNP and on Scottish independence, as though they were already fighting a referendum on the issue. On the other hand, the SNP, anxious to demonstrate that we proposed to work constructively in the new Parliament, concentrated on policies within its powers. In a list of ten objectives, nine were such policies and independence was the tenth. This did not mean that independence was being abandoned as the main objective, but it could be, and was, represented in that way. This was a serious tactical error. We were in the paradoxical position of Labour fighting the independence referendum in advance and concentrating, negatively, on this single issue while the SNP in effect advocated policies for devolution.

Almost certainly, the real reason for the decline in the SNP vote was the combined assault of almost the whole of the Scottish press. *The Herald* was virtually alone in fair and balanced reporting but the others were vicious in their hostility towards the SNP. For example at a debate between the four party leaders for Channel 4 television, which I attended, Donald Dewar was fumbling and long-winded, Jim Wallace competent, David McLetchie sharper and more confident than anyone expected, but Alex Salmond was clearly the most impressive and convincing. That was not the impression given by the press which generally claimed that Alex, and the SNP as a whole, had lost their grip. During the campaign a *Newsnight* poll showed that many of the Labour candidates agreed with SNP policy on Trident, public expenditure and arrangements for the funding of public works with the participation of private sources of finance. But the press continuously represented the SNP, not the Labour Party, as split.

Why did the Scottish press behave like this? Was it because it is mostly English-owned, or because the Labour Party had millions to spend on advertising (they tried to influence *The Herald* by denying them a share of it), or simply because many of the key journalists have close connections with the Labour Party? Perhaps it is merely because the owners of the papers, and the editors and journalists, are genuinely opposed to Scottish independence. Even if that is so, would they be justified in misrepresenting, or denying a voice altogether, to a point of view which is held by a large part of the Scottish population?

In spite of all of this, the SNP emerged from the election as the second largest party, but with insufficient support for my election as one of the list candidates for the Lothians. This was certainly one of the biggest disappointments of my life because so much of my thought, time and energy had been devoted for years to the achievement of the Parliament. I wondered whether I should have tried harder to push my own personal claim, about which I had been very reticent. Of course, there were compensations. It meant that I had more time for other things, including writing this book.

My failure to be elected also abruptly excluded me from the inner circles of the SNP. Attention, inevitably and properly, focussed on the thirty five elected members and they took over all the Shadow Cabinet positions. I was present at the opening working session on 12th May (as distinct from the formal opening by the Queen on 1st July) because I happened to run into Michael Russell who gave me a ticket. The only event to which I was invited was a reception at which the *Claim of Right* (not the full report, but the brief statement signed by Labour and Liberal MPs) was handed over to the safe-keeping of the Presiding Officer (hideous title), David Steel. This brought together many of the stalwarts of the Campaign for a Scottish Assembly, such as Jim Ross, Alan Lawson and Hugh Millar.

Shortly before the great and memorable day of 1st July, and there is general agreement that it was such a day, Barbara Daiches phoned me. She said that they had noticed reports in the press that some VIPs had declined invitations to the opening. Would it be possible for David and herself to have tickets? I had to say that I had not been invited and had no influence in the matter. But I saw the proceedings on television and enjoyed, in particular, Sheena Wellington's singing of 'Is there for honest poverty?' and Tom Fleming's reading of a poem by Iain Crichton Smith.

The press, which had given such support to the Labour Party in the Election campaign, largely turned against them in the first year of the Parliament. Admittedly, the Labour administration was inept but the blame for their failings tended to be directed at the Parliament as an institution. It seemed for a time that the triumph of 1st July might be short-lived and that popular feeling might turn against the Parliament in which so much effort and hope had been invested. In fact, it is already clear that the Parliament is not only firmly established, but that its existence alone has transformed the status of Scotland. In the eyes of the world, there is now no doubt that we exist. Edwin Muir's remark that Scotland was ' falling to pieces, for there is no visible and effective power to hold it together' is finally refuted. Our Parliament, restored after nearly three hundred years, is such a power.

I have already had two examples of the difference which the Parliament has made in the matters with which I have been concerned, the National Theatre and the Scots language. At the Book Festival in August 1999 Edwin Morgan gave the Post Office lecture on 'Scotland and the World'. He ended by saying that we now had a great chance to re-enter the community of nations. We should look to Ireland and the Scandinavian countries. 'Are we a nation? Almost, almost. Another little push and we shall be there.' The reception afterwards was attended by the recently appointed First Minister, Donald Dewar, and by his minister for the Arts, Rhona Brankin, and by the Chairman of the Scottish Arts Council, Magnus Linklater. The matter of the National Theatre was fresh in my mind because I had recently written an essay about it for *The Herald*. So I tackled all three of these people separately on the subject. I reminded Dewar that he had written to one of my predecessors as President of the Saltire Society, Sir Robert Grieve, to say there could be no opposition to the concept of a national theatre. 'Yes,' he replied, 'but I also said that there were obvious problems of resources.' I agreed, but added that the resources needed would not be enormous. (I wondered, to myself, if he really remembered the letter or whether he always inserted such an escape clause in all such letters.) Rhona Brankin gave me the sort of meaningless reply which is customary when politicians want to make no commitment, but to offend nobody. The nothing ruled out, nothing ruled in, careful consideration, wide consultation, type of thing. Magnus Linklater was brutally honest, and in fact, confirmed what I had suspected had been the attitude of the Scottish Arts Council for some years, although they are usually careful to conceal it. 'We already have enough trouble,' he said, 'with the existing national companies without having another one round our necks.'

A month or two later, I heard that the parliamentary committee on education, culture and sport was about to discuss the National Theatre and that I was to be invited to give evidence. *The Herald* published my essay about two weeks before the committee meeting on 1st December 1999. It ended by saying that with the Parliament, we had at last a body with the power to achieve the National Theatre, which had been an aspiration in Scotland for the best part of a century. One of the arguments which the Scottish Arts Council had used to delay, or avoid, action had been that there was no consensus within the theatre community. Shortly before the meeting, I heard that the Federation of Scottish Theatres, which represents thirty theatre companies in Scotland, had destroyed their excuse by producing an agreed scheme for a National Theatre. They proposed that it should be an organisation, modelled on the Edinburgh International Festival, which would commission work 'from existing theatre artists and companies to deliver productions of world class quality.' Hamish Glen of Dundee Repertory Theatre, Giles Havergal of Glasgow Citizens (who had remained detached from the campaign for a National Theatre in the past) and Kenneth Ireland of the Royal Lyceum all spoke eloquently in favour of the project. When I spoke, I welcomed the proposal as a step in the right direction, although drama would be a poor relation among the performing arts until the National Theatre had a company and a home of its own. When the Committee published its report on 2nd February 2000 they endorsed their position by recommending the establishment of a National Theatre company to commission work 'as a starting point which, if successful, would allow the development of more advanced models.'

In response, the Scottish Parliament in December 2000 set up a working party to develop the proposal and its chairman was Donald Smith, who had played a very active part in the National Theatre Campaign. I am optimistic enough to hope that I shall see the first performance of the Scottish National Theatre.

On the Scots language we are still at an early stage, but Irene McGugan MSP has established a cross-party group on the question, at which the Saltire Society, the Scots Language Society, the Association for Scottish Literary Studies and Scottish PEN are all represented. I have written a draft declaration about the nature and value of the language and what should be done about it. I hope that it, or something like it, will eventually be endorsed by the whole group.

These are, of course, only two examples of the way in which the Scottish Parliament is beginning to transform and enrich the life of Scotland. There are many pressing problems in our social structure, but now at last we have a Parliament with the responsibility to confront them.

For a least the last 120 years Scotland has been striving for cultural and political renewal. The cultural achievement in virtually the whole of that time, in literature, painting and music, has been substantial. The political advance has been much slower. It has taken more than a century to achieve even a partial Parliament. But that has been a decisive step. The essential provision of the Treaty of Union was the abolition of the Scottish and (in theory, but only in theory) of the English Parliaments. That no longer applies. What then do those who talk about preserving the Union mean? If they mean the maintenance of a close and friendly relationship between Scotland and England, that will be enhanced when the restrictions on the Scottish Parliament are removed. Scotland will then be no longer an impatient and discontented dependency, but a friendly partner in the Commonwealth and the European Union. I have no doubt that we shall soon advance to that status.

The Scottish Parliament can only function effectively, and Scotland can only play a full part in the European Union and other international organisations, when she becomes as independent as any other member state. We should then look, as Edwin Morgan said, to the Scandinavian countries and Ireland. They are similar in size and geographical conditions to Scotland and their example can help us to find solutions to many of the problems that face us.

There is much that is highly unsatisfactory in the current state of Scotland. Indeed the failure of the Union is obvious if we compare conditions in Scotland with those of our neighbours who have always been, or have again become, independent. They are in a much happier state by almost any standard of measurement. Certainly there are also many problems to which there is no easy solution, which we share with the rest of the world – excessive commerical greed, gross inequality, poverty, pollution and the destruction of the environment, drugs and crime. An independent Scotland will have to tackle all of these, in cooperation with our partners in Europe, but we are well capable of making a valuable contribution. When Compton Mackenzie gave his rectorial address in Glasgow University in 1931 he said:

> It is not because I believe that Scotland is dying, but because I
> believe that Scotland is about to live with a fullness of life
> undreamed of yet, that I count it the proudest moment of my
> career to be standing here today.

I quoted these words in my rectorial address in Dundee in 1989 because, as I said, they express my own feelings precisely. I do not think that this optimism is misplaced because, as the journalist Murray Ritchie has written, this is the age of the small nation. The most prosperous per head of the members states of the European Union, Luxembourg, is also the smallest. At a symposium in the University of Uppsala in March 1995 Johan Olsen of the University of Oslo said:

> Many smaller European states have a good historical record
> when it comes to democratic development, peaceful co-existence,
> prosperity, welfare, equality between social classes, districts and
> gender, life expectancy, cultural development, and ecological
> consciousness.

David Hume and John Millar said much the same in Scotland in the eighteenth century. Since then, it has become still more advantageous for a state to be small for two reasons. Firstly, it is easier for them to adapt to changing circumstances in the global market and inter-dependent world. To quote Olsen again:

> . . . smaller and weaker states with open political, economic,
> cultural and social systems, have more experience than larger,
> dominant ones, in adapting to events and decisions over which
> they have little control.

Secondly the effect of international oranisations, such as the United Nations and the European Union, is to curb the power of the larger countries and increase the influence of the smaller ones. Prime Ministers of Denmark and Ireland, for instance, have said that this has been their experience in the European Union.

Many of the problems that face us are global and can only be solved by international cooperation. This is true, for instance, of the industrial pollution of the environment, of the research, manufacture and trade of weapons of ever greater power, of the pressures against cultural diversity. The large powers do most of the damage. No small country on its own can do much to overcome worldwide tendencies. But each of us can become a focus of resistance. Also, most countries are small and by working together we can begin to change the climate of opinion, which in the end no government can resist.

There is one respect, in particular, where Scotland should be able to make a contribution, valuable both for ourselves and for other countries. That is education where Scotland once, but no longer, set an example to the world, and where the tradition of the Democratic Intellect and the Scottish Enlightenment are still relevant. The decline in educational standards is visible, not only in our poor record of attainment in mathematics and science compared to other countries, but in something so basic and essential as the cultivation of sceptical and rational habits of thought. There is evidence everywhere of intellectual laziness, dumbing-down, loss of critical standards, gullibility and vulnerability to manipulation by advertising, and by the pedlars of popular fashion and the merchants of political soundbites. One of the first objectives of education should be to encourage habits of rational examination of the evidence and of resistance to advertising and propaganda.

We should aim at a new Enlightenment. We cannot tackle the problems that face us without an educated population. We have aspired to this in the past and, with control of our own affairs, I am sure that we can do it again. So I think that we stand on the brink of an exciting new age, one which needs effort and determination, but which will transform the quality of life in Scotland and make some contribution to the rest of the world. Future generations will say of it, as Wordsworth said of the French Revolution:

> Bliss was it in that dawn to be alive,
> But to be young was very heaven!

ENVOI

To Paul

Your life
an open book,
you have offered to me,
unreservedly.
Memories of a past existence,
unfamiliar to my heart.
Words at times written
by whom I do not recognise.
My only reality
our years together:
to share them with you
is unceasing happiness and fulfulment.

Laura
Edinburgh
August 2001

Paul with Laura at Scott's View near Dryburgh, after the inauguration of the
Anne Carrick exhibition in Smailholm Tower, July 1983

Other books of biography from Argyll Publishing

The Last of the Chiefs
Alasdair Ranaldson Macdonell of Glengarry
Brian D Osborne
1 902831 27 6 256pp pbk £9.99
The life and times of 'Wild Alasdair' who embraced the new – sheep and land clearance – but clung to the old Highland ways.

The Ingenious Mr Bell
Henry Bell – pioneer of steam navigation
Brian D Osborne
1 902831 28 4 256pp pbk £9.99
Henry Bell's *Comet* heralded the age of shipping on the Clyde.
'authoritative' *Lloyd's List*, 'scholarly and readable' *Ships Monthly*,
'absorbing' *The Herald*

Far from the Rowan Tree/
Around the Rowan Tree
Margaret Gillies Brown
1 874640 69 6 & 1 902831 06 3 240pp pbk £6.99 each
A family migrate to the Prairie lands of 1950s Canada, and then return to Scotland. 'classics of Scottish autobiography' *Duncan Glen*,
'compellingly personal' *Scotland on Sunday*

A New Kind of Life
Helen Lillie
1 902831 06 3 256pp pbk £6.99
From Scottish middle class respectability to 1930s New York, Helen Lillie carved out a new kind of life.
'unique insight' *Milngavie & Bearsden Herald*, 'an amusing memoir' *Radio Times*,
'epitomises the woman of the twentieth century' *The Herald*

Available in bookshops or direct from
Argyll Publishing, Glendaruel, Argyll PA22 3AE Scotland
For credit card and other enquiries
tel 01369 820229 email: argyll.publishing@virgin.net
or visit our website www.deliberatelythirsty.com